# LABOUR PEOPLE

# LABOUR PEOPLE

*Leaders and Lieutenants,*
*Hardie to Kinnock*

KENNETH O. MORGAN

OXFORD UNIVERSITY PRESS
1987

Oxford University Press, Walton Street, Oxford OX2 6DP
Oxford New York Toronto
Delhi Bombay Calcutta Madras Karachi
Petaling Jaya Singapore Hong Kong Tokyo
Nairobi Dar es Salaam Cape Town
Melbourne Auckland
and associated companies in
Beirut Berlin Ibadan Nicosia

Oxford is a trade mark of Oxford University Press

Published in the United States
by Oxford University Press, New York

British Library Cataloguing in Publication Data
Morgan, Kenneth O.
Labour people: leaders and lieutenants
Hardie to Kinnock.
1. Labour Party (Great Britain)—
Biography
I. Title
324.24107'092'2  JN1129.L3
ISBN 0-19-822929-1

Library of Congress Cataloging in Publication Data
Morgan, Kenneth O.
Labour people.
Bibliography: p.
Includes index.
1. Labour Party (Great Britain)—Biography.
2. Labour Party (Great Britain)—History.  3. Great
Britain—Politics and government—20th century.  I. Title.
JN1129.L32M67  1987  324.24107'092'2[B]  86-23753
ISBN 0-19-822929-1

Printed in Great Britain by Butler & Tanner Ltd
Frome and London

# PREFACE

IN this book, I examine about thirty key personalities in the history of the British Labour movement between 1900 and 1987. I also try to explore what kind of typology of leadership emerges. This is, inevitably, a highly personal selection, in part reflecting my own interests, outlook and background. I am conscious of many omissions, for example Blatchford, Snowden, the Clydesiders, Tawney, Crosland, or Jack Jones; but no selection of this kind can be wholly comprehensive. I hope, nevertheless, that the main kinds of Labour leaders, parliamentary politicians, trade unionists, machine apparatchiks, intellectuals, journalists, prophets, and others are truly represented. There is, I am aware, at least one illogicality, namely including Beatrice Webb among the 'founding fathers'. But I could not think of any alternative terminology, and certainly intend no offence to feminists or others. The reader will observe that I have found positive things to say about almost all the personalities considered here. This is not, perhaps, surprising, since they reflect the British political tradition in which I generally feel most comfortable. To borrow from the preface of my old mentor, Richard Hofstadter, in his book on the American *Age of Reform*, my criticisms are criticisms from within. I hope, however, neither to have been unduly partisan nor uncritical. Above all, I trust that I have avoided the university teacher's besetting vice, that of being patronizing. I have certainly tried.

I am greatly indebted to Sir Henry Phelps Brown and Dr David Howell of Manchester University, two old friends who have read through the entire manuscript and made many valuable comments and criticisms. I am also most grateful, amongst others, to the Rt Hon. Douglas Jay, Lord Longford, Lady Phillips, Leslie Stone, David Hill, and Ken Peay for help with, and illuminating comments on, individual chapters. The errors or misconceptions that undoubtedly remain are, of course, wholly my responsibility.

A number of the chapters included began life as reviews in the *Times Literary Supplement* or *New Society*. All have been entirely re-written and extended, but I am nevertheless grateful to the editors of those journals for permission to include certain thoughts and passages that originally appeared there. As always, I am grateful to Jane, David, and Katherine for keeping me cheerful in a disillusioning world.

K. O. M.

*Oxford*
*October 1986*

# CONTENTS

# ABBREVIATIONS

| | |
|---|---|
| ACAS | Advisory, Conciliation and Arbitration Service |
| APEX | Association of Professional, Executive, Clerical and Computer Staff |
| ASTMS | Association of Scientific, Technical, and Managerial Staffs |
| BSP | British Socialist Party |
| CND | Campaign for Nuclear Disarmament |
| COMISCO | Committee for International Socialist Co-operation (Socialist International) |
| DEA | Department of Economic Affairs |
| EEC | European Economic Community |
| EFTA | European Free Trade Area |
| EPU | European Payments' Union |
| FCRB | Fabian Colonial Research Bureau |
| GLC | Greater London Council |
| HELP | Higher Education for the Labour Party |
| ILP | Independent Labour Party |
| IMF | International Monetary Fund |
| LCC | London County Council |
| LRC | Labour Representation Committee |
| MFGB | Miners' Federation of Great Britain |
| MLR | Minimum Lending Rate |
| NAC | National Administrative Council (of the ILP) |
| NCB | National Coal Board |
| NEC | National Executive Council |
| NEDC | National Economic Development Council |
| NUDAW | National Union of Distributive and Allied Workers (later USDAW) |
| NUM | National Union of Mineworkers |
| NUPE | National Union of Public Employees |
| OEEC | Organization for European Economic Co-operation |
| PEP | Political and Economic Planning |
| PLP | Parliamentary Labour Party |
| PPS | Parliamentary Private Secretary |
| SDF | Social Democratic Federation |
| SDP | Social Democratic Party |
| SPD | (German) Social Democratic Party |
| SWMF | South Wales Miners' Federation |

# ABBREVIATIONS

| | |
|---|---|
| TGWU | Transport and General Workers' Union |
| TUC | Trades Union Congress |
| UDC | Union of Democratic Control |
| UDM | Union of Democratic Mineworkers |
| URC | Unofficial Reform Committee |
| WEA | Workers' Educational Association |
| WSPU | Women's Social and Political Union |

# LIST OF ILLUSTRATIONS

*Between pages 178 and 179*

# INTRODUCTION

THE British labour movement has always venerated the collective ideal. Its key images have focused on solidarity, mass endeavour, the common good. Yet it is one of the paradoxes of our culture that a party that came into being as a protest against the excesses of individualism can go to extreme lengths to perpetuate the cult of personality. More than the Conservatives have ever done, Labour draws constant inspiration from the ideas and achievements of key individuals, in both the political and industrial spheres. Indeed, it could well be argued that, since Labour necessarily arose to represent the poor and inarticulate, its need for charismatic individuals has been all the greater than that of its better-endowed opponents. More than other parties, too, Labour has always been a deferential party— witness the uncritical reverence with which a patriarch like A. V. Alexander was regarded by his Sheffield constituents in the 1940s. Welsh constituency parties, apparent models of social equality, were also famous for their recognition of the BAs and PhDs of their academic members. Of course, in some ways, the emergence of a new kind of populism in the party, notably in inner-city areas, may have modified this tradition of deference over the past fifteen years or so. Yet, the new left has been as aware of the impact of personality and leadership as was the older regime. Without the charismatic presence of Tony Benn, the movement for conference and constituencies' power in the 1970s would never have made such progress. The new appeal of municipal socialism found its essential focus in Ken Livingstone. Without the orchestrating personality of Arthur Scargill, immortalized in football-type songs as someone to be supported for ever more, or a prophet who walks on water, it seems improbable that the miners would ever have attempted their final, despairing stand to prevent the disintegration of their industry. Across the party spectrum, on the left wing as much as the right, Labour has flourished or declined in terms of the triumphs or defeats of significant individuals. So has it done throughout its eighty-odd years of existence.

One of the striking features of the labour movement as a cultural group, indeed, is its evocation of former heroes, and the creation of an alternative history thereby. More than any other party, it has praised famous men (and, just occasionally, famous women as well), and has perpetuated their imperishable memory. This is not really the case with the Conservatives, apart from the special case of the cult of Disraeli and its by-product in the Primrose League. Otherwise, Conservatives are relatively unsentimental about past celebrities; they do not go to great lengths to venerate the memory of Austen Chamberlain, Stanley Baldwin, or Anthony Eden. Similarly, they are far more ruthless than Labour tends to be in discarding present-day leaders. By contrast, Labour is rich in symbolism. Lectures abound to commemorate the varied achievements of Herbert Morrison, R. H. Tawney, Arthur Horner, or Dr Rita Hinden. Housing estates or old people's homes bear the names of Clement Attlee, Ellen Wilkinson, Nye Bevan, or (in his 1964–6 phase only), Harold Wilson. Keir Hardie has been perhaps the most omnipresent symbol of all, his name appearing almost everywhere from memorial halls to school-boy football competitions. At times, of course, the slate has to be wiped clean, as with the sad fate of Ramsay MacDonald after 1931, or other politicians who have lapsed in popular favour. But the principle of individualism and its celebration marches on.

So, too, does another permanent feature of Labour's history and style—its appeal to the past. For a party supposedly harnessing its energies for the founding of a socialist commonwealth in the future, looking to the dawn when England shall arise, it has been captivated, even obsessed, by its history. This especially applies to the trade-union movement, fascinated by past heroic, or tragic, events from Tolpuddle to the General Strike or beyond, and by the charismatic working-class leaders who led the charge. But the political party, too, has an ineradicable tendency to turn to the past to provide the touchstone for the policies and the ethic of today. 'If Keir Hardie were alive today' is no merely idle phrase, any more than Arthur Henderson's evocation of 'This Great Movement of Ours'. Neither is the singing of 'Auld Lang Syne' at the end of party conferences a mere indulgence to amuse political journalists (the role of 'The Red Flag' is more ambiguous). The very chorus suggests a party confident in the triumphant saga of the past, less certain (or maybe less willing) to proclaim or delineate the future social order.

At all points, therefore, Labour's progress or decline has been bound up with major individuals and with the concept of leadership. The movement, of course, has prided itself on being democratic and directly responsive to the grass roots, quite different in character from the hierarchical Tories whose leaders dictate to them from the saluting base, and whose claim that annual conferences are genuine debates is simply a fraud. This belief on Labour's part is not just a myth. As Lewis Minkin showed in an important book in 1978, the annual party conference, with all its uncertainties, does reflect a populistic ethic not found in other parties. The idea of intra-party democracy survived even in the years of Attlee and Gaitskell when the parliamentary party seemed in autocratic control; since 1970 it has notably flourished. The attempt by the late Robert McKenzie to argue (from the standpoint of the mid-1950s) that the Conservative and Labour parties were identical in their structure and both authoritarian in form now seems outmoded, especially in the light of the upsurge of grass-roots pressures in the unions, the constituency parties, and the party conference since 1970. Even at the time, it was notable that McKenzie largely ignored the immense extramural presence of the trade unions who have loomed so dominantly in decision-making in the party in 1931, 1969, and countless other occasions. This has made the question of the distribution of power within the Labour Party a peculiarly complex one, with an immense range of answers provided from Ostrogorski in 1902 to Duverger in recent times.

But it can still be agreed that leadership is a consistent phenomenon in the Labour Party which the historical record amply illustrates. It can take a variety of forms, depending on historical circumstances. At the very summit of the party in parliament, MacDonald's formal adoption of the title of 'leader' in 1922, as well as merely that of 'chairman' which had served Hardie, Henderson, Barnes, MacDonald himself, Adamson, and Clynes well enough between 1906 and 1922, was testimony to his power and personal charisma after the First World War. MacDonald thereafter came to embody both the potentialities, and even more the perils, of party leadership. After the fateful split of 1931, MacDonald's identification with the notion of leadership seemed to embody all the autocratic tendencies of one remote, irresponsible individual, blind and deaf to the wishes of the movement as a whole. Again, Harold Wilson's temporary dominance in 1963–6 focused attention on his highly personal leadership, and led to current talk of 'prime ministerial government', kitchen cabinet and all, on the lines of Lloyd George in a previous era. Thereafter, a reaction almost inevitably set in as

Wilson's star waned. The subsequent turmoil of opposition was, in part, a consequence of the decline of Wilson's personal authority, just as that of 1979–80, continuing into the period of Michael Foot's leadership, resulted from Callaghan's fall from grace after another election defeat. Clipping the wings of the leader, over the drafting of the manifesto, patronage, and other key issues, was a major Bennite demand from 1979 onwards. The electoral college was felt to be a permanent guarantee of control by the party at large over the parliamentary superstructure, and more especially its potentially authoritarian head. Neil Kinnock since 1983 has shown clear signs of trying to reassert the role of the leader in policy matters, in determining strategic priorities and above all in the expulsion of far-left dissidents, though without the authoritarianism of MacDonald or the deviousness of Wilson in the past.

Leadership in the Labour Party, then, is a complicated phenomenon. The very concept often fills party workers with guilt, suspicion, or even contempt. Perhaps Labour's most successful leader to date, one who headed the party for twenty years from 1935 to 1955, was Clement Attlee. He was, above all, a leader who appeared not to lead, a self-effacing egoist, a deliberately muffled, prosaic, lack-lustre character who concealed immense reserves of will and self-belief within himself. The decline of Labour in Attlee's last phase, 1951 to 1955, both created and was precipitated by novel problems over both organization and policy. But, whatever form it takes, however varied by political circumstances and individual crises of authority, the fact of leadership, and the existence of lieutenants to buttress or challenge it, is an enduring feature of Labour's history.

Labour has always thrown up an immense range of leaders of all kinds, in accordance with the complex institutional structure of the party, and its extraordinary variety as a political movement. Tony Crosland in *The Future of Socialism* (1956) listed, in passing, twelve different strains that went to the making of the movement, including Owenite, Morrisite, Fabian, ILP, syndicalist, municipal, and the planning ethic, not forgetting, to a limited but crucial extent, Marxist socialism. Crosland left out quite a few other components, including the corporatist idea produced by the first world war, Social Christianity, and minority movements such as the nationalism of Wales and Scotland. Each of these has evolved its own kind of leadership; each has found its echo somewhere in the structure, institutions, or ideology of the party. The party essentially began, of course, as an alliance of trade-unionists, who predominated, and a small minority of largely middle-class socialists. In the years before 1914, it was overwhelmingly working class in composition; all fifty-one Labour MPs between 1900 and 1914 were of working-class origin. But middle-class socialists—ILP, Fabian, or SDF—exercised a disproportionate influence. The party was becoming increasingly a popular front, and the early cadres of the party leadership reflected the fact. Keir Hardie, originally a miners' official in Ayrshire who became the effective leader of the ILP socialists, a man who straddled both the worlds of workers' class-consciousness and of middle-class activism, was in himself the indispensable embodiment of the alliance in the flesh. So, too, were autodidacts like MacDonald and Snowden.

But there was always a variety of contending individuals and movements within the Labour coalition. There were isolated rebels like Victor Grayson. Always, too, there was a variety of fringe or associated movements to bring in new forms of leadership, such as advocates of industrial unionism or neo-syndicalism, the pre-1914 women's movement, the municipal socialists, or the 'new theologians' of the nonconformist conscience, strong in Wales and the North. Within the trade-union world, the conflict between different kinds of leadership was often bitter, as that between the ageing Lib-Lab, 'Mabon', and Noah Ablett, the youthful voice of Marxist revolt, in South Wales. In the event, the future was to belong to neither, but not until after the General Strike was the outcome totally clear. After the first world war, the broad domination of the unions over the structure of the party was overwhelming, despite their relative lack of political homogeneity. This was shown by the central presence of Arthur Henderson, along with lesser figures such as J. R. Clynes, J. H. Thomas, Ben Turner, and Vernon Hartshorn. On the other hand, the ILP wing, reinforced by the inrush of disappointed ex-Liberals repelled by the first world war, continued to bring in new kinds of leaders at all levels. Hence the dominant role of MacDonald in the twenties, as a man who could appeal both to centrist ex-Liberals and to old ILP socialists, a politician who appeared somehow right-wing and left-wing, an insider and an outsider at the same time.

After 1931, the mix of leadership within the movement changed. Ernest Bevin and many in the TUC attacked the split of that year as a betrayal by the intellectuals, who had drifted away from the trade-union bedrock. In fact, however, an important consequence of the thirties was that a younger generation of middle-class intellectuals, symbolized by the university-trained economists and planners who revolved around the important presence of Dalton, came increasingly to the fore as generators of new ideas. The trade unions, co-ordinated by the apparatchik figure of Citrine, the TUC general secretary, took a more indirect role in party organization. The political movement was increasingly moulded by professional politicians and a machine-man like Morrison. Down to 1939, however, Labour's strength and weakness both largely resided in the fact that, while it claimed to be a national party, it was really more of a sectional pressure-group on behalf of the workers, rooted in the older industrial areas of high unemployment, weaker in areas of new light industry and middle-class suburbia, almost non-existent in most rural areas in England and Scotland.

The second world war brought in new kinds of leadership again, which largely dominated the party and its rhetoric until after the general election of 1970. These were the technocratic and pro-fessional vanguard of the years of power—the planners, economists, social administrators, educators, health workers employed in the public service, together with fluctuating elements of the middle-class intelligentsia, captivated by the planning blueprints of the war years and committed to a belief that Labour could implement them. Labour, it was believed, was the party of the thinking (and chattering) classes. Their hopes were vested in the Attlee government after 1945, and in the welfare services and corporate public institutions that that government created. The trade-union influence over the party became more indirect still, especially after the death of the crucial figure of Ernest Bevin early in 1951. By 1951 there were only four trade-unionists in the Cabinet. Since they included senior figures such as Shinwell and Griffiths, their experience of the trade-union world was necessarily remote. The unions, however, still acted as brokers for the political leadership at party conference and on the NEC, with the famous right-wing troika of Deakin, Lawther, and Williamson, custodians of the card vote, in charge for a full decade after 1945. At the top, led by elderly figures and by Attlee himself (that characteristic late-Victorian figure, the public school phil-anthropist), Labour presented a singularly traditional and senior image of leadership.

In the sixties and the early seventies, Labour was poised between a still powerful, but continuously declining, trade-union element, and the upward thrust of largely middle-class politicians and planners inspired by the ethic of revisionism. Gaitskell was strongly associated with the latter—indeed too much so, since his leadership seemed to important sections of the movement unduly limited and even sectarian. Wilson after 1963 was an interesting contrast, a wartime planner of technocratic outlook, new born as a putative man of the left in the party infighting of the 1950s. It looked in 1964 as if he could present a multi-dimensional appeal, speaking in the accents of Northern nonconformity, yet also evoking the technological revolution to appeal to the middle-class professional man and woman. On balance, the attempt failed, for reasons examined below. A plausible attempt to remodel the leadership of the party, on a much broader social and ideological base than had been tried since the thirties, came to nothing. Amongst the unions, the transition within the Transport Workers from Arthur Deakin in 1946 to Frank Cousins in 1956 to Jack Jones in 1969 and finally to Moss Evans in 1978 illustrated a growing detachment of the organized manual workers from the formal processes of the party. The massive division between government and unions in 1969 over attempts to impose some kind of statutory wage restraint revealed the ideological gulf that had opened up. It is highly significant that the unions won, and the elected Labour government had to retreat in humiliation.

Since 1970, Labour has experienced a variety of other changes, some destructive for the party, others more hopeful. The continued erosion of the traditional, homogeneous working class, speeded up apace by the deindustrialization of older industrial areas and by prolonged unemployment, has further loosened the ties between the unions and the political leadership. The miners are a prime exhibit here. The presence of a mere dozen miners' MPs in 1983, the rise of as openly anti-political a president of the NUM as Arthur Scargill, indicated the gap that had emerged between Labour's political oligarchy and its mass proletarian base. The winning over of new middle-class and professional sympathizers, briefly heralded in 1964 and 1966, was not sustained. Labour could not retain the mandarin allegiance of the great and the good, the quango classes. By the 1980s, many of them were defecting to the Liberals or the new SDP, or losing patience with politicians entirely as economic decline continued remorselessly.

In part compensation, Labour had found new strength since 1970 in the public service unions such as NUPE, and in white-collar unions like ASTMS and APEX, in education, health, and the social services. Journalists have also discovered the so-called 'polycracy', those polytechnic lecturers, teachers, and social workers, invariably on the left, who predominated in many urban constituency parties in the 1970s and early 1980s, to the exclusion of blue-collar trade-unionists. A recent study found that sixty-two per cent of the local party in Sheffield were middle class, mostly from the public sector; the same obtains for many other urban constituencies. Other new elements of strength came in inner-city areas, often caught up in extreme social decay. Thus, black ethnic minorities, spokesmen for the new long-term unemployed, and women's groups emerged as powerful voices of protest here, capable of giving Labour new impetus. The confrontation between Denis Healey and Tony Benn in the fight for the deputy leadership in 1981 was sociological as much as ideological. It was a trial of strength between the newer left of the public sector and ethnic and other minorities, and an older style of Labour coalition, still basically run by the larger manual unions of white, male workers, and its parliamentary spokesmen. The former was defeated, though very narrowly. On balance, though, the elements powerful in the party since the 1970s have often tended to add to Labour's sectionalism, as shown in the disastrously miscellaneous manifesto produced in 1983. Projected against all this was a background of steadily falling party membership, from a peak of over a million individual members in the year 1952–3 to an official figure of just over 297,000 by 1982–3. (In reality, the figure is probably considerably smaller, though some increase has occurred latterly.) In many of its inner-city strongholds, the formal Labour Party, as opposed to a range of supportive community movements, was a mere rump. The attempt to project a different kind of leadership in the party in the mid-1980s was conducted against a background of endemic weakness, just as earlier it had flourished in a mood of hope and self-sustaining advance.

The typology of Labour leadership has often been attempted over the years. After 1908, Robert Michels's famous study of labour organization, the work of a disillusioned German socialist, focused on the 'iron law' which made oligarchy and the necessities of the machine preponderant in a party. The fact of minority participation in politics at all, and the veneration of dominant and technically expert leaders by the rank and file, all reinforced the rise of centralized leadership. 'Organization implies the tendency to oligarchy', in Michels's famous phrase. His analysis is, however, far more applicable to the Prussian-led Social Democrats of his native Germany than to the loosely structured, decentralized British Labour Party, though the advance of men like Henderson and Morrison in the party, supreme as organizers and centralizers, does illustrate aspects of Michels's diagnosis, which he believed to be of universal application.

Egon Wertheimer's 'portrait' of the party in 1929 was impressed by the dominance of intellectuals in the Labour Party, and the easy access that the Fabians, ex-Liberals like the Buxton brothers, or an individual like Tawney enjoyed in the highest circles of the movement. He also emphasized the extraordinary variety of popular participation, including some renegade aristocrats, and new groups drawn from teachers, black-coated workers, and the scientific classes, apart from the working-class base. It was, he thought, a relatively harmonious alliance, united by faith in its leaders, especially in MacDonald, 'the outstanding figure of International Socialism'. In fact, Wertheimer was expressing doubts about parts of this scenario even before August 1931. Thereafter, the portrait he offered was difficult to recognize. In particular, the role of intellectuals became very fragmented, potentially influential with the planners of the thirties, but with major figures like Cole, Tawney, and even (as a theorist) Laski increasingly marginalized in the party. It was basically professional politicians of the type of Attlee, Dalton, and Morrison who gave the party coherence thereafter, and the prospect of victory by 1945. In so far as Labour drew new inspiration from intellectuals during the war, it derived largely from Beveridge and Keynes, both of course Liberals.

Certain key types constantly re-emerge in the history of the party. Organizers, as noted, above loom large—Henderson, Morrison, and perhaps Callaghan all fit into this category, though each required an extra ingredient. Henderson had his union backing, Morrison his base in London, Callaghan his broad contact with both the unions and the constituencies. The Labour Party-machine politician is not usually a figure to conjure with. Men like Jim Middleton, Len Williams, or Ron Hayward have played a relatively invisible role over the years, though the position of Morgan Phillips in the 1940s and 1950s added some additional ingredients. Publicists in the press have always been important, especially in the weeklies. Laski was perhaps more important as a journalist than an academic political theorist; while since 1945 such different personalities as Michael Foot and Rita Hinden have been testimony to the power of the socialism of the word. Intellectuals, however defined, have played a more intermittent role in Labour's history than might be imagined from the international reputation of such as the Webbs, the Coles, Tawney, or Laski. The very creation of the Labour Party at all in 1900 marked a defeat for the Webbs; from 1931 onwards the Fabians have been essentially a forum for ventilating ideas rather than an influence in their own right. Figures like Tawney and Cole became increasingly peripheral. Much of the time, intellectuals have been marginal to the operations of the party, and forced into the role of scapegoats or punchbags for union barons like Bevin or Deakin. There is, however, the unusual role of someone like Tony Crosland, who was both a major revisionist theorist and a leading politician who could give the socialist ethic a powerful new impetus in the fifties. John Strachey had tried to play a somewhat similar role, initially from a Marxist standpoint, but with less enduring impact. The most impressive recent illustration of a significant Labour intellectual might well be Denis Healey, though his main influence has been in specialist areas of foreign and defence policy rather than on the broad philosophy of the party. On the whole, the Labour Party has been a frustrating, even dangerous, territory for the left-wing intellectual. It is not surprising that he or she now appears to be a dying breed.

Equally, the unions have found their role in the party to be more and more indirect since the 1920s. It has long ceased to be common for union bosses of the type of Henderson, Curran, Barnes, Thorne, Clynes, or Thomas to enter parliament. No longer does a man like Henderson embody in his own person the solid alliance of the TUC and Head Office. Even when a union celebrity like Frank Hodges entered parliament in 1924, it was a sign that he had left the world of the organized workers behind him, his union career tainted with the charge of betrayal. The engagement of the unions with politics since 1945 has been more and more tangential. Union-sponsored MPs have declined in number and impact from 1945 to 1983, while the unhappy experience of Frank Cousins in government in 1964–6 does not immediately encourage further participation by union officials. Yet the alliance between the unions and the Labour Party remains as powerful an axis of British politics as ever, as emphatic in the move to the left at party conference and on the NEC after 1970 as in the years of right-wing domination after 1945. After the 1983 election, the 104 union-sponsored MPs numbered almost half the parliamentary party. The influence of the unions certainly extends far beyond industrial policy; Labour's policy on nuclear weapons or the Common Market, for instance, was largely dictated by the left-wards thrust in major unions. Yet the gulf that has opened up, since at least the 1960s, between the key officials of major unions and the political leadership has been a central, determining feature of modern British politics. The union presence remains, but the effect is to make Labour more sectional in its outlook and policy-making than a coherent driving force with a national appeal. The prolonged difficulties over incomes policy, from the days of Cripps in 1948 to renewed attempts at anti-inflation pay policies in 1986, are evidence of a wider weakness.

On balance, the most effective types of Labour leaders have been not the union bosses, nor the intellectuals, nor again the machine men of Transport House, but the pragmatic operators, with national figures like Henderson, Attlee, Morrison, Wilson (up to a point), Callaghan, Hattersley, and Kinnock to provide unity and a sense of cohesion, along with a roll-call of local-government patriarchs (or godfathers) like Jack Braddock in Liverpool, T. Dan Smith in Tyneside, Ike Hayward in London, or Llew Heycock in Glamorgan. Patronage has always provided invaluable cement for the structure of Labour rule. But people like this have always coexisted with the prophets, apostles of the old faith. Hardie, Lansbury, Ellen Wilkinson, Cripps, Bevan, the different styles embodied in the Old Left of Foot and the New Left of Benn have always been essential ingredients in the mix, too. A continuing problem for Labour has always been to find a national leader with the capacity to combine both the realism of the pragmatists and the charisma of the prophets. At times in the fifties, the attractive and irreplaceable figure of Aneurin Bevan seemed capable of supplying both. Whether Neil Kinnock proves to be, ideologically as well as geographically, his heir in this respect remains to be seen, though it is certainly possible.

Whether the Labour Party in Britain has been less successful in generating an appropriate range of leaders, compared with other European socialist parties, is a matter for debate. It is still a party, despite all the recent accretions, deeply wedded to the unions, blue-collar and white-collar, and to the organized working class. Its strength has flowed from the fact that it has, over the years, retained the proletarian base denied to the French or Italian socialists through the challenging presence of large Communist parties in those countries. It has also avoided the regional or linguistic divisions endemic in recently growing socialist parties in Spain or Greece. Labour has not produced the highly personalized or institutionalized leadership shown by socialist leaders in Latin or southern European countries, such as Mitterrand in France, Gonzales in Spain, Papandreou in Greece, or (with special provisos) Craxi in Italy. It is testimony to British Labour's deep native roots within our society that it has not needed to. After all, Craxi in Italy, to take one extreme example, presides serenely over a party that gains barely ten per cent of the Italian vote.

In other European countries, there have been some remarkable changes in leadership structures. It is noticeable that the French Socialist Party, ever since the 1930s, while retaining industrial strongholds such as the Pas de Calais, and old centres of agrarian socialism or even Jacobinism in the south and Languedoc, has become steadily more bourgeois in membership and in leadership. Tony Judt's analysis of the French Socialist Party shows, even for the period 1920–36, a clear decline in its working-class or artisan strength, and a growing support amongst the *employé/fonctionnaire* groups, government employees, small shopkeepers in rural towns, and professional workers such as schoolteachers. This bourgeoisification of French socialism was even more noticeable in the revival under Mitterrand after 1971. The 1981 Mitterrand government included amongst its thirty-seven members not a single proletarian, compared with a variety of *hauts fonctionnaires*, university teachers, company directors, bank managers, doctors, journalists, and others. The comparatively working-class Prime Minister, André Mauroy, was himself a technical school teacher by occupation. Later he gave way to the patrician 'Enarche' (or product of École Nationale d'Administration), Laurent Fabius. Compared with the British Labour Party, French socialist leadership, nationally and locally, shows an absence of any secure trade-union foundation.

This has always been less true of the German SPD, whose support from the 1880s to the 1970s has always come largely from organized workers and the unions. Before the First World War, the German socialist world was an enclosed, proletarian culture, almost hermetically sealed off from the imperialist, capitalist regime all around it. Yet the increasingly bourgeois character of the party's leadership, and the dominance and upward mobility of professional politicians, was shown by the prominence of men like Ebert, Scheidemann, and Noske, even in the early years, for all their working-class antecedents. In the years after the adoption of the 1959 Godesburg Programme, with its renunciation of Marxism, and even more under the chancellorship of Helmut Schmidt between 1974 and 1982, a new technocratic, distinctly pragmatic kind of socialism was clearly emerging in Germany. Its very legitimacy as a socialist party at all was openly questioned by the Young Socialist 'Jusos' and others on the far left. By 1980, the employed middle-class (white-collar workers, professionals, students) claimed forty-five per cent of the SPD membership, as against thirty per cent who were working class (the remainder were housewives and pensioners). A new leader like Johannes Rau, the centre-right minister-president of North Rhine Westphalia and candidate for the chancellorship, seems likely to perpetuate the trend in this direction. Meanwhile, the Dutch Labour Party has illustrated this kind of movement even more emphatically, although here the effect has been rather to loosen and democratize the internal party structure, somewhat on the lines urged by Tony Benn in Britain.

The most consistently successful Social Democratic Party in Europe from 1932 to the mid-1980s has unquestionably been that of Sweden. Originally based on unionized skilled workers, the growth of the public sector and of welfare services, combined with much social mobility, gave the Social Democrats a broad appeal across the nation. They enjoyed forty-two years of unbroken rule. Under Olof Palme, himself from a patrician line of higher civil servants, bankers, and lawyers, the ideological commitment to equality became more pronounced, along with radical stances in foreign policy. But the increasingly bourgeois character of Swedish socialism and its leaders remained as clear as ever. Indeed, a general conclusion about recent Swedish politics reached by political scientists is the marked decline of class-based voting. A 'reform bureaucracy' ethos predominates.

All these major socialist parties elsewhere have shown the capacity to adapt. This is apparent, for example, in the increasing role played by women in the Swedish, Dutch, German, and even French socialist parties. The last is the more remarkable for a nation where women received the vote only after the second world war. Yet by 1978 almost a third (200,000) of the French Socialist Party's membership was female. The old confessional aspects which inhibited the growth of socialism are less apparent, too. As evidence of this, there is the successful post-war SPD challenge to Catholic social philosophy in Germany, and signs of new strength in Bavaria and the south. The Austrian socialists showed similar tendencies in the Kreisky era. In France, the 1970s saw a growing appeal of the French socialists among Catholic voters, the more startling for a party long associated with anti-clericalism and Freemasonry. By 1981, almost half of French Catholics were voting 'left', while a moderate socialist like Michel Rocard was proving attractive in socialist missionary areas such as conservative Brittany.

The socialist parties of Sweden, Germany, and France have shown much skill in projecting themselves amongst economically thriving, upwardly mobile sections of their societies. To this extent, they have offered a more consistently effective image of both leadership and policy than the British Labour Party has managed to achieve in the years since the Attlee government. Party membership as a proportion of the vote tends to be much higher with continental socialist parties. On the other hand, these European parties, in the main, lack British Labour's traditional roots among the working class, skilled and unskilled, which has made the party by far the most internationally influential of the non-Communist left parties in the world, perhaps since 1918. The very reliance of the French or German socialists on more atomized and volatile middle-class support is a source of potential weakness. Some of it could easily migrate to other havens such as the West German, Austrian, and Dutch 'green' environmentalists. Indeed, for this, as for other reasons, the 1980s have usually seen socialist parties in retreat in most continental European countries, with heavy defeats for the German SDP in 1983 and the French socialists (for all the high hopes of Mitterrand's election) in 1986; electoral setbacks in the Netherlands, Belgium, Norway, Denmark, and Portugal, though emphatically not in Spain; in Austria some signs of erosion after Kreisky's resignation in 1983 and the loss of the presidency in 1986, not wholly due to anti-Semitism released by the Waldheim campaign. Even in Sweden, there was evidence of fragility in the long-impregnable Social Democratic Labour party even before Palme's assassination; indeed, the 1976 elections in Sweden actually led to six years of Conservative rule. The most hopeful countries for the socialist movement have been Spain and Greece, ex-fascist countries where the very roots of democracy at all are somewhat slender. On balance, therefore, it may be concluded that the lessons the British Labour Party need learn from its variegated European comrades are distinctly limited.

Labour's capacity to generate new kinds of leadership at all levels in the 1980s is critical for the future of British politics. Commonly, the problem is associated with a popular diagnosis of long-term decline. In the 1983 general election, Labour performed catastrophically, gaining less than twenty-eight per cent of the vote, its worst performance statistically since 1918. Many have seen Labour as crumbling locally, too, with the disappearance of the old industrial heartlands and the decay of the inner cities. Old socialist strongholds like Poplar, the Gorbals, or the Rhondda are losing population fast, and are in manifest decline. Professional people and the intelligentsia have shown a lessening enthusiasm for the party—and indeed for political participation in general, amidst a widespread disillusion in the country. Lack of faith in Labour as an instrument of reform is part of a broader decline of legitimacy in our key institutions, which takes in parliament, industry, the universities, and the police among its varied victims. Some of the discontented have found their haven in the Social Democratic Party, though their divisions, fragile character, and difficult relations with their Liberal allies on defence and other matters suggest that they are an insecure alternative. To date, the dreams of Limehouse in 1981—that the mould of Labour–Conservative two-party domination will be broken—have not been fulfilled.

On the other hand, Labour's prospects are certainly capable of major repair. The fashionable talk of a 'swing to the right' amongst intellectuals, in which not merely socialism but even Butskellite Keynesianism had lost its appeal since the mid-1970s, now seems implausible. The left has certainly taken some recent changes on board. It has accepted the need for reforms of the practices of the trade unions and their need to accept anti-inflation policies on labour costs, side by side with controlled reflation, to restore employment. The acceptance of the sale of council houses marks another important shift in policy. Otherwise, the political consensus of the nation is still largely dictated by the heritage that Labour created after 1945. The relative unpopularity of the Thatcher government in the mid-1980s might well stem from the simple boredom which afflicts all long-serving administrations and prime ministers. But it has been fuelled powerfully by the government's consistent attacks on public spending and public services. The Thatcherite assault on basic premises of the post-1945 revolution, including full employment, regional development policies, the maintained schools, the National Health Service, and the fabric of the social services, together with accretions from the 1960s such as expanded higher education and support for the arts, has caused nationwide alarm. The ethic of privatization and the market economy is viewed with consistent suspicion by a wide range of major social groups including pensioners, residents in remoter rural areas, black voters, deskilled manual workers, the disabled, working mothers, students, and young people generally. The creed of the majority of the nation, from 'wet' Tories through the Alliance to most reaches of the Labour Party not blighted by the Militant contagion, is still 'Labourish', as understood over the past forty years.

The intellectual climate since 1945 has not, in fact, fundamentally changed. This is because it chimes in with a popular instinct, rooted deep in our history, for individual freedom combined with social fairness. In the mid-1970s there was alleged to be a philosophic revolution taking place, launched by the new right. In this new atmosphere, it was argued, the orthodoxies of Keynesian economics, public provision, redistributive taxation, and social welfare were being dethroned. This was the thesis offered, for example, by an interesting, largely Thatcherite symposium, written by dons and others and published in 1976. Yet its main arguments now seem infinitely dated. It is more out of date than, say, Douglas Jay's *The Socialist Case*, which appeared almost forty years previously. The counter-revolution, broadly, has not happened. Its advocates resemble old Bourbons rather than young Turks. Monetarist economics have lost their lustre as their intellectual premises have lost credibility, along with M3 and other once-fashionable indicators. There have been signs of flagging faith even in the London Business School, while it would be hard indeed to claim that the political writings of Roger Scruton and his colleagues of the *Salisbury Review* herald any kind of intellectual renaissance. The right-wing alternative to the Fabians and Tawney, even to Beveridge and Keynes, simply has not materialized. All around there are the signs of unfulfilled expectations and new dangers. Conservatives in the West Midlands, for example, have witnessed the relentless contraction of the motor industry, the pivot of their local economy. More generally they have seen the continuing evidence of an economic system failing to use up fifteen per cent of its capacity, and of a large deficit in manufactured goods for the first time since Britain became an industrialized nation. Repeated pleas in Conservative ranks in 1984–6 for reflation, a rebuilding of the public infrastructure, investment in the social services rather than tax cuts for the wealthy, more 'caring', compassion, and the like, are not merely intelligent anticipations of possible electoral catastrophe in 1987 or 1988 for the British right. They are also a vindication of the mainstream Conservatism pursued by administrations for a hundred years from Disraeli to Heath. They provide a commentary on the basic strategic and philosophical failures of the mandarins of the new Conservative creed. They testify to the continuing intellectual dominance of the British moderate left. Even under Mrs Thatcher, we remain almost all quasi-socialists now.

Labour, then, in many ways still has the ideological tide behind it. What it also needs is the kind of leadership to give its priorities expression in contemporary and intelligible form. A greater political sensitivity among trade union leaders would help powerfully. Indeed, there have been many recent indicators that the self-absorbed nihilism that led to the 'winter of discontent' in 1979 and thus inaugurated a near-decade of Tory, anti-union rule is now being rejected. Even the trauma of the miners' strike had some political benefits. Union leaders of the old left like Ron Todd of the Transport Workers, as well as right-wing figures like John Edmonds of the Municipal Workers or Bill Jordan of the Engineers, all embody the new realism. It may be hoped, therefore, that the unions' leadership will involve itself more positively and vigorously in the national political process, rather than in sectional pressure group activity solely for the supposed benefit of their members. A TUC general secretary like Norman Willis has the opportunity to act as a figure on the national political stage, instead of the more restrained role of the Tewsons, Woodcocks, and Murrays, of the past. One hopeful pointer may be that union-sponsored MPs tend increasingly to consist of young graduates in professional posts rather than the mainly elderly full-time union officials who predominated until well after 1945. Over a third (34.7 per cent) of the union-sponsored MPs in 1983 had received higher education, and the entire Trade Union Group of Labour MPs was becoming transformed in character.

Locally and nationally, new life should be injected into Labour's leadership cadres. They should, for instance, certainly reflect the growing centrality of women (including black women) in the workforce and in our professional life. Bringing in more representatives from the women increasingly employed in health, education, banking, electronics, or office employment—indeed, almost all the growth sectors of the labour force—would give the party a far broader appeal. It might also counter the more strident, inbred feminism recently vocal in constituency politics, and which, for instance, weakened the popular appeal of the campaigners on Greenham Common. There is also a paramount need to mobilize black and other ethnic groups, disillusioned nationalists in Wales and Scotland, the comparatively apolitical or disillusioned young, including students, and a great range of middle opinion anxious about the environment and the effects of nuclear and other pollution. In this last context, it might be noted that there is no need at all for Labour to be in the least defensive about its anti-nuclear defence posture. Amongst the articulate middle class, the anger provoked by recent inroads into higher and other education (shown in the sharp rebuff to the Conservatives in 1985 when Mrs Thatcher's proposed honorary degree at Oxford was emphatically voted down) could also provide new dimensions of support. The kind of intellectual and professional sentiment mobilized by the left in the lead-up to 1945 could be won over again. The recruitment for HELP (Higher Education for the Labour Party) is a possible portent, as is the new politicization of scientists and the sharply anti-Tory mood amongst educationalists of all kinds since the teachers' strike. The civic potentiality of socialism has been given new currency by leaders such as Ken Livingstone and David Blunkett, though some enforced privatization of services, falling local revenues and an enervating sense of economic decline make old-style municipal socialism a less powerful cause. The sad case of Liverpool is a warning of the isolation that can result if the parliamentary and legal framework is rejected, and if socialism does not emerge through consent. But the elements of new life and new hope for Labour are certainly there in abundance: the 1986 local government elections perhaps confirmed this. The younger generation symbolized by Kinnock and Hattersley (both of working-class stock) could provide an encouraging framework for it, assuming that the party can drag itself away from introspection and arguments about internal purges, and look at wider objectives and the pursuit of power. It is no longer self-evident that Labour cannot win.

There is no easy diagnosis for Labour to generate a new, more contemporary style of leadership throughout the movement. In part, the problems of the party are a facet of a wider decline in political participation and a plain lack of interest in politics at all, in a world where the mechanics of computerized technology can drive the content out of politics, and where endless economic crises can destroy the spirit of hope. Perhaps, then, a passing glance at history could provide some limited help, even if it means the argument coming back full circle. Labour has too often been a prisoner of its past, and a devotee at the shrine of ancestor worship. Yet it can still learn by looking back. There is abiding value and instruction in analysing the types of leadership it has produced from the time of Keir Hardie onwards. After all, a remarkably high proportion of the personalities discussed in this book had careers which were outstandingly creative and successful. The legacy of the past, the record of the strikingly gifted men and women who rose up as practitioners or prophets in Labour's history, may help suggest new models, perhaps new myths, to which the movement can respond in the electoral challenge that lies ahead. The immediate future may continue a process of twenty years of Labour decline; it may produce muddled, inconclusive results; or it may even rekindle a new progressivism and social consciousness along the lines of 1906 or 1945. But, whatever the immediate outcome, the historian can risk one prophecy: the high probability remains that, despite the serried ranks of flinching cowards and sneering traitors, Labour's cult of personality will continue to flourish.

# I

## FOUNDING FATHERS
### 1900–1931

# KEIR HARDIE

KEIR HARDIE personifies the necessary myth of the British labour movement. His career was in some ways a remarkably uncomplicated one. He never held—or, indeed, sought—public executive office of any kind, unless we count a temporary membership of the Auchinleck School Board back in 1881. More than any other of Labour's founding fathers, he symbolizes the idea of permanent opposition, of Labour as the party of protest, the voice of outrage. The popular image of him was summed up by *The Times* on the occasion of his death in September 1915—'He was the most abused politician of his time ... No speaker has had more meetings broken up in more continents than he.' And yet it is clear that, to a unique degree, his long-term influence upon working-class history was creative and constructive. He was one of those rare figures of whom it can be said that British politics would have followed a very different course had he never lived. Almost by accident, he became the architect of a social and political revolution, as well as an abiding inspiration who still casts his spell over the working-class movement today.

The main historical problem with Hardie is trying to disentangle the man from the legend. Long before his death (at the relatively early age of fifty-nine), he had achieved immortality as 'the man in the cloth cap'. He was a man of the apocalypse. A Welsh disciple, Wil Jon Edwards, saw him as 'a latter-day Jesus' (the biblical imagery comes naturally in this context). Edwards went on, 'The man and his gospel were indivisible'. Ramsay MacDonald, by contrast, compared Hardie with Moses, a prophet leading the children of labour out of the wilderness towards the promised land. Hardie, indeed, remains one indisputed hero for the British labour movement, one of the saints who from their labours rest. Years after his death, Labour Party conferences could be galvanized into fraternal unity, if only for a time, by intoning the beguiling phrase, 'If Keir Hardie were alive today ...'

Hardie's followers saw him as an incorruptible idealist. His enemies, inverting the point, treated him as a wild extremist. He was, it seemed, the very model of full-blooded socialism, red in tooth and claw. An India Office civil servant had to persuade Lord Crewe in

1912 that there might be some tactical advantage in treating Hardie as a human being for once—though he made the suggestion without much enthusiasm or conviction. Hardie's flamboyant entry into parliament, his outspoken attacks on the Queen and the royal family, his advocacy of such terrifying doctrines as socialism, feminism, pacifism, and colonial freedom all prejudiced conventional opinion against him from the start. Baron Corvo's play *Hadrian VII* depicted Hardie in the guise of Gerry Sant, a mad Aberdonian anarchist who assassinates the pope. With Hardie, any extravagance of speech or action appeared credible.

So, to try to subject Hardie and his role in the British labour movement to proper historical scrutiny, we have first of all to try to cut through the swathes of legend created by disciples and detractors alike. One legend—alas!—has to be discarded from the start. The 'man in the cloth cap' did not actually wear one at all. Contemporary accounts and photographs make it clear that what he wore on that famous day in August 1892, when he entered parliament as member for West Ham South (preceded by a cornet player striking up the *Marseillaise* in the absence of any agreed socialist anthem) was, in fact, a deerstalker, reminiscent of Sherlock Holmes. The point is of more than decorative importance—though an interesting field for study would be the sartorial imagery associated with successive labour leaders, through Jimmy Thomas's dinner jacket down to Harold Wilson's Gannex raincoat and Michael Foot's donkey jacket. The point about Hardie's headgear in 1892 is that he was not then, or ever afterwards, a typical cloth-capped working man, straight from the factory floor or the football terraces. He was rather a romantic, a Bohemian, a contemporary of Aubrey Beardsley and the *Yellow Book* and *fin-de-siècle* aestheticism. He was an outsider in the labour movement who pursued a tortuous, but heroic, path all his own.

The real Hardie, as opposed to the figure of legend, was a man with at least five lives, and five different kinds of entry into the world of labour. First, an aspect often forgotten in his later political years, he was in his youth a notable figure in the so-called 'new unionism' of the 1880s. As secretary of the Ayrshire Miners' Union and stormy petrel *par excellence* of the Lanarkshire and Ayrshire coalfields, he was a powerful rebel, both in Scottish mining unionism and in the Trades Union Congress. His fierce personal attack on Henry

Broadhurst, long-serving secretary of the TUC Parliamentary Committee, at the Swansea congress in 1887, was laughed out of court at the time. The barons of King Coal and King Cotton, and their allies amongst the craftsmen, brushed it aside. But Hardie's challenge spelt the downfall of the Lib-Labbism and the ethic of class collaboration which had been the ideological hallmark of the TUC in the early phase of its history. It heralded the emergence of the British unions from prehistory into history.

Secondly, Hardie was the supreme, consistent champion of the idea of Labour's political independence. To this end, he took on both the Lib-Labs and the intellectual Fabians in dialectical combat, and defeated them all. He embodied the proud ethic of independence in his own prickly personality. He was the main founder of the Independent Labour Party at Bradford in January 1893, its chairman in its formative years, and its dominating personality right down to the twenty-first anniversary, an emotional occasion again held at Bradford, in 1914. Beyond that, Hardie carried the ILP ethic forward into forming the Labour alliance between the trade unions and the socialist societies, which bore fruit at the famous meeting at the Memorial Hall, Farringdon Street. Here was born the Labour Representation Committee, the forerunner of the Labour Party, the essential vehicle for Hardie's creed of independence.

Thirdly, he was a considerable parliamentary figure, far more so than contemporary dismissals of his sometimes maladroit or incoherent performances in the House of Commons would suggest. As member for West Ham in 1892–5, and even more as member for Merthyr Boroughs from 1900 onwards, he was often an effective voice for his class on unemployment and other themes. He later became the first chairman of the Parliamentary Labour Party in 1906–8. This was not his happiest period in politics, certainly. Yet even here there were successes to record, notably the adoption by the Liberal government of Labour's Trade Disputes Act of 1906, which freed the unions from the legal shackles of the Taff Vale verdict some years earlier.

A fourth career, again one often neglected, was that of journalist and all-purpose, all-weather propagandist. Nothing is more moving about Hardie's early career than how this illegitimate, virtually uneducated young Scots miner taught himself to read and write, and how he acquired the skills of Pitman's shorthand by scratching out the characters on a blackened slate with the wire used by miners to adjust the wicks of their lamps, in the dark depths of a Lanarkshire pit. He found delight in the writings of Carlyle and Ruskin, George Eliot and Dickens. Throughout his career, Hardie attached immense importance to the power of the written word in making socialists. He founded the weekly *Labour Leader* in 1894, itself a notable vehicle for the socialist cause, in which Hardie was everywhere—editor, manager, publisher, even author of the women's column under the soubriquet, 'Lily Bell', and of a children's column under the name 'Daddy Time'. When he was forced to sell the *Leader* in 1904, he fought hard to ensure that it would remain a free, independent editorial voice of socialism. Years later, in 1911, he helped launch a famous weekly in his Merthyr constituency, *The Pioneer*, featuring among other things a Welsh-language column from the exotic socialist preacher–bard, the Revd Thomas Nicholas, 'Niclas y Glais'. In addition, Hardie was a ceaselessly active pamphleteer and author, with famous tracts to his name on the physical exploitation of his chemical works by the Scots Presbyterian philanthropist, Lord Overtoun, on the horrors of 'sweated Dowlais' and on the shooting down of workers by troops during the 1911 rail strike at Llanelli, *Killing No Murder*. He attached much importance to Labour journalism, and campaigned without success on Labour's NEC to secure the party's backing for a national Labour daily newspaper. The *Daily Citizen* never really fitted the bill. In the 1980s, with Labour's projection in the press dependent on the tender mercies of capitalists such as Robert Maxwell, Hardie might well have wondered into what directions his campaign for a Labour press had led.

Fifth and finally, Hardie was a considerable internationalist. At a period when British labour took its participation in the world socialist movement much more seriously, when socialists like Jaurès, Bebel, or Adler could feel themselves to be, in some sense, citizens of the world like the men of 1789, Hardie was an important figure. He was active and influential in the Second International (whose founding meeting at Paris in 1889 he attended), in forging links between British Labour and European, American, and empire socialist parties, and in the world-wide peace movement. He and the Frenchman, Edouard Vaillant, crusaded in vain before 1914 on behalf of an international workers' strike against war. Hardie died in September 1915, tragically, amidst a total war which provided an obscene mockery of his values of fraternalism and international solidarity. But, here again, was an area in which he wrenched the British labour

movement, and British history generally, into significantly new directions.

Now, in approaching the historical problem of Keir Hardie, there is
certainly no need for hero-worship. Like all of us, he was a somewhat
flawed individual. As noted above, he was far from being that reassuring stereotype, 'the typical working man', whatever that might mean
precisely. He was in himself a complicated, emotional, self-con-
tradictory individual. For all his solid family life in Cumnock with
his retiring and unpolitical wife, his private life was marked by
frequent warm attachments to young socialist women, of whom
Sylvia Pankhurst was the most celebrated. He acknowledged his own
role as a permanent outsider, even within the labour movement itself
in some ways. He described himself as 'an Ishmael in public life',
who gloried in his isolation. He lived in something of a private world,
marked by an intense belief in spiritualism and palmistry, in magic
and fairies. Indeed, his participation in spiritualist seances was a
crucial bond between him and his close friend, the Salvationist
prophet, Frank Smith. In later life, Hardie took part in seances
with young socialists at Abercynon in his own constituency. It was
claimed by one of them thirty years on that Hardie returned to their
presence in July 1945 to give his benediction to the new Labour
government.

He also indulged in a personal variant of the cult of nature. His
newspaper columns were full of sentimental references to country
streams and glens, to lambkins gambolling over Celtic hillsides. Of
course, the dream of a pre-industrial arcadia was powerful in the
socialist movement of the nineties and later; hence the enduring
appeal of Blake's 'Jerusalem' as a class hymn. But Hardie's interpretation gave his mystical ideology and his brand of Christian populism
a highly distinctive flavour. He was also a touchy, sometimes difficult
colleague or comrade, especially over money matters. Matters such
as the bequest from the Misses Kippen or the sale of the *Labour Leader*
shares in 1904 caused much bad blood. There was even a row over
the Kippen money between Mrs Hardie and the ILP after the terms
of Hardie's will were announced. Contemporaries such as Ramsay
MacDonald and Bruce Glasier often found Hardie very hard to work
with—though, of course, the judgement of that Highland prima
donna and of Glasier, an over-sensitive and often jealous art nouveau

craftsman and poet, needs to be viewed with scepticism. Still, let us agree that Labour's folk hero was no plaster saint.

In more public terms, Hardie had two limitations of particular importance. First, he was almost wholly ignorant of any element of economics. Socialism, he wrote, 'is not a system of economics'. He had no theory of economic management, no understanding of trade cycles, of budgetary finance. He had picked up a few scraps from his favourite economic historian, the liberal Oxford scholar Thorold Rogers, who depicted the joys of daily life in the fifteenth century. But that was about all. Hardie once wrote to the young Fenner Brockway that his view of socialism concentrated on general principles, such as were expounded in his *From Serfdom to Socialism*. Hardie disliked 'specifics', especially economic specifics. He usually took refuge in an ethical, evangelical, almost utopian vision of socialism, the creed of 'the Christ that is to be'. In this, of course, he was typical of the ILP and the labour movement of his time. Socialists need not attend to the mysteries or deceits of economic policy-making within the capitalist order. The details of taxation or finance were seen as the sole province of Philip Snowden, and there matters remained (down to 1931, in fact). Hardie's general neglect of economics was wholly characteristic of Labour in its formative years, until the deluge.

Again, Hardie was never comfortable with the realities and compromises of power. John Burns's verdict on him at the time of his death in 1915 was 'the leader who never won a strike, never organized a Union, governed a parish or passed a bill—Barren Cumnock in the Duchy of Doctrinaire'. This is exaggerated and unfair—and Burns himself was no administrative genius as a Cabinet Minister during eight dismal years at the Local Government Board. But it still contains an important kernel of truth. Hardie was supremely unhappy with the pressures that attended his time as chairman of the Parliamentary Labour Party in 1906–8. It was, wrote Bruce Glasier, 'a seat of misery' for him. He saw his party as an instrument of protest. His instinctive reaction to social injustice was to respond with agitation outside parliament, as orator or pamphleteer. Thus, for instance, his attitude towards the fiery particle of Victor Grayson, who burst meteorically on the scene when elected for Colne Valley in 1907, was distinctly ambiguous. On the one hand, Grayson was an incorrigible adventurer, improperly nominated, who imperilled party unity. He was a young man who threatened 'men who have grown grey in the movement'. On the other, he represented a real thrust from grass-roots radicalism. Hardie, almost alone of the NEC, sent Grayson a message of support at Colne Valley. Later on, he was distinctly more sympathetic to 'Larkinism' in Ireland than were Henderson and the party regulars. Hardie, more than anyone else, more even than Lansbury or Michael Foot, symbolizes Labour cherishing its doctrinal purity in the wilderness. Aneurin Bevan would have classed him, along with the middle-period Jennie Lee, as chief amongst the political virgins. MacDonald certainly was much more effective than Hardie in applying himself to the realities of power, especially parliamentary power. Tawney once wrote of the need for socialism to acquire 'a hard cutting edge'. Certainly, to achieve this kind of vitality, it would be necessary to move far beyond the legacy of Keir Hardie.

But these limitations—shared, to a large extent, with the labour and trade-union movement of his day—were massively outweighed by Hardie's quite extraordinary achievements. Defining them is not an easy task. However, it may be suggested that his special contribution to British socialism lay equally in the realms of policy and of strategy.

In policy-making, Hardie pursued an enormous range of causes. Some of them (for instance, republicanism) proved unfruitful and even damaging to the party. But several of his major policy priorities have proved to be of enduring importance for the British left, and deserve to be resurrected.

There was, for example, the cause of unemployment. Hardie's proudest label when he first appeared in parliament in 1892–5 was that of 'the member for the unemployed'. During the 1880s and 1890s, unemployment entered public debate (and, some have claimed, the English language) for the first time. Hardie, for all his limited understanding of its economic origins, became the most powerful voice in politics demanding its redress. Following the 'under-consumptionism' popularized by the Revd Herbert Mills and others at the time (and shortly by J. A. Hobson), Hardie pressed for more intensive state intervention to provide work. He urged the case for state aid for poor-law guardians in necessitous or deprived areas such as his own West Ham dockland, for new schemes of publicly financed outdoor relief, for national protection of what came to be called 'the right to work'. In 1904–5 he emerged from a trough of internal party controversy to lend his powerful voice and pen to a new nation-wide campaign on behalf of the jobless, now embarking on the first 'hunger marches' of the twentieth century—and meeting with the same rough treatment from the Manchester police as their successors were to do in the thirties. Hardie's unlikely ally in this crusade was the Jewish-American soap millionaire and land taxer, Joseph Fels. Hardie was sufficiently undogmatic to welcome the Employment of Workmen Act passed by the Tory government in 1905, under the unlikely aegis of that backwards-looking squire, Walter Long. In the years down to 1914, the campaign against unemployment became a key to wider critique of the capitalist order. It helped differentiate the fledgling Labour Party from the reformist 'New Liberalism' put forward by Lloyd George and Winston Churchill. Hardie was not the most informed or penetrating critic of the spread of unemployment in service industries. Some of his proposed remedies, like labour colonies in such areas as the Hackney marshes, were not very realistic. The unemployed themselves were hard to mobilize as a coherent force. But he saw both the long-term political potential and the wider social implications in the issue of unemployment. It was an enduring theme that he made very much his, and Labour's, own.

By 1905, however, Hardie had moved on to wider radical themes. In particular, he had been caught up increasingly in the campaign on behalf of the rights and status of women. He was a major advocate of British feminism. A chapter on 'Socialism and the Woman Question' was a powerful passage in *From Serfdom to Socialism*. He was very closely linked with the suffragette movement, partly out of general moral commitment, of course, partly because of his personal friendship with the Pankhursts, mother and daughters. With the young Sylvia, as has been noted, he struck up a highly emotional rapport; she may even have been his mistress. In the *Workers' Dreadnought* in 1915, Sylvia wrote an anguished appreciation of her dead friend. He was 'the greatest human being of our time'. Hardie's gut commitment to the cause of women's suffrage even led him to defy majority opinion at the time of the party conference at Belfast in 1907, when he insisted on backing the immediate, if limited, suffrage for women that the WSPU demanded, rather than the general adult suffrage which most delegates favoured.

But he added to his feminism a social commitment, which he shared with (and partially derived from) Sylvia Pankhurst. After all, she was the most socially involved of the family as well as the most radical. After the first world war, in which Mrs Emmeline Pankhurst endorsed the 'patriotic' cause and sister Christabel actually became a Tory candidate for parliament, Sylvia briefly joined the new Communist Party. Hardie's commitment to the suffragette cause drew frequent criticism. It was said that the WSPU, after all, consisted mainly of middle-class women (or even aristocrats like the Countess of Warwick), while Hardie was said to be allowing his feminism to swamp his socialism. But in fact, he had carved out another crucial priority for the movement, one that made it the more appealing to radical progressives (such as the Pethick-Lawrences or Bertrand Russell). He helped not only to promote the cause of female suffrage, won soon after his death, but to provide a more secure status for women as wage-earners and participants in a welfare democracy. He also fought for women's unionization, along with pioneers such as Mary Macarthur. In this area, ironically, an enduring obstacle in later years proved to be the impermeable chauvinism of the trade-union movement and its well-known camp follower, Andy Capp. Perhaps the women's support groups set up during the 1984–5 miners' strike represented some kind of posthumous victory for Hardie's outlook.

Another theme of wider radical appeal to which Hardie attached himself was the defence and advance of democracy. Britain at the turn of the century was, of course, far from being a democratic polity, with barely sixty per cent of adult males—and no females, of course—having the vote. Hardie trumpeted the cause of democratic advance, though in his own way. His solution for the conflict between the Lords and Commons in 1909–11 was to end, rather than mend, the upper house of hereditary legatees. But this, like republicanism, was a lost cause among the incurably deferential English, who dearly loved a Lord. Even in 1983, Tony Benn's advocacy of the abolition of the Lords was taken, along with calls for industrial democracy, peace, and other dangerous demands, as a clinching proof of near-insanity. More profitably, Hardie turned to the defence of civil liberties, especially in the 1910–14 period. He spoke out against the violent conduct of police in coal, dock, and rail strikes, and the growth of a nationally organized police force, backed up by the army, free from democratic restraint or accountability, during Churchill's brief but ominous time at the Home Office in 1910–11. Hardie was among the first to draw attention to the expanding role of the police in putting down industrial protest by free trade-unionists—assisted by troops called in by police chiefs like the appalling Captain Lindsay in Glamorgan, without the necessary requisition by magistrates. Lives were lost at Tonypandy, Liverpool, and Llanelli during the tense pre-war years, and blood spilt freely elsewhere as far afield as the Cornish clay pits, with no public enquiry or hint of official regret. In however inchoate a form, Hardie had alighted on a theme pregnant with alarming possibilities for Labour and for civil liberties in years to come.

As a democrat, Hardie also advocated local decision-making. He was not only a champion of the municipal socialist ideal. He was also, in the jargon of the 1970s, a devolutionist. He claimed in Merthyr Tydfil to be a Welsh nationalist, not of course in the sense of Plaid Cymru today, but on behalf of a socialist self-governing Wales, and Scotland and Ireland as well. 'That is the kind of Nationalism that will be emblazoned on the Red Flag of Socialism.' The Red Dragon and the Red Flag would be united. Like another later spokesman come from elsewhere to the valleys, Michael Foot, Hardie was passionate in his defence of Wales, its language, culture, and democratic ideals. He wrote cordially of the national *eisteddfod* which (with his usual free way with historical evidence) he claimed had been set up in the Middle Ages to defend the professional interests of medieval bards against literary blacklegs. At bottom, Hardie saw his socialism as emerging from a rooted local culture. This was the basis of his case for local democracy, decentralization, and accountability. He wanted the fraternal socialism of the ILP to steer clear of the megalith of bureaucratic power advocated by the SPD in Germany. His diagnosis of institutional structures and mechanics was always hazy, and certainly the devolution model finally put forward by Labour in the 1970s for Scotland and Wales proved to be something of a well-meant fiasco. But, however unformed, the populism of Hardie and the ILP of his day remains a valid theme in the disunited Kingdom of the later twentieth century. We have not heard the last of devolution.

Overseas, Hardie was the first leader of the Labour Party to become directly involved with colonial liberation, rather than a vague and abstract hostility, to imperialism *per se*. He saw for himself. He liked travel, and he journeyed far afield to encourage nationalist movements in Africa and Asia, ranging as far as modern Malaysia and Japan. In South Africa, he spoke out on behalf of black African rights at Johannesburg, and he was howled down and his meeting broken up. But the episode was prophetic at a time when British radicals were inclined to sentimental sympathy for Boers on the Veldt. His visit to India in the autumn of 1907 caused an immense sensation. He was excited by Indian, especially Hindu, culture and religion. It 'appealed to the mystic and the seer in him', wrote Philip Snowden. He addressed *swaraj* (home rule) meetings in Bengal, and called for Indian self-government. There were cries for him to be deported; the Secretary of State, John Morley, that pure Gladstonian intellectual, was vicious in his condemnation. Hardie's speeches, like his last book on India in 1909 which is still worth reading, made it perfectly clear that his approach to Indian independence was gradualist and non-violent. But he identified British Labour unambiguously with Indian nationalism and the liberationist impulse of the Congress movement, comprising Hindu and Muslim alike at the time. He was a pioneer on the road that led to the transfer of power in 1947. Indeed, the present writer's correspondence has confirmed that, for many Indians in the 1970s and 1980s, Hardie remains a prophet of freedom.

Finally, Hardie harnessed Labour to the cause of world peace. He was, as noted, a considerable figure in the Second International. He travelled widely to Canada, Australia, and New Zealand as well. He visited the United States three times, where he visited the American socialist leader, Eugene V. Debs, in Woodstock gaol. Everywhere, he strove to mobilize the international socialist movement on behalf of a new initiative for peace. Indeed, opposition to war was indissoluble in Hardie's creed ever since his election for Merthyr and Aberdare during the jingo hysteria of the Boer War in 1900.

Like other socialists, Hardie viewed with deep alarm the growth of international rivalries and the build up of naval and other armaments from 1904 onwards. He led a furious attack in the Commons on the *entente* with the hated regime of Tsarist Russia—which led to his exclusion from Buckingham Palace garden parties by Edward VII, a disappointment which Hardie bore with some equanimity. From 1910 he and Vaillant tried to have the Socialist International committed to a general strike against war. The idea was, of course, a mirage. Yet it was also a more realistic strategy than has often been thought, and regarded with genuine alarm by the ruling élites of London and Berlin. His last year was a time of unbearable strain. He was howled down in his own constituency by a jingo mob at Aberdare on 6 August 1914. He spoke sadly of Gethsemane and crucifixion.

He tried during the war years to argue the case for a compromise peace. But in September 1915 he died, perhaps broken-hearted, at any rate worn out, a very, very old man of fifty-nine. At the subsequent by-election at Merthyr, Hardie's seat was captured by a proto-fascist miner, Charles Stanton, preaching hate against 'the Hun'. Labour's commitment to peace was muffled then, and remained erratic thereafter, especially during the cold war era after 1945. But enough of Hardie's pacific message survived to give renewed inspiration to the crusade against nuclear weapons in the 1960s and 1970s. With all his limitations, Hardie remains a viable inspiration for the modern peace movement.

Hardie's influence on Labour strategy may be dealt with more briefly. It may be summarized by saying that he was a consistent advocate of a middle way between the collaboration of the Lib-Labs and the extremism of theoretical revolutionary Marxism. In the nineties, he fought equally against the Liberal embrace, and the idea of 'fusion' with the Marxist Social Democrats. One consistent theme was that the party must be solidly and uniquely based on the mass working-class, trade-union vote. Without the unions, amongst whom he had risen to influence in Scotland, the 'labour alliance' would be nothing. Even if the leaders of the unions were not necessarily socialist— indeed, they were very much the reverse in many coalfields and textile communities—it was vital to ally with them on behalf of common objectives. They would come over in the end. In this, Hardie, a rough, self-educated miner, out-argued with sheer logical power the intellectual Fabians whom he regarded as an inbred, middle-class debating society. Equally, he argued successfully in the press and on the platform against the class-war ideology of the Social Democrats who simply alienated the British workers with their violent talk. For Hardie, the broad mass of unionized workers, non-revolutionary but deeply class-conscious, were the bedrock.

At the same time, Labour should be much more than simply a workers' party. Its constituency of support should be ever broadened. Middle-class progressives should be brought into the ILP to 'blend the classes into one human family'. Even an eccentric aristocrat like the Countess of Warwick, Edward VII's former mistress, was acceptable within the fold. The presence in the 1945 government of old ILP middle-class products like Attlee, Dalton, Pethick-Lawrence, and Creech Jones was testimony to Hardie's long-term success.

Always, he was prepared to collaborate with middle-class radicals on behalf of progressive objectives, as he did at West Ham and as he often did with his fellow member for Merthyr, D. A. Thomas, the coalowner of Tonypandy notoriety. Labour should avoid the doctrinal rigidities of the German socialists. Socialism in the future did not rule out social reform in the here and now. Welfare measures such as free school meals for working-class children or attacks on female sweated labour in themselves advanced the ethic and the logic of socialism. Minimum as well as maximum socialism was permissible to speed on the new social order.

He was at all times a constitutionalist. He never favoured the potential violence of 'direct action'. He was alarmed by the growth of pockets of syndicalism in the Rhondda and elsewhere in South Wales, and took issue with the doctrines of the *Miners' Next Step.* Labour should use the state, and capture its commanding heights by parliamentary means. It should not destroy it, or take the law into its own hands. He opposed the idea of class war. 'Socialism made war on a system, not a class.' On the other hand, he was a realist too. His class, he recognized full well, needed to defend itself by all available lawful means, especially when troops and Metropolitan police were patrolling Merseyside and the Welsh valleys in 1910–11, and Chief Constables like Lindsay were on the prowl. In an illuminating debate with Snowden in the *Labour Leader* in 1913 (a debate which Hardie manifestly won), Hardie strongly defended the workers' use of strike action. 'The strike and the ballot went hand in hand.' Class solidarity and disciplined industrial militancy in labour disputes were needed to make the ballot effective. They would filter into the political consciousness of the working class, the more so as unionization took firm hold. Hardie argued throughout for a fusion of political and industrial strategies. Together, they helped make Labour the leading democratic socialist party in the world after 1918.

But beyond these strategic and tactical nostrums, there was something else, something hard for the historian to define. Hardie never lost sight of the notion that socialism was an ideal, a secular faith. It was not just a matter of pragmatic calculation, technical planning, or managerial techniques. It meant a different kind of society, with equality and fraternity built into the new commonwealth. He had a passionate belief in the symbolism of May Day—'a thing of joy and beauty . . . a sacred day devoted to the cause of labour and humanity'. His very imagery revealed him as a man of passionate religious

conviction. Indeed, his evangelical background in the Scots Morrisonian sect, including his commitment to temperance, was a vital
ingredient in his creed. He was a prophet in an age of waning faith.
His charismatic appeal over the working class in his generation arose
from the fact that he embodied his faith in his own person, his own
independence, strength, incorruptibility, and dignity. No assessment
of Hardie can be satisfactory if it does not reach out beyond the
surviving records and suggest this added dimension of magic and
prophetic inspiration.

When Hardie died, Bernard Shaw wrote that, although he lay mould-
ering in his grave, his soul would go marching on. Well, does it? His
relevance to the labour and socialist movements of today, to the
usable past of Neil Kinnock and Roy Hattersley, is not altogether
clear. In so many ways, the style of his socialism belongs to some
previous age—the crusading style of the chapel-reared radicalism of
late-Victorian Britain with its passionate quest for a new Jerusalem.
The battle-scarred, disenchanted history of the Labour Party since
1915 reveals an immense range of fissures and tensions of which
Hardie would have had little conception, and which would undoubtedly have dispirited him.

Yet, in many ways, he is still a highly contemporary figure. The
issues for which he campaigned have not lost their resonance. The
concern with mass unemployment is indeed more central for the
modern labour movement than for Hardie's Edwardian years of
relative prosperity. Continued discrimination, overt and latent,
against women and ethnic minorities, the concern aroused by police
behaviour during the miners' and other recent strikes, the unimaginable horrors of nuclear weapons, including Cruise missiles, sited
without popular consultation on British shores, all follow directly
from themes that Hardie made very much his own. His strategy also
remains extremely valid. His vision of a Labour Party which was
based ultimately on the unions but was also a popular front of
radicals and activists, constitutional in method but fusing political
and industrial militancy for common objectives, is largely the pattern
the movement has pursued over the years. The need to harness the
energies of the labour alliance for united dynamic action remains as
imperative in the era of Mrs Thatcher as in that of Mr Asquith.

The truth, perhaps, is that Hardie's legacy is somewhat hard to
define because of its essential ambiguity. Indeed, the overlay of legend

makes the task harder still. In so many ways, his ethic was that of the broad church, gradualist, tolerant, solid, subordinating doctrinal divisions to practical action on behalf of specific objectives. Attlee, Gaitskell, Callaghan could claim to be legitimate heirs of Keir Hardie, the apostle of mainstream constitutionalism. At the same time, it is a great mistake to exaggerate Hardie's respectability or willingness to conform. The contemporary charges of extremism and fanaticism cannot be dismissed as just the accusations of paranoid capitalists contemplating the seeds of their own decay. At bottom (as the young Attlee wrote in 1920), Hardie was essentially an agitator of genius, a socialist of a fundamentalist stamp. He could see almost any form of lawful grass-roots activism, home and overseas, as worthy of encouragement, even when spearheaded by such erratic champions as Victor Grayson in England, James Larkin in Ireland, or B. G. Tilak in India. Philosophically, as well as temperamentally, he shades off from the opportunist parliamentarianism of a MacDonald as well as from the 'calculating machines' of Butskellite and other eras. His message could even be spuriously employed by the Communist Party in the 1920s as cannon-fodder against the current Labour leadership. The Bevanites of the fifties and the Bennites of the seventies could, with equal validity, claim to be his heirs too. Ken Livingstone, if hardly the Trotskyists of Militant, could claim him as a comrade. Hardie is the prophet of the sectaries of true believers as well as the latitudinarians of the broad church.

Perhaps one way of reconciling these confusions might be to relate Hardie's approach to a different and more loosely structured form of labour movement. His party, after all, was the product, if not of the classic slum, certainly of the traditional mass working class of the late Victorian age. Now that class is eroding fast, the process speeded by deindustrialization and unemployment in Labour's old heartlands, British society is infinitely more complex and fragmented in its socio-logical gradations. In this new context, Hardie's message could be used to promote a labour movement which still exalts the surviving working class, but which is able to reach out to a range of other protest groups, including the women's movement, the ethnic communities, residual national sentiment in Scotland and Wales, anti-nuclear environmentalists, and the peace movement. At any rate, it is more relevant than many more formal statements of the socialist message to our current dilemmas. It was part of the greatness of Hardie that the vision of socialism that he articulated so passionately reached out in so many different directions. Aneurin Bevan wrote, years later, on how 'the capacity for emotional concern for human life was the most significant quality of a civilized human being'. On that test, Hardie remains a touchstone of civilization (not only to socialists), for our society, our century, and our world.

# RAMSAY MacDONALD

THE shades of Keir Hardie and of Ramsay MacDonald dominate the mythology of the early British Labour Party. They were, of course, comrades-in-arms, fellow pioneers, in the Independent Labour Party, the Second International, and Labour's first years in parliament. MacDonald wrote a moving introduction to the authorized biography of Hardie by William Stewart in 1921. Yet their legacies for their successors are totally different. They symbolize the twin poles of Labour's ever-ambivalent attitude towards political power. Hardie's legacy is a positive one—a tradition of socialism as a pure and uncorrupted moral crusade which unites Labour's left and right in common devotion. MacDonald's memory is in total contrast—a parable of how a great working-class leader succumbed to the pressures of a 'bankers' ramp' and the insidious wiles of the 'aristocratic embrace' (literally so, in the case of Lady Londonderry) to destroy the party which made him. If a Labour politician sighs affectedly in one breath, 'If Keir Hardie were alive today', in the next he will declare 'but I will not be another Ramsay MacDonald'.

Few modern politicians have suffered a more cataclysmic decline in their reputations than has MacDonald. None has been more traduced by contemporaries or despised by later commentators. The pioneering days before 1914, when MacDonald just as much as Hardie was an inspiration to the labour movement, and far more creative in formulating its ideas and policies; the period of courageous protest against the hysteria of the first world war; MacDonald's leadership in 1924 and 1929 in making Labour's warring ranks an effective parliamentary force; the magnetic force of personality which led even Beatrice Webb to call him 'the greatest artist of his time'— all these have long been forgotten.

The turning-point, of course, was the political and economic crisis of August 1931. Those desperate days have blackened MacDonald's name with the British left for evermore. For the left since then, MacDonald is the very symbol of treachery and conspiracy. Hostile, even vicious accounts of his career have swept the field, epitomized in *The Tragedy of Ramsay MacDonald* (1938) by L. MacNeill Weir (once his private secretary). Since 1945, memories of MacDonald's delinquencies have been constantly evoked to rally Labour morale, and to ward off yearnings for coalition. Even in 1966 Harold Wilson had to tread most delicately when suggesting that MacDonald might have genuinely believed in 1931 that he was putting the interests of country above those of party. In the 1980s, the evil spectre of MacDonaldism still haunts Neil Kinnock as he contemplates the dangers of an electoral or other agreement with the Alliance parties. More than most, Labour does not love coalitions.

If the left have branded him as a plain traitor, the centre-right have dismissed him as a woolly-minded, somewhat pathetic incompetent. 'Ramshackle', 'the boneless wonder', 'a substitute for a leader' (Beatrice Webb's phrase) and similar abuse suggests a politician hopelessly out of his depth when confronted with economic collapse, with only an empty, out-of-date rhetoric to resist the terrifying pressures of a new century and a new world. Distinguished academic historians from Charles Mowat in 1955 to Robert Skidelsky in 1967 reinforced the view of MacDonald as foremost of the 'pigmies' and 'second-class brains', who led Britain to its lowest point of depression and dishonour. If Hardie, at least for his own supporters, remains one of the saints, MacDonald is commander-in-chief of the publicans and sinners, his coffers overflowing with thirty pieces of silver at the current market rate.

Until David Marquand's definitive biography appeared in 1977, there had been no worthwhile study at all of MacDonald and his role in British twentieth-century history. There had been a few revisionist studies of specific episodes, such as the minute dissection of the crisis of July–August 1931 by Reginald Bassett. But this was the work of a former National Labour man—an exotic breed, indeed—and therefore held to be suspect. There had been monographs on foreign policy which shed a more positive light on MacDonald's ideas of disarmament and international reconciliation in the twenties and early thirties. But for his career as a whole there was nothing, a silence informed by innuendo. Marquand's biography, securely based on a vast range of new unpublished material (notably MacDonald's papers, with their rich seams of private correspondence, diaries, and personal notebooks, all now stored in the Public Record Office at Kew) has magnificently redressed the balance. The nuances of Mac-Donald's strange, introverted personality, and his brooding, self-pitying temperament, are etched in with grace and subtlety. For his subject's political career, Marquand, himself a Labour MP for eleven years (as well as a trained historian from the A. J. P. Taylor stable of thoroughbreds) has provided an analysis that is never less than compelling, especially for the critical middle years from 1914 to 1931 when the MacDonald papers appear to be most profuse. The first and second Labour governments, and the split in 1931, are unforgettably described. Certainly, in the decade since Marquand's biography was published, Ramsay MacDonald has been rescued from the calumnies and myths of prehistory. How complete a rescue operation can be mounted, however, is quite another matter.

MacDonald's political outlook was moulded in the frontier period of the Labour alliance down to 1914. Second only to Hardie (like himself, an illegitimate boy from a desperately poor Scottish household), he was its architect. After a brief flirtation with the Scottish home rule movement, he emerged from the cocoon of Lib-Labbism in the nineties. After a short flirtation with the Marxist SDF, he joined the ILP in 1894, shortly after being turned down for the Liberal candidature for Dover (in fact, a seat that was solidly Tory from 1874 to 1945). But MacDonald retained strong affinities with advanced Liberalism. He was a member of the Rainbow Circle of intellectuals in the mid-nineties (significantly enough, its only prominent member who was in the ILP) and a member of the London County Council, where he worked comfortably enough with Liberal colleagues. His advance in the fledgling labour movement was a rapid one. He rose, from joining the National Administrative Council, the executive of the ILP, in 1896, to become the first secretary of the Labour Party (or LRC) in 1900, later the MP for Leicester in 1906, and finally chairman (and first real leader) of the Parliamentary Labour Party in 1911. His emergence was inseparable from Labour's rise from *fin-de-siècle* pressure-group radicalism in Gladstone's last years to becoming virtually an estate of the realm. By the eve of the first world war, his towering ascendancy over the party was beyond question.

His early importance had two main features. In the first place, he was Labour's main strategist. He was the creator of the famous Progressive Alliance, that partnership of a supposedly purely independent Labour Party with an increasingly radical Liberal Party, which dominated politics between the Boer War and the war of 1914. MacDonald it was who negotiated (without consulting any colleague, save, somewhat casually, Hardie) the secret *entente* of the

LRC with the Liberal whips in 1903. Without this deal, Labour could never have established a parliamentary foothold. Thereafter, MacDonald bent all his energies to ensuring that the tactics of Labour and the policies of the Liberal government were co-ordinated. He even backed the 1911 National Insurance Act, based as it was on the distinctly non-socialist idea of a poll-tax. In March 1914, there were prospects of a still closer relationship when Lloyd George suggested a possible formal coalition with a place for MacDonald in Asquith's Cabinet. This trap was avoided—though MacDonald was briefly tempted—since the ILP retained a fierce belief in Labour's independence as a prerequisite for ultimate victory. Still, it could well be argued that by 1914 MacDonald had helped give Labour a creative constitutional role within a wider progressive context. He had steered clear of the shoals both of trade-union sectionalism and of industrial direct action. With Henderson's reorganization of the party machine to assist him, MacDonald had ensured that Labour was poised to claim its inheritance.

Secondly, and complementary to this, MacDonald was Labour's leading political theorist. This may now seem very strange. Though subsequently derided as a romantic waffler whose ideas, and even syntax, were barely intelligible, he was hailed by Hardie in 1911 as 'the biggest intellectual asset of the movement'. His books in these pre-war years, *Socialism and Society*, *Socialism and Government*, and *The Socialist Movement*, seem distinctly dated today, with their stilted Darwinian jargon and dreamy Utopianism. They are also as repetitive as their titles suggest, with much recycling. Yet at the time they struck just the right note. Labour's programme was projected as the inevitable outcome of the world as it was, of an organic, evolutionary collectivism of a kind that appealed to MacDonald's scientific training: his first original work had been on 'The Geology of Bristol'. Yet it was also firmly built on the basis of the older radicalism, too. 'Socialism', MacDonald reassured his readers, 'retains everything of value in Liberalism.'

The emphasis in all his writing was on the evolutionary, orderly, peaceful route to socialism. The tensions and antagonisms of a brutish world would be set aside. The key to it would be the ever-extending role of the modern state. Far from withering away on the Marx–Engels model, the state would respond dynamically to the growing complexity of modern society by taking on an ever-wider range of functions. Always, MacDonald rejected the class-war doctrine of the Social Democrats, and the nationalism and jingoism of Blatchford and Grayson. Peace and order at home went alongside peace and fraternalism overseas. All this chimed with the mood of the politicized section of the largely artisan working class in the pre-1914 period, and with the more advanced 'sturdy radicals' of the Dilke type as well. It was the theoretical mainspring of Labour's drive to power, and was largely MacDonald's work.

In the pre-1914 years, MacDonald was culturally a period piece. As Marquand says, 'he lived on the margin of several worlds' in these years. He was deeply involved for a time with the secular nonconformity of the Fellowship of the New Life. He hobnobbed with the 'two Hobs', Hobson and Hobhouse, his Liberal progressive colleagues on the Rainbow Circle. He dabbled in Fabianism. A special inspiration was his wife, Margaret Gladstone, who turned his mind to women's suffrage and other advanced causes of the time. The effect upon him of her early death in 1911 was devastating and permanent. He wrote a deeply moving private memoir of her. In its published form, it conveyed at least some of his personal anguish, though it never assuaged it. The result was to lend a peculiar blend of toughness and vulnerability to his political style from that time on.

MacDonald's career down to August 1914 was that of a relatively orthodox Edwardian progressive. Then his world was turned upside down by the cataclysm of war. His life thereafter was totally transformed. From being a standard, left-centre radical with close access to government circles, he suddenly found himself a rebel and an outcast, the unquestioned leader of a new kind of left. MacDonald loathed war and violence of all kinds. He had been, along with Hardie, a major figure in the peace crusade of the Socialist International before 1914. War for him was a plague, a pestilence, an obscenity, a crime. It was the product of sinister covert diplomacy and corrupt capitalist greed. Its very existence shattered his faith in rational, orderly progress. It made nonsense of the idea of organic evolution. He spoke out with rare courage against the war from August 1914 onwards, and he suffered for it, as did his children. No socialist leader has faced more intense persecution than MacDonald did in these wartime years, but he emerged from the flames triumphant.

He gave up his leadership of the Labour Party to Henderson, and opposed the wartime coalitions of Asquith and then Lloyd George. He lost his seat at Leicester in the 1918 'coupon election', and was almost hounded out of public life. Yet it is deeply significant that MacDonald's opposition to the war took the form, not of simple pacifism, nor of the methods of the No-Conscription Fellowship which urged conscripts to defy the law and found many of its leaders in gaol as a result: MacDonald preferred collaboration with such radical Liberals as shared his viewpoint. The Union of Democratic Control, that famous body committed to open diplomacy, disarmament and a peace settlement, was founded in late August 1914. It was the work of Liberals, MPs like Ponsonby, Trevelyan, Morrell, and that passionate Francophobe, E. D. Morel, supported by assorted intellectuals such as Hobson, Angell, and Bertrand Russell.

Most of the ILP leaders, men like Hardie and Snowden, kept aloof from the UDC: they viewed the war from a socialist, not a populist, standpoint. But MacDonald unhesitatingly joined the UDC from the start. His name was placed first on all its official communications. In war, as in peace, he lived for the Progressive alliance, now ranged in opposition to the jingo advocates of a 'knock-out blow'. Like others on the left he responded passionately to the Russian revolution of February 1917, though not to its successor in October. He felt that 'a sort of spring-tide of joy had broken out all over Europe'. Snowden and others were similarly stirred. But MacDonald was immediately alert to the need to resist the revolutionary impulses of the new Bolshevik regime, lest a new and more oppressive despotism rise up from the ashes of Tsardom. When peace came, he bent his efforts to keeping the ILP away from the clutches of the Communists and to prising the Second International away from the Third, an offshoot of the Comintern.

In effect, as a founder member of the UDC, MacDonald was already measuring his distance from the militant ILP rank and file. As before 1914, he was scathing about the 'direct action' proposed by the Triple Alliance, especially when it was voiced by wild Welshmen, or immigrant Welshmen, like Arthur Cook. Nevertheless, as disillusion set in with the Lloyd George coalition in 1921-2, and unemployment mounted, MacDonald stood out as the leader of a new kind of broad-based left. His opposition to the war had given him a new charisma. More than anyone else in public life, he symbolized peace and internationalism, decency and social change. He made his audiences, in Molly Hamilton's words, 'hear the dark rush of the wings of the Angel of Death as they fanned the hot tormented faces of the wounded'. Here was a man seemingly reborn in the cauldron of war, unmuzzled by the Lib-Labbery of pre-1914, the idealist's answer to the crookedness and corruption of Lloyd George. When he was elected to parliament for Aberavon in 1922, he was the natural choice as the leader of Labour. He was, or had become, the voice of conscience, of the suffering millions still in vain pursuit of that promised land fit for heroes.

In the twenties, MacDonald was the dominant personality in British politics. His socialist credentials were refurbished. Indeed, he gave them fresh emphasis in his prolonged, and highly successful, campaign to crush Lloyd George and the Liberals as rival claimants for the leadership of the left. He had, indeed, been elected Labour's leader in 1922 as the left-wing alternative to J.R. Clynes; all the Clydesiders voted for MacDonald. He was proposed by Emanuel Shinwell, the left-wing member for Linlithgow. As Prime Minister of Labour's otherwise unremarkable first administration, MacDonald was to prove an inspiring and charismatic leader. His personal isolation—Beatrice Webb called him 'the mystery man'—underlined his ascendancy. It was, in many ways, an unhappy government. It was dependent on unreliable Liberal support, and was divided within itself by the deep antagonism between MacDonald, Snowden, and Henderson, its three key figures. It was a constant prey to sniping from the left, not surprisingly when this Labour government chose to use Lloyd George's anti-strike emergency apparatus against a stoppage by Bevin's transport workers. The government eventually fell, through the incompetent handling of the prosecution of the Communist, J. R. Campbell, by MacDonald himself—though this messy affair was the responsibility of many others as well, including the Attorney-General, Patrick Hastings, and even Tom Jones, the deputy secretary of the Cabinet who took the minutes.

Despite the Campbell fiasco, though, MacDonald emerged with an enhanced reputation with the wider public. In particular, the priority given to foreign affairs gave him a new stature. The proposed Geneva Protocol, however flimsy it later appeared and however shaky Mac-Donald's own commitment to it, seemed to herald a new era in Anglo-French relations. The French withdrew their troops from the Ruhr. The Dawes Plan cleared some of the difficulties over reparations, and there was a significant trade treaty with Soviet Russia. In so far as MacDonald argued that the key to economic revival lay in a new kind of foreign policy, and in finding new and stable markets in central and eastern Europe for British manufactures, it made socialism plausible on grounds of efficiency as well as morality.

After surviving attempts within the party to depose him as leader, MacDonald proceeded to come out well of the 1926 General Strike. He kept his distance from the advocates of industrial action, but he also led the attack on the Baldwin government's reprisals on the trade unions, while he also used his good offices with Churchill to try to bring the miners' lock-out to an end. By 1927–8, indeed, MacDonald had achieved a personal dominance over his party matched by none of his predecessors—nor perhaps equally by his successors either, save for Wilson briefly in 1963–4. MacDonald was fully engaged in the battle of ideas as well. He listened with apparent sympathy to the 'living wage' schemes of Hobson and the ILP to stimulate purchasing power, and to Mosley's monetary novelties, though he later disavowed 'flashy futilities' of this kind. He punctured effectively some of the more inflated claims of Lloyd George in the 'yellow' and 'orange' books. There were, after all, problems in transporting thousands of unemployed miners to distant parts of the country to build roads and install telephone wires. As Labour prospered in the late twenties, so did its leader. He took office as premier for the second time in June 1929, with a far stronger parliamentary position than in 1929, and with the highest hopes. As Egon Wertheimer wrote at the time, 'he was the focus for the mute hopes of a whole class'.

The expectations of that second Labour government were destroyed soon enough. They barely survived MacDonald's ticker-tape welcome in New York that cheerful summer. All this is a familiar theme. What is less familiar is that MacDonald was more innovative than has often been supposed in exploring new ideas to defeat the slump which menaced his administration almost from the outset. The Economic Advisory Council (whose members included economists like Keynes) was his creation; he also appointed the highly influential Macmillan Committee. When confronted with prolonged unemployment, by a huge and growing budget deficit, and finally by a banking crisis and a disastrous run on the pound, MaDonald dithered—but so, too, did everyone else. The line sometimes drawn between 'economic radicals' and 'economic conservatives' is an imprecise one. Keynes himself spoke with several voices, even about going off gold. Mosley's schemes for a managed currency certainly provided a theoretical alternative, and MacDonald was far from dogmatic about them. But Snowden shot them down in Cabinet, and Mosley's vanity and egoism led him to premature resignation and the political wilderness. All the main remedies for depression were debated at length, but rejected in turn. Public works, mainly for road-building, were turned down when Ministry of Transport officials, backed by the minister, Herbert Morrison, proved their superficiality. Import quotas conflicted with the deep-seated free trade convictions of Snowden, Henderson, and Graham, as did the plan for a revenue tariff. One interesting theme is how agriculture—in particular, the wheat import quotas and control boards proposed by the energetic ex-Liberal, Christopher Addison—became a major battleground for the recasting of the government's economic programmes. Indeed, since Addison was a major bridge to Lloyd George and the Liberals, Labour's economic and political difficulties came together at this point. But by the early summer of 1931, no firm policy at all had been agreed. The budget deficit widened, the dole queues lengthened alarmingly, the optimistic noises from ministers such as Jimmy Thomas seemed increasingly fatuous.

And yet, despite all the internal bitterness and MacDonald's regular bouts of despair ('I have lifted the cup to my lips—and found it empty', he wrote on unemployment), the administration was not without hope. There were achievements in foreign affairs—the London naval agreement, the French withdrawal from the Rhineland, further modification of French claims for German reparations. The Round Table Conference on India was certainly not a failure. Above all, the government seemed on the verge of a new lease of life. After endless wrangles over voting reform and land taxes, the Labour government seemed in June 1931 much nearer a firm arrangement with the Liberals on whose support they depended. Lloyd George might enter the Cabinet. The Progressive alliance of pre-war years might be generated anew, and MacDonald's career triumphantly turn full circle.

The outcome, of course, was a coalition of a totally different kind. The 'National' government was formed under MacDonald's leadership on the afternoon of 24 August 1931. After the run on the pound since mid-July and the shattering cuts proposed by the May Committee to the tune of £97m., MacDonald seemed in retrospect to have been left with little alternative other than a coalition with the

Tories, especially since his Cabinet was hopelessly divided with nine ministers offering their resignation over cuts in unemployment benefit. But was this the case? Ever since Sidney Webb's famous article in 1932, the air has been thick with rumours of conspiracy, with the King, Montagu Norman, Samuel, Baldwin, and others involved. There is evidence that MacDonald and Baldwin had managed a kind of personal rapport for many years, unusual among party leaders. After all, they had a common interest in liquidating Lloyd George, against whom they had both in their different ways rebelled in the past. Writing to the American liberal, Oswald Garrison Villard, in June 1923, MacDonald had even described Baldwin as 'a Conservative but an enlightened one ... on foreign politics his views are, as near as matters, the same as mine. Really a good type of cultured liberal Conservative.'

Nevertheless, there is no evidence that MacDonald had any real thought of coalition with the Tories until his government submitted its resignation to the King late on Sunday, 23 August 1931. That very evening, he announced his intention of leading his stricken party into opposition, and confirmed this to his daughter and close confidant, Ishbel. But, by the time he went to bed, there were hints that he might be changing his mind. Several factors played their parts in turning the scale. The unbridgeable divisions in Labour's ranks over the proposed cuts in unemployment benefits; the refusal of Bevin and the TUC to countenance any meaningful cuts at all; a second visit to George V, which brought a powerful personal appeal from the King to MacDonald's sense of patriotism; the urgings of Neville Chamberlain and others that MacDonald's leadership was vital to ensuring foreign confidence in the new administration—all these, no doubt, played their part.

But the decisive factor lay in something deeper, in MacDonald's outlook and psychological make-up as they had emerged throughout a long career. On domestic issues, he was fundamentally a consensus man; socialism, as he defined it so opaquely, was part of that communal consensus. He totally rejected the class or sectional view propounded by Henderson and the TUC in 1931. He was always deeply wedded to late-Victorian Liberal orthodoxies of stability, cohesion, and evolutionary change. In 1914, these had led him into the minority camp of the anti-war radicals. In 1931, more typically, they led him to uphold the prevailing view of 'the national interest', with only Snowden and Thomas as major allies from his own party.

Another kind of leader would have interpreted the options very differently. Given MacDonald's progressive past, it is difficult to see him following any other course than obeying his monarch's request to form an all-party administration. It was the supreme gesture, and the supreme tragedy, of his career. It was a matter of duty, wrote his son Malcolm, 'and damn the consequences'.

The last phase in MacDonald's life is usually seen as a painful anti-climax. So, largely, it was. It began with the decision to go off gold in September, quite at variance with the pledges that surrounded the formation of the National government three weeks earlier. There followed the miserable episode of the 'doctors' mandate' general election in October, in which Labour was crushed, apparently beyond recovery. MacDonald himself notably added to the bitterness of the campaign by brandishing worthless German marks as tokens of the financial irresponsibility of his late Cabinet comrades. He stayed on as Prime Minister for almost four years more, isolated, unhappy, increasingly ill. It was 'nae his ain hoose'.

Yet this period is still worth some examination. He played a major part in the successful outcome of the 1932 Ottawa Conference which jettisoned a century of free trade. He was always something of a free-thinker in finance, as in religion. He was a dominant figure in the Lausanne Conference on reparations, and the main architect of British foreign policy until mid-1934 or so. He retained his old faith in the beneficent effects of the Anglo-American alliance, despite such bruising episodes as Roosevelt's blitzing hopes of currency sta-bilization (for very good reasons, let it be said) at the World Economic Conference of 1933.

But MacDonald, like almost everyone else, was quite out of his depth when confronted with the phenomenon of Hitler. Resolution and rearmament were no policy for an old ILP/UDC dissenter who still insisted, to impressionable young aesthetes like Kenneth Clark, on his socialist credentials. The 1935 defence white paper was a shattering defeat for MacDonald's impact on British foreign policy; it was the beginning of the end. By now his role in his own govern-ment was becoming increasingly ethereal. He worried about the government's drift to the right—'its appeal to the country is anti-Socialism'—and the extreme feebleness of its National Labour wing. He was defeated on several issues in the Cabinet, including the repeal of Labour's 1931 land duties, a re-run of some of Lloyd George's

People's Budget. Edwardian Progressivism was being buried fast. MacDonald left 10 Downing Street just after the King's jubilee in 1935, and not a moment too soon.

The last stages were exceptionally painful. There was MacDonald's humiliating defeat by his old supporter, Manny Shinwell, at Seaham Harbour in the 1935 general election, and his pathetic period thereafter as a Scottish university member. There was the disgrace of his old colleague, Jimmy Thomas, over a budget leak. All the time, vitriolic abuse flowed from his old associates in the Labour Party. It inflicted fresh wounds each time. Old and broken, he compared himself in his diary to a drowning man. 'Sinks below surface & person becomes vaguer & dimmer & is at last lost.' He finally sank beneath the waves in November 1937. 'MacWonder' had ended up the forgotten man of British politics.

Ramsay MacDonald's career should undoubtedly be viewed as a whole. To see him just as a noble idealist who lapsed unaccountably from the faith in 1931 is totally superficial. His failures after 1929 only make sense if they are related to the triumphs of earlier years. The inspiration he gave the labour movement before, during, and after the first world war, was based essentially on the Edwardian premises of the Progressive Alliance. MacDonald then was the supreme British embodiment of social Darwinism in its most optimistic form. While his strategy after 1918 was directed towards wiping out the Liberals as foremost rivals on the left, his philosophy was still based on the imperatives of the peaceful and evolutionary change of society, and an almost Burkean respect of the past, not on the disruptive dialectic of class conflict. Socialism was relegated to an increasingly distant and obscure future. This gradualist approach amply succeeded. It played a vital part in making Labour not merely a movement of protest but an instrument of government. After Marquand's biography, MacDonald will surely always be seen as an outstanding and dominating democratic leader in the first three decades of this century, a spellbinding orator, a masterly parliamentary tactician, a superb party organizer, with that rare touch of Celtic magic to touch the souls as well as the minds of the mass electorate.

Even after 1929, these qualities of greatness did not wholly disappear. MacDonald towered over the more pedestrian virtues of Henderson, the dogmatic rigidities of Snowden, the timidity or ignor-

ance of most of his colleagues, to emerge as one of the most dominating party leaders in our history. And there was another side
to this difficult and complex man—his abiding personal loyalty to
colleagues such as Jimmy Thomas, his unadvertised crusades on
behalf of outcasts such as Oscar Slater, victim of a cruel miscarriage
of justice, his selfless love for his wife and children. Previous authors
have been so intent on focusing on the warts which flawed Mac-
Donald's features that the face beneath almost disappeared from
view. That can never be so again.

And yet, the rehabilitation of Ramsay MacDonald, so nobly
attempted in Marquand's massive biography, can never really be
complete. In spite of everything, he remains doomed, perhaps
damned, by his fatal miscalculation in August 1931. No doubt, his
financial ideas were out of date by this time. No doubt, his relative
ignorance of economics was shared by almost all his Labour colleagues in 1929–31. The point of devaluing sterling was simply not
grasped at all. But there is a fundamental sense in which MacDonald's
ideas were always out of date or at least out of place, for the leader
of a predominantly working-class party, committed to sweeping
social change, class equality, and the transfer of economic power
into collective hands.

MacDonald was always, to some degree, the Lib-Lab *manqué* who
never wholly forswore the ethos of the Southampton Liberal Association. (It is appropriate that his distinguished biographer has, since
his book, left Labour to become a founder member of the Social
Democratic Party.) MacDonald was a conservative force even within
the ILP which, after all, was in its confused fashion committed to a
class-based view of politics. As one ILP leader, Bruce Glasier, shrewdly
noted in his diary in 1906, MacDonald 'lacked the instinct of agitation'. He was by inclination a political insider. In this respect,
Hardie, Lansbury, even Maxton, were nearer the essential dynamic
of British socialism. MacDonald was instinctively out of sympathy,
as he was with those class alignments which arose from structural
changes in the British capitalist economy between 1880 and 1920.
It is significant, for instance, that, among his many essays in evolutionary organicism, a concept like 'nationalization' seldom appears.

By the twenties he was isolated within the ILP, painful though the
process undoubtedly was for him. The pattern was soon repeated
within the Labour Party generally, even if his lonely eminence
masked the fact for so long. It is in this context that August 1931

remains central to an interpretation of MacDonald's career and the fatal flaw that it contained. In a supreme crisis of the capitalist system, one long prophesied though not really anticipated on the British left, MacDonald felt instinctively alienated from the organized working class on which his party was based. Henderson guessed right where MacDonald guessed wrong. In 1931 MacDonald felt intuitively drawn towards placating Treasury orthodoxies at home and 'foreign opinion' (that is, bankers' and speculators' opinion) overseas. The facts that the very premises of a 'national' government meant dividing the Labour Party and branding it as sectional and disloyal; that the new government resulted from the deflationary obsessions of the May report which had scant relevance to a financial crisis in August 1931 that arose from an external run on the reserves, not an internal disequilibrium of the budget; that the May Committee itself consisted not of detached observers but mainly of right-wing industrialists; that the crisis had partly been assisted by the incompetence in handling foreign exchange policy by a Bank of England whose judgement was now held sacrosanct; that only the Tories could possibly derive political capital from the new alignment of parties; and that the cuts in benefit involved scandalously disproportionate sacrifices for the unemployed and their families—all these were swept aside in frenetic pursuit of the abstraction of 'the national interest'. This was not Bolshevism, but Idealism run mad. Hegel was repeating himself, in August as tragedy, in October as farce.

From the most honourable of motives, MacDonald miscalculated appallingly, as perhaps inevitably he must. The deep-seated ambiguity of his role as a social democratic leader of the working class was devastatingly laid bare, and its essential emptiness exposed. Here may be added his well-known friendship with wealthy society women. Perhaps (as with Hugh Gaitskell later) too much has been made of his relations with such as Lady Londonderry, Cecily Gordon-Cumming, Princess Bibesco, *et toute cette galère*. As an ageing widower, MacDonald was a desperately lonely man. David Marquand shrewdly commented that, like many Celts, MacDonald could move into, and out of, the English social hierarchy at will. Even so, when all allowances have been made, it is hard to imagine other Celtic outsiders—Parnell, Hardie, Bevan, Lloyd George himself—involving themselves in the pathetic upper-class fantasies of 'Circe' and 'Hamish the Hart'. For all his great qualities, MacDonald lacked their kind of alienation, commitment, perhaps ruthlessness. The injustices of his society roused him to moral protest, but not to insensate rage. He inspired, he orated, he made a unique contribution to the political triumphs of the Labour Party in its early years. Even 1931 can be plausibly defended. Yet to behold such a leader dominating a party, through so fundamental a social and political revolution, is perhaps to see why, neither in 1931, or indeed in 1945 or later, could it ever truly be Socialism in Our Time.

# THE WEBBS

THE Fabians largely inspired the revolution in government in our century, just as surely as did the Benthamites in the nineteenth. Not only Britain bears the Fabian imprint. Many third-world nations imported their social and administrative ideas largely from the Fabian strongholds of the *New Statesman* and the London School of Economics. Over huge ranges of national and local government, welfare, and educational policy, programmes for industrial relations and colonial development, the Fabian stamp has been omnipresent, their gospel of discipline, efficiency, and order seemingly irresistible.

Of course, their impact has been greatest on the Labour Party, even though the Society was opposed to the party's coming into existence in 1900, and left much of the early campaigning to the ILP. The first world war, especialy the Emergency Workers' National Committee, brought the Fabians firmly into the mainstream of the labour movement. The New Fabian Research Bureau of the thirties gave the Fabian ethic a new impulsion. Indeed, Tony Crosland's *Future of Socialism* in 1956 ended with a *cri de cœur* for democratic socialists to re-emphasize the values of freedom and beauty, and to free themselves from the stifling, joyless austerity of the Webb tradition. But the Fabian gospel of collectivism by stealth has permeated far wider than simply through the Labour Party. Through the extension of municipal socialism, through institutions designed to promote the social sciences, through the ever-growing centralism of Whitehall, through such men as 'the microbe' Thomas Jones, Fabian doctrines transcended parties and ideologies. In the Butskellite era of the fifties and sixties, an era which endured in broad terms until the mid-seventies, it could indeed be said that we were all Fabians now.

Sidney and Beatrice Webb were far from being the only important Fabians, even though they feature so prominently in the historiography. The 'Old Gang' who founded the society in 1884 and dominated its history for the next thirty years included other formidable intellectuals such as Sidney Olivier, Graham Wallas, and most spectacularly, Bernard Shaw. In the Edwardian years, personalities such as Hubert Bland and H. G. Wells caused many a *frisson*, ensuring that the Fabian Society, for all its primness, had no shortage of bed and circuses. By the twenties, there were the Coles to rival the Webbs as a major intellectual powerhouse. Even so, it is understandable that it is the Webbs who overshadowed the historical treatment of the Fabians in their first fifty years of life. As prophets, permeators, and planners, they provided the Society with its intellectual drive, momentum, and continuity. From the late eighties, they maintained a ceaseless routine of evolutionary and didactic improvement. In discussing the Fabian legacy, it is impossible to liberate oneself from the presence of this overwhelming, terrifying partnership.

Until the 1970s, the Webbs did not appear to speak directly to us. Their monuments lay about us, but they themselves remained decently obscure. They stayed the *éminences rouges* of the Fabian Society, less accessible to later generations than, say, Shaw or Wells. Sidney Webb, in particular, rose without trace: he left surprisingly little personal record. Margaret Cole's editions of Beatrice's diary were heavily purged of much of its individuality. From the mid-1970s, however, Norman and Jeanne MacKenzie have been indefatigable in editing the Webb correspondence and Beatrice Webb's diary. They have provided an incomparable archive to illuminate as never before the creators of much of our world.

The impression of the Webbs left by this ample record is at once exhilarating and depressing. One is struck with equal force by their selflessness and their soullessness, by their dedication and their lack of humanity. Gradgrind was never far beneath the surface. It is true that Beatrice's diaries, as published *in extenso* by the MacKenzies, show her as more vulnerable and sympathetic than some stereotypes have suggested. This particularly applies to the 1905–24 period. She spends time pondering the nature of religious experience—'the communion of the soul with some righteousness felt to be outside and above itself'. She frequently prays, though to whom is not quite clear. During the first world war, she feels stirred by the call of 'an Abstract Being'. She also responds, in a highly personal way, to her own femininity, especially in the context of Shaw's plays, and tries (in vain) to appreciate the sexually charged novels of D. H. Lawrence. But little enough of this saw the light of day. Publicly, the Webbs were a kind of machine. They appeared to show little interest in a wider culture beyond the dictates of the 'housekeeping state'. They did not particularly admire the workers they were anxious to organize, educate, and improve. 'They must learn the absolute necessity of strictness of dealing, or self-control and of patient temper', the young Beatrice Potter wrote sternly in 1885. In October 1890, just before their engagement, Beatrice wrote to the hapless Sidney, 'You I believe in but do not love.' The same applies to the Webb view of humanity in general.

The Webbs' personal correspondence is remarkably revealing, especially for the earlier years. Down to 1892, during his amazingly sexless courtship of Beatrice, Sidney, slaving away at his desk in the Colonial Office, emerges as a more romantic and appealing figure than later impressions suggest, with a zest for amateur self-analysis. 'For a miserable man, I am still capable of much enjoyment', he wrote to Graham Wallas. By the nineties, both his public role and his intellectual creed were clearly defined.

Beatrice, by contrast, was a product of social guilt as much as of social compassion. The intensity of her feelings was compounded by her relationship with Joseph Chamberlain, which severely disrupted her self-control for a critical period of her life. During the courtship, it was Beatrice who dictated matters throughout. Her letters to Sidney link discussion of the complexities of their personal relationship with analyses of Spencerian sociology and of Marshall's theory of rent. She repeatedly nags the miserable man for his lack of 'self-control'. 'Let us not be sentimental', she scolds, and packs him off to study the Co-operative Society's views on wages policy. On the other hand, she would not let Sidney depart in peace. 'Let us have a more detailed concordat', she demanded. When they finally got married in July 1892, she asked Sidney for a photograph of his head, since it was the only part of his anatomy in which she took the slightest interest. After all that, we turn with relief to Sidney's expositions of Fabian ideas on municipal socialism, of their investigation of Irish trade societies during their honeymoon in Dublin. Even then, Beatrice, as 'investigator' was driving Sidney as 'executor' remorselessly, nagging him for his slow progress on their joint book on the history of trade-unionism. In fairness, it should be added that she drove herself even more unsparingly, and suffered for it.

Their correspondence—and their relationship—took a somewhat different turn in the period 1892–1912. At times, their judgements were remarkably wrong-headed, as in their accounts of United States society and politics during an American tour in 1898, the

year of the Spanish–American War. They took the imperialist line
during the Boer War. There is wide-ranging, often perceptive, comment, usually by Beatrice, on contemporaries such as Lloyd George,
Churchill, and the philosopher-king of the Cambridge Apostles, G. E.
Moore, whose ideas, with their open hedonism, merely 'disintegrated
the intellects and characters of young men'. Much of this was the
product of frustration, since the Webbs had no clear-cut role during
these years. They played only a fringe part in the labour movement
in the nineties, and were openly at odds with the unions on such
crucial matters as the arbitration of industrial disputes. They were
isolated by the formation of the Labour Party in 1900, which they
broadly opposed. The new party was, after all, the creation of the
crude, unlettered miner, Keir Hardie, and those stolid trade-unionists
whom the Webbs, as intellectuals, planners, and middle-class tech-
nocrats, largely despised.

They pinned their hopes on a series of unlikely champions—on
Lord Rosebery and the Liberal Imperialists whom Sidney congratulated, with absurd optimism, on their ideological 'escape from
Houndsditch'; on a non-party group such as the 'Co-efficients', many
of whom were Tories. Meanwhile, their own Fabian Society was
losing momentum, racked by new controversies, many of them provoked by the volatile personality of H. G. Wells. In 1912, the Webbs
had to swallow their pride and join the ILP. They rejected 'Progressivism' and made their peace with a mass Labour Party, rather
than face a lifetime of sterility and ineffectiveness. The original 'per-
meating' idea of the Webbs had run its course, as had the ideals of
the distinctly Old Gang who dominated it. The way was open for
Sidney and other Fabians to engage with the perils and challenges
of political power.

The Webbs' main achievement in these years (though one sometimes exaggerated by historians) was in exerting some influence over
Arthur Balfour in the remodelling of public education in 1902.
Certainly, Balfour, Gorst, and other ministers frequented the Webb
ménage at 41 Grosvenor Street, for guidance in the intricacies of
elementary and technical education. The Webbs applauded the transfer of elementary education to committees of county councils, as a
victory for 'experts' over amateurs, churchmen, and parents.

The Webbs' main disappointment, by contrast, concerned the
famous Poor Law Commission of 1905–9, of which Beatrice was a
key member. Her own ambitious scheme for a centrally administered

system of public welfare, especially for state regulation of the labour market, led nowhere. Beatrice manifestly exaggerated the gulf between themselves and the authors of the Majority Report, and alienated much of the labour movement as well. They overestimated the appeal of a huge state-run bureaucracy set up to administer the whole range of the social services. Equally they underestimated their opponents, from Lloyd George to Lord George Hamilton, and found it impossible to understand why others obstinately refused to accept their own manifestly rational panacea for the Poor Law. Perhaps the truth was that the Webbs, with their professed worship for facts, really only respected facts that conformed to their own preconceived diagnosis of scientific socialism; when other 'facts' emerged, in public argument and debate, the Webbs treated them with dismissal or contempt. The result was that by 1911 the Webbs' crusade for a 'national minimum' and the recommendations of the Minority Report had got nowhere. Most of the trade unions supported the government's national insurance proposals; Lloyd George had achieved his 'heroic demagogy' in the Act of 1911; the Webbs themselves appeared sectarian and isolated from much of social debate.

Instead, many of their endeavours went towards more pedestrian, though worthwhile, activities such as money-raising ventures to support their own new project, the London School of Economics. On the eve of 1914, the Webbs were still frustrated improvers, evangelists in search of a crusade. On the personal side, things still read bleakly. On their tenth wedding anniversary, Beatrice urged Sidney that 'we must try to keep our health by temperance and guard our minds against any vulgar striving for personal prominence ... It will be delightful to be back at work in our own little home and get to work again on the Poor Law chapters.'

The final phase of the Webbs' pilgrimage, down to their respective deaths, introduces some different themes. It was, in many ways, the most constructive and fulfilling period of their lives. One striking feature is how, against all the odds, Sidney now emerged as the dominant figure in the partnership, with Beatrice unselfishly prepared to play a supportive role. The Webbs were enthusiastic about the first world war, and at first surprisingly so about Lloyd George— 'so extraordinarily alert in intelligence and cheery and calm', wrote Beatrice in 1914. Sidney welcomed the war as an opportunity for 'Universal submission to the National Need'. Both Webbs were used

by Lloyd George in devising new schemes for post-war reconstruction. They also became very active in Labour Party policy-
making, especially on the War Emergency Workers' National Committee, which Sidney turned to valuable effect in putting shrewd
pressure on the Local Government Board in social matters. It evolved
a more precise view of the function of the state in economic direction.
Webb also became central, in partnership with the unlikely ally of
Arthur Henderson, in restructuring the Labour Party from the base.
He drafted much of the party's constitution, including Clause Four
(then Three (d)) and the idealization of the role of 'workers by hand
and by brain'.

After the war, they reconciled themselves to far more active participation in the Labour Party. Sidney served on the Sankey Commission on the mining industry, and, with Tawney and others,
strongly pressed the case for nationalization. In 1922, he entered
parliament as member for the mining constituency of Seaham Harbour in Durham. Beatrice hurled herself into the role of an MP's wife
and made heroic, if embarrassing, efforts to entertain miners' wives
in the constituency over afternoon tea. Sidney served in the Labour
Cabinets of 1924 and 1929, and entered the House of Lords as Baron
Passfield. As a minister, he was not a great success. The Webbs were
really social administrators, not economists, and proved to be as far
adrift in the economic maelstrom of the 1920s as anyone else. Sidney
voted with MacDonald and Snowden in cutting unemployment benefit in August 1931; the trade-unionist ministers wisely took the
opposite view. Sidney's comment on the later decision to go off gold
became a classic—'Nobody told us we could do that.' Nor were the
Webbs any more attuned to close collaboration with the trade unions,
whose history they had devotedly written. Beatrice criticized the
TUC's belief that 'any increase to the income of wage-earners is a
good thing in itself'. Sidney's distaste for the General Strike in 1926
had been particularly marked. In 1931, he commented, 'The General
Council are pigs: they won't agree to any cuts'. His time as Colonial
Secretary in 1929-31 had also been undistinguished, with repeated
failures in handling the problems of India, Egypt, Kenya, and most
of all Palestine, where Beatrice's hostility towards Zionism and the
ideas of Dr Weizmann were a permanent stumbling-block.

After 1931, the Webbs, now approaching old age, had no clear
niche in British life. The movements of the thirties, such as the New
Fabian Research Bureau, largely passed them by. Not surprisingly,

they looked overseas for their promised land and produced their absurdly uncritical book on the Soviet Union, which perturbed many friends in the Labour Party. The Coles, who also visited Russia at this time, steered clear of these excesses, if narrowly. The Russian authorities treated the Webbs like 'minor royalty', and to good effect. Sidney wrote enthusiastically on the collective farms, Beatrice on the Russians' success in handling unemployment. In a passing reference, she commented prosaically on 'Stalin incidentally liquidating the kulaks'. She warmly defended the Moscow show trials in 1936—'I think on the whole the Soviet Government has acted in wise restraint.' It was a rather pathetic last phase. They pottered about in Passfield Corner, their days enlivened by visits from the Soviet ambassador, Maisky, and Lloyd George, amongst others. The Nazi–Soviet pact of 1939 'knocked them senseless'. Beatrice died in 1943, Sidney in 1947, a socialist government at the helm, but their planned antiseptic Utopia still far away. At Shaw's insistence, a plaque to their memory was placed in Westminster Abbey, the shrine of the capitalist establishment.

On the whole, it is hard to love the Webbs after the massive revelations of their correspondence and diaries. Their Comtean religion of humanity seldom led to human sympathy for men and women in particular. Time and again, they forgot the dying bird. They specialized in a form of social and intellectual élitism which the more gregarious Coles (or at least Dame Margaret) managed to avoid. In Shaw's terms, they were comparatively unsocial socialists. Their creed of Germanic discipline and rigour was alien to the warm, chapel-reared radicalism from which the ILP derived much of its vitality. As Eric Hobsbawm pointed out long ago, in a famous chapter, they reflected the ethic of the *nouvelle couche sociale* of the administrator, bureaucrat, or scientifically trained manager, a stratum of society more common in Germany or France at the time. Only a minute fragment of the membership of the Fabian Society (well under ten per cent, on any reckoning) was proletarian. The Society was a hymn to suburban middle-class improvement and self-sufficiency. The Webbs' work added enormously to an understanding of welfare policy, the labour market, industrial relations, higher education, and local government. But it was accompanied by a relative ignorance of the realities of economic, social, or political power which made their legacy of limited value for later socialists. They wished to uplift the toiling working man, but never understood him, knew him, or sought his company. Sidney toyed with eugenics and publicly lamented the deterioration caused to the imperial racial stock by Irishmen, Jews, and Chinese. With their puritanism, austerity, and zeal for bureaucratic control, the Webbs were all too typical of some strains in the making of British democratic socialism: it is noticeable that both the young planners of the 1930s and the Croslandite revisionists of the 1950s rebelled against their influence. In their authoritarianism and plain lack of humanity, the Webbs were quite alien to the essence of the socialist message. They ignored the basic fact that socialism is about people even more than it is about order.

In one particular area, the Webb ethos is particularly open to attack, namely their attitude towards the arts. In some ways, this encapsulates the limitations of their entire credo. No doubt, the Society has been misrepresented in some ways. Certainly a Fabian movement which could capture the imagination of an artist like Walter Crane, a critic like Holbrook Jackson, or a drama producer like Harley Granville-Barker could hardly have been wholly lacking in cultural appeal. The conventional wisdom that sees the Fabians as austere, humourless philistines owes much to the dominant influence of Beatrice in the available record. She wrote bleakly in *Our Partnership* of how, 'owing to our concentration on research and municipal administration, we had neither the time nor the energy to listen to music and the drama, or to visit picture galleries'. In fact, Sidney as a young man was deeply stirred by Goethe and Heine, and by Italian renaissance art, in the evolution of his socialism—at least, he was until Beatrice got hold of him. On the London County Council, he was active in trying to expose the urban masses to the visual and other arts. Like Shaw, he wanted to link social engineering with aesthetic inspiration, just as Shaw condemned the frivolity, almost the nihilism, of the 'art for art's sake' school or the ideas of the *Yellow Book*. There was a Fabian Arts Group, while the Fabian summer school would offer entertainment that varied from improving drama by Ibsen or Chekhov to impromptu musical revues. One of these was adorned by 'a full beauty chorus' and devoted to the theme of 'The Socialist State of the Future as portrayed by its Opponents'. The Fabian summer school later reported, with reference to this last spectacle, that 'the hilarity engendered cannot often have been surpassed'—which one may doubt.

Even so, the rehabilitation of the Webbs and other Fabians as cultural experimentalists and patrons of the arts cannot be taken very far. The history of the Fabian Society was littered with artists and writers who broke away because of the severity of its ethic. William Morris was one: the medievalism and anti-industrialism of the Morrisian critique was far removed from the Fabian worship of modernity and machine-made efficiency. Holbrook Jackson and A. R. Orage rebelled totally against the artistic puritanism of the Old Gang. Along with others, they retreated to a variety of havens, including the Nietzschean metaphysic of the *New Age*, the atomism of Cole's Guild Socialists, the artistic communities of Eric Gill, and the aesthetic pluralism advocated by Edwin Muir and Herbert Read.

There were perhaps two main reasons for this flight of artists from the Fabian fold. First, there was the Fabians' relentless insistence on austerity and the ascetic ideal. Cultural avant-gardism was all very well, but it must be disciplined always by a 'sense of purpose'. Artistic experiment for the masses was harmful if it led to elevating 'pleasure above purpose'. This was hardly a trap into which Sidney and Beatrice were likely to fall. The Webbs' balance between free self-expression and restraint in the arts was a difficult one to achieve. Hubert Bland, the ardent disciple of Walter Pater and the husband of the much-abused Edith Nesbit, was one who found it impossible to attain. This earthy aesthete took refuge in founding the Anti-Puritan League in revolt against Webb-style prudery. He died, embittered and disillusioned, in 1914.

The other major problem was that of 'art for whom?' The Webbs may have persuaded themselves that their vision of art was intended for Everyman, for faceless, anonymous industrial workers in their slum tenements and mining villages, as much as for the emancipated, middle-class Hampstead aesthete. But when they came across authentic forms of working-class culture they reacted with incomprehension bordering on alarm. Beatrice's contempt for the Victorian music-hall, and the journalism of Robert Blatchford's *Clarion*, rich with allusions to pubs, pints, and chorus-girls, was an extreme response. But for the Fabians generally (including those like Annie Besant, not normally associated with the ethic of puritanism), Marie Lloyd, Vesta Tilley, or George Robey could hardly be viewed as worthwhile exhibits in the socialist hall of fame. Popular sport such as association football was little more than a cultural nightmare. Even Fabian enthusiasts for popular music in the form of folk-song or ballads, like Cecil Sharp himself, were undermined by a Utopian unrealism which made them hesitant about the value of the tradition they were trying to preserve.

The Webbs' view of the arts—and of life generally—was, therefore, élitist and didactic. As the young Rupert Brooke suggested, in a lively Fabian lecture at Cambridge in 1911, their outlook was shot through with contradictions. Claiming to elevate the cloth-capped mass proletarian, they actually took their stand on the assumptions of a small, inbred, educated coterie. In Calvinist terms, they felt themselves to be 'an infinitesimal group of the infinitely elect'. Like other Messiahs for the underprivileged, they ended up representing largely themselves. At a deeper level, the Webbs' careers cast some doubt on whether philosophical socialism ever can, or ever should, be a really popular movement. Time and circumstance make Leninists of us all.

# VICTOR GRAYSON

LIKE other parties of progress, the Labour Party is a prisoner of its past. Myths and romantic idylls are inseparable from the onward march of British socialism, from Tolpuddle onwards. But few individuals have more dramatically captured the Labour imagination than did Victor Grayson, the very embodiment of what American Indians call 'the legend that walks'—or perhaps staggers, in this case. Grayson was catapulted to instant fame by a sensational by-election victory at Colne Valley in July 1907 when he was only twenty-five. He was a spell-binding stump orator, with a kind of film-star charisma, a supreme rebel propelled from nowhere to smash down the crumbling edifice of British capitalism. The future leadership of the left, many surmised, lay within his grasp.

Yet it was all cruelly deceptive. Grayson was to prove himself burnt out at twenty-eight. Defeated at Colne Valley in January 1910, he rapidly retreated from the political limelight into a private *demi-monde* of self-indulgence, drink, and bisexual extravagance. By 1914 he was already a spent force, and he migrated to Australia and then to New Zealand. When he returned to Britain after war service, he was a shadow of the titan he once had been. Finally, in a famous episode in September 1920, he walked out of a London hotel (precisely which one seems uncertain) and disappeared for ever. Although sightings of Grayson between 1921 and 1948 were almost as frequent as for that other monster resident in Loch Ness, he was never positively identified. His domicile, style of life, and precise date and place of death remained mysterious to the end.

However brief his effective career, though, the Grayson mystique lived on, as it had captured the enthusiasm of a fiery young socialist like Manny Shinwell in Glasgow back in 1907. Grayson's name was one to conjure with—and to perpetuate, too, as in the Christian names of Victor Grayson Hardie (Vic) Feather, later general secretary of the TUC in the early 1970s. Grayson made Victor a popular name for British socialist babies, as did Eugene Victor Debs for American. An interesting, if brief, life was written by Reg Groves in 1975. A fuller one appeared in 1985 from the hand of David Clark, Labour MP for South Shields, who had been in 1970–4 the member for

Colne Valley himself (like Grayson before him, he was defeated in 1974 by a Liberal). This new biography, assisted by vivid recollections of Grayson from his daughter and from elderly socialists in both Yorkshire and New Zealand, gives renewed and abiding interest to an astonishing career.

Grayson first emerged, curiously enough, from the obscurity of training for the Unitarian ministry in Manchester. He was an unsuccessful student and found new scope instead for his remarkable oratorical gifts in the Manchester ILP and in socialist evangelizing in textile villages on both sides of the Pennines. As a result he was unexpectedly nominated by the local 'Labour League' in Colne Valley early in 1907. His nomination was unconstitutional under party rules, and failed to obtain the official endorsement of the Labour Party national executive. On the other hand, the ILP did eventually give him its backing. Snowden and Clynes both spoke on his behalf at Colne Valley, while Hardie, typically, sent a message of support— though his tour around the world prevented his having to appear in person. Colne Valley was a promising battleground for the young socialist campaigner. A Labour Union had been formed among the scattered textile villages as early as 1891. It was followed by a rash of Labour clubs and churches, and several impressive polls in local elections. It was evidently socialism rather than mere 'Labourism' that inspired the Colne Valley Labour Union as the adoption of Tom Mann as parliamentary candidate in 1893 suggested.

But it was also a very private constituency, sprawling across the base of the Pennines between Huddersfield and Oldham, from Slaithwaite in the east to Mossley in the west. It was localized, introspective, with myriad divisions within the valley. Slaithwaite, where most early members of the Labour Union came from, was a world of its own. Nearby Marsden boasted an esoteric socialist festival known as 'the Red Stir'. Saddleworth, which had many Tory voters, was quite distinct again. Colne Valley held aloof from the ILP inaugural conference held at Bradford in January 1893, though it did affiliate a year later. But its relationship to the national ILP was always ambiguous. The first wave of Labour activism petered out in 1895 when Tom Mann, now emerging from a Christian Socialist phase into a distinctly hedonistic approximation of Marxism, came bottom of the poll. In the early years of the new century, there was only a gradual recovery.

In 1907, however, Grayson rekindled all the old fire, and much more besides. His unorthodox campaign drew heavily on West Riding nonconformity, which responded warmly to the fiery pulpit-trained ethical socialism he preached. At least forty clergymen, Anglican and nonconformist alike, worked on Grayson's behalf, including the giant curate of Thongsbridge, 'six foot a socialist and five inches a parson', according to Robert Blatchford. Grayson's party workers crusaded for 'Socialism—God's Gospel for Today'. 'Jerusalem' was regularly sung at Grayson's meetings, along with 'England Arise' and 'The Red Flag'. The fine summer weather encouraged large outdoor meetings, which Grayson kept in an ecstasy of passionate excitement. He embodied a new morality and a younger, less deferential style of Labour leadership. It brought him an astonishing electoral triumph against all the odds, amidst scenes of revivalist hysteria. The stormiest petrel of the entire socialist flock had arrived at Westminster, at the summit of power.

Yet Grayson's subsequent two and a half years as an MP proved quite disastrous. He was wilful, quarrelsome, careless in his parliamentary and constituency duties. He was often drunk, and a generally impossible colleague. He did well in a public debate in Manchester in early 1908 with that arch-reactionary, Sir William Joynson-Hicks; but what stuck in the gullet of Labour supporters was that Grayson chose to appear in formal evening dress. In a famous contrived scene in the Commons debate on the 1908 Licensing Bill, he denounced his Labour comrades, one and all, as traitors to their class. He was also involved in splits within the ILP which saw the party's big four, Hardie, MacDonald, Snowden, and Glasier, resign from the National Administrative Council, the Party's executive, in 1909. Labour as a political force was seriously disrupted by Grayson's free-lance activities. Hardie quarrelled with him publicly after a meeting at Holborn Town Hall in November 1908, ironically enough designed to promote 'socialist unity'. And yet in his own home base, in the textile villages of Lancashire and the West Riding, Grayson's charisma as a socialist evangelist, a latter-day Savonarola, was unparalleled. Women in particular were enthralled. As veteran party workers recalled years afterwards, 'People went mad at his meetings ... He was ready to set things on fire.'

After his defeat at Colne Valley in January 1910 (when he came bottom of the poll but still gained a creditable vote), Grayson tried to carve out a new career as the founder of a militant form of nationalist-socialism. This saw him ally with men like Hyndman of the SDF and

Robert Blatchford, editor of the *Clarion* (who called the handsome Grayson 'Mr God'), as well as with the discontented left of the ILP. They launched a new British Socialist Party to counter the Utopianism and pacifism of the ILP. It was the beginning of the end. The BSP was a quarrelsome band of brothers, powerful in the high command with not much of a rank and file. Grayson broke, with his new allies and lapsed into a haze of alcoholism and nervous exhaustion. His new role as a journalist was a failure. With his hapless actress wife he left for Australasia, where his aggressively pro-war views and *bon viveur* image won him few friends. He joined the New Zealand army, and fought bravely in the trenches in France, where he was gravely wounded. He then went back to Britain, a much diminished force physically, politically, and morally. He was hounded by charges of fraud and sexual misdemeanours (apparently with both men and women, with impartial gusto). He evidently developed secret links with Horatio Bottomley and the sinister Maundy Gregory of 'honours scandal' fame in 1919–20. He certainly seems to have been caught up somehow in Gregory's subterranean world of titles, espionage, blackmail, and bisexual liaison, though David Clark does not endorse one sensational suggestion that Gregory actually sought Grayson's murder, along with that of his mistress, Edith Rosse. Despite many intriguing stories (including that of a septuagenarian 'Victor Garston' who turned up in London in 1948), the later phases of Grayson's life remain shrouded in obscurity for ever. Not only is the date of his death unknown. His birth seems mysterious also, with some hints of aristocratic parentage, and even an alleged relationship to Winston Churchill. To the end Grayson remained an enigma.

In one sense, his story is mainly of personal or psychological interest, a tale of how a uniquely brilliant young orator could take the working-class movement in the North by storm, and then casually toss his career aside. He was never 'Labour's lost leader'. To compare him with either Oswald Mosley or with Tony Benn is unfair to these very different personalities since neither of them (both effective ministers, after all) began to approach Grayson's record of instability. More important—and well worth further reflection—is how that sprawling mass of local splinter groups which coalesced to make up the Edwardian labour movement could be so captivated by the style and rhetoric of so rootless a person as Grayson. How could the solid, respectable, nonconformist cotton and woollen workers of

Colne Valley, close to much older forms of industrial production, relatively well-housed and well-paid, and almost all in regular employment, allow themselves to be so swept up in the millenarian intensity of Grayson's crusade in 1907, more redolent as it was of the Ranters of the seventeenth century than the radicals of the twentieth? One obvious comparison is with the almost contemporary Welsh religious revival of 1904–5 which erupted in the very similar world of the mining and tinplate villages of east Carmarthenshire; its Messiah, Evan Roberts, like Grayson, ended up in mysterious confinement, his nervous system shattered. Victor Grayson is, indeed, an ambiguous figure. His contempt for the trade unions and his relative lack of contact with the realities of working-class life were oddly juxtaposed with a compelling moral indictment of a fractured society and an economic system already in latent decay. To examine the relationship between these contradictory positions is to lay bare some of the essence of early British socialism—and to begin to explain the real mystery of Victor Grayson.

# MABON AND NOAH ABLETT

SOUTH WALES was the cockpit of the British labour world in the early twentieth century. In the bitter, often violent, confrontations between the Miners' Federation and an obdurate Coalowners' Association—the era of the Taff Vale verdict and the Tonypandy riots—a new generation of labour leaders came of age. Already by the First World War, the socialism, even the syndicalism of the Welsh coalfield had become legendary. It had become, government spokesmen complained, a kind of 'El Dorado' for every kind of extremist doctrine. After the war, tension continued to mount. The Welsh coalfield threw up hard men like Arthur Cook, and later Arthur Horner. Through their influence, as well as through young neo-Marxist politicians like Aneurin Bevan and S. O. Davies, the passions of the pioneering years were kept alive and aflame during the unemployment and stagnation of the inter-war years as they had been during the expansion and industrial advance of the pre-1914 period. As South Wales went, so, to a degree, went the nation. It was the Welsh miners who largely swung the affilation of the Miners' Federation of Great Britain to the Labour Party in 1908. It was they also who carried industrial relations to unimaginable depths of class confrontation in the years up to 1914, during the war itself and on to the General Strike in 1926. Even after that, young militant unemployed miners carried the passions of the valleys to such unlikely places as Oxford and Slough, Coventry and Dagenham; the Welsh were catalysts of social revolution as the Irish had been in the past. In Glamorgan over this period, under the aegis of the fanatical chief constable of the county, Captain Lionel Lindsay, himself a product of the Egyptian army in the time of Sir Garnet Wolseley, with his frequent recourse to troops and the new operational violence adopted by the local constabulary, South Wales became the battleground of the class war, British style.

Two men particularly symbolized the struggle within the labour world for the hearts and minds of the Welsh proletariat—William Abraham ('Mabon'), the very model of Welsh nonconformist Lib-Labbery, and Noah Ablett, the incandescent young Marxist ideologue who erupted to leadership in the Rhondda in 1909–10. The struggle between the ethic of Mabonism and the ideology of the *Miners' Next*

*Step*, the neo-syndicalist tract published by the Unofficial Reform Committee at Tonypandy in 1912, of which Ablett was the inspiration and part-author, reached deep down into the psyche of the Welsh working class. Through their dialectic, a wider battle was fought out throughout the working-class movement in Britain as a whole between the idea of class collaboration and of class conflict. The outcome was a mixed one, in which both the aged Mabon and the young Ablett emerged as part losers. But its course, and the violent passion that accompanied it, dictated much of the nature of British labour relations in the first quarter of the twentieth century.

Mabon was a typical product of the nonconformist radicalism that galvanized and democratized Welsh politics and society after the general election of 1868, uniting tenant farmers in the countryside with industrial workers in the mining valleys against the common feudal, Tory enemy. He grew up during the first development of the Rhondda coalfield in the late 1860s and 1870s. Born in 1848, he had emerged, by the time he had entered his thirties, as a formidable leader of the Cambrian Miners' Association, one of the fledgling unions in the Rhondda. He was a faithful nonconformist, a deacon of Nazareth chapel, Pentre, and a fluent and effective speaker in both English and Welsh. His fine tenor voice, which won him the eisteddfodic *nom de guerre* Mabon, was also of value in times of industrial tension. Mabon, it seemed, had only to strike up the Welsh national anthem for the most angry assembly of miners to be transformed into a peaceful and united gathering. General Smuts was to marvel at Mabon's style of musical diplomacy during the First World War. Ironically—and significantly—when Mabon sought election to parliament in 1885 as the first Welsh working-class MP, the local Rhondda Liberal Association refused to endorse even so quietist and undeniably orthodox a Welsh Liberal as Mabon. He had to fight, and beat, a Liberal coalowner at the polls. But the episode left no bitterness. In parliament, he proved himself a wholly loyal supporter of the young middle-class nationalist Liberals of the *Cymru Fydd* school, such as Tom Ellis and Lloyd George. Disestablishment, land reform, education, temperance, even a vaguely conceived Welsh home rule were Mabon's political priorities. His quiet recital of the Lord's Prayer in Welsh on the floor of the House of Commons shook many a cynical Tory back-bencher. Built like a prop forward, Mabon was the sturdy proletarian embodiment of the Welsh *werin*, the folk myth of his people.

In industrial relations, his outlook was moral rather than economic. He adhered, as Professor Arthur Beacham once wrote, to 'the simple truths of the New Testament, not the tortuous canon of Karl Marx'. Indeed, there was a prophetic, biblical quality about Mabon himself—'five feet by four feet, correct measurement' (according to Keir Hardie), with his long black beard, and patriarchal appearance and mode of speech. The South Wales sliding scale on wages, agreed by the coalowners and the miners' leaders in 1875, was Mabonism in action. He was its vigorous champion against more militant critics who accused him of being a bosses' man, enjoying cigars and other hospitality in the managers' offices. In fact, the sliding scale was largely to the disadvantage of the colliers themselves. It depressed wages (without any limit stated) while maintaining the owners' profit levels. An agreed scale of wage rates was achieved at the cost of infrequent audits, small percentage increases, and a built-in tendency to depress the price of coal, on which wage assessments depended. The price of industrial peace was acceptance of the terms of the owners, with their casual, even criminal, disregard for the physical safety of their men. In 1880, even the minimum wage provision of the sliding scale was swept away, and Mabon was left to propose such dubious expedients as compulsory emigration to America.

However, the sliding scale and Mabonism held the field until the massive six-months' coal stoppage—in effect, an owners' lock-out—from March to September 1898. It was a shattering defeat for Mabon, a decisive turning-point in his career as in the history of the Welsh miners as a whole. Symbolically, 'Mabon's day', the miners' holiday on the first Monday of each month, was abolished in the holocaust. Mabon had indeed 'fought tooth and nail for his day'; but the owners were implacable. The South Wales Miners' Federation (popularly revered as 'The Fed') was formed shortly afterwards in 1899, shaking the valleys and pit villages into class unity. Mabon became its first president, with William Brace, (once an enemy of his) the vice-president. But it was clear that his influence, and the creed of Lib-Lab conciliation, were on the wane.

In the first years of the new century the remnants of Mabonism were rapidly cast asunder in a period of extraordinary industrial turmoil in the valleys. Coal production soared to unimaginable heights, and Cardiff became the major coal exporting port in the world, followed closely by its *arriviste* neighbour, Barry; together, they dominated the international carrying trade. A third of the world's coal exports came from South Wales. But at the same time, a huge rise in immigration from England, and much sociological upheaval in the coalfield, reinforced an intense bitterness between owners and men. The sliding scale was formally rejected by the Fed in 1902. These years were a time of continuous retreat for Mabon— the merger of the Welsh miners into the Miners' Federation of Great Britain, and affiliation to the Labour Party; a nation-wide campaign for a minimum wage; an explosion of anger at the effects on wage rates of the Mines Eight Hours Act; demands for the standardization of wage rates against the hazards of 'abnormal places' where the cutting of coal was difficult. Tension was built up still further by a series of appalling mining tragedies, from explosions and other mishaps, with the death of 439 miners at Senghenydd in 1913 the crowning tragedy. All this meant a decisive breach with the older chapel-reared Liberalism to which Mabon automatically subscribed. He was the venerable victim of the conflict that scarred the road that led to Tonypandy.

The Welsh miners were ripe for another Messiah. Indeed, the use of religious and eschatological terms comes naturally enough to an analysis of the coalfield at this period. The 1904 religious revival, which galvanized Wales in the next two years from its starting-point at Loughor near Llanelli, had a powerful impact on the consciousness of many young miners. They included men like Frank Hodges, Arthur Cook, Arthur Horner, S. O. Davies, and others moved by religious experience to become part of the vanguard of industrial revolt. One of these was Noah Ablett, the most remarkable Marxist ideologue to surface in any part of the British coalfield in this period. Born to a large mining family at Porth in the Rhondda in 1883, his early enthusiasm was kindled by the community life of the local chapels, and he was soon preaching the gospel in local pulpits. However, a pit accident, which prevented his moving on to a post in the minor civil service, led to his continuing as a working miner underground. Over the next few years, he became fired by the theory of socialism, and of the message of Marx's *Kapital* in particular. He was an outstanding student at Ruskin College, Oxford, in 1907-9, where he became closely associated with an older Welsh miner and fellow Marxist, Noah Rees. Ablett returned to the Rhondda in 1909 a fierce and learned advocate of extreme socialist views, coloured additionally by the syndicalism of Sorel in France and the industrial unionism of Tom Mann now flourishing in Australia. Ablett was, indeed, a remarkable young man, a rebel of cosmopolitan, perhaps cosmic, importance. As an educator and ideologue, he was unique.

He now set up Marxist tutorial classes in the central valleys of the Welsh coalfield, the Rhondda and Cynon Valley in particular, using the chapel Sunday schools he had known in his childhood as something of a model. His Plebs League, founded in January 1909, led to the eventual creation of the Central Labour College, a militant and class-conscious organization which led to a fierce revolt amongst working-class students in Oxford against the quietism of Ruskin College. Between 1909 and 1912, Marxists such as Ablett and other young ideologues like Will Mainwaring and Will Hay were ceaselessly active throughout South Wales, contributing to Tom Mann's syndicalist publications, expounding the truths of Marxist economics and sociology, propounding a class-based attitude towards the industrial controversies of the day. Ironically enough, Ablett was hailed locally as illustrating the dialectical and philosophical skills of 'the Oxford man', hitherto associated only with bourgeois institutions such as Jesus College. His main activity focused on the Unofficial Reform Committee based on Tonypandy, in the heart of the Rhondda. It was essentially a rank-and-file protest against the caution of Mabon, Brace, and other older leaders of the Fed. It was also a revolt at the grass-roots (or rather the pit-head) against the autocratic position of senior miners' agents within the federalized framework of the miners' union which emphasized local autonomy.

In *The Miners' Next Step*, published at Tonypandy in 1912, the doctrine of Ablett (one of the six authors) was spelt out with frightening clarity and language of Biblical intensity. Not only the timeworn Lib-Labbery of Mabon was condemned. The Labour Party's call for parliamentary leadership and the state nationalization of the coal mines was equally rejected, in favour of industrial unionism, workers' control, pit-head democracy and the running of mines by miners' syndicates at the point of production. Public debates that took place between Ablett and (ironically enough) Frank Hodges, for the neo-syndicalists, and T. I. Mardy Jones and George Barker, for the socialist nationalizers, were forums for a crucial debate between the idea of 'the mines for the nation' and of 'the mines for the miners'. Under nationalization, so Ablett argued at Trealaw in November 1912, the same depressed wages, the same lack of basic safety provision, the same absence of industrial freedom would prevail. 'Where there are state workers', he proclaimed, 'there is always a condition of servility.'

In 1910–12, the battle lines were drawn up between the old ethic embodied in Mabonism and the angry class ideology of Ablett and his friends. The valleys were locked in intense ideological crisis. With the background of the terrifying violence of the Tonypandy riots, almost equally alarming events in Aberdare, the loss of life at Tonypandy in November 1910 and then at Llanelli in August 1911 during a rail strike, South Wales was the arena for an immense industrial turbulence. The whole British labour movement seemed poised at a historic parting of the ways. Ablett at this time was, by all accounts, a figure of Lenin-like charisma, a great teacher, a brilliant orator and pamphleteer. Young miners like Arthur Cook, Arthur Horner and Aneurin Bevan were swept up by his gospel of industrial revolt; they never forgot it throughout their subsequent careers. Within the SWMF, the fortuitous death of three members of the executive in a train accident, led to the election of three militants, Will John, John Hopla, and Tom Smith, in their place. Ablett himself was on the executive from early 1911, as representative of Maerdy. In addition, he helped launch a new publication, *The Rhondda Socialist*, the self-proclaimed 'BOMB of the Rhondda workers'. Renamed *The South Wales Worker* in 1913, it claimed a circulation of over six thousand. From his base in red Maerdy, where he still worked as a checkweigher, Ablett acted as the one-man Comintern of the coalfield.

Mabon by this time was becoming an increasingly ceremonial, even pitiable, figure. He remained MP for the Rhondda until his retirement, at the age of seventy-two, in 1920. He stayed on the executive of the Miners' Federation of Great Britain, and travelled widely abroad. During the first world war, of which he was a powerful supporter, his public image reached a zenith of respectability. He entered the privy council and was conferred with a doctorate of laws by the University College of Wales, Aberystwyth. He was a powerful advocate of conscription. He also lent his name—and his beard—to the advertisement of tobacco and tomato sauce. He became a director and major shareholder of several insurance companies. At his death, his biographer, Dr Eric Wyn Evans, tells us, 'he was a wealthy man by any standards'. Ideologically he had outlived his usefulness by at least twenty years. The myth had consumed the man. He seemed an incongruous survivor from the years before 1898, the middle ages of mining trade-unionism. In plain terms, as the then syndicalist, Charles Stanton, told him bluntly at Aberdare in 1910, he should 'move on or move out'. Mabon did neither, and his irrelevance to industrial history was only the more vividly underlined as a result.

Yet the future in South Wales, and amongst the miners generally, did not really belong to Noah Ablett either. Despite the alarm raised by the *Miners' Next Step*, the Unofficial Reform Committee did not greatly extend its influence beyond its original power base in the Rhondda. In 1912, the elections to the SWMF executive saw a marked reaction against the class-war militants like Ablett. Mainstream advocates of orthodox trade-unionism like Brace, Hartshorn, Onions, and Barker were elected instead. By 1914, the URC was a declining and localized splinter group. The early years of the first world war, in which patriotism was surprisingly rife in the coalfield and in which Welsh miners volunteered in vast numbers, also saw Ablett in eclipse. He remained, however, a powerful teacher and strategic influence. His role was an important one in the Welsh miners' official strike in July 1915, in which they defied Lloyd George and the government, and won a significant wage advance. In the latter stages of the war, Ablett returned to prominence as the Unofficial Reform movement resurfaced, especially after the excitement generated by the Bolshevik revolution in Russia. Ablett became miners' agent for Merthyr in 1918; he served on the MFGB executive from 1919 to 1926; and, with supporters such as Mainwaring, Cook, and S. O. Davies, he was active within the so-called Minority Movement within the Fed, in effect proclaiming the industrial policy of the Communist Party of which he was an early member. Reports from the excitable Special Branch sent to the Cabinet mentioned Ablett, along with Cook and S. O. Davies, as a revolutionary figure, bent on establishing 'the Soviet system of government' in South Wales. As late as the 1926 General Strike, he was prominent enough to be arrested. The legend of Noah Ablett, the guru of Marxist industrial economics and the prophet of the class war, lasted long beyond his lifetime (he died in 1935, a totally spent force at the age of fifty-two). Labour historians have faithfully recreated it anew in recent years.

But, for all his charisma, the future for the Welsh miners, and indeed for the British proletariat as a whole, did not lie with Ablett any more than it did with the antediluvian conservatism of Mabon. In part, this may be a comment on Ablett's own personal decline.

Like other Welsh miners' leaders before and since, the pressures of his public role led to his succumbing increasingly to the solace of alcohol. In his later years, he was thereby effectively removed as a significant force in mining trade-union circles. This was the unspoken reason why Arthur Horner and other Welsh militants threw support behind A. J. Cook rather than Ablett in the election of a successor to Hodges as secretary of the Miners' Federation of Great Britain 1924.

Beyond these personal aspects, Ablett's appeal to direct industrial action, focusing on the localism of individual pits and valleys, cut against the class solidarity of the mining community. To many Welsh miners, Noah Ablett from Porth, translated to Maerdy, was simply parochial. In addition, his brisk dismissal of parliamentarism, local government, the chapel ethos—the values of South Wales communal life as it had emerged over five decades—was too complete and total to win many converts, even amidst the storms of Welsh labour relations between 1910 and 1926. The Central Labour College itself folded up in the late twenties, with much bad blood (and allegations of financial malpractice) all round. As South Wales emerged from the maelstrom after the General Strike, defeated and embittered but with its pride and local institutions intact, the leaders of the miners, in the main, conformed to a different style. It was best personified by a man like Vernon Hartshorn of Maesteg, the outstanding Welsh miners' leader of the post-1918 era, who served in the first Labour governments of 1924 and 1929. Along with Hartshorn went other distinctly centrist figures like Arthur Jenkins, Enoch Morrell, Charles Edwards, Oliver Harris, and the coming man of the thirties, James Griffiths. All of them were pragmatists, practical negotiators rather than ideologues. With men like these, the appeal of community was fused with the call of class. Through the capture of community power, in local government, in the local branches of the Fed, in adult education and in a variety of local services, a new leadership élite was created. It was freed from the outdated ethos of Mabon and all his works, but it was totally detached from the adversarial creed of Ablett as well.

By all accounts, Noah Ablett was a remarkably selfless, sincere, devoted man. He died in October 1935 as he had lived, comparatively poor (he left effects worth £230), revered within Maerdy and his own local circles, but proudly contemptuous of the honours and blandishments of a wider world. As with the Scottish Clydesiders—or some of them—his very dogmatism was both his strength and his downfall. It led him into destructive paths, and into an unrelenting commitment to class stereotypes, from which even such a militant associate as Will Mainwaring finally managed to free himself. Mainwaring moved on to Westminster, and so later did S. O. Davies. The ethic of industrial unionism remained articulate in South Wales, especially in the Fed through men such as Horner and other gifted Communist leaders. But it proved to be too parochial and backward-looking to provide an effective critique for coming to terms with a world in which industrial technology, world markets, and a wider social culture were generating immense changes. In the new, more affluent circumstances that the Welsh coalfield experienced from 1945 to the mid-1970s, with full employment and industrial diversification, there was little room for the ideas Ablett had promoted. Even his disciple, Arthur Horner, who served as secretary of the NUM from 1946 to 1960 and became an indirect prop for the Attlee government during the first phase of nationalization, moved into more positive channels; the old poacher even briefly considered turning gamekeeper and joining the National Coal Board, but declined the offer after some thought.

Ablett will remain a romantic legend for the apostles of an 'alternative', counter-factual labour history, full of bravura, panache, and schizoid turbulence. In the more humdrum, real world, the *Miners' Next Step* proved to be a step too far.

# ARTHUR HENDERSON

ARTHUR HENDERSON has become honoured over the years as one of the undisputed heroes of British labour. More than any other of his contemporaries, he embodied the rock-solid alliance of the unions and the Labour Party, with all the pragmatic accommodation that this implied. Lenin would have seen him as the very model of working-class 'economism'. Indeed, Lenin's *Left-Wing Communism: An Infantile Disorder*, written in April 1920, included a fierce personal attack on Henderson as a petty bourgeois opportunist of the stamp of Kerensky, Scheidemann, or Turati. Amongst British labour supporters, Henderson is revered above all for two famous, central episodes in his career. The 'doormat' incident of August 1917, after which he broke away from Lloyd George's wartime coalition and master-minded the new organizational independence of the Labour Party, gave him a totally new stature. And, at the end of his career, he achieved near-immortality by leading those who resisted cuts in unemployment benefit in August 1931 and insisted on following the dictates of the TUC rather than the international bankers.

Henderson, then, is imperishably identified with the proud independence of the labour movement, fighting free from the shackles of coalition with the capitalists in 1917, asserting its gut responsibility for its own mass supporters within the trade-union world. Even so, his reputation as an apostle of party independence is in many ways curious. He began life as a nonconformist free-trade Liberal; he did not greatly change throughout a long career. He was the embodiment of the artisan commitment to the progressive alliance, one of the Webbs' classic 'new model' unionists. Far from being a founding father of British socialism, he was not associated with any socialist body at all until he quietly joined the Fabians in 1912.

Arthur Henderson was also in personal terms not at all what he was commonly represented as being. The lovable, warm-hearted 'Uncle Arthur' of popular legend was a proud, prickly individual. His surviving correspondence in the Labour Party archives shows him to have been the terror of laggard party workers, sometimes a bully. He and MacDonald had a particularly difficult relationship. In many ways, they were two prima donnas locked in combat. In the first

Labour government, in January 1924, to the dismay of colleagues, MacDonald even tried to exclude Henderson from the administration altogether. With very bad grace, Henderson went to the Home Office, in whose affairs he took little interest. MacDonald tried to exclude him from the Foreign Office in 1929, ludicrously suggesting Jimmy Thomas as an alternative. Henderson is manifestly one of those giants of the early labour movement who demands a decent, up-to-date biography. Molly Hamilton's affectionate portrait of 1938, which embalms him in historical preserving fluid for ever more, urgently needs to be replaced. Fortunately Chris Wrigley is now engaged on this vital task. Until his book appears, Henderson, like the intellectual G. D. H. Cole, remains 'a bit of a puzzle'.

His stamp on the movement was many-sided and all-pervasive, but it operated above all in three main areas. First and always, he personified Labour's bedrock in the unions. It was as a trade-unionist that he grew up in the movement, within the Ironfounders of the North-East. He became a strong proponent of industrial conciliation and arbitration, and served as secretary on the North-East Conciliation Board of the industry formed in 1894, when he was thirty-one. He felt it entirely compatible with his role as a trade-union organizer to act simultaneously as election agent for the Liberal capitalist, Joseph Pease, from 1896 onwards. It was essentially as a Lib-Lab adherent of the LRC that he was elected for Barnard Castle, over Tory and Liberal opposition, in a famous by-election in 1903. Though rapidly diverging from the simple artisan Liberalism of men like the railwaymen's leader, Richard Bell, he retained his strong trade-union connection thereafter, and became president of the Ironfounders' Union in 1910.

During the first world war, Henderson's trade-unionism became decisive in moulding the character of the movement. He took a strongly 'patriotic' line in 1914, and was the main architect of the famous Treasury Agreement with Lloyd George and the Asquith government in March 1915. Later, this was strongly attacked as sacrificing the right to strike and imposing shackles on the labour movement without any compensating sacrifice from profiteering wartime capitalists. At the time, though, it seemed a great triumph. Henderson spoke not merely for his own ironfounders but for the corporate identity of the unions as a whole. For engineers, shipbuilders, boilermakers, metal workers and many others, the Treasury Agreement embodied a new commitment by the state to a national partnership with organized labour. There were tangible material benefits in return for concessions over the 'dilution' of skilled labour and demarcation of particular skills. During the war years, union membership doubled to over eight million; a new status was given to union executives in concluding national, rather than purely local or regional, wages and hours agreements; a new access to Whitehall and Downing Street was permanently achieved, with Henderson's presence in Lloyd George's five-man War Cabinet in December 1916 the symbol of it. These changes would surely survive the events of the war years.

When the Labour Party emerged with new purpose after the 1918 constitution and structural reforms, it was Henderson who ensured that the unions dominated the machinery of the party at every stage. He entered on a carefully chosen tour of mining and other areas to ensure the unions' acceptance of the new structure: even the famous Clause Four, committing Labour to nationalization, merely re-enacted the unions' view of wartime collectivism. In the twenties, far more so than at any other time in its history, Labour was the trade-unionists' party even if its leader was the *déclassé* Ramsay MacDonald. The party embodied the unions' vision of class solidarity. The alliance of party and unions emerged all the stronger after the trauma of the general strike, in which Henderson played a comparatively marginal role.

In the final crisis of July–August 1931, Henderson's views went through many gyrations. But always the ultimate touchstone was the outlook of the General Council of the TUC. When the TUC finally pronounced against the cuts in social benefit that MacDonald's government proposed, Henderson, along with such other ministers as Clynes, Lansbury, Adamson, Alexander, Greenwood, Graham, and Johnston, instinctively followed the call of class loyalty. (This applied perhaps even to Johnston, the son of a licensed victualler who went to Glasgow University.) With all his many intellectual and other limitations, Henderson's strength, then as always, was that he embodied the class base of the movement, the positive rather than the defensive aspects of late-Victorian Lib-Labbism. Henderson changed comparatively little between the 1890s and the 1930s, from the Gladstonian artisan radical he originally was. He showed himself to be a firm, even fanatical, teetotaller, a devoted Methodist lay preacher, intellectually cautious and distrustful of 'flashiness'. He reflected a latent social revolution which saw trade-unionists like

Henderson, and men like Vernon Hartshorn and Jack Lawson else-where, capture power at local level and move out to form a new cadre of leadership. Not for nothing was Henderson imperishably identified with that famous concept, so mercilessly parodied by journalists later on, 'This Great Movement of Ours'.

Henderson seemed to many a dullish dog. But, in the second main area of his historical significance, as party organizer and secretary of the Labour Party in its formative phase from 1911 to 1934, he was anything but dull. Indeed he was aggressive and dynamic, a tremendous force fully comparable with Morrison in later years. His association with the Labour Party early on had been distinctly sectional. He became a Labour MP and temporary chairman of the parliamentary party in 1908–10 as a unionist pure and simple. When he became party secretary in 1911, there was some criticism that he was not linked with any socialist organization: hence his membership of convenience in the Fabians. However as general secretary of the party he found a highly congenial role; indeed his strong insistence on Labour's 'independence' indicated how much he diverged from older Lib-Labs like 'Mabon' or Richard Bell. He proved to be a superb technician, utilizing the administrative skills first developed in the nineties while serving J. A. Pease as his election agent. These qualities were especially marked in the heyday between 1917 and 1924 when the modern Labour Party was born. Henderson devoted much of his working year to tours of outlying constituencies, often with Arthur Peters, the national agent (succeeded by Egerton Wake in 1918), instructing local party workers in organizational techniques, the arcane mysteries of registration law, the broad prin-ciples of party finance. As a peripatetic one-man link between Westminster and the grass-roots, he developed a national vision of the movement that was unique.

He helped rally the party in the face of the legal rebuff of the Osborne Judgement which seemed to undermine the very validity of Labour's involvement in politics, not merely in supporting union-sponsored candidates, but at any level of local and national govern-ment. Through Henderson's efforts, the outcome was the endorse-ment of the political levy by union after union in 1913 (reaffirmed triumphantly in 1985–6), the build-up of local party organization, and the emergence of a position by the summer of 1914 in which Labour could legitimately claim to fight a far wider range of seats, perhaps a hundred or more, as their price for the maintenance of the progressive alliance with the Liberals.

During the war, Henderson, while active both in Asquith's and Lloyd George's wartime Cabinet as a token Labour representative, maintained an active organizational role outside parliament as well. He was a classic instance of the insider–outsider role that Labour acquired during the first world war, to its great good fortune. He also used the War Emergency Workers' National Committee to strengthen the party nation-wide, and to bring in intellectuals like Sidney Webb, with whom he struck up a firm, if improbable, alliance, to give the party new policies. It became clear in the course of 1918, especially after Henderson's resignation from the government, that Labour was drifting away from a corporate relationship with the state towards an adversarial role. Henderson now struck with the ferocity of a tiger. He kept his eye consistently on the objective of harmonizing the activities of the party and the unions: this was the nub of his famous 'Memorandum A' for overhauling the party organization, in October 1920. Always he was the great centralizer, Labour's Bismarck, putting down local revolts from Celtic separatists in Scotland and Wales, or syndicalist dissenters in the *Daily Herald*, with a firm hand. The ascendancy of Head Office became omnipresent: one early victim of it was the Labour Research Department, which had enlisted such bright young people as Hugh Dalton and Barbara Wootton, but which clashed with his idea of central control.

These successes in the party machinery were achieved at some cost. Henderson was never fortunate in finding a reliable parliamentary seat. At various times, Barnard Castle, Widnes, Newcastle East, Burnley, and Clay Cross afforded him refuge. But his very mobility enhanced his relationship with party workers, with whom he built up an influence of an intimately personal kind. From Transport House committee men to the humblest office typist, Henderson could establish a rapport. On a parliamentary plane, he reinforced these skills with his work as party chief whip in the 1924–9 sessions. Throughout the party machine, he introduced a new generation of young organizers, including Jim Middleton, Arthur Greenwood, William Gillies, and his son Willie Henderson. As an organizer, Henderson could be emollient and encouraging. If thwarted, he could be strict, even brutal. His work had its limitations, without doubt, especially the abolition of the promising Labour Research Department. But the achievement was still impressive in so centrifugal a party. Perhaps the greatest implicit tribute to Henderson came in his last years, when his party, and the machine he had so patiently built up, were able to recover from the defeat of 1931 and re-emerge as a credible challenge for power. The Liberals after 1922 could have done with the organizational skills of an Arthur Henderson. His own party could use them again at the present time.

In his wider outlook, Henderson appeared the very model of British insularity, with an unconcern for other nations reminiscent of characters in Gilbert and Sullivan. Yet the third, and most remarkable, thread of his career lay in his unquestioned internationalism. He knew no European languages, and had scant knowledge of foreign geography or history. Yet his sturdy class-consciousness as a late-Victorian artisan impelled him towards a sense of international kinship, just as Applegarth and the union 'junta' of the 1860s were moved to launch the first workers' International in 1864 with as improbable a bedfellow as Marx himself. Henderson became a key figure in the links between the British and European socialist movements. Before the war, he served as secretary of the British section of the Second International. In this capacity, he argued strongly against Hardie's call for a world-wide workers' strike against war. He travelled with Hardie to the momentous conference of the International Socialist Bureau at Brussels in late July 1914. But, unlike some trade-unionists and the bulk of the ILP (which he always distrusted), he swung to endorse Grey's policy and the entry into war. Whatever Henderson was, he was never a pacifist.

It was, of course, the events of 1917 that gave a new dimension to Henderson's international outlook. At first, he was very wary of the new regime in Russia. Indeed, his mission to Petrograd in June 1917 was intended to warn the Russian provisional government of the dangers of making a separate peace with Germany. Nor was he initially in favour of the Stockholm conference, in which German as well as Russian and western European socialists would be represented. Lenin's Bolsheviks he feared and distrusted. Then, in dramatic fashion, Henderson completely changed his mind. He became wholly converted to the cause of Stockholm, and urged Labour's NEC to endorse it. He now saw Stockholm as an essential means of building up a constitutional regime in Russia. Lloyd George, no doubt, behaved with much deviousness in the next few weeks, which led eventually to Henderson's departure from the government on 12 August after the celebrated 'doormat' affair at 10 Downing Street on 1 August. But Henderson's views, expressed with much obstinacy and dourness, were not straightforward either. As Lloyd

George observed in his memoirs, the laconic Newcastle ironfounder had been unaccountably touched with 'the revolutionary malaria'. In endorsing the Stockholm conference at a Labour Party conference on 10 August, Henderson appeared to go against an agreed Cabinet decision two days earlier. From that time onwards, no less than MacDonald, Henderson embodied the new internationalism and solidarity of the socialist movement. Indeed, the two men were largely reconciled by their joint collaboration on Labour's 'Memorandum of War Aims' which called, among other things, for a League of Nations, an international court, and machinery to deal with world economic problems. Henderson also emerged as a powerful leader of European socialism and organized the famous congress at Berne held in January 1919, a kind of People's Versailles, at which revolutionary and non-revolutionary socialists parted company with each other in dramatic fashion. Russia influenced Henderson's outlook in domestic politics too. It encouraged him to reorganize his party on a popular, if not populist, basis, and to commit it unambiguously to a version of socialism acceptable to the unions.

In the twenties, Henderson emerged as a powerful apostle of the League and a crusader for disarmament. He made support for the League the principal base of Labour's stance in foreign affairs. He was fiercely outspoken in his criticism of 'the system of Versailles', somewhat to the embarrassment of MacDonald himself. He condemned the use of war as an instrument of rational policy. At the same time, he insisted that peace needed coercive means to make it a reality. Collective security under the League would make sense only if the nations of the world pooled their resources to enforce it. There were many Utopians amongst the British left in the twenties, who largely ignored the brute factor of power in international affairs. But Henderson was never amongst them.

Although notionally Home Secretary, he and Lord Parmoor were active in Geneva in the late summer of 1924 on the subcommittee that produced that famous, almost legendary, document, the Geneva Protocol. With its subtle combination of conciliation and coercion, it embodied the essence of Henderson's approach to European security. Its interlocking provisions were designed to circumvent international aggression; but the government fell before the Protocol would be given effect. MacDonald was, in any case, very doubtful about the Protocol idea, and the incoming Baldwin government promptly scrapped it in favour of a more distinctly nationalist approach.

Henderson, however, remained a dominant figure in the formulation of Labour's foreign policy throughout the twenties. The
climax of his career came in 1929 when, at his own insistence and
after yet another bitter clash with MacDonald, he went to the Foreign
Office. Here he became an unexpectedly commanding figure, both
over the Foreign Office itself and amongst his European contemporaries, for whom he embodied the temporarily more hopeful
mood of the Locarno era. Henderson had many obstacles in his path
at the Foreign Office, two of them near at hand. Philip Snowden,
with his bitter anti-Germanism, often conflicted with Henderson's
policy of Franco-German conciliation. Snowden, a sternly insular
figure, interfered on such matters as inter-allied war debts and German reparations payments, to harmful effect. But Henderson's
heaviest cross to bear was his own Prime Minister. MacDonald prided
himself on his own insight into foreign affairs, and often clashed
with Henderson. In the particular area of Anglo-American relations,
MacDonald virtually ran affairs on his own. The rivalry between
Prime Minister and Foreign Secretary reached an extraordinary climax in 16–20 July 1931, when each appeared to be playing off the
Germans and the French as weapons in a private conflict against
each other. The London financial conference of 20 July onwards,
which was supposed to be arranging a collective loan to Germany,
was a total failure. The whole episode was an extraordinary exercise
in foreign policy. It had few, if any, parallels in British history, for
the tension at the summit of government that it displayed. Certainly
the bitter conflict between MacDonald and Henderson played its
part in driving the two men apart, with permanent results, in the
arguments over cuts in unemployment benefit the following month.
Henderson throughout seemed to be labouring under difficulties:
some were self-created since he insisted on staying on as party
secretary. Sir Warren Fisher, who controlled all Foreign Office
appointments under the terms of the famous memorandum of 1919,
was another consistent enemy. He secured the appointment, against
Henderson's wishes, of Vansittart as permanent under-secretary for
foreign affairs in 1930. In spite of it all, however, Henderson's
standing as a statesman of international stature seemed immeasurably greater by the time the government resigned. For League
enthusiasts like Robert Cecil, he was almost a god.

His achievements were probably more apparent than real. The
withdrawal of French troops from the Rhineland did not really lighten

the tension in Franco-German relations, especially with the rise of Hitler and the Nazis at the 1930 elections. The German–Austrian customs union of early 1931 was an uncomfortable portent of the *anschluss* of a few years later. Britain's signature to the 'Optional Clause' (which accepted compulsory arbitration for all justiciable international disputes) was a deceptive gesture. Reparations remained as big a mess as ever. Even so, the international atmosphere did show some lightening between 1929 and 1939. France and Germany were at least talking; relations with Russia were becoming normalized; the League seemed a more plausible instrument of international order. For all this, Henderson could claim much of the credit.

After the crash of August 1931, Henderson, soon out of parliament, presided over the world disarmament conference at Geneva. It was a pathetic last act. He battled on with his unenviable task in the face of French hostility, Nazi jingoism, and the freezing indifference of the British Prime Minister, his old comrade MacDonald. The very concept underlying the conference was subsequently derided by 'realists' such as E. H. Carr, an enthusiast for Stalinism who saw Geneva as embodying the absurdities of the Utopian solution for the arbitrament of international disputes. It showed also, Carr thought, the pointlessness of a simple faith in the power of 'world public opinion'. But the truth was surely that Henderson's hopes were simply swamped by events far beyond the Geneva conference hall. The emergence of the Hitler regime in Germany inexorably doomed the talkers and pacifiers at Lake Geneva. Henderson became internationally acclaimed; he even received the Nobel peace prize, a final accolade of futility at that time. But his crusade came crashing down in ruins, leaving Europe in chaos. It also left Labour's foreign policy, including what precise meaning the left attached to the very notion of 'collective security', as vague and ambiguous as ever.

Henderson was a man often underestimated at the time, by colleagues and opponents alike. Like Stanley Baldwin he was 'not a clever man'. Yet on key issues and at critical occasions, his judgement proved decisive and impeccable. After his death, Beatrice Webb, a frequent critic, observed that 'Arthur Henderson will stand out as the wisest and most disinterested of the Labour leaders of 1906-36' (*sic*). Henderson was a much more complex figure than he seemed at first sight. A stolid, almost taciturn, trade-unionist, he could explode with anger or launch himself recklessly into the unknown as in 1917–18. Like many men of God he was a good hater, with Lloyd George and Ramsay MacDonald foremost in his demonology. His soul could be ignited by the heady aspirations of a war-torn world, desperate for peace and the stability of a new international order. The plodder turned into a prophet, even a poet. Nearer home, in 1919–20, he emerged as a powerful and influential champion of Irish independence. He was an organizer, a committee man and administrator of proven skill over three decades; behind the surface was a will of iron and uncynical idealism. There was also an unquestioned honesty, unselfishness, and integrity. He was never a plotter; for all their personal differences, he supported MacDonald loyally enough down to 1931. He was a safe custodian for the movement as flashier colleagues fell by the wayside; he built to last. Labour is right to venerate 'Uncle Arthur', and to see him as the most effective and creative of all its founding fathers.

# 2

## TOWARDS JERUSALEM
### 1931–1945

# HAROLD LASKI

DANIEL MOYNIHAN, erstwhile American ambassador to the UN, once commented ruefully on how the leaders of the emergent nations of Africa, Asia, and the Caribbean had learnt their political ideas from the British Labour Party, the *New Statesman* and the London School of Economics. It was, no doubt, Harold Laski that he had partly in mind. Throughout the inter-war years and on into the years after 1945, Laski was the inspiration for a generation of students from every continent, the mentor of rising politicians from Krishna Menon to John F. Kennedy. He was also extraordinarily productive as a journalist in the socialist press, and as an academic writer on law, political theory, and institutions. In active Labour politics, he bestrode the worlds of the Left Book Club, *Tribune*, and the Popular Front like a pint-sized colossus. He is a part of the legend of the thirties, just as much as Jarrow, Munich, or Guernica. When Churchill and the Beaverbrook press tried to use Laski as a red bogey in the 1945 election campaign, with some success, they were attacking one of the most charismatic and controversial figures in British public life.

Yet since those heady days Laski's name and reputation have gone into almost total eclipse (with the rather curious exception of Japan). In part, there may be a personal explanation for this. Laski's erratic role in the 1945 election and his ill-advised libel action against two obscure Nottinghamshire newspapers (which claimed that he had advocated revolutionary violence at an election meeting) helped to undermine him. He cut a surprisingly ineffective figure in the witness box when confronted with the withering fire and relentless aggression of Sir Patrick Hastings—himself, ironically enough, a former Labour Attorney-General. Laski's public standing never recovered—and neither did his health. He died prematurely just after the 1950 general election, manifestly a waning force.

Quite apart from personal circumstances (which must include the prolonged ill-health of his last years), the ideas promoted in Laski's works now often seem unjustly dated. His numerous large books on sovereignty, authority, or the theory of democracy—even the massive *Grammar of Politics*, which captured the imagination of students on both sides of the Atlantic—seldom excite discussion. The Webbs and the Coles continue to provoke scholarly argument and to inspire major biographies. The Fabian ethic lives on defiantly. That other great Labour intellectual and scholar, R. H. Tawney, remains a name to treasure, regularly cited by Labour leaders from Gaitskell to Kinnock. The very appropriation of Tawney's name by the newly formed Social Democrats in 1981 provoked a passionate outcry within socialist circles, including a memorable and moving rebuke from Raphael Samuel. But Laski, who ranked for so long with them, or even ahead of them, as a major ideological force in his time, provoked no such reaction. There are two biographies, one by Kingsley Martin in 1953, too close to the cold war and too uncritical to be at all satisfactory, another by Granville Eastwood in 1976, a brief and unpretentious study which draws on the testimony of Laski's widow, Freda, and many of his pupils and admirers. But the absence of a major study of Laski's ideas and influence is a massive gap in socialist historiography. Maybe we shall have to rely on the Japanese to provide one.

As an interim assessment, it may be suggested that Laski's influence had three main facets. First and foremost, as his close friend, Felix Frankfurter, wrote, there was 'his central significance as a teacher', mainly at Harvard and the London School of Economics. All the evidence, from pupils as diverse as James Callaghan, Professor John Saville, and Bernard Levin, suggests that Laski was a truly magnetic lecturer and leader of graduate seminars, during thirty somewhat troubled years at the LSE. There were personal disputes galore, notably with Beveridge, director of the London School and another powerful personality who regarded Laski's leftish political activities with a jaundiced eye. Even some of Laski's progressive colleagues found him a tiresome member of common room. Beveridge tried, without success, to argue that Laski's writings in the columns of the Daily Herald impaired the time and energy he had for his pupils, and that in any case they were incompatible with the work of a scholar. Laski was able to prove that the hours he devoted to his students per week were vastly higher than the average. As Beveridge's biographer, Dr José Harris, has commented, the episode led Beveridge to be regarded as an enemy of academic freedom.

On the other hand, there was abundant evidence of the extraordinary warmth, patience, kindness, and humanity that Laski showed towards many of his students, especially those from foreign lands. His willingness to lend or give them books or money became legendary. The war years, when the LSE was evacuated to

Cambridge, and Harold's classes and seminars were transferred to the unlikely locale of a chemist's shop on King's Parade, merely intensified Laski's willingness to give himself to his students. Even more than before, they were enthralled by a teacher of astonishing brilliance, consumed by the pursuit of academic truth, setting his own beliefs, as he advised them to do, 'against the experience of mankind'. He challenged the hard-line dogmatism and Stalinist rigidity of his more revolutionary pupils, but did so without incurring their wrath or resentment. For many students in these wartime years, not only on the socialist left, therefore, Laski's values represented much of the essence of what the war was really all about.

Secondly, there was Laski's vast corpus of writings as an academic political scientist. He launched a vast profusion of mighty works, all precisely argued, mostly extensively researched, produced, somehow or other, amidst the spate of political and other public activity. Perhaps the most worthwhile and enduring of his books was one that achieved somewhat less celebrity at the time, a subtle survey of English political thought from Locke to Bentham. Other works ranged far and wide over the whole theory underlying the nature of democracy and the law in Britain and the United States. Some of Laski's writings, especially the *Grammar of Politics*, strike one now as surprisingly turgid for a communicator of such acknowledged brilliance. The style is always lucid, but seldom sparkling. Others are hopelessly dated; notable among these is a Home University Library volume on *Communism* in 1927, where an analysis of the Marxist theory of the state largely ignores its actual application within the Soviet system as it had emerged in Lenin's time and since. Laski's forte is always his treatment of legal and political theory. He is weakest on social and economic analysis. One abiding gap in his writings, surprisingly for one much influenced by Marxism, is any serious or sustained examination of the concept of class.

None the less, Laski's writings, still repay careful attention. More than any of his contemporaries, he sought to provide intellectual links between liberalism and socialism. His life was one prolonged intellectual engagement with the twin concepts of liberty and of equality. By the early 1920s Laski was a committed socialist. He had been impelled in that direction, quite apart from intellectual considerations, by the personal crisis of his relations with Harvard in 1919 when Laski found himself bitterly pilloried by Boston society for his open sympathy with the local police in a savage strike, put down with unwonted energy by Governor Calvin Coolidge. Laski was also much influenced, even then, by the Marxist analysis of the nature of property relationships and their bearing on the distribution of power within the state. At the same time, he also had a powerful inheritance from the classical liberalism of nineteenth-century England. He grew up as a disciple of the New Liberals of Edwardian days, men like J. A. Hobson and L. T. Hobhouse. He paid obeisance, more surprisingly perhaps, to John Stuart Mill, from whom, he told Oliver Wendell Holmes, 'we still have a damned lot to learn'. He approached the notion of personal freedom and self-expression in a remarkably pure and uncomplicated way. This led him to become uneasy with the Idealism of T. H. Green and the neo-Hegelian school who, he thought, unduly exalted the power of the central state. He first became involved seriously with political theory through his interest in medieval constitutional law, especially the work of Maitland—his favourite historian—and Otto Gierke. He was fascinated by the corporate position of religious communities and the guilds in the later Middle Ages, and the way in which they preserved their autonomy against the increasing encroachments of the national state. Laski, this aggressively agnostic Jewish socialist, found inspiration in the high Anglican writings on these themes of the Reverend J. N. Figgis, a Cambridge college chaplain and the author of such academic treatises as a study of later medieval thought from Gerson to Grotius, and of the divine right of kings.

Laski's intellectual interest in the enduring vitality of independent corporations, religious and lay, chimed in with an instinctive feeling for individuality. Indeed, he became a forceful advocate of libertarian ideas against the bureaucratic power of central government. In the *Grammar of Politics*, he took issue equally with Hobbes and Rousseau over the alleged unifying effect of authority. He urged a bill of rights for Britain itself, a notion fashionable with sections of the British right in the 1980s. Laski served on the Donoughmore Committee on ministerial powers in 1929–32, and became a fierce critic of the despotic implications of the quasi-judicial powers being annexed by faceless public servants in impenetrable government sanctums.

Squaring the circle between a socialist commitment to state direction and a libertarian commitment to individual freedom and consent is far from easy; it may perhaps be insoluble. It has certainly taxed the mental resources of socialists of all shades from William Morris to E. P. Thompson. Laski came closer than most to providing a

satisfying intellectual answer. This lay in the magic concept of pluralism, a notion that appealed naturally to Laski with his feeling for
American society and federal forms of government. Political relationships should become functional, and power decentralized. In the
*Grammar of Politics*, Laski combined a broadly Fabian view of the rise
of the providing central state with a plea that sovereignty should be
located in a diversity of institutions and social groups. It was the
social and economic aspects of pluralism that Laski emphasized,
rather than the legal or juristic. It enabled him, he believed, to
propound a form of creative devolution which escaped the futility of
the Guild Socialists (for whom he had little sympathy), the stark
reaction of the Chesterton–Belloc gospel of 'distribution', and the
potential violence of the Sorelian syndicalists. The legislative, executive, and administrative aspects of the pluralist state were spelt out
in much detail. They were linked with a distinctly Utopian plea for
an interdependent world order, restructured on federalist lines.

In the thirties, Laski's sympathy with Marxism became ever more
pronounced. Beatrice Webb recorded in July 1934 how Laski and
his wife 'were in a state of exhilaration about the hope and adventure,
the social equality and universal activity in the land of the Soviets'.
From 1936, he was a leading figure in the Left Book Club, preaching
the cause of an alliance between Labour and the Communists. Yet
there was no question that his insistence on libertarianism and
individual self-expression were still central to his outlook. In *Liberty
in the Modern State*, published in 1930 and reissued with only trivial
amendment in 1937, he emphasized yet again the limits to political
power—and to economic power as well, since one of his themes was
to enlarge the freedom of the consumer. Much of the book is a hymn
to civil liberties in highly traditional Millite terms. Appropriately, he
was a prominent member of the National Council for Civil Liberties,
formed in 1934 to monitor abuses of power by the central government and, more especially, the police.

Laski's ideological impact was never as great as he intended (or
perhaps believed, for all his apparent air of modesty). Nor did his
*Grammar of Politics* achieve the influence he sought as the work of a
latter-day Aristotle. He conceived it as a major statement of political
theory; but it mouldered away, unheeded and unread. In 1938, Laski
appeared to disavow its main thesis himself, and to dismiss his
earlier ventures in pluralist theory as the product of a semi-mystical
attachment to medieval corporatism which could only have reac-

tionary consequences and boost the power of the capitalist. Even so, the change in Laski's position was less radical than Kingsley Martin's biography seems to imply. He continued to exalt freedom above all other values, though now defined as 'positive freedom' which should 'assume a wider context'. The underlying theme even of *Reflections on the Revolution of Our Time* (1943), his most radical work, published during the war when enthusiasm for the Red Army was at its height, was the need to reconcile economic planning with personal self-expression. It is a book that starts and ends with the free autonomous individual, though admittedly there are some intellectual adventures along the way. Laski was no Leninist, scarcely even an orthodox Fabian. His students of the LSE were always aware that his background was social democratic, never Communist or Stalinist. He should not be classed with the advocates of a juggernaut of faceless, centralized bureaucratic power, but with socialism spelt out in human terms of localism, devolution, regional and personal accountability. We need not confront Laski drunk with Laski sober, the unreflective centralist of the forties with the wary critic of the state apparatus in the twenties and thirties. There is an abiding thread of individualist liberalism evident throughout his career, with his passion for the United States an essential part of it. As an unthinking commitment to centralization and state control melts away in British socialist ranks, Laski deserves to be resurrected. As a thinker, he retains a surprising freshness and modernity.

His pluralistic philosophy had implications for his third career. Sadly, this was the most frustrating of them all—his work as a Labour Party activist. Elected to the NEC for the constituency party section in 1937, he was a ceaselessly goading voice on the left over the next nine years. He called for a 'unity front' with the Soviet Union. During the Second World War, he was a ceaseless critic of the prevailing consensus. He urged that the experience of total war be harnessed to promote a socialist commonwealth and a revolution by consent. *Reflections on the Revolution of Our Time* included an overt call for socialist ownership and a total transformation of the means of production and the underlying social structure. It criticized Labour ministers in Churchill's coalition for not trying to alter the fundamental relationship of production, in effect for compromising with capitalism.

Laski was, in particular, a ceaseless critic of the impassive Attlee. This brought him more than once to the verge of serious disciplining, even possible expulsion. At one time, he even suggested to Ernest Bevin that he should replace Attlee as party leader, but was snubbed for his pains. Herbert Morrison was more frequently his favoured candidate, for all his right-wing stance on most issues. Events reached a climax during the election campaign in May–June 1945 when, as luck would have it, Laski was newly installed as party chairman to succeed Ellen Wilkinson. Even at the LSE, Laski was not a good committee man, and he was never one of nature's chairmen. He now openly told Attlee that he should retire as leader, adding the unhappy analogy of the removal of Auchinleck in favour of Montgomery just before the victory of El Alamein. Morrison was his nominee for the Montgomery role. The climax came when Laski urged Attlee, just before the polls, that he should accept the premiership subject to the approval of the National Executive, and that he should attend the Potsdam conference with Churchill as 'an observer only'. What Attlee termed Laski's 'constant flow of speeches and interviews' merely confirmed a widespread national distrust of political intellectuals in general, and Jewish ones in particular. As noted, Laski— 'this hitherto unknown person'—was grist to Churchill's mill in election broadcasts, the 1945 equivalent of Derek Hatton or Bernie Grant.

Without doubt, Laski's interventions in general were ill-phrased, mistimed, often simply foolish. Attlee spoke for the vast majority in suggesting that a period of silence on Laski's part would be valuable. It had the effect of entrenching Attlee in the loyalties of his followers. On the other hand, Laski had the uncanny gift of analysing the dangers of Labour's being sucked up by the patriotic euphoria of a bogus wartime consensus which belied the social divisions beneath. His view of the role of the party executive and conference in directing policy-making and the pronouncements of party leaders became the conventional orthodoxy of the Labour left in the 1970s. Attlee himself was punctilious, even in 1945, in acknowledging the sovereignty of the annual conference. Laski was too often tactically maladroit. But during the war years and in 1945 he said awkward things that needed to be said, whose resonance continues down the years.

Laski's last years were at anticlimax after the excitement and the notoriety of the libel case which upset him deeply. He wrote sadly on what it felt like to be 'the most unpopular man in England'. He remained on the NEC until 1949, invariably supporting gadflies on the left, but also prepared loyally to endorse the agreed majority line.

He voted, reluctantly, for the endorsement of military conscription and the expulsion of Zilliacus, Hutchinson, and other rebels. This was not surprising: he had, after all, not actually opposed the expulsion of Cripps from the party for his Popular Front activities back in 1939. Even Palestine did not strain Laski's loyalty to the party beyond the limit. He now came under increasing fire from the Russians and from Communists in general for his attacks on Stalinism. His advice to French and Danish socialists not to merge with the Communist parties in their countries led to Laski's being formally branded a social fascist by the Kremlin. Laski, once Churchill's favourite red bogey, was now condemned by *Pravda* as 'a prop to bourgeois civilization'. For the Communists discovered that academician Laski was not merely an abstracted university professor who advocated intellectual experiment: he was also a long-standing Labour loyalist who believed equally in solidarity with the party and its creed of democratic socialism.

His career is certainly far more than a period piece. It has intense and enduring human interest as a tale of a man of transcendent intellectual integrity who strove to reconcile socialist planning with a liberal and pluralist view of democracy. Nothing was more ludicrous than Sir Patrick Hastings's insistence in the famous libel case that Laski had been preaching revolutionary violence over the years. In responding, Laski did not do himself full justice in the witness box. He was nervous, and also prevaricated disastrously when asked whether the possible violence he mentioned could arise from the socialist workers, and not merely from counter-revolutionary capitalists. Hastings was much helped by an extraordinary performance by the presiding judge, Lord Chief Justice Goddard, a man of notoriously reactionary outlook, who allowed Hastings to proceed at length with a series of extracts from Laski's writings in the past, all wrenched out of context. Goddard also directed the jury that it was not merely a question of whether Laski had actually used the disputed words about possible violence, but also 'Are these the sort of words which Mr Laski would be likely to use?' But, even in the confused atmosphere of the courtroom, it emerged clearly enough that Laski had been arguing, with copious historical examples from the fall of Rome to the Russian Revolution, that the alternative to social change by consent (which he advocated) might well be some form of violent confrontation. He was saying little different from liberals in the 1970s or 1980s who commented that dissident groups—perhaps blacks, the unemployed, Ulster Catholics, or the Scots and the Welsh—would turn to direct action unless positive, sustained attention was paid to their grievances. To depict Laski as some kind of English Trotsky was absurd.

The furore caused by the *Reflections* of 1943 is also curious. Certainly it did include some unduly lenient, or plain inaccurate, observations on the government and social system of the Soviet Union. But that was common form at the time. Like Orwell, Priestley, and other democrats, Laski saw the war as an apocalyptic moment, a crucible of social transformation. The nub of his programme as advocated in 1943 was remarkably close to the distinctly finite programme actually enacted by Attlee and his colleagues after 1945—excluding some details such as public ownership of the banks. Even in that left-wing work, Laski's commitment to parliamentarism, consent, constitutionalism, and the rule of law shines from (almost) every page.

His career is interesting in another respect. It also shows how a Jewish middle-class professor of English political theory could infuse an insular movement with a genuine internationalism. He learnt much from the French jurist, Duguit, and the German, Gierke. In this respect, his lifelong attachment to the United States, so often a bogey country for British socialists, is of much interest. His intellectual relationships with Holmes, Frankfurter, Brandeis, Morris Cohen, and many others testifies to its centrality. No doubt, Laski did not move widely in American society beyond the academic and literary circles of Boston, New York, and the intelligentsia attached to *New Republic* and *The Nation*. The South and the West were largely unknown countries for him to the end; he knew little of the blacks at first hand, for all his zeal for racial equality. Still, Laski kept alive, even during the rigours of the cold war in his last years, a warm enthusiasm for America as a democratic society of a unique kind, born free. In key respects, he shared the assumptions of the progressives of the early twentieth century, and of the New York *Nation* for which he wrote freely. Like them, he was alarmed at the growth of capitalist domination over US social and political institutions, and the rise of brute monopoly economic power. In his last major book, *American Democracy* (1949), a work flawed by a distinctly sketchy and outdated range of sources for American history, Laski called for the ethic of Americanism to be adapted to the demands of a new age. Yet, like the Progressives, he was essentially an optimist about

America. Like them, he believed that the land was fundamentally sound, rich with promise, and fully capable of moral salvation, perhaps with a new Lincoln or Franklin Roosevelt as a presidential saviour.

Laski found a particular inspiration in American jurisprudence, especially as modulated in the relativist outlook of a giant like Oliver Wendell Holmes. The venerable American jurist found in Laski a kindred spirit. 'There is no other man I should miss so much' he wrote to the twenty-seven-year old Laski in 1920. It is consonant with his friendship with Holmes that, for a generation of American liberal intellectuals, Laski's reputation was higher even than it was amongst British socialists. His writings still figured in the thought-world of US campuses in the sixties as living documents, when they were dead texts in his own land.

For Laski, despite his practical limitations and frequent personal tiresomeness, was far more than just a megaphone for the left in Britain at a particularly critical phase in its history. He was an international inspiration who offered passion and intellectual excitement which survived him—and certainly survived his forensic battering by Sir Patrick Hastings. Some day, it may be hoped, a proper biography will do justice to this unassuming little titan whose monuments, suitably disguised, still lie all around us, landmarks of the revolution of our time.

# ELLEN WILKINSON

ELLEN WILKINSON was arguably Britain's most important woman politician. Of course, she did not attain Mrs Thatcher's supreme position and never looked like doing so. She did not show the executive flair of Barbara Castle; nor was she ever inflicted with the all-weather sentimentality with which a gullible press used to drown Shirley Williams. For all that, in the years down to 1945, when she became Minister of Education in Attlee's government, Ellen Wilkinson made the role of women in high politics credible and effective as no one had done before, with powerful consequences for her sex and her class. As trade-union organizer, as journalist and international propagandist, as a major figure on Labour's national executive, above all as an inspirational orator and ubiquitous crusader, she placed an unforgettable imprint on the mind of the British left.

She was uniquely identified with the passions of the thirties, with anti-fascist campaigns, with the Popular Front, above all with the moral outcry against mass unemployment and poverty. Her leadership of the march from Jarrow, the town she represented in parliament from 1935 onwards, and her remarkable Left Book Club volume, *The Town that was Murdered*, had a dramatic, perhaps decisive, impact on the public conscience, long before the new egalitarian passions of the Second World War. The last phase at the Education Ministry in 1945–7 was less impressive, even anticlimactic, though it is reasonable to argue that her early death at fifty-five cut her off in her political prime. Her lifelong career as champion of the disinherited is now largely forgotten, like much else of the middle ages of the labour movement. It is admirable that it should be celebrated again in an excellent recent biography by Betty Vernon, which sets the record straight once and for all.

It is clear that the grey, artisan Methodist world in which Ellen was brought up in Manchester did not reflect her character and personality. She was an out-going, red-haired romantic who partially expressed her strong emotions in some rather curious novels, and in a fussy concern for her dress and coiffure that is reminiscent of some of the more baroque passages of Mrs Castle's diaries. It is evident, too, that Ellen Wilkinson's passionate nature overflowed into a complicated maze of personal relations. Among the various men with whom she had a close attachment were Walton Newbold, the first Communist MP (to whom she was briefly, and disastrously, engaged); a Yorkshire miners' agent; a Czech propagandist; Frank Horrabin, the socialist cartoonist and journalist; and, most remarkably of all, Herbert Morrison.

Ellen Wilkinson was, at least until 1939, usually identified with the far left, Morrison with the Tammany right. Yet their friendship became increasingly close from 1931 onwards. Apart from personal considerations, she also admired Morrison as a charismatic organizer and above all a man of action, who had impeccable working-class origins as well. Morrison's biographers have concluded that Ellen was probably not Morrison's mistress. Mrs Vernon seems to think that she was. The point is not of great importance either way, save to underline Ellen's close involvement with him in the thirties, and her efforts to promote him as party leader in 1935 and again in 1945, shortly after the election results were known. The relationship remained veiled to the general public. Morrison did not refer to Ellen in his autobiography. In February 1947 he failed even to send flowers to her funeral. Yet, in the complex and ambiguous stands that made up the British labour movement in the years of recovery after 1931, the Morrison–Wilkinson affair is worth its modest historical niche. Perhaps only a novelist could really do it justice.

Ellen Wilkinson's emergence as a leading socialist in the years down to 1931 (when she was forty) in many ways seemed typical of its time. There was the conversion to a messianic form of ethical socialism, after a brisk read through of William Morris and Blatchford. There was the inevitable membership of the ILP, with the impact upon her of Bruce Glasier and even more of his remarkable wife, Katharine Conway. There were campaigns against the First World War, followed by temporary membership of the newly formed Communist Party. Later came predictable phases of political activism, election to Manchester city council, involvement in the Labour Research Department, and finally election as Labour member for Middlesbrough East in 1924, Labour's sole woman MP. It was a classic progress for a socialist pilgrim, rudely shattered by electoral calamity after the formation of the National government under MacDonald in 1931.

Yet there are many features which lift Ellen's career out of the ordinary. There was the unusually enduring impact of Methodism.

This was a lifelong commitment, not merely a phase of adolescent revivalism as it was with so many Labour pioneers. 'I am still a Methodist', she told the Marxists of the Left Book Club in 1939, 'you can never get its special glow out of your blood.' There was her extensive higher education, which included the gaining of an upper second degree in History at Manchester University under the great Professor Tout. (Did young Ellen, one wonders, come into contact with Tout's suffragette wife?) Then there was her astonishing appointment as women's organizer of the Co-operative Employees in 1915, at the tender age of twenty-four. There followed involvement in the shop-assistants' union, NUDAW, important both for its far-left politics and its organization of women workers. There was also an amazingly eclectic association with almost every known species of Labour activism from the Fabians to the Labour College movement. Finally, and most important, there was the fact that she was a woman.

Ellen's personal charisma evidently transcended her apparent basic disqualification as a mere woman, in a movement where feminism ranked close to Toryism as a term of abuse. She showed much toughness both as a stump orator and as a determined union negotiator. Even in the earthy male stronghold of the steel town of Middlesbrough, her qualities won her nomination as a Labour candidate, against strong male competition, in 1924. She confirmed her durable qualities during the General Strike, where she acted as chairman of a women's committee for the relief of miners' families (and toured America on its behalf). Despite the debacle of 1931—and a record of some instability including a brief flirtation with Oswald Mosley's panaceas for economic recovery—it is clear that Ellen Wilkinson's political reputation had been firmly established by the time of her parliamentary defeat in the 1931 election. Of no other woman prominent in the Labour Party, including the dour Margaret Bondfield who had actually served in MacDonald's Cabinet, could this be said.

The thirties were her golden age. On the face of it, Ellen was associated with a succession of lost causes—the Socialist League, the Unity Front, Morrison's bid for the party leadership in 1935, a sequence of confused anti-fascist or quasi-pacifist movements during the period of the Spanish Civil War and Munich. Yet it is transcendently clear that she was a crucial figure in giving the movement new inspiration and zest for the good fight throughout that unhappy decade, especially after her election for the shipbuilding town of

Jarrow in 1935. In passing, it may be noted that her career suggests that the Labour left was less narcissistic and ineffective than some recent accounts have argued. The Jarrow march and the Left Book Club revealed her genius as an agitator and propagandist. So, too, for a time did the columns of *Tribune*. But she also demonstrated a new realism and tough-mindedness, especially in her renewed commitment to the parliamentary wing of the Labour movement. Although a long-term member of the ILP, she never lapsed into the sectarianism of Jimmy Maxton and his Glasgow comrades. Although an advocate of the Unity Front with the Communists, she would not undermine the party by blind adherence to the cause of Cripps, although it is true that she was the sole member of the NEC to vote against Cripps's expulsion in January 1939. But she was never one of Cripps's root and branch supporters. 'He is a bad leader but a magnificent lieutenant', she observed of him.

She left the editorial board of *Tribune* in March 1939, perhaps just in time. It was apparent that she was now moving to a more centrist position in the party after years of rebellion. With her personal friendships with cross-party associates such as Boothby and Macmillan, she was an ideal representative of the new popular consensus that arose after the outbreak of war in 1939. At the Home Office under Herbert Morrison, she showed new and unsuspected qualities of executive drive, notably in directing civil defence during the blitz. She was not one of those swayed sentimentally towards Russia by the wartime achievements of the Red Army. On the contrary, the war years reinforced a growing gut repugnance to Communism. She was a charismatic chairman of the party in 1944-5, and played an important part in persuading Attlee, Morrison, and Bevin to break with the Churchill coalition immediately after VE Day. In July 1945, after the election, she gained Cabinet office, not simply as a long-serving member of the NEC, nor as a relentless campaigner on behalf of Herbert Morrison, certainly not as a token woman, but on her own proven merits.

Her time at the Education Department until her death in February 1947 has often been attacked for its inertia and institutional conservatism. Undoubtedly, she did little to promote the cause of multilateral forms of secondary schooling, while her handling of private and direct-grant schools was generally cautious. A group of left-wing teachers, headed by the Welsh ex-syndicalist, W. G. Cove, bitterly attacked her in her last few months, and subsequently trained their fire on her successor, George Tomlinson. In fact, Ellen Wilkinson's policy was inevitably determined by the passage of the monumental Butler Act of 1944 which Labour broadly endorsed. The new government could merely try to work it as effectively and humanely as possible. Nor does her deep attachment to the grammar school as a unique channel of working-class advancement and improvement seem so absurd now, with the chaos surrounding the comprehensive experiment in so many parts of the country. Labour in 1945 believed in the grammar schools. Through their academic excellence and social inclusiveness they would rout Eton and Harrow in peaceful coexistence and competition, as the Welsh 'county schools' had made the few private schools in the principality such as Llandovery or Christ's College almost an irrelevance. Ellen would have been horrified to have heard Tony Crosland (Highgate School and Trinity College, Oxford) calmly tell his wife in 1965, 'If it's the last thing I do I'm going to destroy every fucking grammar school in England. And Wales. And Northern Ireland.'

In view of the political and financial constraints that dictated Labour's freedom of manoeuvre in 1945, too, her general record seems less negative. There was a major school-building programme, while Ellen did force through the raising of the school-leaving age to fifteen, in the face of opposition from Treasury ministers—and, ironically, from Herbert Morrison himself. As Cabinet minister, Ellen was neither dynamic nor inspired; but even the last phase (cruelly cut short by an accidental drug overdose) is far from being to her discredit or to that of the government.

Ellen Wilkinson's main importance lies in the way she helped to translate the passions of the thirties into the experience of power from 1940 onwards. It was the inspirational side of the thirties that she embodied as the kind of red-haired British *La Pasionaria* she was so often represented as being. The tougher, more intellectually demanding aspects of Labour's experience in that decade—the new policies that were embodied in the 1937 interim programme; the economic ideas maturing in the XYZ group and in the group of brilliant young economists assembled by Dalton; the more informed understanding of international relations which Bevin, amongst others, reflected; and the development policies for the colonies worked out by Creech Jones and Rita Hinden—tended to pass Ellen Wilkinson by. Yet she remained unique as a voice for social justice in her generation. Further, in the inter-war years, she was foremost amongst those who gave their lives to flagging radical causes. She helped redirect the creativity of the ILP when it was losing the central role it had enjoyed in the great years of Hardie and the Glasiers. She helped the women's movement, somewhat in the doldrums in the twenties, from a formalistic and somewhat limited campaign for votes and civic status to a wider concern with working and living conditions for women as workers and citizens. And she did so with a style, gaiety, and charm which moved A. L. Rowse, amongst other unlikely allies, to warm admiration. *Pace* Bernard Shaw, she was a very social socialist.

She was also an organizer of no mean talent, especially on behalf of the poor shop-assistants and factory workers of the Co-operative Employees. And, grafted on to the class tension and emotion of the depression years was a passionate libertarianism, half imbibed from Laski during membership of the Donoughmore Commission perhaps, with a staunch commitment to parliamentarism and civil liberties as vibrant as it had been for Tom Paine in the past. This emphasis was crucial. The Jarrow march of 1936 (which started in a town that, after all, was distinctly respectable in its ethos, dominated by the Palmer industrial dynasty and usually Conservative in politics) was a stimulus to democratic socialism, not a substitute for it, or a form of escapism. It was extra-parliamentary but not anti-parliamentary. After making their powerful point in London, the marchers returned to Jarrow by train to continue the good fight. They did not contemplate a mass occupation or sit-in, or industrial disruption, and they were the more influential for it.

At first glance, the left that Ellen Wilkinson represented in the thirties seems far removed from the Bennite battalions of the 1980s. But the connection may be more direct. Michael Foot, a spiritual heir of Ellen and indeed a warm personal friend, succeeded to the party leadership in 1980, to renew the fight for the old values. His successor, Neil Kinnock, upholds a broadly similar ethic. Through them and their successors, 'Red Ellen' may yet win the posthumous victory.

# THE PLANNERS

For the British left, the 1930s were the day after the deluge. The events of July and August 1931 had a traumatic and lasting effect. Superficially, the fall of the second Labour government could be taken as showing that a socialist administration would always be sabotaged from within by the banks, the civil service, the politicians, even perhaps the King. The 'bankers' ramp' legend was born, to popularize this reassuring and deceptive belief. But, at a far more profound level, it was the sheer emptiness of Labour's economic thinking, in the face of a total collapse of trade and employment, and the flight from sterling, that was truly disturbing. On the main themes of macro- and micro-economic policy, official Labour had simply nothing worthwhile to say, as the antique Cobdenism of Snowden at the Treasury between 1929 and 1931 amply confirmed. Only the ILP's, 'living wage' scheme, and Bevin individually, offered anything at all. British socialism had always emphasized the distribution of wealth rather than its creation. It had always implicitly assumed the health of the capitalist order. Now its credo was exposed as the pathetic illusion it always was. One response to 1931, of course, was a sizeable lurch to the left, with the neo-Marxism of the Socialist League and the later exciting crusades of the Left Book Club and the Popular Front. But these emotional revivals, to which much literature and research have been devoted, got nowhere. They had virtually no impact at all on the policies of the Labour Party thereafter; their main exponent, Cripps, was to be expelled for his pains. By the end of 1934, the Marxist upsurge of the party conferences of 1932 and 1933 seemed no more than an emotional spasm.

Far more important—indeed, quite decisive in revolutionizing the economic ideas of the British left—were the vigorous, if much less flamboyant, activities of an extraordinary generation of young left-wing academic economists, including men like Gaitskell, Jay, Durbin, and Meade, as well as Clark and Dickinson. Their work bore fruit through the New Fabian Research Bureau, the XYZ group, and in discussions that took place at Nicholas Davenport's stately home at Hinton Manor, near Oxford, a comfortable citadel for the progressive cause. These busy little groups led to the substantial revamping of

Labour's economic programmes by the time of the Interim Programme, drawn up in 1937. For the first time in its history, Labour could claim to have a credible, sophisticated approach towards prices, money supply, exchange rates and investment policy, trade, employment, and public ownership. The influence of these youthful academic crusaders was slow and indirect; its progress is not easy to chart. Not until the war were they in a position seriously to influence the course of national economic policy. But they had, almost in spite of themselves, created a programme for power. The economic consensus of 1940-51—a legacy that endured robustly until the monetarist counter-revolution after 1979—was thus made possible.

Much the most important work on these developments has been written by Elizabeth Durbin. She is the daughter of Evan Durbin, one of the brightest stars in the firmament among this gifted generation, a man of great talent and intellectual curiosity whose career as an MP was tragically cut short when he drowned while on holiday in 1948, when he was forty-two. In part, therefore, Miss Durbin's book offers an implicit tribute to her father. In this context, it is perhaps unfortunate that it is cut off somewhat abruptly in 1938. This means, among other things, that Evan Durbin's most influential work, *The Politics of Democratic Socialism* (1940), is not really discussed. But this is far outweighed by the transcendent merits of the way in which the author supplies a wealth etailed and deftly processed information about the activities and ideas of these young socialists. Not the least of the book's many virtues is the use of revealing material drawn from survivors of that inspired generation, many of whom remain active and productive fifty years on. This, then, is a study of the first importance for an understanding of the British left, and the economic odyssey of modern Britain.

The young socialists of the thirties came from a variety of backgrounds and intellectual positions. The public schools, especially Winchester, loomed large. In addition, Oxford, and to a lesser degree Cambridge, was always a point of reference. It was socialism from, though not necessarily for, the cloister. Among many other things, the history of the young planners of the 1930s offers a contribution from those ancient universities more positive and palatable than the *mélange* of nihilism, pacifism, espionage, and sexual deviation, flavoured with self-indulgence and self-pity, on which so many recent books have concentrated. A variety of groups came together in the period after the crash of 1931. There was the 'Cole group', an academic gathering which had originally emerged in Oxford in the late twenties; Hugh Gaitskell and subsequently James Meade were amongst its major luminaries. There were the financiers, journalists, and academics of Berry's XYZ group, which brought in Douglas Jay and Nicholas Davenport among others, formed to redress Labour's almost total ignorance of the banking and monetary system prior to 1931. Again, there were the social engineers of the New Fabian Research Bureau, a somewhat different body again but with Evan Durbin and again Gaitskell prominent amongst them. There was an important Cambridge influence provided by Colin Clark (in fact, educated at Winchester and Brasenose College, Oxford), and the somewhat contrary stimulus offered by some of Lionel Robbins's pupils at the London School of Economics.

Finally, to give these young academics and theoreticians of the socialist think-tank coherence and political thrust, there was the orchestrating presence of Hugh Dalton, chairman of the Labour Party Finance and Trade Committee. He was an acknowledged expert on public finance, the patron and benefactor of young left-wing intellectuals, and at the height of his considerable powers. From his energy and drive, allied to the administrative skills of Morrison, there emerged a new democratic socialist programme. It was outlined, somewhat hesitantly and sketchily, in the left-wing proposals of *For Socialism and Peace* in 1934, and, more convincingly, in *Labour's Immediate Programme* in 1937. This proclaimed boldly that 'the community must command the main levers which will control the economic machine. These are Finance, Land, Transport, Coal and Power.' Among the measures laid down as first priorities for a Labour government were the nationalization of the Bank of England, and a national investment board. It was in these documents, even more than in the social upheavals and new radical consensus of the Second World War, that the road to 1945 and the policies of the post-war Attlee government can be said to originate.

During the thirties, the ideas of these youthful economists and planners necessarily went through many gyrations. Although they were friends, they were far from monolithic in their outlook. There were frequent clashes of approach and emphasis. G. D. H. Cole himself was always under some suspicion for his adherence to an updated version of the well-worn Edwardian creed of under-consumptionism. Gaitskell and Durbin, rationalists both, criticized his lack of theoretical rigour, and what they saw as a kind of sentimentality or romanticism towards the working class. Such weaknesses offended the rigorous academic canon of the new planners: Cole gradually faded from a central role. On the other hand, Webb-style centralization and collectivism were flatly rejected on libertarian grounds. Indeed, as the Webbs' visit to the Soviet Union impelled them towards a new worship of statism, the gulf between them and the new generation of socialist economists became even wider. Gaitskell himself evolved new concepts of socialist planning from 1932 onwards, especially in relation to market pricing and redistribution. This brought him into conflict with those such as Cole and Barbara Wootton, enamoured of Soviet planning policy at the time, who preferred a more rigorously government-controlled system of pricing, reinforced by substantial physical controls. But at least the outlines of a socialist programme for the allocation of resources were emerging almost for the first time.

The impact of Keynes upon these economists is somewhat problematical. It was Douglas Jay who went perhaps furthest in fusing Keynesian models for explaining aggregate output and a new employment policy with a socialist approach, as the basis for a new progressive consensus. This was the basis of his book *The Socialist Case* (1937), the most powerful exposition of the new economic creed. Jay was probably the most enthusiastic Keynesian among the entire group. He does, however, point out in his memoirs that his ideas on 'total effective demand' in *The Socialist Case* had already been worked out in the winter of 1935–6 before the publication of Keynes's *General Theory*, later in 1936, gave them general confirmation. Evan Durbin, by contrast, was somewhat wary of the influence of Keynes. 'He never swallowed Keynes whole', his daughter tells us. As early as 1933 in *Purchasing Power and Trade Depression*, he contested Keynes's view that 'forced investment' would promote economic recovery, though Durbin later greatly modified his opinions here. He also felt that Keynes underestimated the dangers of inflation. Durbin was (at least in the early thirties) much influenced by the business cycle theories propounded by Professor Hayek at the London School of Economics, while sternly rejecting the reactionary social philosophy of that gloomy prophet.

James Meade, with the support of Roy Harrod, dissented from Durbin on this point. He favoured an immediate expansionist policy, including flexible exchange rates, and a marked emphasis on public ownership, towards which Durbin was generally cool. Over many key issues—notably the nationalization of the joint-stock banks which appeared in Labour's 1934 proposals but was deleted in 1937, despite protests from Gaitskell and Meade—fierce argument continued to rage. Yet out of the cataract of debate, a consensus clearly emerged. Fundamentally it meant that Labour appropriated the idea of 'planning'—for investment, employment, trade, and even, to some degree, wages policy—as the basis of its economic rationale. The vogue for planning, as has long been noted, was widespread in the middle and later thirties amongst what has been called 'middle opinion', ranging from Harold Macmillan's 'next five years' group to followers of the ageing Lloyd George. It was much stimulated by the collapse of the international economy after 1931, and the apparently successful examples of collective planning visible in Russia or the American New Deal. A body like the new PEP was the embodiment of this fashionable idea. In political terms, the important fact was that planning was linked with the intellectual renaissance of the idea of socialism, long dormant where Keir Hardie had left it. Planning meant the application of scientific reason to economic affairs. Its youthful advocates would be the Newtons of the social sciences. A flexibly planned, democratically accountable socialist economy would provide a coherent and credible alternative to the inefficiencies and inhumanities of market capitalism. Evan Durbin wrote in *New Trends in Socialism* (1935) of how 'the first stages of socialism' (in effect, the first five years of the next Labour government) would be judged by how far prosperity would be restored during the lifetime of the government. Planning was the key to efficiency, and ultimately to social equality as well. Updating Harcourt's *obiter dictum* of the 1890s, Durbin cheerful claimed that we were (almost) all planners now.

Even after reading Elizabeth Durbin's fascinating book, it is still somewhat difficult to determine precisely how politically influential these young planners really were. Of course, none was close to the party machine, let alone parliament. None had as sensitive and central a role as Michael Young of PEP, drafted into Transport House during the latter stages of the war. The young planners' main political influence lay through Dalton, and it was he who put Durbin, Clark, Gaitskell, and Jay on Labour's intellectually highly impressive Finance and Trade Subcommittee in late 1937. But in the later thirties, he was moving into wider spheres, including a heavy involvement with foreign policy and the international socialist movement. Without his direct backing, young men like Gaitskell, Jay, Durbin, and Meade were on the fringes of great events, while policy-making, under Labour's cumbersome institutional processes, was never easy. Gaitskell, Durbin, and Jay presented to Attlee and the shadow Cabinet in April 1939 a powerful paper on 'The Conscription of Wealth', which advocated among other things a special annual 'defence levy' on capital, to last as long as conscription continued. But the parliamentary party, still somewhat bemused by old-fashioned pacifism, turned it down. Jay's memoirs eloquently recall the personal disappointment that he and his friends felt.

It was, clearly, the war years that suddenly gave them a far broader impact and impetus. Their private, even introverted, world of seminars, committees, and discussion groups suddenly found practical fulfilment in the transformation of the government structure and policy perspectives from May 1940 onwards. Among many other things, this meant that their patron, Dalton, moved to high office, ending up at the Board of Trade between 1942 and 1945. Under his aegis, Gaitskell and Durbin moved into government service: Gaitskell became Dalton's PPS in May 1940 and an adviser of much influence. They were joined by Douglas Jay, who moved to the Ministry of Supply to work with Oliver Franks in late 1940. Later he also served Dalton at the Board of Trade, a major instrument of the industrial diversification and full employment policy carried out in the former 'depressed areas' in the last two years of the war. It was a policy sanctified for the post-war period by the Distribution of Industry Act passed by the Churchill coalition in 1945, and meant a dramatic renaissance for areas such as the North-East and South Wales.

Equally important was the new Economic Section of the Cabinet Office. This became a major forum for such leftish Keynesians as Richard Stone' and especially James Meade whose influence was paramount in the formulation of the 1944 white paper on full employment (a document which Keynes himself criticized as unduly timid). Within the Labour Party, a new energy was kindled in the Finance Committee, on which Dalton was a key figure. It gave substance to the kind of fusion between democratic socialism and Keynesian demand-management to which Labour adhered after the war ended. When the election results were announced on 25 July 1945, Gaitskell and Durbin were among the two hundred new Labour MPs elected; Jay was a private secretary to Attlee from

September 1945, and also soon to become an MP. Labour's governing mandate was emphatic. Equally clearly, the party was intellectually prepared for the economic realities of power in a way inconceivable at any earlier time in its history. It was the academic blueprints of the thirties which had made it so.

Necessarily, an examination of the ideas of the planners of the thirties is mainly a task for the specialist macro-economist. It is a task that extends not only into arcane realms of high theory but into the wider, chequered course of British economic policy-making for thirty years and more after 1945. These were years in which the planners of the thirties and their disciples were broadly dominant. They set the parameters of post-war Britain. They offered a diagnosis, some of the difficulties of which they themselves came to acknowledge by the 1970s—notably, their comparative lack of attention to the pressures of cost-push inflation and a general over-optimism about the potentiality for self-generating economic progress. On the other hand, their programme offered also a scheme for thirty years of unparalleled affluence, full employment, economic growth, and (until the seventies) social peace. The nation could exploit the boom in world trade, American investment, and European technological advance. After the bleakness and callousness of the thirties, it was a priceless legacy.

Beyond economic considerations, however, two wider aspects strike the later student of the ideas of this generation—their moralism and their nationalism. The planners of the thirties were trained as economists; Jay wrote that 'the case for socialism is mainly economic and it rests on facts'. Yet wider human, perhaps spiritual, considerations, were always central to their debate. In fashioning a new economic methodology and language, Durbin, Jay, Gaitskell, and their colleagues were anything but the 'desiccated calculating machines' of later legend. They were, first and foremost, committed socialists who rejected with equal fervour the Marxism of the far left and the 'bizarre and unconvincing hedonism' of Keynes. Their programme was to be linked to political strategy and to the democratic mechanisms that provided the mainspring for non-Marxist socialism in Britain. Contrary to one avowal, they did not believe that 'the gentleman from Whitehall knows best'. Indeed, it was precisely for such a reason that they broke with older, more centralist forms of socialism such as that of the Webbs. Jay wrote in *The Socialist Case* that, over a large part of the economy, 'the value of free consumers' choice is almost impossible to overestimate'. They also blended their economics with ethics and with the creed of fraternalism. The instruments of planning were designed for democratic and ethical ends. Evan Durbin is particularly notable in this respect, as in the way he introduced elements of social psychology into his work. His study of the roots of aggression and the spirit of conflict in modern society provides a striking passage in *The Politics of Democratic Socialism*. For him, socialism meant not just a more productive society, an antiseptic Utopia, but a living world in which 'men and women may sing at their work and children may laugh at their play'. Not for nothing was Durbin a child of the Baptist manse: his name, Evan, was given him after the Welsh revivalist, Evan Roberts, active in 1905, the year of his birth. His writings were a reaffirmation of the nonconformist 'forward movement' of the 1890s, suitably updated in neo-Keynesian terms.

There was something else latent in the world-view of the young planners, something that has been largely lost from the socialist and radical armoury of the past twenty years—a robust patriotism of distinctly Anglo-Saxon lineage, and a confidence in national, even imperial, institutions. For them, as for George Orwell, a consummation of British history came in 1940 when Britain indeed stood alone but could draw uniquely on native instinct and genius to defend and rebuild itself. Witness Durbin's passionate commitment to his people in 1940—'I feel the life of a strong and quiet people about me; more deeply united than they realize, more creative than they ever suspect.' In a book review in the *Economic Journal* in 1945 he strongly rebuked his old teacher, Hayek, for suggesting that Britain was on the German-style road to slavery. Durbin expressed surprise that continental *émigrés* should not rather say, 'Here is a people that have [sic] had no civil war for nearly three hundred years, who have led Europe in an ever-changing search for liberty, who have practised tolerance and kindliness before we were born— here they must have mastered some secret that is still hidden from us.' Durbin's patriotism, no less than his socialism, was deeply affronted by Hayek's pessimistic predictions. The professor had failed to acknowledge that, as the transport hoardings had it, 'British was Best'.

On balance, the planners' ideas for national regeneration in the thirties had been conceived largely in insular terms. Douglas Jay presents *The Socialist Case* basically in a British context, with some occasional favourable comments on Australia, New Zealand, and Scandinavia. Some of the thirties' economists responded enthusiastically to Roosevelt's New Deal in the United States, but on balance it was far too remote from the British experience to offer any particularly useful model for them to follow. (It is revealing that Elizabeth Durbin's book, dealing with the economic policies of the thirties, does not mention Roosevelt at all.) Indeed, on the strictly economic side, the American New Deal had only limited success, with unemployment running up to ten million until 1941, and a serious recession in economic activity as late as the winter of 1937–8. The socialist planners of Britain, with democracy disintegrating in Germany, Italy, and elsewhere in Europe, necessarily saw themselves as working out their own salvation and thereby providing hope for socialist movements overseas. Continental ideas played little part in their ideas. The 'syndicalism' of pre- and post-war France had seldom made much penetration beyond such working-class strongholds as the Rhondda Valley or Clydeside. Evan Durbin called for the trade unions to root out the last vestiges of syndicalism as a prelude to intelligent industrial planning. G. D. H. Cole himself had long forsworn the devolutionary corporatism of his guild socialist youth.

The only foreign country that had any impact at all on the thirties' planners was one distinctly more isolated—Sweden, a potentially socialist state which boasted a Social Democratic government, pursuing a Keynesian-type approach including deficit financing, from 1934 onwards. Like American liberals such as Marquis Childs, the young socialists of Britain praised Sweden for its 'middle way'. A book edited by Margaret Cole and Charles Smith for the New Fabian Research Bureau in 1938 sang the praises of Swedish Social Democracy. Cole, Postgate, and G. R. Mitchison were amongst its authors, and so was Gaitskell who wrote on Swedish banking and monetary policy. The authors noted enthusiastically that in Sweden, alone in Europe apart from the Soviet Union, the socialized sector of the economy was already extensive. It included the Post Office, most of the railways, most electric power, forests, the Riksbank, air transport, radio services, tobacco, liquor, and even some iron-ore mining. Even so, for a young socialist like Gaitskell, the appeal of Sweden lay not in its modest experiments in public ownership, but rather in weaving together exchange rate policy, deficit budgeting, and a public works programme. Sweden was hailed as a socialist regime committed to efficiency and modernization, and to the achievement of consumer affluence at a time when, in the light of the second Labour government in Britain and the Popular Front in France, socialism and prosperity seemed to be incompatible. But, other than the marginal case of Sweden (an abiding point of reference for Gaitskell long afterwards in the fifties when he was party leader), the idea of nationalization and economic planning in Britain was conceived largely in insular terms. In the unique circumstances of the second world war, this insularity was turned into triumphant practical achievement.

After the war, this approach was in many ways beneficial. It gave a self-confidence, a panache almost, as apparent in the planning programmes of the Gaitskellites as in Aneurin Bevan's belief that Britain was a unique beacon of socialist freedom in the world, and a third force of incalculable moral appeal. For Gaitskell and his colleagues, from the Cripps period at the Treasury from late 1947 onwards, the way forward lay in pursuing the cause of the detached, altruistic public servant, treading the path of civic duty, managing economic and social institutions in a way that would transcend sectional division and invest the new society with a kind of Platonic purity. Their vision had imperial overtones, too. It was a progressive, domestic version of the model of colonial rule once offered to the young Attlee at Haileybury, and to the Wykehamists and others who joined him after 1945, a kind of social imperialism with the common touch. It is worth mention that, among the thirties' generation of socialists, largely public school boys, Gaitskell's father was an Indian civil servant while his brother developed irrigation schemes in the cotton fields of the Sudan. Durbin was the son of a Baptist minister who had been a missionary in Ceylon. Jay's imperial connections were more indirect, but his works such as Socialism in the New Society (1962) show much enthusiasm for the Commonwealth as a free, inter-racial association which could provide the model for a new world order. The Victorian empire (much admired by Bevin, Morrison, and other ministers after 1945) had been Joseph Chamberlain's Birmingham writ large. The public boards, economic councils, and development agencies in Britain after 1945 were Chamberlain's empire writ small. Their chairmen (sometimes retired industrialists or even generals) were cast as the Cromer or Lugard de nos jours.

Gradually in the 1960s and 1970s, however, the cocoon of confident insularity in which the movement for planning had developed began to dissolve. There was a retreat from empire at Gadarene pace overseas. At home, the structural weaknesses of the British economy became embarrassingly clear. The state lost much of its legitimacy and moral authority, notably among the children of Commonwealth immigrants. Equally, the mystique of the detached public servant, the patrician symbol of the great and the good, began to fade. The decline of the vogue for planning and public ownership in Britain mirrored—and partly grew out of—the decline of empire overseas. In these circumstances, the disciples of the planners of the thirties found their basic assumptions under challenge.

Yet the attachment to national values remained. In 1962 Gaitskell followed a basic commitment to nation and Commonwealth, and rejected British membership of the Common Market. He was partly swayed by an evasive performance by Jean Monnet at an XYZ dinner arranged by Roy Jenkins in April 1962, when Monnet's mysticism about the European idea offended Gaitskell's rationality. Douglas Jay became a passionate opponent of attachment to a European Community whose very premises, he argued, meant a rejection of the basis of British prosperity, based on cheap food imports, that had endured at least since 1846. In addition to his strong (indeed, unanswerable) arguments against the EEC, he claimed that the countries of EFTA, including the Scandinavian nations and Switzerland, were far closer to British democratic traditions than were the nations of the Six—especially post-Hitler Germany, and France whose history was an alternation between 'Bonapartism and anarchy'. He remained a passionate patriot, devoted to cricket, Shakespeare, and the English countryside. Even after Britain's distinctly hesitant move to join the EEC in 1973, the attitude of several of the disciples of the thirties' planners remained cool or hostile—though, of course, others, including Roy Jenkins and Shirley Williams (daughter of George Catlin and Vera Brittain, two more thirties' progressives), became devoted 'Europeans', and eventually defected from the Labour Party partly for this reason.

The young planners of the thirties were members of a remarkable, even inspired, generation. They comprised an alternative, more worldly and useful, Bloomsbury group. They retained faith in their movement, their country, their values, and their inheritance, despite the deluge of slump and dictatorship they saw around them at that time. The experience of war made theirs the conventional orthodoxy after 1945 and for two generations to come. It is no diminution of their extraordinary intellectual achievement in socialist thought and policy-making to say that the newer Jerusalems of the 1980s must necessarily emerge from a wider, more eclectic frame of reference. Fraternalism and the international sense must be reawakened if the planners of the past are to be effectively succeeded by the social engineers of today.

# HUGH DALTON

FRATERNITY has seldom been the most obvious characteristic of the Labour Party in its eighty-seven years of fitful life. But few if any of its leading figures have aroused quite the passion and unpopularity incurred by Hugh Dalton. With his loud, bullying style and wounding belligerence at the dispatch box and in personal relationships, Dr Dalton of the LSE, above all other socialists, drew the violent dislike of his political opponents. He seemed to pick quarrels with any Tories he came across almost as a private hobby. Once, when lunching at the House of Commons while Chancellor of the Exchequer, he gratuitously turned on an unoffending, silent Conservative MP at a nearby table. 'What's the suburbanite looking at me for? ... Come on, let's show him how we in the Labour Party behave.' Whereupon the Chancellor ostentatiously began to shovel peas into his mouth with his knife.

Churchill (whom Dalton himself much admired in an awestruck, deferential way) simply loathed him. 'Keep that man away from me', Churchill would demand. 'I can't stand his booming voice and shifting eyes.' On another occasion, he confided to Lord Moran, 'Dalton's a swine.' Other Conservatives considered that Dalton's style, the deliberate posturing of an upper-class renegade, his Mephistophelean asides, even his curious physical appearance, topped by a vast dome, symbolized everything they detested about British socialism. Dalton, it may be added, gave as good as he got in this and other directions. His diary references to 'Sir H. Quisling' (Horace Wilson), 'Horeb Elisha' (Hore-Belisha) and 'Lord Hyde of Cowes' (Lord Leathers) show how numerous and colourful were his dislikes among the unappealing massed battalions of the British right.

On the other hand, he was hardly a well-loved personality within his own party either. The story of Dalton striding into the Cabinet chamber, 'eyes blazing with insincerity', became legendary in Labour circles. Attlee he much admired for his unruffled demeanour, loyalty, and total integrity—and also for his possession of the magic gift of silence, which Dalton himself so conspicuously lacked. On the other hand, with Morrison, Bevin, and Cripps, the other members of Labour's 'big five' after 1945, he always had difficult and tense relationships. They condemned him as a conspirator and intriguer. A working-class politician like Emanuel Shinwell ('Shinbad the Tailor') viewed him with cold hatred. Dalton also aroused strong feelings among his civil servants and departmental aides, and especially within the diplomatic world.

Most remarkably of all, King George VI, usually so reticent in giving vent to his views on politicans of the day, freely confided to Gaitskell and others his vivid dislike of Dalton, the 'anarchist son' of a canon of Windsor who had been a close friend of his father, George V. Indeed, the King's hostility may have played some part in denying Dalton the Foreign Office in July 1945. When Dalton virtually destroyed himself with an extraordinary indiscretion through leaking budget secrets to a lobby journalist (at least, it seemed extraordinary then, when leaks were far less commonplace than in the 1980s), there were many in the Palace, Westminster, Whitehall, and Fleet Street who rejoiced. Even an amiable man like A. P. Wadsworth, editor of the *Manchester Guardian*, was flatly unforgiving.

And yet this difficult, contradictory, oversensitive, clumsy, profoundly lonely man was, without question, a figure of towering political stature. He exercised immense influence in the emergence of Labour as a party of power, and in evolving the theory and practice of democratic socialism in Britain, in the 1930s above all. He played a central role in Labour's revival and recovery of morale after the schism and débâcle of 1931. He was supreme among the architects of the electoral landslide of 1945. In addition, he was a vigorous and creative government minister in a variety of major posts between 1940 and 1951; at times, the party leadership itself seemed to beckon. He deserves much of the credit for the regional policy which dispelled the mass unemployment of the 'depressed areas' and for the fiscal basis of the welfare state after 1945. Within Labour's ranks, even if he aroused widespread enmity, he could never be disregarded. Meanwhile, in his patronage of young socialists—from Gaitskell, Jay, and Durbin in the thirties to Crosland and Abel-Smith in the fifties— he powerfully assisted in giving new life to the socialist idea.

Until 1985 Dalton was usually recalled as the omnipresent diarist of the Labour Party between 1931 and 1951, whose verdicts have coloured the views of later historians as profoundly as the other prolific chronicler, Richard Crossman, did for the 1950s and 1960s. While major biographies were written to honour Attlee, Bevin, Morrison, and Bevan, Dalton long remained a less familiar figure. The gap has been triumphantly filled at last by Ben Pimlott, who is now adding to his achievement by an admirable edition of Dalton's diaries as well. His biography is particularly valuable for its sensitive treatment of Dalton's personal friendships with a variety of male colleagues, from Rupert Brooke before 1914 to Tony Crosland in the later years, with Dalton's homosexual impulses always present in the story. Pimlott also deals honestly and convincingly with the wretched details of Dalton's miserably unhappy marriage to Ruth, including the permanent rift created between them by the tragic death of their young daughter, Helen. The unhappiness of his marriage, leading to the couple's living apart for much of the war period, is shown to be a vital clue in explaining the insecurity and erratic behaviour which cast their shadow over so much of Dalton's career.

Dalton's emergence as a leading Labour politician by 1929 was an unusual story, even by the standards of the British Labour Party— that remarkably generous refuge for social eccentrics. He attended Eton and King's College, Cambridge. Sensibility and social conscience, developing from his friendship with Rupert Brooke and the homosexual entourage of Edward Carpenter, impelled him into the Fabian Society and the Labour Party. He also recalled how stirred he was by the dignified bearing of Keir Hardie in a meeting at Cambridge in 1907, broken up by a violent mob of delinquent undergraduates. King's also began a thirty-five year association, difficult and uncertain on both sides, with his one-time tutor, Maynard Keynes ('Jeremiah Malthus' as Dalton christened him privately). Significantly, though, Dalton never followed Keynes into the narcissistic circles of the Apostles, and rejected the nihilism of the Bloomsbury world.

Dalton left Cambridge determined to become a socialist politician and teacher. A lectureship at the London School of Economics (at the second attempt—the first time he was defeated by the unknown Clem Attlee!) impelled him in this direction, as did a Ph.D. thesis on the social origins of the inequality of incomes. Another powerful early influence was grim battle experience on the western front, including the horrors of the Somme, and further heavy fighting in Italy. This left him with a virulent hatred of the Germans as a people (Dalton would say, as a race), which never left him, as well as an abiding love of Italians. After the war, he moved into the Labour

Research Department, with Barbara Wootton, until Arthur Henderson closed it down for left-wing deviation. Then Dalton became a Labour MP, his ultimate fulfilment, first for Peckham in south-east London and then (after much constituency bickering there) for Bishop Auckland in the Durham coalfield, his political base and ideological barometer of public opinion thereafter.

As well as being an active politician, he also achieved much fame as a teacher: indeed it was Dalton's didactic, even hectoring style which reinforced the Tories' hatred of him. His *Principles of Public Finance*, although an orthodox enough pre-Keynesian work, provided some basis for rethinking Labour's fiscal programmes. Without doubt, by the end of the twenties, Dalton was a coming man. Beatrice Webb, characteristically for her, denounced him as an insincere poseur; but she also recognized his great powers of intellect and oratory. The other rising patrician in Labour's ranks at this time was Oswald Mosley, with whom he was often compared. But it is evidence of Dalton's many qualities, that very early on he rumbled 'Tom' Mosley as the rootless, egocentric, anti-democratic adventurer he really was.

The watershed in Dalton's career came with the second Labour government of 1929–31. He had a busy time as junior minister under Arthur Henderson at the Foreign Office (which gave Dalton ample scope for indulging in his well-known phobia against diplomats). But the great split of August 1931 gave his career a quite new significance. Although, quite unexpectedly, he lost his seat at Bishop Auckland in 1931, he now achieved, as a member of the NEC, as writer, ideologue, and personal mentor, a more powerful impact on the recasting of Labour's ideas on both domestic and foreign policy than anyone else in the movement. These were truly Dalton's great years. At home, as noted in the previous section, he led the fight to give the party a new, credible, social-democratic economic programme. No one more effectively harnessed the idea of planning for the socialist cause. Through his encouragement of gifted young economists like Gaitskell, Jay, and Durbin, and the entourage of the XYZ group, he effectively built up that 'alternative civil service' the party had demanded at the time of the new constitution in 1918. Dalton helped give Labour an intelligible economic programme for the first time in its history. He was especially active and important on the Finance and Trade Subcommittee of the NEC from 1932 onwards, a powerhouse of new ideas.

His main policy statement appeared in *Practical Socialism for Britain*, a path-breaking book indeed, first published in March 1935 and rapidly reprinted. In retrospect, some features of its argument may strike the modern reader as decidedly primitive, notably its distinctly pre-Keynesian views of budgetary policy and the idea of planning. The multiplier and deficit finance are both conspicuous absentees. On the other hand, the book does contain both a robust and detailed programme for the nationalization of industries and utilities (in 1929 Labour had specified coal alone, and that very timidly), and a central treatment of banking and monetary policy. Dalton also shows a characteristic interest in the amenity and environmentalist aspects of planning, including National Parks, forests, and the National Trust, appropriate for this country lover. His book looks totally unlike anything that any Labour leader might have written on financial and economic policy prior to 1931. As the publishers, Routledge, proudly proclaimed, it was indeed 'indispensable to Socialists—and to their opponents'. Dalton was ideally placed to give these policies practical effect. As chairman of the NEC in 1936–7, a major author of the 'Immediate Programme' of 1937, and head of the Distressed Areas Commission, Dr Dalton could turn his prescriptions into hard reality.

In foreign affairs, his impact was equally decisive. His views were powerful and highly personal—anti-German as he had been since the battle of the Somme; pro-Italian (again a wartime legacy), with an unexpected penchant for Mussolini's public works programme; somewhat wary on Soviet Russia. His enthusiasm for the Spanish Civil War was distinctly muted: 'Arms for Britain' roused him far more than did the heady slogan of 'Arms for Spain', which he saw as assistance for a fractured Spanish left that played its own shabby part in undermining Spanish democracy and aiding the rise of Franco. But the main thrust of Dalton's views on international policy was unambiguous. As early as 1934, he was outspoken in urging that Labour should vote for rearmament programmes, and aid collective security, so wantonly threatened by a Nazi dictatorship that had already crushed workers' freedoms in Germany. His own close links at this time with the German Social Democrats, now beginning their flight from Hitlerism, and with the international Jewish community, gave his views an added pungency. In a famous coup in 1937, he succeeded in getting the parliamentary party to stop voting against arms estimates. More than any other leading figure in the movement, Dalton's views on appeasement and the need for rearmament in the thirties were consistent and courageous. More continuously (and coherently) than Arthur Greenwood in September 1939, Dalton truly 'spoke for England' over the years. With all his quirks, his patriotism helped ensure that his country entered the war in 1939 as a united society, the class and party disputes of the past years set aside.

Dalton had a good, exciting war. Between 1940 and 1945 he was busy in several major departments. As Minister of Economic Warfare under Churchill between May 1940 and February 1942, he was conspicuous for his unrelenting pursuit of the blockade of Nazi Germany, whatever the cost in civilian suffering. He added, on more than one occasion, to drive the message home, 'More darns in your socks means more bombs on Germany.' One result of these years was that Dalton rapidly cut his ties with the German Social Democrats, many of whose leaders were now in exile in London. They found themselves increasingly frozen out, their patrons like Dalton cold and unhelpful. All Germans, it seemed, were bad Germans to him, and to the fiercely anti-Teuton William Gillies, of Labour's International Department. It was wholly in character that Dalton applauded a plan by the American, Henry Morgenthau, under which post-war Germany would return to a largely pastoral economy, the industrial empires of Krupp, Thyssen, I. G. Farben, and the rest dismantled until the end of time. Dalton also founded SOE, the Special Operations unit for allied espionage behind enemy lines. This appealed to his flair for the conspiratorial. Churchill called Dalton's department at the time—approvingly—'The Ministry of Ungentlemanly Warfare'. His achievement, however, faded during a long quarrel with Brendan Bracken who, with Churchill's backing, acquired control over wartime propaganda, and thereby dismantled Dalton's empire of espionage.

Dalton moved on to the Board of Trade, and stayed there until Labour left the Churchill coalition shortly after VE Day in 1945. It was a fortunate portfolio to be given at such a time. Here was a constructive, planning role for Dalton to play, and he seized the opportunity avidly. He had fierce clashes with the coalowners over fuel rationing, and what they rightly suspected was his socialist zeal for state control of the mines. He had no difficulty in showing the coalowners to be quite appalling; but Churchill and right-wing members of the government managed to ward off outright nationalization.

Most creative of all was Dalton's devoted work for the redistribution of industry in former 'distressed areas' like South Wales and his own Durham, a triumph for 1930s' planning, and a vindication of Labour's Distressed Areas Commission of 1936–7. With gifted younger associates like Douglas Jay and much enthusiasm within the governmental machine, nationally and regionally, Dalton was able to adapt wartime physical controls constructively and far-sightedly, so transforming the industrial prospects for the post-war years. The 1945 Distribution of Industry Act, a prime source of economic recovery for the older industrial regions after the war, was Dalton's triumph. *Practical Socialism* had found glorious fulfilment, ten years on, and added immeasurably to human happiness in Britain's poorest areas.

Always, though, there was partisan dispute about Labour's role in the Churchill coalition, and the effect of wartime governmental experience on the party's concept of socialism. Dalton was much involved in all this. Indeed, his diaries cast a radically different perspective on the received wisdom of historians that the war saw a clear radical consensus emerging, with Labour as its self-confident and predestined spokesman. History was never so simple or clear-cut. Between 1943 and 1945, there was a series of rows in the party, over nationalization, over welfare policy in the light of Beveridge, over Harold Laski, over overseas issues such as a post-war German settlement and policy towards Greece after liberation. Many in the grass-roots feared that the war, far from driving Labour further to the left, was neutralizing its commitment to socialism. A bitter struggle was already in the making between revisionism and fundamentalism, well before 1945. Hugh Gaitskell and Nye Bevan, the first a key civil servant, the latter a stormy petrel on the backbenches, already had more than walk-on parts in these ideological disputes whose shadow was to loom over so much of the post-war history of the party.

The famous 'Reading resolution' carried, *nem. con.*, at the December 1944 conference by Ian Mikardo, against the wishes of the national executive, was but one famous manifestation of this rank-and-file disaffection and suspicion of the leadership. It reflected a fear in the constituencies that, amidst the conformist, consensual mood of wartime coalition, Labour was getting used to the idea of industrial control and economic management in place of the nationalization of the commanding heights and socialism in our time. Dalton played a somewhat mixed role, not without guile and success. He, like Attlee, Bevin, and others, was sufficiently moved by the experience of wartime government to seek a possible continuation of the coalition, at least for the early part of the post-war period. On the other hand, he remained more committed than most to the socialist objective. Unlike Morrison, he responded very positively to the Reading resolution. It was Dalton who made sure that the party manifesto would include a clear commitment to widespread nation-alization, including the highly controversial (and, it was feared, electorally damaging) case of iron and steel. Like most others, Dalton was astonished at the Labour landslide in July 1945, even though his own triumphant election meetings, quite apart from wartime by-elections and the much-derided Gallup polls, might have told him the way the public mood had swung Labour's way. But, unlike many of his colleagues, he was ready for action and a decisive step forward, towards the promised land for which he and other socialists had contended for decades past.

Dalton was obviously going to be a major figure in the new govern-ment. When the coalition broke up, he had thrown himself with renewed relish into the party battle. His reward ought to have been the Foreign Office, where he had served in 1929–31 under Henderson. But, at the very last moment, Attlee transferred him to the Treasury instead. Ben Pimlott lays much stress on the King's personal dislike of Dalton, fostered anew by a recent quarrel between Dalton and Dalton's sister over the disposal of their mother's estate. (Dalton had apparently sold off a tea service and other gifts from the royal family.) But other factors should also be noted, of course, including the famous animosity between Bevin and Morrison which would have made collaboration on the home front very difficult. As a result, Dalton went to the Treasury, for which he was undeniably uniquely qualified, both in terms of theoretical understanding and ministerial experience. He presided over Labour's socialist march in its most buoyant phase. He seemed almost unbearably confident at the dispatch box, deliberately provoking the Tories with insults, and proclaiming his socialist faith (specifically with reference to the Development Areas) 'with a song in his heart'. Even a mundane event like nationalizing Cable and Wireless (which already had a strong public investment element) could be injected with drama by the unsinkable Chancellor. 'Yesterday, it was coal. Today it is cables. The socialist advance, therefore, continues.'

His period at the Treasury certainly had its effective and positive side. He presided over the launching of the Beveridge-style welfare state. He gave his blessing to immediate family allowances and heavily subsidized council housing. He sketched out a bold new policy for achieving full employment, with a strong emphasis on the central direction of licensing and pricing, and much use of physical controls. He pressed ahead with public ownership, steel and all, while his initial 'cheap money' policy (the impact of which, admittedly, can be exaggerated) helped with investment and reducing the cost of financing the National Debt, so hugely swollen after the war. He was also active in foreign affairs, including the important decision to withdraw British troops from Greece in early 1947 which led to the Truman doctrine being proclaimed by the Americans. As always, emotional factors and prejudices intruded too. Dalton opined, 'I regard the Greeks as a poor investment'; he had been hostile to Greek pretensions of grandeur ever since the Chanak crisis in 1922. The Greeks never matched up to his beloved Italians, and, once again, his elephantine prejudices reinforced the call of financial prudence. He also had much to say about Palestine, although in the event he was unable effectively to counter Bevin's policy, which he saw as basically anti-Jewish. Throughout, Dalton appeared as the voice of an expansionist, optimistic Treasury, not a negative, restrictive department pursuing a deflationary policy such as the nation had endured after 1918 and which had made Britain a land fit for *rentiers* to live in. He saw the American loan of 1946 as providing the lifeline for such a forward-looking policy. A year of sustained economic growth in 1946 seemed to confirm his judgement.

There is much to be said in favour of Dalton's policy as Chancellor. The contrast sometimes drawn between the inflationist Dalton and the austerity-minded Cripps can be overdone, though a comparison of their personalities might lead the unwary in that direction. The most disinflationary budget of the post-war years was actually Dalton's final one of November 1947. At the same time, it is hard to see his tenure of the Treasury as a saga of success. Apparently the most technically expert and financially literate of Chancellors, perhaps since the time of Gladstone in 1852, Dalton's mind was really cast in the pre-war, pre-Keynesian mould. In particular, he gave insufficient attention to external finance. His policy was hamstrung throughout by an inadequate understanding of overseas financial constraints, the implications of the dollar shortage above all. He was not helped by the weakness of Eady's Overseas Finance Department, though Dalton ought to have overhauled it long before August 1947. In many ways, for all his bravado, Dalton was a strangely timid Chancellor. He strongly rebuffed James Meade and the Keynesians of the Economic Section of the Cabinet Office when they tried to push him towards a more active budgetary policy and demand management. He did not want a remodelled system of national accounting and assessment to disturb the glory of budget day. His nationalization of the Bank of England, much trumpeted, was not much of a measure, and failed to place effective control of investment and movements of capital in the hands of the government. His issue of cheap government stock at 2 per cent (nicknamed 'Daltons') in November–December 1946 proved to be a fiscal disaster. The 'flapping penguins' of the City (as Lloyd George had called them) had their revenge over the unduly optimistic Chancellor.

Worst of all, Dalton culpably failed to anticipate the coming of sterling convertibility into other currencies in July 1947, as decreed under the terms of the US loan. No doubt this policy would have led to difficulties anyway. Keynes had been as guilty as others in underestimating the dangers. But Dalton, misled by the Bank of England and the Treasury Overseas Department, allowed an orderly retreat to turn into a rout. In August 1947, Britain under a Labour government, which prided itself on its productive efficiency and mastery of planning, faced acute external crisis. The welfare state and Labour's other reforms were potentially under threat. Dalton never seems to have grasped the roots of the external problem, of which growing balance of payments troubles from the start of 1947 gave ample warning. Interestingly enough, the very word 'convertibility' appears only infrequently in his published memoirs. From that time onwards, the Labour government was under siege and its programmes in sad disarray. Dalton's autumn budget of 1947 had to impose £200m. of additional taxation. Cripps emerged as the man of the moment to underpin, perhaps undermine, Dalton's position. Attlee was probably relieved in November 1947 that the budget leak episode, trivial in itself and treated with some generosity by Churchill, gave him an opportunity to dismiss a minister tainted irredeemably with failure.

Dalton never recovered from this sad setback. But he had many parts still to play. He returned to the Cabinet in May 1948 as Chancellor of the Duchy of Lancaster, as noisy as ever. This role gave him special opportunity of venting his anti-Germanism to the full. He was vehement in his rejection of anything resembling European integration. He dismissed the Council of Europe as 'a collection of chatterboxes', the invention of foreign capitalists, with the Vatican lurking in the background. He joined in the belated protests over the withdrawal from Palestine, but without much success. When he moved to the Ministry of Town and Country Planning in February 1950, and then the Ministry of Local Government in January 1951, he built a good many houses, with less fastidious attention to the niceties of internal provision of space and toilet facilities for working-class tenants than had been shown by the previous minister, that proletarian artistocrat, Nye Bevan. In an important move in December 1950, Dalton successfully persuaded Attlee to fly to Washington to meet Truman and convey British disquiet over the possible use of atomic bombs by the Americans in Korea. In May–July 1951, he helped check Morrison's bellicose approach to the Abadan oil crisis. But when Labour fell from office in October 1951, Dalton was amongst those who gave the administration the air of an enfeebled group of pensioners, as he was the first to acknowledge.

After 1951, he warmly backed up his protégé, Gaitskell, against Aneurin Bevan, and helped promote him to the party leadership in 1955 on Attlee's retirement. At the same time, with his commitment to 1930s'-style nationalization and his strident anti-Germanism in foreign policy, he remained in many ways a man of the left. There were commentators who, mistakenly, saw him as a possible recruit for the Bevanites in the 1952–3 period. He certainly flirted with both the Gaitskellite and Bevanite camps, and was fully trusted by neither. His go-between, Desmond Donnelly, made him doubly suspect. His final achievement was a purely personal one—the defeat of his old associate, Herbert Morrison, whom he had strongly backed twenty years earlier, for the party leadership in the autumn of 1955. Only as the patron of young intellectuals did Dalton still have a viable role. Towards the end, pointlessly, he took a peerage. When he died in 1961, he seemed almost an anachronism, recalling an earlier, more robust age.

In many ways, Dalton's career was marked by disappointments, personal and public. Some of his lifelong causes, such as the defence of Zionism and opposition to the rearming of Germany, came to little.

He lived long enough to see Labour suffer its third successive electoral defeat, its heaviest since 1931, under his protégé, Gaitskell, in 1959. His period as Chancellor was compared unfavourably, by journalists at the time, and by academic economists like Sir Alec Cairncross later on, with that of his successor, Cripps. The latter's export drive was more effective, while he also conveyed a much more visible sense of command. Dalton's linking of socialism with wartime physical controls seemed increasingly dated. In terms of personal relations and the image of socialism that he created in the media, while being a powerful parliamentary debater, he was too often unsuccessful and maladroit.

And yet, in that vital decade between 1931 and 1940, more than any other man, Dalton remade the face of British left-wing politics. Like art deco and Alex James, he belongs to the thirties; that is why he is included in this particular section of the present book. The thirties, with its commitment to *dirigiste*, pre-Keynesian planning, its vigorous anti-fascism and resurgent patriotism (including a sense of empire and colonial development) were Dalton's classic phase. By 1945 his main work was done. As a publicist and practitioner he gave British socialism a new intellectual force and belief in itself. Through gifted young disciples like Jay, Crosland, Callaghan, Healey, and Abel-Smith, his influence lived on for a generation to come.

Hugh Dalton was an odd, contradictory personality. He was an urbanite with an intense love for the countryside; an egalitarian committed to the public schools and the rowing fraternity at King's; a planner who rejected budgetary controls as a kind of mumbo-jumbo; an internationalist with deep-rooted, irrational racial hatreds, which led him to turn savagely against the exiled German socialists he had once patronized; an anti-colonialist whose private views could reveal a kind of contempt for the cultural values of African and Asian 'niggers'; a Zionist who could lapse into anti-Semitism. He was a permanent outsider within the establishment world in which he had grown up, volatile, vulnerable, and insecure. But, as a constructive and creative figure in Labour's formative phase, he was unique. The party owes him an enormous debt, one not always recognized, at least until Pimlott's fine biography. The affection attaching to his memory among his political disciples and many civil servants who worked with him is still immense, and testimony to his influence. For all his transparent faults, he helped give Labour faith in its crusade, and practical instruments with which to give it effect. In particular, his use of public finance to redress inequalities of property and income (especially taxing inheritance and large fortunes) was a crucial victory for democratic socialism in Britain. As his achievements sink beneath mass unemployment, the psychosis of pessimism, and the cynicism of the market-place, as his beloved Durham coalfield lapses after the 1984 strike into decline and defeat, it is right to be reminded that once, well within living memory, England arose.

# 3

## THE YEARS OF POWER
### 1945–1970

# CLEMENT ATTLEE

CLEM ATTLEE is our really unknown Prime Minister. Compared with him, Bonar Law (to whom the term was originally applied) was a model of transparency. Attlee's enigmatic, reticent style was celebrated, perhaps notorious, during his lifetime. His autobiography, *As It Happened*, is so unrevealing as to be almost comic. 'Quite an exciting day' was his measured verdict on 26 July 1945, the day he went to the Palace to become Prime Minister. A favourite adjective, applied for instance to the Gallipoli landings, was 'interesting'. His volume of interviewed reminiscences, *A Prime Minister Remembers*, has been described by A. J. P. Taylor as being notable for showing what a Prime Minister forgets. None of the memoirs of the period of Attlee's heyday, from the diaries of Dalton to those of Crossman, have shed much revealing light on Attlee's personality, his ideas, hopes, fears, inner tensions, or uncertainties. Television interviews in his last years proved equally unsuccessful. Appropriately enough, his private papers in Oxford and Cambridge are sparse and uncommunicative, though the family correspondence, edited by Kenneth Harris, and the curious little poems printed by Dr Golant provide a shade more. But the private records tell us little of the mighty events that punctuated his premiership between 1945 and 1951. These were years that saw the winning of a world war, the building up of the welfare state, the founding of NATO, the independence of India, the development of Britain's nuclear weapons. Yet they seem one with Tyre and Nineveh, almost dust in a career which, on the surface at least, embodied the useful, if limited, qualities of a minor public school headmaster or a small-town solicitor, transmuted into a kind of genius.

Kenneth Harris's biography in 1982 comes closer than any other work to date to uncovering the essence of this impenetrable Prime Minister who managed, almost by stealth, to transform the course of British domestic and international history over six momentous years. His book has its shortcomings, no doubt. In the Public Record Office, he made good use of the Cabinet Papers, but apparently none of the Prime Minister's files (PREM) which are more revealing of Attlee's views on major themes such as Palestine, India, or economic policy. The Foreign Office files could have also been used to advantage, since Attlee was a major figure in the conduct of foreign affairs, especially after the departure of Ernest Bevin in early 1951. On the other hand, Mr Harris's new material, notably private sources from the Attlee family and extensive interviews with politicians (including Attlee himself in old age), civil servants, aides, and many others, more than redresses the balance.

With Attlee as with others, of course, biography as a method can be misleading. Close concentration on Attlee's leadership of party and government tends to downgrade his close colleagues, sometimes with unfair results. Herbert Morrison usually appears in Mr Harris's pages as a self-seeking intriguer—'couldn't stand the fellow'. Morrison's autobiography is dismissed by Attlee as 'a fine work of fiction'. The manager of the legislative and parliamentary machine for six years seldom surfaces. Aneurin Bevan is another constant thorn in Attlee's flesh—unstable, erratic, always liable to 'emotional spasms' at awkward moments. His building up of the National Health Service and vigorous exposition of the ideas of democratic socialism cannot emerge in this context. No wonder, with two such colleagues, that Attlee cast his vote for Gaitskell in 1955. Again, the Colonial Secretary, Arthur Creech Jones, was simply 'one of my mistakes' to Attlee, not the planner of a new and far-seeing colonial development policy. Presumably the ground-nuts fiasco buried everything else. But biography can never analyse a government or a movement as a whole. Nor can it provide a study of the structure or typology of a party which could throw up such an improbable leader at such a time. In this case biography, in Mr Harris's capable hands, can powerfully illuminate the dark, hidden centre of a powerful government, and this is a major service to history and to political understanding. It enables us to propel the Attlee administration out of the swirling mists of legend into the more demanding world of historical reality.

The main features of Attlee's unremarkable early career are a well-known story, though some features deserved added emphasis. He had a wholly conventional, late-Victorian, middle-class upbringing, leading on to Haileybury and University College, Oxford. Perhaps out of sheer boredom, he ventured into a boys' club at Stepney in London's East End in late 1905, clad, we are told, in the silk hat and tails of the trainee barrister. Quite unexpectedly, this began seven years of intense social work amongst the East London poor. It propelled Attlee's entire career into new directions. He evidently first saw Stepney in terms of the charitable paternalism of the Charity Organization Society; by 1912, though, he was a socialist and distinctly on the left. He had no settled occupation in these years. A brief and unsatisfactory time at Toynbee Hall (which he thought bourgeois and patronizing) was followed by various temporary posts as a part-time lecturer. His main activity, without question, was in organizing the Stepney ILP, which he had joined in 1907. Finally in 1912 he gained a lectureship at the London School of Economics, defeating Hugh Dalton for the post.

These Edwardian years in Stepney must have had a galvanizing effect upon Attlee's ideas and sense of social purpose. Yet, then and later, it is difficult to discern any particular sense of commitment other than an awareness of social waste and inefficiency, a prosaic urge to deal with the practical evils of slum housing, malnutrition, and casual employment in a matter-of-fact way. No wider social diagnosis came from Attlee's pen at this time. Even his later book, *The Social Worker*, written in 1920 when his socialist credentials were at their most extreme, is really a recapitulation of the well-meaning, charitable outlook of the late-Victorian Liberals against whom the young Attlee had supposedly rebelled. Much of the argument concentrates on providing links between professional social workers and voluntary bodies. While he includes a fierce attack on the individualist ethic of the Charity Organization Society, he extols the work of settlement houses, religious agencies, friendly societies, and the WEA. The main thrust of the book is to enlist the enthusiasm of middle-class professional people for the principles of social service, to add an extra dimension to Greek ideals of citizenship and civic pride. It is an admirable tribute to his seriousness, integrity, and utter lack of pomposity. It is in no conceivable sense a blueprint for revolution.

Attlee's social passions, kindled in the slums of the East End, were entirely compatible with a loyalist, conformist attitude towards King and country. He had no qualms about enlisting in the army in 1914 or fighting with much courage thereafter. The anti-militarism of ILP leaders like Hardie, MacDonald, and Snowden made no impression on him. Promoted to the rank of major, he took a notable part in the Gallipoli campaign (the work of his later colleague and opponent, Winston Churchill), and was seriously wounded there. The effect of war service and such inhumane carnage on a mass scale must also have been an immense formative influence upon the young socialist. Again, it is difficult to discover from his speeches and writings any quickening of the pulse. He returned to work in the East End much as before.

From mayor of Stepney, he rose to parliament and was duly elected for the Stepney, Limehouse constituency in the 1922 election as 'Major Attlee'. The next nine years in parliament, a stormy time in the history of the labour movement, were relative free from crisis for him. He held a junior post at the War Office in the 1924 Labour government, and a more substantial role in 1929-31 as Chancellor of the Duchy of Lancaster, and then Postmaster-General. He impressed colleagues such as Addison by his high administrative competence in office, but he steered well clear of the high political crises of the time. Fortunately for him, he did not have to take a view for or against the cuts in unemployment benefit which fractured Mac-Donald's Cabinet in August 1931. The most traumatic experience for Attlee in this period was rather his decision to serve on the Simon Commission on India in 1927-30. Both his membership of it, and his adherence to proposals that fell far short of effective self-government, aroused some criticism from the left. But it was soon swamped in the wider anxiety about mass unemployment and the run on the pound. In the long term, Attlee's acquired expertise on India was another latent asset.

His election as party leader in 1935, over the heads of better-known men like Morrison and Greenwood, both of whom had been Cabinet ministers, was almost wholly unexpected. He had kept his East End seat in 1931 by 551 votes, and was inevitably a most active front-bench spokesman on a great range of issues for the diminished rump of forty-six Labour MPs. But he made no wider impact. A brief period of left-wing rhetoric in 1931-2 did not last. His quiet talents as committe man and party administrator were muffled by a deliberately prosaic style and lack of oratorical flair. However, there were strong feelings against both his rivals, Morrison and Greenwood, in 1935, while Attlee had had the luck not only to be in parliament after the landslide of 1931 but to act as leader during Lansbury's illness in 1934-5. Almost by default, he was elected. Even then, for several more years he failed to impress. It was Dalton and Bevin who largely directed the party away from neo-pacifism and appeasement. Down to 1940, there were repeated criticisms of him, mainly from left-wingers like Ellen Wilkinson and Laski, but also from ambitious colleagues like Morrison. But Attlee rode his luck. When the party decided to join Churchill's war coalition on 11 May 1940, there was no real dissent. Henceforth Attlee's position as leader, almost without effort, was impregnable.

During the second world war, Attlee certainly acquired new stature. He was much more than just an anonymous chairman of committees, important though his domestic co-ordinating role was during Churchill's frequent absences overseas, and involvement in war policy. Attlee also became an active policy-maker, both in discussion of a post-war settlement for Germany and on social reform at home. He forced Churchill to set up the Cabinet's Reconstruction Committee in 1943, which became an important platform for Labour ministers in pushing the coalition towards social change. When the Prime Minister dragged his feet on welfare policy, Attlee bluntly slapped him down. At the same time, he was adroit enough to beat off challenges to his leadership. He allowed a memorandum by Morrison in October 1944, aimed at committing the Cabinet to widespread programmes for the socialization of industry, to founder. Thereby, his main possible rival as leader lost a vital degree of credibility. On the NEC, repeated sniping by Laski, both about Attlee personally and the unwillingness of Labour ministers to proclaim the socialist cause, got nowhere. Never was Attlee's indirect, non-confrontational style seen to greater effect.

Most important of all, Attlee evolved during the war a powerful critique of the techniques of Cabinet government, based on the remodelling of the machinery of government achieved during wartime. Not since Peel had there been a minister with such grasp of the central institutions of government. There were those who felt, later on, that Attlee showed some excess of zeal in this direction, and that the existence of no less than 148 Cabinet standing committees and 313 ad hoc committees by October 1951 made governmental life needlessly complicated. He did not want to leave the Churchill coalition in May 1945, and was under repeated attack from Harold Laski on the left flank during the subsequent election campaign. But he came through with ease, while his calm rebuttal of Churchill's attacks on the Labour Party's structure during his election broadcasts—rebuttals which sounded more convincing at the time than they read now—added to his stature. When he went to the Palace on 26 July 1945, he was derided by many as a colourless, humdrum substitute for the mighty Churchill. Jibes about empty taxis, and grubs becoming queen bees, became commonplace. In fact, both in terms of his knowledge of the party and his understanding of the apparatus of government, no Prime Minister was more fully equipped for the highest office than was Clement Attlee in July 1945.

The years of the premiership between 1945 and 1951 are Attlee's claim to greatness. They built up a legendary reputation for the all-wise, taciturn leader which has provided the touchstone for all Labour leaders since, from Wilson to Kinnock—not to mention defectors to the SPD, for whom Attlee remains a model of 'sensible socialism' who still inspires reverence. The quality of Attlee's premiership is, however, hard to capture, not because of a shortage of evidence but rather because of the massive fall-out of paper from the Public Record Office, saturation bombing by document. It can, however, safely be stated that Attlee was far more than just a grey, anonymous director of a myriad of interlocking Cabinet committees. At least in the great period of socialist advance from July 1945 to the financial crisis of July 1947 he was a strong, clear-headed leader, who often intervened in Cabinet and in departmental policy-making with devastating effect. On matters ranging from bread rationing to the founding of the National Health Service (where Attlee swung his support strongly on Bevan's side), the Prime Minister's intervention was decisive. In one key area of social policy, housing (where the ministers concerned, notably Bevan, seemed to be lagging behind the pace of events), Attlee himself chaired the new Cabinet Committee that was set up. As a result, much overlap between departments in the allocation of manpower and raw materials was ironed out. Labour's housing policy began to match the credibility of its other social commitments, on health, education, and employment. Attlee kept his government on the move—and firmly to the manifesto. Backsliding from its pledges was avoided. But so, too, were policy novelties such as equal pay for women, the permanent abolition of capital punishment, or tinkering with the governmental structure of gerrymandered, Tory-run Northern Ireland—the latter an area in which Attlee was outstandingly cautious.

He became particularly involved in foreign and defence policy, especially in relation to policy towards Germany, rearmament, Palestine, Marshall Aid, and the founding of NATO. In each area, he was more than merely a passive supporter of Bevin's policy, immense though his admiration for 'Ernie' undoubtedly was. Thus Attlee had his own, well-formed views on a post-war reconstruction of both the political and economic structure of the western zones of Germany under allied occupation. Wisely, he resisted Montgomery's demand that the Rhineland should be detached from Germany. He also had a strongly developed sense of the need to establish Britain's independent role within the framework of an enduring alliance with the United States. His first visit to Washington, in November 1945, was in many ways a disillusioning experience, with the Americans unwilling to implement the wartime Quebec agreement on nuclear policy. It left him with an acute sense of America's unreliability for post-war collaboration on nuclear power and atomic information. One result was that Attlee was a powerful force behind the fateful—and wholly secret—decision in the winter of 1946–7 for Britain to pursue its own nuclear weapons programme.

Many of his interventions on foreign affairs in this period marked him out as amongst the radicals of the government. Perhaps this is what lies behind Kenneth Younger's somewhat surprising claim that Attlee was 'the extreme outside left of the government'. However, Attlee could proclaim, but he could not necessarily insist. His memoranda in late 1945 on the pointlessness of an east of Suez defence strategy and the declining value of imperial defence outposts in the Persian Gulf and the eastern Mediterranean strike one now as fresh, vivid, and far-sighted. But they had no effect on Bevin. The Attlee government came to its end with British forces strongly entrenched from Aden to Cyprus, military expenditure per capita higher in Britain than in the United States, and the imperial mission as vigorously upheld as by any Tory imperialist in the past. Left-wing critics like Brockway or Crossman, anxious for 'a socialist foreign policy', were slapped down for the besetting sin of 'woolly idealism'.

In one area of policy, as is well known, Attlee's personal role was quite decisive. On India he could claim a special expertise, dating from Simon Commission days. At every stage of Cabinet deliberation in 1946–7, Attlee's influence was crucial; even the great Bevin could be reprimanded for residual imperial nostalgia. It was Attlee who dictated the vital parallel decision to speed up independence for Burma as well. It was Attlee who sacked Wavell, the old Viceroy, as defeatist (though, ironically, Wavell's 'breakdown' plan for withdrawal by mid-1948 gave Britain twelve months longer to prepare for the succession than did the Labour government's scramble to get out). It was Attlee, too, who personally appointed Mountbatten to negotiate a transfer of power, with plenipotentiary authority to speed up the withdrawal. Mountbatten's aide could write of Attlee at this period that 'the man burns with a hidden fire'. The rapid withdrawal from India in August 1947, with the huge communal carnage that followed, is widely controversial. Attlee saw it in a wider context of the long-term relationship between Britain and the ex-colonial peoples in Asia and Africa. He wanted to avoid the horror of what France was currently enduring in Indo-China, and was to endure again in Algeria with fatal results for the Fourth Republic. Here, he succeeded to the full. He emerged as a liberator, the leader of his government and the architect of the new Commonwealth.

After the financial crisis of August 1947, Attlee's reputation somewhat slumped. Indeed, his very leadership was briefly under challenge, though he negotiated the crisis with great skill by giving Cripps, the foremost conspirator, an offer of supreme economic command that he could not refuse. In 1948–50 Attlee's style somewhat changed. The image of the pipe-smoking, unruffled, taciturn leader, conveyed erratically across the country by his wife's ancient car while her husband grappled with *The Times* crossword on the back seat, was now born. Even so, his authority, refurbished and subtly reinterpreted after the near-disaster of 1947, was never in doubt. In 1950–1, he emerged again as a powerful leader of his government. This appeared particularly in foreign policy during Bevin's last ailing months and Morrison's somewhat uncertain tenure of the Foreign Office. Attlee's visit to Washington in December 1950 was surely less effective in restraining the Americans over the possible use of nuclear weapons in Korea than was claimed at the time. But, domestically, it gave Attlee a new boost.

As a result, in 1951 he threw his authority behind the conduct of foreign policy in such weighty matters as Anglo-American policy differences over China, the rearmament of western Germany, the defence budget of January 1951, and the Abadan oil crisis with Iran. On balance, Attlee gave a firmness and consistency to British policy at a time when his government was gravely weakened by the loss of Bevin and Cripps, and buffeted both by internal party differences and external difficulties with the balance of payments. His government fell from power in October 1951 very narrowly, with Attlee's personal prestige as high as ever.

This view of Attlee's qualities of leadership, perhaps more vigorous than many accounts of his reticence used to suggest, has now become widespread. There is no need to revise it radically just for the sake of novelty. Attlee had supreme skill in handling prima donnas like Morrison or Cripps. Lesser ministers such as Pakenham or Jay have testified to his mastery of men and situations. He could take on obstreperous colleagues and unsentimentally cut them down to size. He was also consistently effective in handling potentially explosive meetings of the parliamentary party or the national executive, while his command of the party conference was considerable. Indeed, between 1946 and 1951, the euphoric mood of that traditionally quarrelsome assembly of delegates is probably unique in the entire history of the Labour Party. Attlee presided over the plaudits of the assembled comrades as surely as did Stalin or Mao preside over socialist gatherings of a distinctly different colour.

At the same time, it is surely a mistake to build up an Attlee myth of a different kind. He was certainly very far from the timid mediocrity portrayed by Tory opponents. But he was no superman either. In the handling of ministers and Cabinet, Attlee was at his best piloting the party quietly and efficiently along a predestined and well-charted course, as in 1945–7. In the difficult parliamentary session of 1950, his very personality was a tranquillizing and reassuring force throughout. But he could not take control when complex events were throwing the government off course, when the winds of change gave way to a hurricane. In the financial and political crisis of 1947, Attlee failed to offer any real lead. It was Cripps (together with American bailing out) who rescued the Prime Minister and his government from the brink of financial disaster. In the devaluation crisis of the summer of 1949, Attlee again offered a muffled lead. It was left to much younger ministers like Gaitskell and Jay, neither of whom was even in the Cabinet, to convert key ministers to the need for a swift, radical devaluation, with Attlee agnostic, remote and silent.

The most disastrous example of his failure to lead came in March–April 1951, with the mounting crisis between Bevan and Gaitskell over proposed charges levied on the National Health Service. Attlee had ample time to see the crisis building up. After all, Bevan had threatened resignation on precisely the same issue in the spring of 1950. On that occasion, Cripps retreated. Bevan's leaving the government was no surprise, though Wilson's certainly was. Yet Attlee failed to exert any particular influence. He was, it is true, in St Mary's Hospital, after an operation on a duodenal ulcer. But he was far from incapacitated. Indeed, two weeks after Bevan resigned, Attlee was back at work in Downing Street. He failed either to suggest any viable compromise over NHS charges (even the dying Ernie Bevin did better), or to try to influence Aneurin Bevan. Indeed, he treated him to a historical disquisition on the undesirability and danger to one's career of resigning over the budget at all, as shown by Lord Randolph Churchill back in 1886. This was both irrelevant and so wide of the mark as to be insulting. Attlee also began the canard, sustained by later gossip and some historiography, that Bevan had only come out against the rearmament programme at the very last moment. Attlee, in short, bears part responsibility for the widening of the breach between Bevan and his colleagues which did such immense harm to the party for the next decade.

In this connection, it may be added that Attlee's last, somewhat inert, phase of leadership from 1951 to 1955 served to widen the breach. He seems to have believed that his continued presence at the top could help moderate the feud between Gaitskell and Bevan, and to resolve policy difference over German rearmament and the bomb. He did produce a compromise on German rearmament, but elsewhere his inability to supply any initiative made things rather worse. The gulf between Gaitskellite right and Bevanite left, only latent before 1951, became a chasm. The withdrawal of the whip from Bevan in April 1955 was the final blow, though Attlee managed to prevent his expulsion from the party. In the end, it is difficult to believe that Attlee's lingering on as leader for four more years, until he had reached the age of seventy-two and was obviously a waning force, had much purpose other than to ensure that his near-contemporary, Morrison, would be excluded from the leadership. This strongly emerges in *The Road to Brighton Pier*, by Leslie Hunter, a *Herald* journalist close to Morrison. In Attlee's last years, which included the loss of the 1955 general election after Labour had led in the polls for much of the past four years, Labour was inadvertently removed as a credible party of government. Attlee had offered no initiative. His inability to inspire or innovate, coupled with a passive attitude towards the media, had become crucial liabilities. He had become his own grave-digger.

This failure to exert leadership was linked with the one great gap in his intellectual armoury—his slight understanding of economics. In this area, as Harold Wilson has written, Clem Attlee was 'tone-deaf'. His view of socialism centred on social administration, infused with Christian morality. In *The Social Worker* he had criticized an economics that was 'abstract and academic'. Attlee's down-to-earth approach was quite remote from an understanding of modern economic problems. The crises of August 1947 and August 1949 were not helped by Attlee's inability to grasp the main issues at stake, either in the reasons for the loss of currency reserves or in the basis for devaluing the pound. In the end, he chaired the Cabinet's Economic Committee, which took Britain through the crisis in each case. He also had the precious gift of sensing the value of advice from men like Gaitskell and Jay who did understand the technical issues at stake. But he was a presiding figure, not a fount of ideas, at least in the economic field. He was thus unable to question the statistical basis of the manifestly ill-conceived rearmament programme of January 1951 which did such political and economic damage all round. Meanwhile, his originality in industrial policy had diminished after the petering out of the wave of nationalization in 1947–8. Indeed, by allowing the Cabinet to debate the crucial case of iron and steel for so long, and so divisively, in the summer of 1947, Attlee again inadvertently helped to weaken party morale, and to make men wonder whether the socialist fire of 1945 had been extinguished for ever. From the official standpoint, Sir George Mallaby, a Cabinet secretary, considered Attlee's chairmanship of the Cabinet 'only a negative success. He was like a schoolmaster who kept order very well but did not really teach you much.' But this may be unduly harsh.

By 1951, and even more by 1955, Attlee symbolized a Labour Party whose capacity to generate new ideas seemed spent. He himself spoke privately of his veteran status. 'I think of "The War" as the Boer War—that was the war that was on when I was in my late teens.' Few able young men had been promoted by his government, which by 1951 was distinctly elderly, almost senile. An era foreshadowed in Edwardian days, amongst the social workers and upper-class philanthropists of the East End, pursuing the path trodden by Charles Booth and his investigators in the nineties, had reached fulfilment in 1945–7. The programme was complete, and finite. England had indeed arisen, and Attlee's idea of socialism had nothing else to offer.

The career of Clement Attlee, inevitably, leads on to wider reflections on his private personality and political style. He was, without any doubt, a highly conservative figure in personal life. He stayed devoted to the public school ethos of Haileybury, and treasured the progress in his government of Old Haileyburians such as Mayhew and de Freitas. His private tastes were as conventional as his family and household were models of humdrum, middle-class domesticity. He liked pottering about at home, leaving his wife, 'Vi', to tidy up the flower-beds. He disliked modernity and innovation, at least in so far as it affected himself, including any assertion of feminism. While he wrote warmly on the moral outlook of Ruskin, Lethaby, and Morris, he was no aesthete, and disliked (perhaps feared) modern art. As Prime Ministers tend to do, he read some Gibbon. His other main enthusiasm was for cricket. This, indeed, was one bond between him and that over venerable Edwardian survivor, Lord Addison, his closest friend in the government after Bevin.

Attlee was, for all his professed socialism, a dedicated enthusiast for King and country, a patriot who took pride in his career of gallant war service. He became especially attached to George VI, and even rearranged the election date in October 1951—disastrously for Labour's prospects—to accommodate an intended royal visit to Africa. Attlee was said to have shown rare emotion in public on hearing of his King's death early in 1952. Along with a love of country went a veneration of empire inherited from Haileybury days. Attlee combined an intellectual anti-colonialism with an emotional feeling for Britain's paternalist role in raising the condition of lesser breeds in far-flung continents. The Commonwealth, with Britain's presiding role made clear, meant much to him. He saw little wrong with South Africa, at least when the unquestionably racialist Smuts was in charge. In December 1950, Attlee delighted to instruct Truman and the disbelieving and cynical Dean Acheson on how Britain, with its centuries of experience in Asia, simply understood the oriental mind and the inclinations of black, brown, and yellow-skinned people far better than did the *arriviste* Americans. In quasi-imperial gatherings, from Prime Ministers' conferences at Lancaster House to meetings at the MCC at Lord's, Attlee was in his element, emotion recollected in tranquillity.

A deeply conservative man, he was also no intellectual. He was certainly not a man with a zest for the interchange of new ideas, as leaders such as Gaitskell, Wilson, and perhaps Callaghan have been at times. Bevin called Attlee 'our Campbell-Bannerman', which is perhaps not altogether a compliment. When Kenneth Harris asked Attlee of which other country he would have liked to be a citizen, the immediate answer was Denmark. Attlee saw his party in the most humdrum of terms. In 1935 he compared it with a country garden in which there should be regular pruning (perhaps by party members' wives), 'lest the coarser growths take all the light and air from the delicate'. The Labour Party for Attlee was less the new Jerusalem, more the Hampstead Garden Suburb *in excelsis*.

But he was a strong, self-sustained man, with an indomitable will and iron courage. The *New Statesman*'s portrait of him in the mid-fifties was rightly entitled 'The Egoist'. His reputation for modesty was wholly false. In old age, he wrote a little limerick, to mark his being enrolled a Knight of the Garter:

> Few thought he was even a starter
> There were many who thought themselves smarter
> But he ended PM
> CH and OM
> An earl and a Knight of the Garter.

He was an immodest little man with plenty to be immodest about. His inner strength and total self-confidence enabled him to take a firm, unsentimental view of the limitations of almost all his colleagues—Cripps, Morrison, Dalton, Bevan, Shinwell, and Gaitskell included. Only George VI, Bevin, and the septuagenarian Addison roused him to automatic enthusiasm. He disliked rootless adventurers above all. Beaverbook he considered 'the only evil man I ever met'. Throughout, Attlee's slow-burning, taciturn qualities were turned to advantage. He illustrated perfectly the old Roman tag that, if you remain silent, you are thought a philosopher. Yet here was a man whose talents were unique and indispensable, at least for his Labour Party at the stage it had reached in 1945. He embodied in his own Strube-type 'little man' personality Bagehot's definition of the statesman (first applied to Peel): 'the powers of a first-rate man and the creed of a second-rate man'.

Like all the great political leaders, like Pitt, Peel, Gladstone, or Asquith, like Lloyd George or Churchill, Attlee was buoyed up by his own sense of indispensability. The party, which he led for a record twenty years, was created in his own image. Nor did he totally desert his ILP heritage, despite the conservative (or Conservative) outlook of Mrs Attlee. As noted, from the nationalization of hospitals to the recognition of Communist China, Attlee instinctively belonged to the radical camp. His qualities enabled him to hold together an extraordinary team of powerful personalities, to weld them, his party, and his movement into a mood of united purpose unique in their history, to transform his beloved country into a welfare democracy, and the old empire into a free, multiracial Commonwealth. He imposed his own elusive personality on a whole generation. No doubt there are dangers in taking the mystique of Attlee to excess, and building up a myth of his instant wisdom and prescient leadership which the evidence can hardly sustain. But the legacy remains. A. J. P. Taylor, long a fierce critic of Attlee, especially of the cold war policy pursued by Bevin under him, recently said to me 'Attlee grows on you. He was the greatest of Labour's leaders and Prime Ministers.' If this is the considered view of our greatest living historian, our most incorrigible of academic rebels, which of us can reasonably disagree?

# ERNEST BEVIN AS
# FOREIGN SECRETARY

To the outside world, Ernest Bevin was easily the dominant personality of the 1945 Labour administration. 'That great mountain of a man', wrote W. J. Brown in 1946, 'while his health lasts, is pivotal to the future of the Socialist government.' In western Europe, in the Commonwealth and third world, above all in the North Atlantic alliance where he achieved a remarkable rapport with secretaries of state like Marshall and Acheson, Bevin seemed the transcendent figure of the age, a dockers' John Bull, a British Foreign Secretary of Chatham- or Palmerston-like proportions. When he died in April 1951, at the height of the Cabinet conflict between Gaitskell and Bevan over NHS charges and the cost of the rearmament programme, the departure of this massive figure left a huge gap within his party and his nation.

Yet none of the Labour ministers after 1945 has aroused more controversy since his death. As the cold war tensions and power polarizations of Bevin's day have melted into a more fluid international system in which the post-war alignments seem less relevant and less rigid, the passions of those far-off years when Bevin and Molotov abused each other at the conference table seem extraordinarily remote. Naturally, Bevin has faced the most withering fire from the far left. E. P. Thompson, for instance, has attacked him for failing to nurture that nascent socialist revolution in Europe in 1945 which Mr Thompson believes he detected while a serving soldier in Italy during the war. Many other commentators, far removed from this stance, have also found the blunt nationalism, gut anti-communism and sheer belligerence of Bevin's outlook inexplicable, perhaps repugnant. It is difficult for socialists or anyone else in the 1980s to warm to Bevin's proclamation in November 1946 that the Union Jack ought to fly over the atomic bomb—this as a serious justification for Britain's pursuing her own secret nuclear weapons programme rather than work for multilateral disarmament. Certainly, no British Foreign Secretary has tried to emulate Bevin's style since. Selwyn Lloyd, of Suez fame, was a much more guarded,

almost feline, figure; George Brown (another TGWU man) was widely
regarded abroad as an eccentric, too often drunk or otherwise
unstable to be taken seriously. Trying to make sense of Bevin's
impulses and instincts is clearly central to understanding the international pretensions of British Labour in its years of power after
1945. But it is a task which the passing of years and the transformation of international forces makes progressively more difficult.

Alan Bullock's triumphant third volume of his trilogy on Bevin,
published in 1983 was thus an immense contribution to historical
understanding. Of course, he had described, in two earlier magisterial
volumes, the extraordinary impact Bevin made on British domestic
history, as the tsar of the Transport and General Workers down to
1940, and then as Minister of Labour and supremo on the home
front under Churchill during the war. Bevin came to the Foreign
Office with a vast wealth of experience of social and economic change
in Britain, viewed at the highest level, for over a quarter of a century
past. But his involvement with foreign affairs had been episodic. He
had established a wide range of contacts internationally through the
world-wide transport workers' organization. He had been foremost
in the fight to commit Labour to rearmament and a vigorous response
to fascism in the thirties. His brutal crushing of the veteran pacifist,
George Lansbury, was rightly seen as a crucial bench-mark in
Labour's maturing understanding of foreign policy. Bevin had
reflected widely on the international macro-economic aspects of the
depression and financial collapse of the thirties. He had also some
contact with wartime external policies, notably—and disastrously—
in the Allied intervention in Greece in late 1944.

But he was in no sense a man with an authoritative or sustained
grasp of foreign affairs. As is well known, his original portfolio in the
Attlee government had been the Treasury. He was moved to the
Foreign Office instead, as we have seen, partly through the King's
dislike of Dalton, the putative Foreign Secretary. But Bevin flung
himself into this unfamiliar world of international diplomacy with
astonishing single-mindedness and strength of will. Alan Bullock's
third volume memorably spells out the nature of the achievement in
rich detail. He gives us a portrait of a beleaguered, lonely titan thrust
into a desperate post-war world, a man with few friends, with no
hobbies or relaxations (other than curt telephone discussions with
his wife about cooking), a person of strong prejudices and much
irrationality, but one who was in his rough way a creative artist.

Understandably, Bullock refers only incidentally to Bevin's position in the Attlee government generally as the voice of trade-unionism. It is, therefore, worth additional emphasis that Bevin had a far wider role within the government than simply that of Foreign Secretary. He was the most powerful trade-unionist alive, and perhaps the only genuine manual proletarian (and the official voice of manual workers in the mass) amongst Labour's key ministers. It was Bevin who was the vital link with the unions in sustaining the unity of the movement, on matters ranging from the repeal of the hated 1927 Trades Disputes Act (which he moved himself in the House) to the implementation of a wage freeze in 1948, which Cripps originally somewhat mishandled. He also turned, spasmodically, to the insistence that trade-unionists be represented on the boards of nationalized industries that he had first proclaimed against Morrison in 1932–4, the origin of their long feud. Bevin's position in the Cabinet was unique, and Attlee frequently deferred to him, as he did to no-one else. On a vast range of domestic questions, including labour and demobilization, wages policy, housing, the nationalization of steel (which he supported, albeit cautiously), food production, and much else besides, Bevin would intervene in Cabinet at length, with the mininum of grammatical precision but the maximum of impact. Even at the very end, in March 1951 when he was a dying man, he was active in trying to produce a compromise over a ceiling on NHS expenditure for 1951–2 which would avert Bevan's resignation, the dangers of which he sensed, for all his dislike of his volatile Welsh colleague. Bevin's wider impact on the domestic strategy and logistics of the Attlee government is a major theme, still to be fully explored.

But the main focus in Bullock's book, rightly, is Bevin's struggle to propel the foreign policy of his country and his class into radically new directions after 1945. He spoke repeatedly of 'my foreign policy', and clearly saw his initiatives in highly personal terms. This needs further examination. Certainly, Bevin was nobody's poodle or puppet, and to see so strong-willed and class-conscious a man as clay in the hands of smooth Foreign Office mandarins is manifestly absurd. At the same time, the almost universal Foreign Office admiration for Bevin, voiced by Strang, Kirkpatrick, Dixon, Jebb, Kelly, Roberts, and many others, arouses questions, perhaps suspicion. Perhaps his robust style of self-expression and of behaviour at the UN and elsewhere kindled their partisan enthusiasm for a Foreign Secretary who could speak up for his country in so forthright, almost pugilistic, a fashion. Perhaps this most socially exclusive and inbred of departments revered the mystery of their token, semi-literate, proletarian mascot, a man scarcely capable of wielding a pen or completing a grammatical sentence, but who fought the good fight with muscular relish reminiscent of Hazlitt's account of the prize ring. Undoubtedly they liked Bevin for his directness, reliability, and integrity.

At the same time, he was notable for being a Foreign Secretary with a fascination for broad conceptual flights of policy rather than for the pedantries of detail. Bevin was chief among the delegators; he favoured the presidential mode. He deliberately chose a style which kept him aloof from the pragmatic working out of policy on the spot. No doubt this is partly why the Foreign Office so preferred their 'Ernie' to the fussy and temperamental Eden. But in practice it meant that much latitude was granted to departments and embassies, giving policy-making almost a momentum of its own. Bevin did not like being badgered by officials. Sir Frank Roberts describes him once complaining to senior advisers, 'The ink's hardly dry on the words from my mouth when you are back again wanting new instructions.' Especially in relation to the Middle East, where strongly pro-Arab views had been deeply entrenched for decades, this method gave a distinct thrust to British policy which Bevin influenced only at a somewhat remote level. The Foreign Office, to a man, worshipped Ernie, in part for the freedom and sense of international self-importance he gave them.

Unhindered by divisions within his own department of state, Bevin could proceed to conduct foreign policy in a relatively uncluttered way. He enjoyed, as has been seen, a unique status in the Cabinet. There was no Foreign Affairs Committee, while Attlee largely gave him a free hand in most areas other than India. Bevin repaid him with unswerving loyalty, notably during the attempted '*putsch*' by Cripps and Dalton in September 1947. There were moves to get Bevin moved into No. 10 at this time. 'Who do you think I am—Lloyd George?', was one of Bevin's more printable responses. There were no effective restraints on him from within the government, certainly not from his personal enemy, Morrison, who endorsed the broad drift of Bevin's policy, nor from such possible leftish critics as Bevan or Strachey, who found that on issues such as Palestine they were too remote from policy-making to have much effect.

In parliament, of course, Bevin was in unfamiliar territory, but his failure to master parliamentary procedure seldom mattered much.

The parliamentary party usually gave him little serious trouble, despite an occasional revolt over Greece, Palestine, or conscription. The back-bench Foreign Policy Committee, set up under Morrison's reforms to placate MPs, provided a natural platform for Zilliacus, Platts-Mills, Sydney Silverman, and other left-wing gadflies to annoy Bevin. But these regular bouts of pugilism were an irritation to Bevin and a trial for his patience, but little more. The annual party conference usually responded in respectful deference to Bevin's *tours d'horizon* of foreign affairs. After his fierce rebuke to Crossman and others in May 1947 for the Commons 'stab in the back' motion on foreign policy back in November 1946, there was seldom much trouble again. Morgan Phillips's dexterity with the rule book and the trade-union block vote ensured that dissenters were evaded or crushed. The 'trouble-makers' (to use Alan Taylor's imperishable term) found 1945–51 a frustrating time.

But the main reason why Bevin's position within the party and movement was so secure was that his policy anyway produced general agreement. Not only the centre and right of the party applauded his vigorous anti-Communism and the build up of the western alliance. *Tribune* by 1949, edited by Michael Foot and Jennie Lee, pronounced that Bevin's foreign policy commanded the broad support of all wings of the movement. Most left-wing critics were disarmed by events in 1947–8 from the 'coup' in Prague to the Berlin blockade and the Tito–Stalin split. Only a few incorrigible fellow-travellers or pacifists, such as S. O. Davies or Emrys Hughes (Keir Hardie's son-in-law), were left to complain, and Bevin could brush them aside with disdain.

The only restraint on Bevin at home, indeed, lay in his own uncertain health. This is an important factor since he spent so much of the years 1945–51 suffering, directly or indirectly, from illness. Back in 1943, a doctor had declared that Bevin had not one sound organ in his body apart from his feet. After the war, he suffered a series of minor heart attacks. But he bounced back astonishingly each time. Only in late 1950, perhaps, could it be argued that his failing health was seriously impairing his performance as Foreign Secretary, for instance over Egypt or in anticipating the looming Anglo-Iranian crisis over the oil refinery at Abadan. Until the last few months, he was supreme not only in Britain but in the western world generally, in the moulding of the post-war world. The process reached an astonishing climax in the period from Marshall's Harvard speech of

June 1947 (which Bevin perhaps took more seriously than Marshall did himself—Denis Healey called Marshall's speech mere 'waffling aloud'), through the founding of OEEC and the Brussels defence pact to the birth of NATO in April 1949. The Russian climb-down over the blockade of West Berlin came at much the same time. However assessed, as a phase of enduring long-term achievement, it is a record unmatched by any Foreign Secretary in our history.

Bevin's ultimate purpose was to give Labour a credible stance in international affairs. From its earlier history, and especially from the thirties, Labour had inherited a confused bundle of sensations, socialist, populist, neo-pacifist, anti-imperialist, deeply suspicious of reality and power in world affairs. Despite the change in the later thirties and the reassessments brought about by the war, these confusions were still far from resolved in July 1945. Many voices then, within the party and outside, called, with more passion than precision, for 'a socialist foreign policy'. This idea, however ambiguous, did register the genuine belief that the 1945 election would mean a revolution in Britain's foreign as well as its domestic policy, after the shameful pre-war record of the right-wing appeasers. Labour came to the Foreign Office, in that sense, with clean hands. Bevin fuelled popular hopes by emphasizing, in a much-misquoted passage, that 'left understands left'. But his move to the Foreign Office soon resulted in calls for a 'socialist foreign policy'—especially when made by such an erratic figure as Richard Crossman, who by 1949 had totally recanted—being exposed as the empty and unrealistic rhetoric it really was.

Bevin's outlook was crucial because Britain in July 1945 manifestly felt itself to be a great power. Britain's post-war decline, like Mark Twain's death, is often exaggerated. Britain was one of the 'big three' who had won the war. It had immense world-wide commitments unique among the nations—strategic, financial, and geopolitical, in the Middle East above all, but also in the Far East, Australasia, throughout Africa, north and south, and in the Caribbean. It was easily the ascendant nation in western Europe, the one major power Hitler had never been able to invade. Of course, Britain's position was in many ways based on an illusion kept alive—especially as regards its financial strength—by such false aids as the sterling balances. The US loan of December 1945 was vitally necessary not only to maintain Britain's world-wide military and naval pretensions, but even to keep the essentials of Labour's programme at home in being.

Bevin's handling of this illusory position, as Alan Bullock describes it, went through three main phases. There was a period of uncertainty and frustration down to the late spring of 1947, with endless deadlock in negotiations with the Russians and much acrimony in the Council of Foreign Ministers. There were no results to show, apart from the clear evidence of British economic weakness, revealed in successive decisions in early 1947 to withdraw from Greece, India, and Palestine. Bevin's bugle note of advance covered a saga of imperial retreat. The merger of the British and US zones in Germany, the 'bizone' of January 1947, was also partly the result of Britain's manifest economic difficulties in feeding and running its own zone of occupation. Then there followed the astonishing phase of achievement and diplomatic triumph of, roughly, June 1947 to May 1949, noted earlier. Finally, there came a time of consolidation and of renewed challenge, symbolized by the outbreak of the Korean War in June 1950. Bevin's policy, especially in terms of the Anglo-American relationship and the future of western European defence arrangements, was still in some flux at the time of his death.

But his legacy stood the test of time; much of it still provides the parameters of our contemporary world. For historians of the British labour movement, Bevin's time at the Foreign Office is fascinating for the transformation in attitudes it implied. For a party long pacifist in its instincts, it meant a long-term policy of high defence expenditure, military conscription in peacetime, and even the covert commitment to Britain's possession of nuclear weapons on an independent basis. For a movement deeply anti-German ('I regard them all as Huns', Dalton sagely observed in 1951), it meant a political settlement with Germany and the gradual association of the Federal Republic with the political and defence strategies of the democratic western nations. Hopes that German steel barons would be nationalized into oblivion were set aside, partly under US pressure. For a party of 'little Englanders' (including many Welsh and Scots), it meant a new involvement of Britain with the defence and security arrangements of continental Europe for the rest of the century, as embodied in the Brussels Treaty of March 1948. And, for men and women sometimes moved by an almost Pavlovian hostility to capitalist America and the omnipotence of Wall Street, it meant a lasting commitment to a military and economic alliance with the United States, dating from early collaboration in facing up to Stalin during the Iran crises of 1945–6, through the forming of the German 'bizone' and the later conception of the Marshall Plan, down to the military arrangements of NATO, and the economic collaboration of OEEC and the European Recovery Programme. The spectre of a return to US isolationism was dispelled for ever. In return, a succession of Labour Foreign Secretaries between 1945 and 1979—Bevin, Morrison, Gordon-Walker, Stewart (twice), Brown, Callaghan, Crosland, and Owen—were passionate exponents of the belief that Labour was the White House party.

Most shattering of all, for British socialists committed to a sentimental tenderness for fellow socialist regimes from 1917 onwards, a feeling rekindled by the victories of the Red Army during the war, it implied a stern, unrelenting hostility to the Soviet Union. Bevin's personal animosity towards Molotov, whom he saw (correctly) as, among other things, a mass criminal, embodied the mood of the time. This all amounted to an astonishing series of redefinitions, even revolutions, in Labour attitudes towards the world outside. But, save for a handful of fellow-travellers or crypto-Communists such as Solley, Platts-Mills, and Zilliacus, the change was accepted with remarkably little dissent in Labour ranks. Even Crossman became almost an Atlanticist. Certainly, he effectively deserted the 'third force' objectives of 'Keep Left'. By 1948 Aneurin Bevan himself was an enthusiastic supporter of most of Bevin's policies. He was anxious to back up the Berlin airlift with the dispatch of a task force of British tanks through the Soviet zone. The Russian aggression towards Tito's Yugoslavia, a country he much admired for its experiments in workers' democracy, made Bevan doubly anti-Soviet at the time. The view expressed by the British ambassador, Sir Oliver Franks, in June 1950, that Britain had achieved a unique international influence since 1947 through its interlocking special relationship to the United States, its headship of the sterling area and the Commonwealth, and its lead in western Europe, could have commanded the general assent of most of the British labour movement at that time. Certainly Bevin, a Bristolian like Franks, endorsed it in every detail. Under no subsequent Foreign Secretary, Labour or Tory, has Britain's international role seemed anything like so imposing since.

But, even at the time, there was criticism of Bevin's policy, both in detail and in broad design. It often betrayed a strident nationalism, for instance in his attachment to British possession of a nuclear arsenal. It was deeply permeated by a traditional attachment to the cult of empire (though his 1950 Colombo plan showed a more creative side). Bevin was unhappy about the transfer of power in India, a rare area of disagreement with Attlee. He had an almost obsessive fascination with the Middle East, a region of which he knew virtually nothing at first hand but which became the pivot of his policy. He claimed to approach the Middle East with radical objectives: 'peasants, not pashas', was his slogan. He aimed to replace the old direct imperialism with a more indirect and equal form of partnership with modernizing regimes in the Middle East, especially in the states around the Persian Gulf. He had some effect, perhaps, in the 'northern tier' of Turkey and Iran.

But the effect of his policy was rather to reinforce Britain's expensive military presence east of Suez. He continued the process of client relationship with friendly, but reactionary, Arab states such as Nuri es Said's Iraq. Bevin saw the preservation of Britain's special role throughout the Middle East as vital for his concept of national survival, for economic reasons in terms of oil supplies, for the strategic purpose of protecting the 'lifeline of empire' in Suez, along the Red Sea and the Persian Gulf, and to ward off the threat of Soviet involvement, real or (quite often) imagined. This could even lead him to ideas of the post-1945 British Commonwealth expanding rather than contracting. In 1945–6 he vainly sought to set its bounds wider yet and wider, adding modern Libya and even perhaps Italian Somaliland to the imperial domain in the Mediterranean and the Horn of Africa. Kipling and Elgar had come again. But it failed, and by the time of his death in April 1951 Bevin's work in the Middle East, and Britain's entire position in that volatile region, were decidedly fragile. William Roger Louis's fine monograph on the 1945–51 period, covering Bevin's policy in the Middle East, is sympathetic to the Foreign Secretary, but nevertheless it depicts a chronicle of failure. Relations were precarious with Egypt; trouble was looming with Iran over Anglo-Iranian oil; Britain's involvement in the Arab world was being partly undermined by the instability in Trans-Jordan, that hyphenated aberration; the Arab League was turning in a pro-Egyptian and anti-British direction; the imperial dominion of the pashas such as Peake and Glubb was increasingly outdated.

Immediately after Bevin's death, the confrontation with Iran over the Abadan refineries underlined the basic futility and failure of Bevin's policy in the Middle East. The withdrawal from the base at Suez in 1954 and the humiliating climb-down of November 1956 by Eden and Lloyd, accompanied by the collapse of Britain's indirect relationship with Iraq, Jordan, and ultimately Aden and South Yemen, left Bevin's policy in shreds. His policy is often invested with visionary, prophetic overtones. In relation to the North Atlantic alliance this is entirely defensible. But in so far as he saw the Middle East as central to Britain's exercise of international influence, his assessments, especially his view of Arab nationalism, can only appear now as inflated and largely misconceived.

Bevin's Middle East obsessions affected the one unmistakable débâcle in foreign policy—the disaster and tragedy of Palestine. Alan Bullock rightly defends him against grosser charges such as anti-Semitism. But he was undoubtedly prejudiced, and culpably so. His understanding of the Palestine problem was fundamentally flawed. He failed to perceive the political, as against the religious, aspects of Zionism. He failed, quite appallingly at times, to gauge how the Holocaust in Europe had charged Jewish emotions to a new pitch of intensity. His handling of the US government was too often maladroit for all the undeniably erratic quality of a Truman administration deeply conscious of the Democratic Jewish vote in the cities. Bevin's crude remarks about the Jews wishing to 'jump to the head of the queue' in migrating to Palestine, or being anxious to move to Palestine because of US quota restrictions which kept them out of New York, struck an alarmingly wrong note. Palestine was a tragic mess in July 1945. It was even worse in May 1948 when the British simply gave up their mandate and ignominiously withdrew, leaving no successor state of any kind in prospect. There was only the certainty of a bloody war for national survival which Bevin expected (and perhaps hoped) the Jews would lose.

On the other hand, Palestine had been insoluble ever since the contradictory pledges given to both Arabs and Jews after the 1917 Balfour Declaration, and by successive governments from that of Lloyd George to that of Churchill. The mandate period of Palestine's history was a saga of intermittent carnage. Bevin's faults in Palestine were, essentially, defects of style and presentation rather than of substance. Never was his crudeness in dealing with the press and the machinery of public relations shown to worse effect. He was, none the less, right in trying to ensure that the US government, however erratic, was directly involved in any permanent settlement of Palestine, partition or no. He was properly anxious to resolve the Palestine question as speedily as was practicable, to patch up relations with the Americans, and to leave himself free to handle other, even more critical, problems in the Middle East, such as the long-standing dispute with Egypt over the Canal Zone. His instinct that any solution, partition or whatever, must be acceptable to Palestinian Arabs as well as to immigrant Jews was surely correct. British Prime Ministers from Churchill to Mrs Thatcher have said much the same. The continuing chaos and violence in the Middle East, recently reproduced in Lebanon and Libya with horrendous effect, reinforced the basic intractability of the problem. Palestine, perhaps, is not wholly to Bevin's discredit. But it does certainly cast an immense doubt over his conception and handling of foreign affairs.

Bevin has also been attacked in another respect, his attitude to European unity. Here there is a more solid case to make for the defence. The circumstances in 1945–51 should not be over-simply equated with those prevailing some years later, whatever one's view of the later EEC. Bevin's view of 'western Europe' was specific and functional. It was shared by Attlee, Morrison, Cripps, and all his major colleagues. It was, effectively, shared also by the Tory opposition, for all Churchill's bombast in the 'European Unity' movement in various European capital cities in 1946–8. Bevin's hostility to the Council of Europe idea in 1948, his blunt opposition to the Schuman Plan for steel and coal in 1950, had only an indirect bearing on whether Britain should have involved herself in the Treaty of Rome in 1956 or the Common Market later on.

It is clear that there was scant economic, political, or legal justification for Britain's joining these French-inspired schemes for European integration in 1948–50, quite apart from the avowed socialist commitment of a British government which had no wish to become a pawn for continental capitalist cartels. The Schuman Plan was not conceived with Britain in mind. Indeed, Schuman himself expected (and hoped) that Britain would reject membership. There were zealots for European unity in the Labour Party in the late 1940s, men like the Australian 'Kim' Mackay, who sought a socialist federal Europe with the erratic collaboration of Mollet or Nenni (though probably not of Kurt Schumacher of the German SPD whose talk of 'reich' and reunification had uncomfortable Hitlerian overtones). But they were a fringe minority. The failure of Britain to involve itself in moves for European unity in Bevin's period is entirely explicable in the light of the prevailing circumstances. It conflicted with Labour's view of the Atlantic and the Commonwealth idea. Bevin could be accused of many things, but not of being a 'little Englander' or an isolationist.

Here and elsewhere, his policy must be measured against the realities of his time. Those who have denounced him as an intransigent cold warrior should measure his response against the quite monolithic rigidity of Soviet foreign policy in Stalin's last phase. With a renewed threat of US isolationism and troop withdrawals in 1945, and a lack of any viable alternative leadership in a ravaged western Europe, Bevin and his nation had to fill a colossal vacuum. In terms of institutions such as Marshall Aid, the OEEC and NATO, he provided solutions that, to a degree, have survived the test of time. The labour movement of his day felt that no other possible course of policy was open. Even British support for US military action in South Korea was applauded even by those on the left, as preferable to the defeatism and deceit of Munich days, for which Labour had attacked the Chamberlainite appeasers at the time.

On the other hand, Bevin's achievement could only be transitory, since it lay on a number of illusions, well understood by several observers at the time. It rested on a gross overestimate of Britain's international role, especially in the Middle East where, even in 1951, the imperial structure was fast crumbling. It rested on a belief in a unique Anglo-American partnership and British leadership in western Europe which, by the mid-1950s, seemed out of date, quite apart from the Suez débâcle. The relations of John Foster Dulles with Churchill, Eden, and Macmillan may suggest many things, but hardly the existence of anything that can meaningfully be called a 'special relationship'. Bevin's policy rested above all on an economic base which was inherently fragile, and imperilled still further by the massive defence expenditure on far-flung imperial outposts which was part of Bevin's policy too. Labour rallied round Bevin's accomplishments in 1945–51 with solidarity and even enthusiasm. But, for the next twenty years, down to the Wilson government's reluctant disengagement east of Suez in the late 1960s, Labour was profoundly divided over the implications of Bevin's legacy. In Gaitskell's time, it became a rock-hard orthodoxy. The rise of CND, romantic and Utopian in many ways, showed that there still existed a deep dismay in the movement and in the country at the scope of Bevin's nuclear policy, adopted almost casually, certainly without public debate or serious inquiry into the scientific or environmental consequences, between 1946 and 1948. The opposition of the physicist, Professor Blackett, to a British nuclear weapons programme, expressed unavailingly in February 1947, was now resurrected. Bevin was a far-seeing, brave man, capable of visionary flights of imagination. Had he lived on, it is possible that he might have tried to adapt his legacy to an international scene in which the cold war, apart from rare confrontations such as Cuba in 1962, became replaced by a wary, but genuine, *détente*. Bevin was the greatest negotiator of his time, supreme in industrial and diplomatic bargaining alike. But 'war, war' rather than 'jaw, jaw' provided the style and substance of his legacy in 1951. Labour has been tearing itself apart about the implications ever since. That, in party terms, is the tragic outcome of Bevin's achievement.

# STAFFORD CRIPPS AS CHANCELLOR

WHEN Sir Stafford Cripps succeeded Hugh Dalton at the Treasury in November 1947, it was popularly seen as marking a decisive shift of tempo and of mood for the Labour government. In place of the ebullient hedonism of Dalton, there would be the stern, monk-like austerity of Cripps. Cheap money would give way to rationing and retrenchment. The buoyant socialist advance of 1945–7 would be replaced by two years or more of hard slog. Above all, morality and high Christian principle would be enthroned anew at No. 11 Downing Street. The *Manchester Guardian* on 15 November diagnosed the new mood with puritan satisfaction: 'Mr Dalton would always yield to the call of popularity. Sir Stafford Cripps will always listen to the call of conscience.'

Of course, in some ways this contemporary contrast between the expansionist Dalton and the Spartan, deflationist Cripps was much overdone. The policy of the Treasury did not change overnight. The most disinflationary budget of the post-war years was, in fact, Dalton's last, in November 1947, just before his enforced resignation over the press 'leak'; it set the pattern for the next three years. It included large cuts in dollar imports (notably food), and a sharp reduction of consumer purchasing power with swingeing rates of purchase tax. Food rationing had existed since the end of the war. Nevertheless, it is hard to deny that, at least at the level of popular psychology, there was a distinct change in the climate thereafter. The Cripps era at the Treasury, which lasted almost three years until the Chancellor's enforced withdrawal from political life through ill-health in October 1950, did project democratic socialism in a totally different way, through the grim imperatives of something resembling a siege economy rather than through glad, self-confident advance. In particular, it meant that the personality and policies of Cripps became totally identified with the ethic of the government. At a time of austerity, cuts, and severe rationing of food and other essentials, Cripps cast his massive shadow over government and nation. He embodied a new morality and sense of public rectitude. Personally, he was a teetotaller and (initially for dietary reasons, but later by choice) a vegetarian. He was obsessive about punctuality. He worked phenomenally long hours, his day beginning with a cold bath at four in the morning. A tendency to insomnia intensified his air of self-flagellation and self-sacrifice. A passionately evangelistic Anglican-ism permeated the land, with the Chancellor ever ready with pro-nouncements on the moral basis of austerity, the evils of materialism, or the Christian's duty of public service. As in Gladstone's day, the Treasury was a citadel of Victorian values.

Both in the 1950 general election and again in 1951 (when he was a dying man), the record of Cripps was the main issue. He had become uniquely identified with the stern public resolve and unbending endeavour of a government associated, Bunyan-like, with all the puritan virtues. 'There, but for the grace of God, goes God', was Churchill's jibe. When the Conservatives under the ebullient Winston returned to power, it seemed somewhat like a cavalier restoration after the grim rule of the saints. Only a handful of com-mentators, then and later, chose to notice that it was the disciplined restraint pursued by Cripps in the late forties that had made possible the affluence and consumer pleasures of the next two decades. Unex-pectedly and ironically, the real legacy of Cripps was to be the so-called permissive society.

This unique personal identification of Cripps with the mood and message of the nation and the party is the more extraordinary because, for most of his career, he was a high-minded maverick, at odds with his comrades and colleagues. Indeed, it is almost impossible to fit him into a conventional political mould at all for most of his life. He grew up in a conventional, affluent, upper-middle-class home in rural Buckinghamshire and Oxfordshire, the son of a Tory MP with strong views on Welsh disestablishment and Church issues generally. Stafford enjoyed a well-upholstered youth, including edu-cation at Winchester and London University, and the comforts of rural life. He began life as a chemist: in 1922, he discovered the inert gas, xenon. When he was in his early thirties, he began a highly successful career at the bar, specializing in the most technical and arcane areas of legal work. His entry into politics, and finally into the Labour Party, came late and in a highly personal way. There were radical impulses in the family background. Cripps was, for example, a nephew of Beatrice Webb. More important still, his father, after moving to the Lords as Lord Parmoor, dramatically turned to the Labour Party after the end of the first world war, mainly because of that party's internationalism and Hendersonian idealism in world affairs, and served in MacDonald's Labour Cabinets of 1924 and 1929.

But the abiding moral impulse for Cripps's socialism, without doubt, was his intense commitment to the Anglican Church, including much active work in the Oxford diocese and the House of Laymen of the Church Assembly. While his brother (a bachelor who inherited the peerage) stayed a Conservative and became a fox-hunting bursar of The Queen's College, Oxford, Stafford moved to the left. His Anglicanism was of a distinctly practical and social kind. His main public activity in the 1920s lay in the World Alliance of the Churches for promoting international friendship. He thus found a focus for his idealism; he also met other Social Christians such as William Temple, then Bishop of Manchester. He did not, however, join the Labour Party until just after the 1929 general election, when he was forty years old. Ultimately, it was the Christian ethic of Tawney and Temple, rather than practical events such as the General Strike, that impelled him into politics. He entered the party (and, shortly, parliament and the Labour government as Solicitor-General in early 1931) in a highly personal fashion. He remained the isolated, inexhaustible pilgrim to the end.

In the thirties, as is well known, Cripps followed his individual credo in remarkable, even revolutionary, directions. Narrowly retaining his seat at Bristol in the electoral rout of 1931, he moved to the further reaches of the far left. In the Socialist League he preached the cause of total socialist transformation, with emergency measures demanded to neutralize the instinctive opposition of Crown, court, civil service, City, and the capitalist class towards an incoming Labour government. He caused a stir by a well-timed attack on Buckingham Palace. After the Socialist League faded away, he then turned his energies to the crusade for a Popular Front with the Communists, Liberals, and all anti-fascists devoted to the fall of the National government. He varied this with the idea of a Unity Front with the Communists alone, fortified by the heady impulse of the war in Spain. Down to 1939, he remained an inflexible advocate of a Popular Front; he used the weekly *Tribune*, which he largely financed from 1937, to promote the cause. In the end, in January 1939, along with Aneurin Bevan and George Strauss, he was expelled from the party. It set the seal on a decade of relentless, if wholly ineffective, left-wing militancy.

Cripps's position, in fact, was less revolutionary than it sometimes appeared. He was no Marxist and no pacifist. He opposed voting for the arms estimates on the grounds that the National government was an imperialist regime which adopted an unremitting hostility to the Soviet Union. Always, his outlook was infused with an earnest, febrile Christianity. He personified the eternal upper-class outsider, a non-fascist Mosley (to whom Bevin freely compared him). What is clear is that, neither by doctrine nor by personal association, did he fit into any recognizable niche within the Labour Party. He had only two brief periods on the NEC, in the mid-thirties, and in October 1937 to January 1939. He stood outside all the main policy reassessments associated with men like Morrison and Dalton after 1932. Naïve, impressionable and erratic, he had no obvious place within a party and a movement advancing to a more centrist and rational position under the aegis of Attlee and Bevin, leaving the old Utopian rhetoric behind. The trade unions regarded him as an enemy. His variously chosen instruments for popular crusading, the Socialist League, the Unity campaign, the Constituency Parties' Association, the Petition Campaign of 1939, all collapsed in turn. It was a record of continuous frustration and failure which left Cripps almost exulting in his isolation in the wilderness.

The war years saw his career take another extraordinary turn, one which took him even further from the Labour mainstream. A strong patriotic commitment to the war effort in 1939 led into new links with liberal Conservatives such as Butler and Stanley—and even with the Foreign Secretary, Lord Halifax, who shared his high Anglicanism and his interest in India. Cripps's call for a new, positive relationship with the Soviet Union then led to his remarkable appointment as ambassador to Moscow by Churchill in May 1940. He stayed there, amidst many storms with his Prime Minister over demands for British aid to Russia, until early 1942. It might have been supposed that Cripps, given his role in the thirties, would have found first-hand exposure to the Soviet regime a further stimulant to his leftish enthusiasms. In fact, he returned from Moscow in more realistic mood, almost as disillusioned with Stalinism as with the policies of the Churchill government. It was a time when, before and after the fall of Tobruk, Churchill's position as premier appeared under threat. Cripps, his stature refurbished after his mission to Moscow, seemed to be the new Messiah. In February 1942 he entered the War Cabinet as Leader of the House and Lord Privy Seal. Leftish

Conservatives, some newspaper editors, military experts like Liddell Hart who had once looked nostalgically to a possible return of the aged Lloyd George, now saw in Cripps the fresh symbol of leadership, planning, and a new executive drive in the supreme command. Cripps's commitment to dogmatic socialism appeared a thing of the past. Orwell was alarmed to find in 1942 that Cripps was oblivious to the doctrinal niceties of capitalism or socialism. Technocracy was all.

Another episode in early 1942 helped impel Cripps to a more centrist position. This was his celebrated mission to India which included the famous 'offer' of self-government to the Congress leaders. Cripps had had a close involvement with Indian politics for several years, and had actually been to India in December 1939 to try to negotiate with the leaders of the Muslim League. In fact, his mission to India, like that to Moscow, was a sobering and disillusioning experience. His 'offer' was rejected, and led to a severe breach with Gandhi, Nehru, and the Congress. After a wave of passive resistance, many Congress leaders were then imprisoned, and nationalist passions in the subcontinent became far more inflamed. Cripps's credentials as a man of the far left had taken a further battering. His own views shifted accordingly.

The great Cripps boom did not survive 1942. Churchill, reinforced in public esteem after El Alamein, finally managed to outmanoeuvre Cripps in November without undue difficulty. Cripps's latest offer of resignation was accepted, and he spent the last two years of the war, in relative obscurity, as a very efficient Minister of Aircraft Production. He remained aloof from his former Labour colleagues. He did not actually rejoin the Labour Party until as late as March 1945. In the 1945 general election, enough of his wartime charisma survived for him to be viewed as a major figure, destined for high office in the event of a Labour victory. His campaign speeches, however, were distinctly bipartisan, with heavy emphasis on communal endeavour and partnership between both sides of industry. He entered Attlee's Cabinet in July 1945 as President of the Board of Trade, still an ambiguous and widely distrusted figure, but with his location in the political spectrum totally transformed by the events of war.

Cripps's future progress, more than that of most members of the Attlee government, seemed peculiarly hard to predict in 1945. In fact, he emerged, along with Bevan, as the one major figure of the government whose reputation rose steadily between 1945 and 1947. No other minister gave such an impression of command, competence, and inner confidence. Conversely, his reputation and ideological position were still distinctly complicated. He still kept, despite all the curious events of the war years, a powerful reputation as a man of the left. He remained on cordial terms with Aneurin Bevan, their friendship dating from the Popular Front and early *Tribune* years before the war. Back-benchers like Michael Foot saw in him a friend in need. He was among the very few ministers between 1945 and 1951 who could be plausibly regarded, both by civil servants at close quarters and the public at large, as a committed socialist. In the great Cabinet debate on the nationalization of iron and steel in the summer of 1947—a kind of litmus test of the government's socialist resolve—Cripps, after some hesitation, threw his weight behind Bevan, Dalton, and the advocates of public ownership. On the other hand, his policy at the Board of Trade was far removed from state socialism. His early announcement that the nationalization of the cotton spinning industry was not on the agenda possibly cost him the resignation of a junior minister, Ellis Smith (another view, however, is that Smith was dropped for simple incompetence), and much argument with his PPS, Barbara Castle, a Lancashire member. He caused a minor sensation in October 1946 by announcing that any kind of workers' control was inconceivable because of the ignorance of the workforce in the skills of management. His policy generally was one of partnership with both sides of industry, symbolized by the 'working parties' set up in cotton, pottery, hosiery, and other industries. He gave particular attention to industrial design. He was the driving force behind the setting up in June 1947 of the new Economic Planning Council under Edwin Plowden, who respected Cripps's powerful Social Christianity and non-party economic approach.

Throughout these years, as the reputations of men like Dalton, Morrison, Greenwood, even Attlee himself fluctuated, Cripps's prestige inexorably rose. It was not seriously impaired by a further unsuccessful visit to India. This was the Cabinet mission he headed in March–June 1946 which conducted inconclusive negotiations with both Hindu and Muslim leaders. Cripps's own commitment to an all-India assembly, and his personal bias towards the Hindus in the Congress, came to little with the eventual partition. Even so, he was plausibly presented as one of the architects of Indian self-government and the creation of a new Commonwealth. India did him no harm, though it might well have done if his own suggestion in late 1946 that he replace Wavell as Viceroy had been accepted by Attlee. Despite India, he remained in the summer of 1947 an immensely powerful, authoritative member of the Cabinet. Nor was his reputation harmed by a somewhat unsuccessful involvement with the fuel shortage early that year, the main blame falling (correctly) on Shinwell.

Then his position was dramatically elevated in the financial crisis of July–August 1947. He alone in a shaken government kept his nerve. He emerged with a clear plan of campaign, and the self-confidence to face up to a huge run on the reserves which had destroyed Dalton, humbled Morrison, and brought the all-conquering Labour government to its knees.

His new authority in the administration was clearly recognized thereafter. Above all, it was recognized by Cripps himself. With his usual political naïveté, he approached Attlee in September 1947 suggesting that he should stand down as Prime Minister. As noted above, Bevin was his favoured alternative, though it was clear that he had in mind another candidate nearer home. Attlee responded with the political deftness that Churchill had shown in similarly frustrating Cripps in November 1942, but with the major difference that Cripps's position in the government was markedly strengthened as a result. On the principle of the higher-minded the man, the higher the offer, Attlee offered him a new post, as Minister of Economic Affairs, with huge powers over trade, exports, and production. He would be backed up by major new Cabinet Economic and Production Committees. The logjam in the machinery of government would thus be by-passed. Cripps emerged as the unquestioned victor from the turmoil of the financial crisis of mid-1947. As the stars of Morrison and Dalton waned, as even Attlee's own reputation slumped, Cripps emerged as uniquely capable of supplying direction, leadership, and a sense of purpose to a flagging, dispirited government. When, through the freak incident of the budget leak, Cripps succeeded Dalton as Chancellor in November, it carried the logic of events to its appointed conclusion. Thenceforward, the very survival of the Labour government, perhaps of the nation, rested in the hands of that reformed maverick and twice-born centrist, Stafford Cripps.

Cripps's time at the Treasury over the next three years is a highly distinctive period of British economic and political history. It saw the promotion of successful new policies for exports overseas, planned consumption and wage restraint at home. But it was above all a triumph of the will, and of one extraordinary man's indomitable spirit and sense of moral purpose. He was, of course, enormously assisted by the Marshall Aid Programme, channelled to Britain under the European Recovery Programme from mid-1948 onwards. Britain was, in fact, to be the recipient of the largest slice of American assistance over the next four years, even more so than West Germany. Nevertheless, the domestic contribution of the government and of Cripps himself was undeniably impressive. The Chancellor had a firm commitment to Britain's becoming economically self-reliant, free from the shackles of unpredictable currency movements or balance of payments difficulties, and free also from dependence on US loans. To this end, an enormous impulse was given to exports and to domestic production.

The year 1948 saw all records broken in an export-led boom. By the end of the year, the horrors of the previous year were a thing of the past, and the balance of payments (in deficit by £443m. in 1947) was actually in surplus. Cripps had before him a target of exceeding pre-war exports (based on 1938 figures) by over 150 per cent. This was easily achieved by 1951. Unemployment, still uncomfortably high in depressed regions like South Wales in 1946, now virtually disappeared. Production of coal and steel rose substantially. Motor manufacturers became exporters on a massive scale: Land Rover sales were particularly successful. Vast inroads were made into North American markets with their precious dollar earnings. Stimulated by the government's active regional policy for relocating new industries in the older industrial areas, regions like Clydeside, the North-East, Cumbria, Merseyside, and South Wales were throbbing with new life. The shipyards of Swan Hunter, Cammell Laird, and Harland and Wolff had full order-books. Coal was again exported from the long-dormant ports of Cardiff and Newcastle, even if only in limited quantities.

To the general public, Cripps's undeniable successes were a triumph for socialist planning. Certainly the entire apparatus of economic direction, with the Economic Planning Staff under Plowden, annual economic reviews issued by the Treasury, and major Cabinet committees, including those for Economic Policy, Production (where, according to Douglas Jay, 'the main work was done'), Import Programmes, Overseas Negotiations, and much besides, appeared to

resemble *dirigisme* of a carefully organized, interlocking kind. At the
apex of the machinery of economic decision-making stood the mighty
figure of Cripps himself. The most politically powerful Chancellor
perhaps since Lloyd George, he combined the old functions of the
Treasury with those carved out for the new Economic Affairs Ministry
in September 1947. The balance of payments and the rates of exchange; budgetary and tax policy; the control of expenditure; wages,
dividends and investment; overseas aid and development all came
within the mighty purview of the Chancellor, with considerable
influence over the Board of Trade and other departments as well.
Never, it seemed, had the British economy, flagging since late-
Victorian days, been wrenched so single-mindedly into decisive
action by one dynamic figure.

In fact, though, it is clear that Cripps's commitment to planning
was more apparent (or perhaps cosmetic) than real. Originally
trained as a chemist, his objective was scientific efficiency, his
method, partnership. As one dedicated to the values of the mixed
economy, with all the zeal of a convert, Cripps sought above all to
collaborate with private industry rather than to coerce or threaten
it. Planning, in Cripps's view, related primarily to the domain of
consumption rather than to production. The main instrument lay
in management through the budget and the command of capital
movements and investment, rather than through direct planning.
Certainly, essential physical controls were retained—those for building, imports, raw material allocation, and the location of new industry. Yet in fact, Cripps's three years at the Treasury were marked by
a steady retreat from planning. Many lesser physical controls were
dismantled, most enthusiastically so by Harold Wilson with his famous 'bonfire', while at the Board of Trade. The rigours of rationing
and licences were sharply modified in 1949–50 (partly at the behest
of Morrison, who warned his colleagues that they were desperately
unpopular among the middle-class vote which Labour was anxious
to retain). The annual economic surveys became indicative rather
than directive; from the autumn of 1948 they largely lost their force,
although they continued to be published until the late 1950s. In the
end, Cripps's planning resembled not so much state socialism but
something resembling the *mélange* of public and private activity that
characterized Roosevelt's New Deal of the thirties. Cripps's public
facade of unbending rigour concealed a policy of a fluid and flexible
kind. But it worked, and famously revived the fortunes and spirits of
the Labour government.

Cripps's eclecticism emerged in financial policy as well. He expanded capital formation until 1949 and then contracted it. He was a budgetary-demand manager rather than a fully-committed Keynesian, though no doubt closer to the Keynesian position than Dalton had been. On broad matters of financial policy, Cripps was agnostic or uncertain. The most spectacular example came with the approach to devaluation of sterling in the summer of 1949. Despite a background of a deteriorating balance of payments in the first quarter of the year, Cripps set his face strongly against devaluation. He told an economic conference at Rome in May that 'it was neither necessary nor would it take place'. Partly, it may have been a moral sentiment after repeated pledges to Europeans and Commonwealth allies that Britain would not devalue. Cripps prided himself on being a man of his word. Partly, there were technical fears about finding the correct rate of exchange and sticking to it. Partly it may have been simple fear of Labour again suffering from a slide of sterling such as brought it down in 1931. One close adviser, Lord Trend, saw Cripps torn between his role as planner and a Treasury Minister of a traditional kind.

At any rate, Cripps was almost the last member of the government to agree to devaluation. In turn, Bevin, Morrison, even Bevan gave it their reluctant assent. Young economics ministers like Gaitskell and Jay (with ambiguous support from Harold Wilson) gave it enthusiastic backing. Cripps remained adamant, until he was removed to a Swiss clinic for treatment for illness (in fact, a premonition of the cancer that was later to kill him). In effect, he was presented with a *fait accompli* by his colleagues, in a statement written by Douglas Jay but presented to him by Wilson who travelled to Zurich to see the ailing Chancellor. With extreme reluctance, Cripps gave way, and the devaluation of the pound to $2.80 was announced in September, after his return to active duty. In effect, the external value of the currency fell by a third. Churchill afterwards accused Cripps of deceiving the nation over devaluation. Angrily, Cripps refused to accept an honorary doctoral degree from him at Bristol University.

However, what Cripps had accepted with reluctance was again turned to advantage. Devaluation proved a mighty boost to exports, and the decline in the balance of payments soon began to be reversed. His final year at the Treasury down to nearly the end of 1950 was thus a further successful period, with the cost of living stable, the balance of payments in the black, and British industry enjoying growth and prosperity unknown since Edwardian days. Cripps had not handled devaluation well, perhaps had not even understood its macro-economic implications, for all his immense intellectual gifts. At one excited moment, he complained to Gaitskell that right-wing civil servants were trying to sabotage his so-called 'socialist' policies. Yet the outcome was to reinforce his policy and his position in the government, and to fuel a belief that Labour had truly turned the corner and that the worst was behind it.

The domestic aspects of Cripps's period are the best-known, perhaps notorious. These saw, of course, extremes of rationing and austerity, with pathetically small quantities of milk, eggs, bacon, and sugar available for the hard-pressed consumer, and 'Bread Units' in operation until late 1948. Petrol was also rationed, as was clothing under the 'points' system. Cripps declared himself against the 'new look' in women's fashion and in favour of distinctly shorter skirts— not for the usual male reasons but because of the savings in textile supplies that would result. These were in many ways grim years, of course, hallowed in popular memory by recollections of whalemeat, reindeer steak, and 'snoek', that unknown and inedible fish from the Indian Ocean. Comedy programmes on a generally hostile BBC, and in the right-wing tabloid press, mercilessly pilloried Cripps and his colleagues, while the self-styled Housewives' League led a populist campaign against the Chancellor and all his miserable works. There is no doubt that much middle-class disaffection with the government resulted, and the defection of suburban and commuter constituencies away from the Labour Party in Greater London and elsewhere in the 1950 and 1951 elections can be clearly foreshadowed.

At the same time, amongst Labour's mass working-class supporters, Cripps and his policies seem to have been generally popular. Rationing was, of course, not welcomed. Neither was the total wage freeze that the unions reluctantly accepted in the 1948– 50 period as the domestic side of a policy of restraint. Devaluation somewhat increased the cost of living for hard-pressed and underfed consumers. On the other hand, Cripps's policies emphatically confirmed the existence of the welfare state, full employment, and full pay packets. Inflation was no problem, and bank rate did not reach 2 per cent. Surplus private savings could be diverted to remarkably cheap sport or popular entertainment, or to such new delights as the holiday camps of Billy Butlin, or the vogue for the dance hall. Football in particular reached new heights of popularity; Stanley Matthews was Stafford Cripps in boots. Labour's battles were being partly won on the playing fields of Highbury or Old Trafford, if hardly of Eton.

Apart from the vogue for sport and recreation, there is much evidence, too, that the converse of the restrictions of rationing was a vastly enhanced basic standard of living, including great improvements in health, housing, and environmental development, for working-class people. Children, in particular, were beneficiaries of social welfare as Cripps interpreted it. The sense of equality, enshrined in the popular slogan of 'fair shares', was manifest. The capital levy in the 1948 budget embodied it. As a result, Labour's fortunes in the opinion polls and in key by-elections notably revived under Cripps's regime. Difficult contests at such places as South Hammersmith in 1949 saw Labour's working-class vote remain solid, and the seat held. Cripps was by the start of 1950 generally seen, not as a popular scapegoat at all, but as perhaps Labour's major asset. Indeed, he might have turned his success to greater advantage had he not insisted on an early, and ill-timed, election in February 1950, for fear of having to introduce an electioneering budget in April to which he objected on moralistic grounds. Even so, the fact that Labour won the 1950 election at all, and that it remained in excellent heart until the new strains fatally imposed by the Korean War from June onwards, represented a great triumph for Cripps and his strength of will.

For much of the 1947–50 period, Cripps was regarded as the strong man of the Cabinet, the most likely successor to Attlee should a change arise. Gaitskell in April 1948 had a strong sense that, in attending a dinner party at Cripps's at which Strauss, Strachey, Jay, Marquand, Wilson, himself, and (eventually) Bevan were present, 'Stafford was surveying his future Cabinet'. The very ambiguousness of Cripps's present and past now served him well. He retained his old left-wing credentials, including his important friendship with Bevan. This enabled him to defuse difficult Cabinet crises with his Welsh colleague over prescription charges in the autumn of 1949 and over NHS charges in February 1950. In both cases, Cripps, unlike Gaitskell a year later, gracefully withdrew. For all the rigours of austerity, Cripps pleased the left by maintaining a high priority for social spending, for welfare and regional employment policies, and for food subsidies, against which Treasury mandarins continued to protest.

On the other hand, his broad economic policy, as refashioned by men like Plowden and Robert Hall of the Cabinet Office economic section, was broadly supra-party; the socialist zeal was squeezed out. The devaluation crisis in August–September 1949 somewhat dented Cripps's reputation, but the major factor in diminishing his position was not political at all, but rather his growing ill-health throughout 1950. On other non-economic issues, he seems to have endorsed the main conclusions of his colleagues—strongly anti-Soviet in foreign policy; committed to the North Atlantic alliance; mainly hostile to moves for European integration (though he showed some sympathy with the notion of the Schuman Plan at first); a warm supporter of the new Commonwealth. In domestic terms, he was a consolidationist like Morrison (and practically everybody). His face was set against further nationalization after iron and steel. The fight for economic recovery was the overriding priority. He opposed the nationalization of insurance companies because of the potential damage to invisible earnings. He remained an aloof figure in many ways. He had little contact with his Bristol constituency, while not until 1949 did he play any part at the annual party conference. Nevertheless, when he retired from the Treasury in October 1950, his successor proving to be Dalton's choice, Gaitskell, rather than Bevan whom he himself preferred, his reputation was at its height. At the end, if only then, Cripps and his party were in perfect harmony.

Cripps's contribution to the history of the labour movement was a decidedly curious one. Down to 1945, he was an eccentric, individual figure, apparently impossible to contain within the mainstream of the party. Perhaps he was not really a Labour man at all. His style of life at Filkins and later was comfortable, even 'squirearchical'. He had a passion for country life; his son, John, appropriately became editor of the *Countryman*, and served for many years as chairman of the Countryside Commission. Much of Cripps's career was almost wilfully negative. Had Labour not won in 1945, it would surely have been viewed as largely a failure, both at home and in external ventures to Russia and India. Yet his achievement as minister after 1945, especially as Chancellor, was colossal. In many ways, he was the most obviously effective exponent of executive power that any Labour government had ever known. He wielded power with a puritan style of a highly distinctive kind. After all, his Christianity derived from the upper reaches of high Anglicanism, rather than from the democratic populism of the chapels from which much of Labour's ethic had been drawn. He applied power, in part, through a battery of controls inherited from the war, which have played a diminishing part in economic policy ever since. Like Tawney, he seemed to view physical controls as an appendix to the Thirty-Nine Articles. Still, Cripps did have a clear, unambiguous policy that Labour's social programmes and its practical idealism must rest on a secure material base.

Almost alone of Labour's Chancellors, he linked the socialist advance with technocracy, modernization, and productive efficiency. And he did so without losing sight of the moral values that had captivated him as a young Christian. He was not a trained economist, but his intellectual power enabled him to turn the Keynesian policies of progressive advisers like Plowden, Robert Hall, and Otto Clarke into effective mechanisms for action. Sir Alec Cairncross, one of Cripps's advisers then, has entitled his masterly survey of post-1945 British economic policy 'Years of Recovery'. Of that recovery, really applicable from September 1947 onwards, Cripps was without doubt the main architect. Many of the rows in which he was involved in his earlier years now seem distinctly dated; his own method of handling them was no model to follow. But he was a man of government, not a leader in opposition. In his years of greatness, he sacrificed himself to ensure that Labour placed hard-headedness alongside warm-heartedness. His achievement was to show that Labour now was truly fit to govern.

# HERBERT MORRISON

BETWEEN 1945 and 1950, Herbert Morrison was universally acclaimed as one of Labour's 'big three', along with Attlee and Bevin. Alone of this supreme troika, his reputation has slumped markedly since his death. Attlee is now acclaimed as the all-wise leader, hailed on the left as the pilot of socialist revolution, revered on the right as the epitome of reformist common sense. Bevin often receives bouquets across the political spectrum, as a Foreign Secretary whose achievement merits comparison with any of his predecessors since the days of Cromwell. Morrison, by contrast, has won no such esteem. His reputation, such as it is, has been viewed from a humbler perspective as belonging to a lower, perhaps disreputable, plane of political machination. At the time, he was frequently condemned as little more than a caucus politician. Charles Key in 1944 accused him of having nothing more than the mind of an election agent. 'A fifth-rate Tammany boss' was Aneurin Bevin's famous epithet. This record continued to pursue Morrison beyond the grave. When writing on Roger Liddle, the amiable SDP candidate in the April 1986 Fulham by-election, Alan Watkins in *The Observer* commented (surprisingly to Liddle's former tutor) that he represented the 'brutalizing tendency' of an old type of socialist. He would have been at home, Watkins added, 'in the Labour Party of Herbert Morrison'. We may be sure that no compliment was intended.

This view of Morrison as a political boss, nationally and locally, arises in part, of course, because that is precisely what he was. He built up his position in the party as the most influential operator of local government politics that Labour has ever known. Further he achieved this in London, which had been down to the mid-1920s a notoriously weak area for the left, apart from the homogeneous working-class strongholds of such areas as Stepney and Poplar in the East End, and Bermondsey and Rotherhithe around dockland. Herbert Morrison virtually created the London Labour Party and made it the most formidable of fighting machines. He was himself the quintessential embodiment of the cockney spirit, chirpy, full of backchat. In a famous victory in 1934 he captured the London County Council for Labour. The new Waterloo Bridge became his symbol of victory over the Tory Napoleonic Old Guard. For six remarkable years he directed Labour's London administration. He launched a period of unbroken Labour control of the metropolis, founded on sound and prudent government, rather than the wider radical causes—feminist, ethnic, Irish, gay lib, and otherwise—identified with the GLC under Ken Livingstone's regime in the 1980s. A new generation of municipal reformers, including Lewis Silkin, Charles Latham, and Ike Hayward took control. Morrison's roots in local government were never forgotten. In the Attlee government he was champion of the municipal and local idea, protesting at the way in which the National Health Service or the public ownership of the gas or electricity services eroded the spirit of civic enterprise and local patriotism. On the other hand, ironically, no politician either was more closely linked with the centralizing force of nationalization.

Morrison's achievement in local government, soon to be explained in depth in a major new study by John Rowett, was an abiding source of pride to him. It left a legacy of a very positive kind in the well-built schools, homes, and development programmes that marked Labour's contribution to municipal socialism in the pre-Thatcher years. But it was always linked with the reputation for Morrison as a fixer, happiest in the secret caucus conclaves of the smoke-filled room. It was a reputation that did him much harm in the wider circles of the party. When he first stood for the party leadership in 1935, his image of ambition and comparative lack of scruple cost him dearly. He was overtaken by the obscure and relatively unproven Attlee, with whom he never really struck up a wholly trusting relationship over the next twenty years in peace and in war. The Prime Minister decided such sensitive matters as the remodelling of the government in September 1947 and the timing of both the 1950 and 1951 elections when Morrison was out of the country, and against his known advice. Attlee seems to have stayed on as leader until the autumn of 1955 to ensure that Morrison made no effective come-back, twenty years on. He lived on to deride Morrison's autobiography and the details of his will which revealed Morrison's estate as being larger than had been surmised. As Attlee went, so went the party. It is indisputable that Morrison did arouse much distrust, both for his internal party manœuvres, in such critical times as the very aftermath of Labour's election victory in July 1945 or the financial crisis of August 1947 (when on both occasions he made a clear bid for the leadership, to the disgust of Bevin and other proven enemies).

For posterity, he can seem cast in a humdrum mould, a man of parochial outlook, not a bad mayor of Hackney, but little more.

There is, indeed, none of Labour's major figures after 1945 who more urgently need rehabilitation, and John Rowett's coming biography will be eagerly awaited as a result. Morrison was in himself an unhappy individual, with a miserable, sexless first marriage, partly compensated for by a long attachment to Ellen Wilkinson, and by various other affairs. He had his friends in the party and the movement, notably journalists such as Maurice Webb and Leslie Hunter. But an array of Cabinet colleagues, Bevin and Dalton, Shinwell and Bevan, disliked him with a bitterness close to hatred. Without doubt, they seriously underestimated him, as historians have often done since, despite the publication in 1973 of Bernard Donoughue and George Jones's excellent biography.

It is clear that Morrison was an outstanding socialist and Labour leader. In many ways he was unique in the entire history of the party, for the example of sheer administrative competence and professionalism that he offered. He was, as noted above, a pioneer of local government of quite exceptional talent and importance. At the LCC in the 1920s and 1930s, he imposed his personality on the politics of the metropolis as no single individual had done since the days of Wilkes. Through his expertise on transport and electricity, he moved on to the wider national stage with aplomb. He was a very skilful Minister of Transport under Ramsay MacDonald, when his London Passenger Transport Board became the model for a new system of public enterprise, including the work of Pick and Holden on architecture and design. Even the bus stops were works of art. During the war years under Churchill, after a brief and unhappy time at Supply, he was a marvellously effective Home Secretary, with a high visibility that made him second only to Bevin in his impact on domestic opinion on the home front. Not only was he a vigorous director of local services, including the vital area of air-raid precautions and repair; there was a more idealistic side also which saw the relaxation of the 18B restrictions upon dissenters, even Sir Oswald Mosley, which provoked much flak from the left. He was less authoritarian than might have been expected from a policeman's son. Since Morrison is commonly regarded as the archetype of the Tammany right-winger, it is also worth recalling that he was never a union nominee as, say, Bevin or Bevan were. He was at times at odds with Deakin and other trade-union barons, for example over

1. Keir Hardie addressing a suffragette meeting in
Trafalgar Square, 1912

2. Ramsay MacDonald while
   Prime Minister

3. Sidney and Beatrice Webb c.1900

6. Miners' Federation of Great Britain executive committee, Scarborough, July 1925: Noah Ablett is seated, in the middle of the bottom row.

5. William Abraham ('Mabon') c.1900

4. Victor Grayson waiting to address a meeting, c.1910

8. Harold Laski, Labour Party conference, Bournemouth, 1946

7. Arthur Henderson leaving for his Burnley constituency, September 1931

10. Douglas Jay as Economic Secretary to the Treasury, 1949

9. Ellen Wilkinson at the time of the formation of the Attlee Cabinet, August 1945

11. Evan Durbin in 1947

12. Hugh Dalton while Chancellor of the Exchequer

13. Clement Attlee while Prime Minister

14. Ernest Bevin meeting Molotov at the Foreign
Office, 11 September 1945

15. Sir Stafford Cripps preparing his budget, 5 April 1949

16. Herbert Morrison and Ellen Wilkinson during 1945 general
election campaign

17. Christopher, Viscount Addison. *c.* 1930

18. Hugh Gaitskell and James Griffiths with Julius Nyerere at
1956 Labour Party conference

19. Aneurin Bevan, while Minister of Health, speaking at Labour Party Conference, Margate, 5 October 1950

20. Hugh Gaitskell in his study after being elected leader of the Labour Party, December 1955

21. Morgan Phillips, with Denis Healey and Len Williams, at Transport House, *c.*1950

22. Rita Hinden in the *Socialist Commentary* offices in the 1950s (the portrait behind her is of Sidney Webb)

23. Harold Wilson entering Downing Street
after being elected Prime Minister, 17
October 1964

24. James Callaghan at Downing Street on
his first day as Prime Minister, 6 April 1976

25. Michael Foot while Labour leader,
11 September 1981

26. Joe Gormley with Mick McGahey at the TUC Congress at
Brighton, 1 September 1980

27. Arthur Scargill at the Orgreave coking plant, near Rotherham, during the miners' strike, 29 May 1984

28. Denis Healey while Chancellor of the Exchequer, March 1976

29. A left-wing trio, Tony Benn, Arthur Scargill and Ken Livingstone, at the Labour Party conference, October 1982

30. Roy Hattersley arriving at Labour Party headquarters, Walworth Road, 12 June 1984

31. Neil Kinnock, observed by Roy Hattersley, 8 April 1986

union pension funds. In the summer of 1939, Morrison was pushed strongly by Laski and Ellen Wilkinson, both impeccable figures of the left, as leader in place of the apparently colourless Attlee. During the later stages of the war, down to the campaign of 1945, Laski continued to promote the cause of Morrison's leadership as a guarantee that an orderly socialist advance would be combined with an understanding of the mechanics of power. Morrison had emerged in the ILP (and in his very early days in the Marxist SDF) as a man of the left, a pacifist during the first world war and a man with a neo-Marxist background, who perceived a stark contrast between socialism and capitalism. In the thirties, he was not commonly thought of as a right-winger. So Morrison's stereotype image, in terms of his interests and his precise place on the party spectrum, is in urgent need of revision.

His great years were the period of the Attlee government. If examined closely, his role in that government over the long term emerges as quite central and indispensable, more so than Bevin or Cripps, perhaps more crucial even than Attlee himself. He was perhaps the one opponent the Tories most feared. In those tumultuous years, Morrison pursued a variety of essential tasks, each of which was quite vital to the effectiveness and unity of the party and the efficiency of the government. At grave cost to his health, including a major heart attack in early 1947, Morrison played a supreme role in Labour's history. He was truly Labour's Carnot, the ultimate organizer of victory. In 1964–70, the Wilson government could well have done with an orchestrator and guide comparable to the position Morrison filled with such distinction for so long. So, too, could the Wilson and Callaghan ministries of 1974–9, since Morrison proved himself at his very best manœuvring in tight corners with small majorities, and the minimum room for error. Labour has never had anyone remotely like Morrison since 1951. It has gravely suffered as a credible party of government as a result.

His work in the Attlee government stood out in four main areas. First, he was supremely effective as Leader of the House of Commons, combining this with a role as deputy Prime Minister. As Leader of the House, he was exceptionally subtle and adroit. He was equally efficient in the excitement of the 1945–6 session when he and Attlee kept a mighty flow of over seventy bills on the move, to make the nearly three hundred parliamentary troops on the back-benches happy and active, and in the quieter times of 1948–50 when the logic of 'consolidation' took effect and the government concentrated rather on sound administration and taking stock. Morrison was also the key figure on the Cabinet's Legislation Committee, along with William Whiteley, the chief whip, and Addison, Leader of the Lords, to ensure a steady flow of efficiently drafted legislation, Virtually no major procedural mistakes were made in five eventful years. Morrison's task was assisted by his decision to make full use of standing committees rather than waste precious time by committing government measures to the floor of the whole House. This proved an effective method of operation, even if it inevitably meant the controversial application of the guillotine to government-inspired measures, a logical step but a great contrast with previous usage. Although something of a reformer in terms of parliamentary procedure, the general image that Morrison projected was that of the classic House of Commons man. He emerged from his experience as Leader with a veneration for the practices of the House which became increasingly uncritical as time went on. His book, *Government and Parliament* (1954), underlined an admiration for the British constitutional system which bordered on adulation. To that extent, it was a text of somewhat ephemeral interest, as well as being disappointingly guarded about his own experience. For all that, his role as the supremely competent and cheerfully confident administrator of the House, no less than his early distinguished work as manager of the LCC, was a major contribution to the effectiveness of the Attlee government.

It was closely associated with a second vital role—that of manager of the parliamentary party. Here again, his capable qualities were seen at their very best. Handling an enormous body of back-bench MPs, basking in a majority of 150, was inevitably a difficult task. For the Labour Party, with its constant propensity for faction and turmoil, it was especially complex. Morrison tackled the task with buoyant energy. He sought to give the back-benchers something useful to do other than act as lobby fodder. An immediate atmosphere of tolerance was established by the suspension of standing orders for the entire 1945–50 period. Thus, a variety of back-bench revolts on topics ranging from Ireland to Palestine were quietly allowed to defuse. A Liaison Committee, under the secretaryship of Carol Johnson, formed a useful bridge between the whips and the back-benchers, though by 1947 its effectiveness was beginning to be questioned.

The most important of Morrison's innovations, though, was the creation of subject committees among the back-benchers. Many of them, notably the Finance Group which Dalton personally hand-picked, worked well and proved a valuable forum of ideas. Much the worst was the Foreign Affairs Group, partly because of Bevin's lack of parliamentary skills, partly because it became the haven for a miscellany of far-left dissenters who often reduced meetings to a series of brawls. In mid-1947, after some criticism, these groups were supplemented by area groups, intended to provide more effective links with the constituency parties, and which had a considerably lower profile than the subject groups which preceded them. On balance, at a time of constant economic difficulty, the existence of a large Commons majority, which has caused anxiety for politicians of all shades from Herbert Bowden in 1966 to Francis Pym in the 1983 election, caused relatively little embarrassment for the Attlee government. No doubt, this mood of comparative unity reflected a general harmony of purpose that brought government and rank and file close together. But it also owed much to the mood of enterprise and tolerance which Morrison helped to create.

In addition to managing the parliamentary party, Morrison was also a close link between government and the party machine. He was a leading member of the National Executive, a member of the party's International Subcommittee and, eventually, chairman of the Policy Committee in the lead-up to the 1950 election, as he had been previously in 1944–5. From his control of the NEC flowed a broad command over the party conference, where he, rather than Attlee or Bevin, usually emerged as the dominant orchestrating figure. With Morgan Phillips, his contact was at first close. They collaborated in ensuring that dissenters, great and small, from Platts-Mills in 1948 to the mighty figure of Nye Bevan in 1951, were quietly sidelined. Morrison's role was especially important in the lead-up to the 1950 election, when he was largely responsible for the drafting of the manifesto with its strongly consolidationist tone. As a result, there was none of the tension between Transport House and the party leadership which added to the difficulties of party leaders from Wilson to Foot in a later period. In 1950–1, however, a growing personal rift with Morgan Phillips saw Morrison's links with Transport House much diminished, and they were never the same again.

Finally, Morrison's credentials were not inconsiderable as a policy-maker. While he remained proud of his working-class origins—

indeed, sometimes prickly about them when his lack of education was hinted at—he may, nevertheless, be garlanded with the deceptive reputation of being an intellectual. Nothing is further from the truth than to see Morrison as just a professional machine man with no wider ideas. Mrs Webb praised him in 1933 as 'a Fabian of Fabians', while as has been seen Laski also much admired him. Morrison, in fact, found the discussion of general principles congenial enough. Further, he was more prepared to turn them into reality than were most of his colleagues, both through informal policy-making and through the more laborious formal structures of the party. As Lord President of the Council in charge of Economic Planning in 1945–7, he gathered round him a range of highly intelligent planners and commentators, headed by Max Nicholson, once of PEP. In his later years after 1951, Morrison took pleasure from his association with Nuffield College, Oxford, where the combination of hard-headed social science expertise and intellectual engagement was highly attractive. The warden, the bluff Mancunian, Norman Chester, was an especially sympathetic figure.

It may be surmised, indeed, that Morrison's role was considerable from the twenties onwards in creating the ideas as well as the practical institutions of the British socialist movement. In particular, it was his highly influential book, *Socialisation and Transport* (1933), which committed Labour to the idea of the corporate public board as the model for nationalization. His plans were refined on the party's Reorganization of Industry Subcommittee from 1932 onwards. Morrison's conception of public ownership has been much criticized ever since, as providing no major organic change from the capitalist order and offering little to hopes of industrial democracy or joint consultation. An official party policy document in July 1986 condemned it as 'an unresponsive monolith'. But it may be noted that his scheme carried the day because no other viable model existed at the time, or even seemed credible. Intellectuals such as Cole and Laski gave it their blessing. No one believed any longer in the theories of guild socialism, while dreams of syndicalism or industrial devolution had perished in the Welsh valleys around the time of the general strike. Morrison alone provided a coherent, intellectually defensible model, which made sense both as an administrative construct, and in terms of the working experience of the London Passenger Transport and the Central Electricity Board, which were already in existence by 1933. In *Socialisation and Transport*, Morrison dealt briskly and knowledgeably with all the main conceptual problems attaching to his idea of public ownership—aspects of competition and consolidation, ministerial control and wider economic planning, management and workers' representation. He went into immense detail on the compensation of stockholders, which he largely worked out by himself. In this work, Morrison thus filled a massive void in Labour's policy-making since no other broad scheme for nationalization, applicable to a wide range of industries and utilities, had hitherto been worked out. Warts and all, it held the field for a generation as the centre-piece of the British variant of democratic socialism.

Morrison's advocacy of 'consolidation' from mid-1947 is another qualification for the title of policy-maker, even if his views have to be culled from policy papers, speeches, and contributions to Cabinet and party debate rather than from a single monograph. Of course, much of his argument rested on electoral considerations and a well-founded belief that the newly nationalized industries were far from being overwhelmingly popular, either with the workforce or with the consumer public. He often cited the black-coated, lower-middle class like his Lewisham constituents. He accepted the possibility of episodic transformation, more so than Crosland was to do in 1956. At the same time, he provided many cogent arguments for concentrating for some time ahead on administrative improvements and improved productive efficiency to give renewed impetus to the idea of socialization, rather than press on recklessly into new areas where the case had not yet been made out. He was a withering critic of the 'shopping list' in 1950 in which the meat industry, water, cement and, most hazardous of all, sugar refining were sketched out as further targets for nationalization. As Morrison had prophesied, the effect on the voters was distinctly negative, especially with the sugar lump 'Mr Cube' brandishing the sword of free enterprise aloft, on every breakfast table in the land. Morrison's case is certainly open to attack. James Callaghan and others may well have been right that he was being too defeatist about the nationalization measures of 1945–50. The fact remains that he won the argument, hands down. By 1951, all significant groups within the party, not only trade-union right-wingers, but even Bevan and Crossman on the left, were clear advocates of the mixed economy, of improving the performance of the public sector and also revitalizing the presentation of their achievements in the media. Time and election setbacks had made consolidationists of them all. For good or ill, Labour has followed in his wake down to the Kinnock–Hattersley era in 1987.

In all these areas, many of them relatively concealed from public gaze, Morrison was an indispensable, pivotal member of the government. In his more visible role as an executive minister of high rank in the Cabinet the record is, however, somewhat more mixed. He was most effective as a co-ordinator, with a special role in harmonizing policy on the home front in relation to the social services, and general domestic policy in the non-economic field. He was a particularly important figure in directing the Socialization of Industry Committee in 1945–7 when all the major nationalization measures, which in all took about a fifth of the economy into public ownership, were efficiently processed through Cabinet.

His main executive function down to September 1947, however, concerned economic planning, which was the responsibility of his Lord President's Committee. Here he was not a success. He was out of his depth with the subtleties of macro-economic thinking, and had much suspicion of Keynes and his disciples in the Economic Section of the Cabinet Office, notably James Meade and Richard Stone. Morrison's mind was still lodged in the physical planning nostrums of the thirties, such as those sponsored by PEP, whose Max Nicholson was a major policy adviser of his. He was deeply hostile to the creation of the Economic Planning Council under Edwin Plowden in the summer of 1947. It was alleged at the time that Morrison was using cronies such as Nicholson and Clem Leslie, the public relations officer of the Planning Board, to hamstring Plowden's activities. What Morrison's economic officials manifestly failed to do in the years down to September 1947 was to plan. Indeed, the Lord President's Council seemed a remarkably frail instrument for so central a function, especially for a socialist government. The main odium for the financial near-catastrophe of July–August 1947 fell, as noted above, on Dalton and the Treasury. But it was also a massive setback for Morrison, newly recovered from a serious heart attack. He found economic planning now removed from his grasp and transferred to Cripps's new Ministry of Economic Affairs, along with newly created Cabinet Committees for Economic Policy and Production. The Lord President's Committee thereafter was a relatively humdrum affair.

Here was an area where Morrison's talents did not really extend. He was a marvellous manager of the machinery of government and co-ordinator of domestic policy. But he was not, and never had been, a specialist economist. He protested bitterly when Attlee removed him from economic planning while he was enjoying a few sunny days of relaxation on the beach at Guernsey in September 1947. His friend, Maurice Webb, loudly complained on his behalf. However, Attlee very reasonably pointed out that with leading the Commons and managing the party, together with his new role as successor to Greenwood as chairman of the Social Services Committee, Morrison had already more than enough to cope with, especially as his health had recently been most uncertain. In fact, Morrison soon shook off his irritation with Attlee, and emerged in 1948–50 more buoyant and vigorous than for some time past.

The other major policy area where Morrison was generally felt to be a disappointment concerned his time at the Foreign Office in succession to Bevin from mid-March 1951. Attlee had been very doubtful about promoting Morrison, and considered a range of other possible ministers including Shawcross and Griffiths. From the start, Morrison's performance at the Foreign Office aroused widespread complaint. He was felt by colleagues and departmental officials to be unconvincing. Attlee noted that 'H.M. always read off a sheet of paper in Cabinet; he hadn't any of it in his head.' Dalton ridiculed him as an imperialist *manqué*, a 'pseudo Pam'. Foreign Office advisers noted with dismay Morrison's ignorance of protocol and even of geography. He responded with defensive anger when Tory opponents in the House ridiculed him for pronouncing the River Euphrates with only two syllables. Dean Acheson saw him as parochial, with a mind that hadn't ranged beyond the sound of Bow Bells. No doubt, some of this may be sheer snobbery by Oxbridge (or Ivy League) public servants who looked on Morrison's humble origins and domestic preoccupations with some contempt (though they had come to worship the even more proletarian Bevin for his rustic simplicity). But criticism by officials as varied as Kelly, Jebb, and Franks cannot be discounted. Morrison, it may be granted, did not have a natural feel for foreign policy. Anyhow, he just wasn't Bevin, and the effect was a natural anticlimax.

On the other hand, Morrison's overall record at the Foreign Office does not seem too bad. He was at his worst in the Middle East, where he more than once threatened military and naval intervention in the summer of 1951 to protect the Anglo-Iranian oil refinery at Abadan, its personnel and their families. By July, Gaitskell noted that he had become quite a fire-eater, and was attacking his colleagues for being too 'United Nationsy'. Had Morrison's proposed 'Buccaneer' plan for military action in the Persian Gulf come about, reinforced by a covert attempt to remove Dr Mossadiq as Prime Minister of Iran, by fair means or foul, Britain might very well have been faced with a crisis similar to that which Eden created at Suez five years later. Fortunately, the combined weight of Attlee, Gaitskell, and Dalton, among others, restrained him—and also Shinwell, whose approach was even more bloodthirsty. At the very end of the government, in October 1951, when Egypt seemed to be threatening the British force stationed in the Suez Canal zone, Morrison was again bent on armed intervention. Attlee managed to curb him once again, and as chairman of the Chiefs of Staff Committee wisely overruled him. Morrison's touch was erratic in the Middle East. As an old patron of Zionism with many links with the Jewish community in London, he did not greatly like the Arabs (including the non-Arab Iranians, for this purpose). Added to this was a residual imperialism which led him to refer in 1946 to the 'the jolly old Empire'. In 1956 it was to move him to warm enthusiasm for the Anglo-French attack on Egypt. Not for nothing had he taken down Bell's life of Palmerston from the bookshelves as basic reading when first appointed Foreign Secretary.

Elsewhere, he fielded a variety of difficult problems, bearing on Anglo-American and Anglo-Soviet relations, quite capably. Difficulties in Korea, Formosa, and above all in western Europe were handled well enough. Morrison was particularly successful in acting as broker between the French and the Germans on defence questions in 1951. Indeed, his greatest achievement during his eight months at the Foreign Office was probably in Anglo-French relations, in giving new harmony to the flagging *entente cordiale* after a myriad of difficulties. Nor did he share Dalton's crude anti-Teutonic prejudices. Like his colleagues, Morrison had opposed any move towards European integration, including the Schuman Plan—he explained that the 'Durham miners wouldn't wear it'. But he did give new impetus to western European defence and economic co-operation in the summer of 1951, and also modified a good deal of the British suspicion of the Council of Europe at Strasbourg. In Western Europe, Morrison, with his wide contacts in the continental socialist movement over the years, emerged as a more commanding and less parochial figure than is often stated. Even so, it must remain true that, on balance, his tenure of the Foreign Office did his reputation harm, and perhaps confirmed some of Attlee's doubts about him. He soon gave up this portfolio when Labour returned to opposition and concentrated on more congenial domestic topics thereafter.

For all his somewhat mixed fortunes in high office, Morrison made an extraordinary contribution to the cohesion and purpose of the Attlee government. More than anyone else, he supplied the ghost in the machine. More than any other minister, he was the prime orchestrator, manager, mechanic, always quick to oil or repair defective parts. To the general public, he was to a unique degree the quintessential Labour voice, a familiar chirpy figure, a kind of political Max Miller, ready to beguile or reassure the doubters. The Festival of Britain, which took place in the summer of 1951, in Labour's last months, saw his qualities of executive drive and humanity at their best. The Festival, despite much sneering in the Tory press and bad luck with weather and strikes by building workers that spring, was a huge success. It paid tribute to the British talent for technical innovation and industrial design, which reminds us of the dominant role that Britain still played in the world economy in those far-off times. The Festival was also great fun, with the Battersea fair an enormous popular attraction. It cleaned up the scruffy South Bank of the Thames in a way pleasing to a devoted Londoner like Morrison, with Robert Matthew's superb Festival Hall as its architectural centre-piece. The whole concept was in many ways typical of Morrison's personal style, self-confident, cheerful, fired with civic zeal and a non-exclusive sense of patriotism. It is extraordinary (and typical) that the succeeding Tory government pulled it down within a few months, with only the Festival Hall left, presiding over a bleak strand and the gaping and hideous car-parks of an unplanned South Bank returned safely to familiar dereliction.

The Festival of Britain seems aeons away from the introspective, defeatist Britain of the mid-1980s. It gave London what Morrison gave to the Metropolis and his nation, a capacity to think big and to match dreams with careful practical execution. It reminds us of how Morrison could transcend his local, municipal origins, or rather use them as a springboard for wider objectives, as surely as did the socialist planners of Red Vienna or the Progressive exponents of the 'Wisconsin Idea' earlier in the century. Herbert Morrison was a difficult, flawed man, but no-one in Labour's ranks has begun to match his all-round capacities in the past thirty years. The void remains as gaping as ever. Whether Ken Livingstone, Labour's most remarkable practitioner of municipal enterprise in the recent past, can provide an updated, modern version of Morrison's civic idea will indeed be a theme to watch in the future.

# LORD ADDISON

THE House of Lords has always had a prime place in Labour's demonology. The idea of a non-elected, hereditary upper house, after all, had enraged radicals in the last century from John Bright to David Lloyd George. 'End it, not mend it' had been the old cry. Inevitably, Labour joined in the attack after the first world war, regarding the Lords as a feudal anachronism, with a built-in Tory majority. Yet successive Labour governments from 1924 to 1979 have done nothing at all to threaten the existence of the upper house, to the impotent fury of the left. Indeed, Labour has almost developed a kind of affection for the peers, especially when their lordships have acted as thorns in the flesh of Tory governments such as Mrs Thatcher's. One of many criticisms by the party orthodox of Tony Benn's left-wing campaigns in the later 1970s centred on his wish to abolish the Lords. Here, indeed, he was wholly consistent since he had, after all, launched a famous constitutional debate twenty years earlier by disclaiming his own succession to the peerage as Lord Stansgate.

But the Lords, like the monarchy, the Church, the civil service, the stock exchange, the public schools, Oxford and Cambridge, the Jockey Club, the MCC, and many other venerable institutions, has hitherto been safe with a Labour government. The 1949 Parliament Act, which cut down the Lords' delaying powers over Commons' legislation to just one year, still left the upper house with significant powers. The only major change to their lordships' composition this century has come, ironically or significantly, from a Conservative government. This was Macmillan's Peerage Act of 1957, which created those life peerages for which even Walter Bagehot had politely called in the middle years of Queen Victoria's reign. Since that time, Labour has refused to tinker with the upper house. Harold Wilson's proposals in 1968, to separate the Lords into voting and non-voting peers, among other reforms, were frustrated in part by Michael Foot and some of the left (in liaison with Enoch Powell) on the grounds that they would unduly increase executive patronage. Also they would make the Lords look more sensible.

Labour's timidity in handling their lordships no doubt has many roots, historical, constitutional, and psychological. Socialists have often loved a lord. Old rebels like Davie Kirkwood and Manny Shinwell were proud to wear the ermine in their time. But a major factor must be the usefulness—or the docility—of the upper house during periods of Labour government.

In this process, the leadership of the Lords by Christopher, Viscount Addison, between 1945 and 1951 is a prime exhibit. A relatively obscure figure to the public at large, Addison was in every way a remarkable member of the Attlee Cabinet. In the first place, he was very old, since he entered the Cabinet when he was already seventy-six; he stayed in office to the end, when he was eighty-two. He died immediately after the polls which saw Labour's defeat, a happy warrior to the end. His political career had begun with his rise as a leading Lloyd George Liberal of strong radical inclinations, and a particular interest, as a distinguished doctor, in public health. For years, he had been a very eminent professor of anatomy, and was known in the House as 'Doctor Addison'. During the first world war he had been Lloyd George's main Coalition Liberal lieutenant, and he served for two years after the war as the first Minister of Health. Then he broke with the Prime Minister on grounds of conscience, after a blazing public row over the axing of his housing programme, and found new sanctuary in the Labour Party. Here he climbed rapidly as a respected ex-minister and served as a very energetic Minister of Agriculture under MacDonald in 1930-1. Then he resigned a second time. To be precise, he was the one professional middle-class dissentient amongst the nine who opposed the cuts in unemployment benefit proposed in August 1931. For the second time his career seemed to be at an end.

Yet, in fact, the sexagenarian Addison found new zest in opposition. He briefly recaptured his seat at Swindon and then went to the Lords as first a baron, then a viscount in 1937. Meanwhile he was a busy policy-making chairman of the New Fabian Research Bureau and an influential writer on agriculture, where his marketing schemes and price reviews had been pioneering efforts. In July 1945, for a third time, he began a major phase of Cabinet office. It was to prove the most rewarding, and in every way satisfying period of his long career. It gave him new stature as Leader of the Lords, taking Labour's vast programme of radical legislation quietly and efficiently through a basically hostile upper house. It also gave Addison himself, sometimes in the past a belligerent or prickly figure whose public brawls with other former Liberal colleagues had hit the headlines, a new tranquillity in his old age. Over six years, the venerable Addison, the oldest even of this singularly elderly government, built up a new role as the acceptable, constitutional face of British socialism. Since his time, Labour's fires of resentment against the upper house have been hard to stoke up effectively.

It should be noted that his role in the Attlee Cabinet was a wide-ranging one. As a very senior figure, whose ministerial experience went back to 1914, and the sole survivor in office of the post-war government of 1918–22, Addison intervened on a wide range of issues, domestic and foreign. He was particularly effective on his old speciality of agriculture, and on health, where he solidly backed up Bevan's proposals for a National Health Service. He was recalled by Harold Wilson as 'a wise old man' who was usually listened to with deference. He was also, until October 1947, at the Dominions Office, no sinecure at a time when the Commonwealth was vital to Britain's defence needs and food supplies. Here, he built up a particularly fruitful relationship with Mackenzie King, the Liberal Prime Minister of Canada, whose somewhat morbid interest in spiritualism consorted oddly with Addison's strictly rational, scientific mind. Smuts, a Cabinet colleague back in 1917–18, was another good friend. Above all, Addison was Attlee's close confidant. 'Chris' and 'Clem', with their respective wives chatting about gardening in the background, would enjoy afternoon tea at Chequers, enjoying the calm of the Buckinghamshire countryside (Addison himself lived at Radnage, a few miles away) and ruminating on Lloyd George, cricket, and other topics of mutual interest. Attlee's regard for Addison went beyond personal sentiment. He made him a highly influential chairman of inter-departmental Cabinet committees. Addison even served on the secret Cabinet committee which authorized the British development of the atomic weapon, much to the later dismay of his daughter, a strong supporter of CND. But it was as Leader of the Lords that Addison had his main significance, and it is here that the discussion must chiefly focus.

For most of the six years of the Attlee government, there was remarkably little conflict between the Commons, with its huge Labour majority, and the Lords, with their built-in Tory control. Of course, much of the reason can be found in wider, tactical considerations. It would be mistaken to lay undue emphasis on Addison's wise handling of their lordships, considerable though his talents in this direction were. With the experience of 1909-11 in mind, the Tory peers were unlikely to charge blindly into a fierce constitutional battle with a Labour government which had received an incontestable mandate at the polls for its measures. In the judgement of Lord Salisbury, the Tory Leader in the upper house, a direct clash with the government might well doom the Lords to permanent oblivion. A strategy of great caution was thus pursued, at least in the 1945-7 sessions, when a stream of over 70 measures, including many acts of nationalization and much social legislation, went through the Lords with little difficulty.

The first real battle came over the Transport Bill to take the railways and road haulage into public ownership in 1947. There were some debatable features of this bill, notably the proposal to take over small road carriers, holding so-called 'C Licences', covering journeys of up to forty miles. But the basic reason for the Lords' revived energy, of course, came from the downturn in the government's popularity, as measured in opinion polls and the sense of country, during the aftermath of the fuel crisis in early 1947 and the subsequent run on the pound during the convertibility crisis. Circumstances which cheered up the Tory opposition necessarily found their echo in the Lords. On the issue of C Licences, indeed, the government did give way in the end, though it should be added that many ministers were unhappy with a clause which appeared to be anti-libertarian and a threat to small operators. Capital punishment continued in existence after the Lords, urged on by Lord Chief Justice Goddard, a fanatic on the issue, had mauled the 1948 Criminal Justice Act. Gas nationalization, however, went through with little dispute.

Iron and steel, though, were known to be far less popular, and to be generating much dispute within the Cabinet itself. The Lords' decision to resist it with much use of delaying tactics was anticipated. To this end, the government introduced the 1947 Parliament Bill, to cut down the Lords' powers of delay of measures passed through the Commons to just one year. An Iron and Steel Bill could thus be passed through parliament prior to the next election. The Parliament Bill was the only measure ever to go through the full procedures of the 1911 Parliament Act, being twice rejected by the Lords until it became law in 1949. By now the Lords were in much more combative mood. 'Cohabitation' was over, and they fought the Iron and Steel Bill bitterly in 1949. A possible constitutional crisis was averted only by

a compromise worked out by Morrison and Addison with Salisbury
and Swinton for the Tory peers, under which the Iron and Steel Bill
duly became law in December 1949, prior to an election, but the
vesting date for the publicly owned iron and steel industry was
postponed until after the next election, in the summer of 1950. Even
so, the Homeric battles over steel nationalization apart, the general
record of relations between the Lords and the Commons in 1945–
51, including the 1950–1 session when the government had a tiny
majority of only two or three, was relatively peaceful. The Labour
government left office in 1951 with the position of the Lords apparently as secure as ever.

Addison's contribution to this in personal terms was considerable.
He had to handle the passage of a huge sequence of major bills,
and to introduce most of them himself, including iron and steel
nationalization which he had opposed in Cabinet. Most of them gave
him little intellectual or moral difficulty. He had been a staunch
advocate of increased collectivism since before the First World War,
and could calmly trace the roots of major measures of state ownership
or social welfare in long-established proposals of thirty or forty years
ago, some of which he himself had helped promote. A particular
delight was Tom Williams's Agricultural Act of 1947, where Addison
could claim a good deal of the parentage. He not only handled
the passage of all these bills, he also helped to process them. In the
Cabinet's Future Legislation Committee, along with Morrison and
Whiteley, the chief whip, he helped ensure a steady flow of measures,
sensibly drafted and in appropriate sequence, to maximize the role
of the Lords as an efficient revising chamber.

One of his important tasks, naturally, was to ensure that the
Labour peers were kept up to the mark. They were, he wrote in July
1946, 'but a tiny atoll in the vast ocean of Tory reaction'. They
numbered only forty-odd, many of them veterans or near-veterans,
such as Lords Pethick-Lawrence, Stansgate, Ammon, Nathan, and
Hall, together with a handful of younger minister peers such as
Pakenham (Longford) and Listowel, Latham, and Winster. Numbers
of Labour peers rose only slowly. Four more were added in the 1947
New Year's Honours List, but even then the tally was less than fifty.
Nevertheless, Addison seems to have handled this small and ageing
group with much tact and effectiveness, with a rota of fifteen or so
appointed to monitor the course of any particlar debate. Addison
himself led from the front, ceaselessly active for all his seventy-

odd years. He acted firmly to ensure good attendance and effective debating performances. One ministerial recruit, Lord Pakenham, has recorded his surprise when, in full flow in the Lords, Addison passed him a short note: 'Take your hands out of your pockets.' But, in general, the impact of Addison on his colleagues was achieved through conciliatory rather than disciplinary methods.

One notable feature of his handling of the Lords was his good relationship with the Tory front bench in the upper house. Many of them he had known well personally in his lengthy career; some, such as Swinton (Lloyd-Graeme), had been ministerial colleagues under Lloyd George in the distant past. He struck up an especially good relationship with the Tory Leader, Lord Salisbury, a man twenty-four years his junior, with whom he struck up a so-called 'father and son' relationship. No doubt the cordial relations between Labour and Conservative leaders aroused the instant suspicions of the critics of the Lords. But, without doubt, it helped the flow of business, made the Lords more usefully effective, and added substantially to the extraordinary record of legislative achievement that distinguished the 1945–51 Labour government. One innovation, the 'Addison–Salisbury agreement' under which government bills will not be thrown out on second reading by the Lords, still governs conventional relationships between the two houses. Addison and his colleagues achieved a notable impression of competence and practicality, not always evident in the mass of crises and confusions that beset the Attlee government. Compared with the gaffes over the fuel crisis, the débâcle of ground-nuts, or the suspicions aroused by the Lynskey tribunal about suspected ministerial corruption, the Lords during Addison's six years in charge was an oasis of calm, measured achievement. Addison's own urbane personality and good humour, all passion spent in a lengthy and often stormy career, added immensely to this process.

The debit side, of course, was that the Lords continued much as before. As in local government, the police, or the organization of the civil service, the 1945–51 Labour administration was not a time for institutional reform. The Lords' delaying powers, as noted above, were curtailed to one year. Otherwise, the upper house, including the flowering of the hereditary principle in obvious conflict with the ethos of the Labour government, remained wholly undisturbed. There were desultory and inconclusive discussions between Conservative, Labour, and Liberal leaders in 1947–8 on a possible reform of the Lords' composition. Clement Davies, the Liberal leader offered a scheme for a new second chamber of three hundred peers with perhaps one hundred 'Lords in Parliament' nominated on a life basis. Addison recorded, for Mackenzie King's benefit in April 1948, that agreement had been reached about abolishing the automatic right of hereditary peers to attend, and on a fairer distribution of peers between the parties. But these talks led nowhere, and were soon swallowed up by renewed conflict between the two houses over iron and steel. Attlee and Morrison both felt that Lords reform was a low priority. Morrison was generally conservative on the matter (his own enthusiasm for the Lords when he received his peerage confirms the point). He was anxious that any reformed second chamber should maintain continuity with the upper house as it was. 'We should not set up something new and different from the past' declared this spokesman of socialism. No proposals for reforming the Lords' composition reached the Cabinet in 1945–51, and none of Labour's major figures was anxious to put any forward. Indeed, the criticism of the Lords by such as Dalton focused rather on the small numbers and great age of the Labour peers. He wanted to boost their strength, not abolish them root and branch. Life peers and other reforming novelties were set aside for the Conservatives to tackle.

Addison's leadership of the Lords was a consuming and highly congenial phase of his life. Buoyed up by a happy second marriage (to a lady who, like Mrs Attlee, was probably a Conservative and venerated the upper house), he found his life given a new lift and sense of purpose. It was a supremely agreeable finale to a remarkable career in Liberal and Labour politics, and in high office after both world wars, the only man with such a record. Even in early 1951, when he was well into his eighty-second year, he was active in Cabinet, as a distinguished doctor and the first Minister of Health, in trying in vain to bridge the gap between Bevan and his colleagues over NHS charges. In this instance, Addison, previously a staunch supporter of Bevan's achievement, threw his support behind Attlee and the majority. Only in the autumn of 1951, when Addison was showing advanced signs of the cancer that was shortly to kill him, did he appear a waning force, though in fact he was still nominally Leader of the Lords when the government resigned.

The positive aspects of Addison's work in the Lords are transcendently clear. So, too, is the impact of his experience and informed judgement within the government. The difficulty was that Addison was simply too successful in harmonizing the Lords with social democracy. He did his work too well. He managed to neutralize the Lords and minimize its potential threat. No subsequent Labour government made much effort to change it. The result is that Labour peers, though somewhat swollen in numbers by life creations, are still a small minority; the Lords remain non-elective and not representative of the populace at large, an obstacle to wider changes with a membership that defies logic or political reality. Meanwhile, the Labour peers battled on gallantly in the 1980s, with the nonagenarian Lords Noel-Baker and Brockway to the fore, and the centenarian Lord Shinwell a prominent independent supporter. Some day, perhaps, a Labour or reformist administration will seize the challenge evaded over the generations and wipe out the Lords as the constitutional anomaly it has been for centuries. But in so doing it will have to contend with the abiding influence, beyond the grave, of its greatest, longest-running Leader, Christopher, Viscount Addison of Stallingborough in the county of Lincolnshire.

# JAMES GRIFFITHS

JIM GRIFFITHS and Nye Bevan are the prototypes of the Welsh entry into the higher reaches of the Labour Party. Bevan, who came from the anglicized Rhymney Valley in the east of the coalfield, represented a sharp break away from the quasi-nationalism of the nonconformist, Liberal past, the world of his Lib-Lab Baptist father. His philosophy was eclectic, relativist, outward-looking; he kept aloof from what he considered the slow-witted miners who dominated the Welsh table at the House of Commons. He poured immense scorn on the first 'Welsh day' debate in the Commons in 1944. How, he asked, did Welsh sheep differ from English sheep? Griffiths, by contrast, was the very embodiment of the way in which Labour flourished in Wales by appropriating most of the old radical heritage. A Welsh-speaking nonconformist from the anthracite coalfield of east Carmarthenshire, deeply patriotic, he worked self-consciously within the parameters of the industrial and cultural past. The fierce debates between Bevan and Griffiths in the late 1950s over whether Labour should commit itself to a Welsh Secretaryship of State were a duel between two visions of socialism, the one centralist and deriving from a broadly Marxist diagnosis of economic power, the other pluralist and seeking the socialist commonwealth gradually and peaceably, through the acknowledgement of local cultures and traditions. Griffiths won the day in 1959, and, on balance, has tended to win the argument ever since. Even the rout of devolution for Wales for 1979 has not eroded Labour's commitment, not only in Wales and Scotland, to relate socialist collectivism to a sense of community, with a due respect for the past. In so far as the Red Flag and the Red Dragon have been reconciled, it is Jim Griffiths, self-styled reconciler-in-chief, who has much of the credit.

Jim Griffiths hailed from the Amman Valley. It is a beautiful green countryside, until recently sprinkled with anthracite mines and tinplate works, extending from Gwendraeth in the west to the Swansea Valley in the east. In the late nineteenth century, this new coalfield proved to be a powerful stronghold of Welsh-language culture, alive with choral festivals and *eisteddfodau* in Jim Griffith's childhood; the heritage never left him. He spoke no English until he was five, and his brother, 'Amanwy', became a local bard of some distinction. A powerful cultural influence on the local community was the Revd John 'Gwili' Jenkins, radical poet and theologian. To the present time, this western fringe of the Welsh coalfield, or what little is left of it, remains intensely Welsh in its cultural outlook. The two outstanding Welsh rugby players of recent times, Barry John of Cefneithin, and Gareth Edwards of Gwaencaegurwen, both miners' sons and Welsh-speaking, were products of this region. Jim Griffiths, then, grew up as a miner with an intense identification with his local society. Appropriately, he was indeed impelled towards socialism as a young man by the religious revival of 1904-5, when he was fourteen years old, which started at nearby Loughor. The 'new theology' of the Revd R. J. Campbell was another inspiration. Griffiths was always to see his socialism as fraternal and ethical, the product of good works and comradeship.

He became active in the ILP as a teenager around 1908, and witnessed from afar giants like Hardie and Snowden at annual conferences. He remained a working miner during the war, but after 1919 he was a student at the Central Labour College, Regent's Park, London. Aneurin Bevan, Morgan Phillips, Ness Edwards, Bryn Roberts, Lewis Jones, and other notable socialists were students there, too, around this time, a new working-class leadership élite. But, unlike others of this inspired generation, Griffiths was never really tempted by the Marxist gospel. It amused him in later years that his first letter to his wife-to-be, Winnie, a Hampshire woman of much common sense and force of personality, was headed 'comrade'.

Griffiths managed to steer clear both of the violence attaching to his own local pits at Ammanford in 1924-5, when he was elsewhere, and of controversies surrounding the end of the General Strike and the subsequent miners' lock-out. Elected agent for the anthracite district in 1925, he became active in the South Wales Miners' Federation, the old Fed, striving to regroup and rebuild membership and finances after the shattering defeat of 1926. After a remarkably swift rise, Griffiths became president of the Fed in 1934. But he represented something distinct. Along with men like Enoch Morrell and Oliver Harris (as noted on p. 76) he symbolized a revival of the moderates in the SWMF, disillusioned by the class-war talk of men like Ablett and Cook which had seemed to have led to disaster. Griffiths emerged as an industrial diplomat of much skill. He was able in 1935 to bring the Welsh miners their first wage advance since the mid-1920s. More importantly, he was able to negotiate out of existence the company unionism of the Spencer-type Industrial Union after the crisis of the stay-down stoppages at Nine Mile Point and other pits in Monmouthshire and Glamorgan. But it should always be added that it was the stern resolve and physical determination of the brave miners who 'stayed down', rather than the emollient diplomacy of Griffiths, which forced the coalowners, and their allies in the local constabulary, to give way.

Most of the Welsh miners who had political aspirations were men modest in disposition and in their talents. Apart from a handful like Bevan and Ness Edwards, most of them were unremarkable cannon-fodder on the back benches who made relatively little impact on the politics of their time. Griffiths was an exception. He had, after all, been Labour Party agent for Llanelli in the early 1920s. He entered parliament for that constituency in a by-election in 1936, and from the start was extremely effective, not only on local themes of unemployment, industrial injury, or lung disease, but also on foreign policy questions like intervention in Spain. In 1939 he was elected to the party national executive, and stayed there until the 1960s. He also became a party expert on the social services. It was Griffiths who moved, at party conference in May 1942, several months before the Beveridge Report, Labour's motion for a comprehensive, cradle-to-grave national insurance scheme. He was also the leader of a back-bench revolt by Labour MPs (plus some Liberals, including the aged Lloyd George) against the government early in 1943 for failing to give sufficient priority to Beveridge's findings.

Griffiths thus attained high office in July 1945, as Minister of National Insurance outside the Cabinet. Here he was in his element. He understood intimately the arcane details of Beveridge's blueprint for social insurance which it was his main task to implement. He handled, confidently and effectively, three major bills, the 1946 National Insurance Act and the 1948 National Assistance and Industrial Injuries Acts. He was sufficiently adroit to respond to Labour back-bench criticisms that the benefits accorded under the National Insurance scheme were too meagre, and he duly improved them, with the goodwill of Dalton, the Chancellor, with whom he always had a very good relationship. In later years, the underlying theoretical basis of Griffiths's bill, with its flat-rate contributory method amounting to a kind of poll-tax, was to be increasingly under fire.

In time, the earnings-related principle was admitted. But it stood the test of time for twenty years, and embodied the conventional liberal wisdom of the time. Griffiths thus became a major architect of the welfare state, and was proud to be so.

He also understood some of the weaknesses surrounding his welfare measures, notably the existence of private schemes which undermined the state system. Thus, although normally on the party right, he joined forces with Bevan in urging the NEC in 1949 to nationalize the industrial assurance companies, whose massive funds were not available for investment in the state scheme. After much passionate argument, Griffiths and Bevan lost the day in the face of the cautious attitude of Morrison, Cripps, and eventually Dalton, and in the face of the hostility of the Co-operative Society which ran various profitable insurance systems it was zealous to preserve. Faced with divided counsels and vested interests, Griffiths had to withdraw, though he never professed regret for his unwonted enthusiasm for further nationalization in this instance.

In February 1950, he took on a quite different responsibility, the Colonial Office, with, of course, Cabinet rank this time. Hitherto, he had not had much contact with external policy. Nevertheless, his success in his new post was considerable, perhaps the more so after the uncharismatic, if earnest, efforts of Creech Jones before him. Indeed, Griffiths's reputation grew to such a degree that he was seriously considered for the Foreign Office as successor to Bevin in March 1951. Apart from anything else, Griffiths was a genuine and unmistakable proletarian, and Attlee was aware of the need to give important office to the dwindling band of trade-union ministers. Griffiths's widow actually states in her memoirs, published privately, that her husband was offered the Foreign Office, but that he turned it down partly to avoid disappointing Morrison. This cannot be verified. At any rate, Griffiths stayed on at the Colonial Office during a time of much change and controversy.

It was an exciting period, bringing him into contact with young nationalist leaders like Harry Lee (Lee Kuan Yew) of Singapore. In later life, Griffiths would reflect on it as a remarkably fulfilling time of his life. Much of his work was spent in following up the implications of Creech Jones's legacy, including the development programmes of East Africa, so cruelly parodied by the ground-nuts affair in Tanganyika. There was also the beginning of real self-government for both Nigeria and the Gold Coast (Ghana) in West Africa. The guerrilla war in Malaya went on remorselessly. Griffiths's main innovation, however, was much more debatable. He took up with some enthusiasm the cause of Central African Federation for Northern and Southern Rhodesia, and Nyasaland, though with a much more solicitous regard for the protests of black leaders like Hastings Banda and Kenneth Kaunda than was shown by his very right-wing colleague, the Commonwealth Secretary, Patrick Gordon Walker. Griffiths saw the Central African Federation in very positive terms as affording scope for massive joint development projects, as well as keeping this vast area of southern Africa free from the apartheid and racialism of the Union of South Africa further to the south. Griffiths was also attracted to the robust personality of the ex-railway trade-unionist and heavyweight boxer, Roy Welensky, a refreshing contrast with the usual type of white settler. However, Griffiths rapidly changed his mind after the Victoria Falls conference in September 1951 which revealed the depth and totality of African resistance. Thereafter, he led opposition to the Federation in the Commons from 1952 onwards. On balance, until the attempted Federation was finally wound up by R. A. Butler in 1963 after its ghostly existence, Griffiths was a consistent voice for sanity in the handling of African affairs.

In the troubled history of Labour in the fifties, Griffiths was a rare symbol of comradeship. He kept his seat on the NEC constituency party section even after the 1952 Morecambe conference saw a huge swing to the Bevanite left. He proclaimed himself a reconciler, and repeatedly opposed the threat of purges or expulsions directed towards Bevan and others. With much goodwill on all sides, he became deputy party leader, in succession to Morrison, in February 1956, defeating Bevan in the process, and worked closely with Gaitskell during the Suez period before giving way to Bevan as deputy leader in 1958. Griffiths was never thought of as a possible leader (as he had been by Dalton and Crossman in 1951). But with his special expertise on colonial matters, in a decade when Central Africa, Kenya, Guyana, Cyprus, and other colonial territories were in the forefront of controversy, he was a powerful figure down to 1959, though less so afterwards. In 1963 he voted as a solid trade-unionist for George Brown for party leader; but although now over seventy he was still a considerable figure in Harold Wilson's counsels.

He became the first Secretary of State for Wales, the 'charter secretary' in Wilson's words, in 1964–6. It was a fitting finale to a long career which had seen his identification with his native Wales quite unshakeable. His period as Secretary of State was mainly a time of foundation, with few important initiatives. The new Welsh Office was not a powerhouse of ideas, rather a co-ordinating ministry for a variety of Whitehall departments within Wales. However, Griffiths did try out one novelty, one that, perhaps fortunately, was snuffed out. This was the idea of a new town somewhere near Caersws in the Severn Valley in Montgomeryshire, to help arrest the decline of population in mid-Wales. Griffiths was excited by the whole new town idea as a way of giving coherence to various scattered local initiatives to bring new industry to declining rural communities. But the tide was turning against schemes such as these. Its defeat prevented what might have proved the most spectacular ghost town since the passing of the old West.

Griffiths gave way to Cledwyn Hughes in April 1966, his achievement accomplished. In fact, Hughes then faced a series of ferocious challenges, barely evident during Griffiths's time as Secretary of State. The sterling crisis of July 1966 heralded renewed unemployment and decline in the valleys. Politically, there were the challenges of the Welsh Language Society and a resurgent Plaid Cymru, even in industrial areas such as the Rhondda. By 1970 Labour's almost unchallengeable hold on Wales seemed as uncertain as its domination of Scotland, now galvanized by the SNP. Griffiths, it is known privately, hung on to his seat at Llanelli until 1970 despite failing health, to prevent a dangerous by-election in which the Plaid Cymru candidate would be the highly articulate Welsh rugby player and coach, Carwyn James.

Nevertheless, Griffiths's approach remained more sensitive and less aggressive than that of George Thomas in a less satisfactory regime in Gwydr House in 1968–70. Griffiths remained to the end an advocate of Welsh devolution and an elected council, as he had been during the Cabinet debates on nationalized industry in 1946–7. He was also a firm supporter of the recognition of the Welsh language and culture, and a genial patron of the renaissance in modern Welsh history apparent in the sixties. In his late years until his death in 1975, he stayed on benignly with Winnie in their house in Wandsworth, reflecting in the press correspondence columns on the Common Market and devolution (which he supported) and unilateral nuclear disarmament (which, though a former pacifist, he opposed). He was also a priceless source of first-hand oral tradition for younger researchers, anxious to have first-hand testimony of the pioneering days of sixty years earlier. He died a happy man, it may be surmised, with a Labour government once again in office if hardly in power.

To the outside world, Jim Griffiths often seemed a largely parochial figure, strongly identified with Wales in speech and sentiment. He would be abused by Ness Edwards in the Commons tea-room for being more of a Welshman than a socialist. Griffiths seemed in his appearance the archetypal Welsh miner, complete with blue scars around his eyes, full of cheery stories of rugby referees and his old mates in the pit. In fact, he was much more eclectic than he seemed, as his time in the Colonial Office and his wide interests in Labour politics in the fifties suggest. His somewhat unrevealing memoirs, *Pages from Memory* (1969) do, none the less, show a man of genuine internationalism of spirit. But it was a source of strength that he was an authentic working-class leader of a very traditional kind, central to a movement that owed almost everything to Methodism (or Congregationalism, in his case) and little or nothing to Marx. With strong local roots and a vivid sense of history, he was an ideal instrument for what Leon Blum defined as the 'conquest of power', in the gradualist, fraternal sense in which Griffiths interpreted the process. In however sentimental a fashion, he spoke for a movement that held fast to local values and the sense of cultural community. Like Hardie or Bevan, he could bridge the enclosed world of the mining villages and a wider political stage, but without losing contact, physically or psychologically, with the world whence he came. His main memorials were always tributes to ideological consensus and compromise, from Coleg Harlech, with its message of working-class self-education, to the broad basis of the welfare state. He could be cunning, but never vicious. He was certainly never even remotely a class warrior. He was one of the few miners, and very few Welshmen, to make a decisive impact on national politics. So long as British socialism keeps alive a sense of its diversity and its particularity, so long as class and community can be reconciled within it, then Jim Griffiths will be a politician to remember.

# ANEURIN BEVAN

In recent years, Nye Bevan, restless rebel and prophet of working-class power, seems to have gone legitimate. At the time of his premature death in 1960, he was Labour's deputy leader, a shadow Foreign Secretary who had strongly championed Britain's retention of nuclear weapons, almost a 'patriot' at the time of Suez. By the 1980s, it had become a journalists' cliché to contrast the parliamentary socialism of the Bevanites of the fifties—'the legitimate left'—with the Marxist extremism of the Bennites in the constituencies a generation later. Asked in 1980 what Bevan would have thought of the 'New Left' of the present time, Harold Wilson briskly replied, 'Nye wouldn't have been seen dead with that lot.'

However, certain things have to be recalled before Bevan is clutched, finally and fatally, to the bosom of the establishment. For nearly all his career, he was thought of as a dogmatic irreconcilable. He was the most hated—if also the most idolized—politician of his time. During the thirties he was a savage critic both of the National government and his own party leaders. He was expelled from the party, along with Cripps, for advocating a Popular Front. In the wartime years, he was a remorseless opponent of consensus, and of Churchill in particular. His years in the Attlee government were often scarred by controversy. To his political enemies, he was 'a squalid nuisance', a 'Tito from Tonypandy', the 'Minister for Disease'. Even his name was mispronounced, with the stress placed on the second syllable, perhaps to distinguish him from nice, right-wing Ernest Bevin, probably just to be offensive. No episode after 1945 caused a greater sensation than Bevan's remark, made during a speech at Manchester in July 1948, ostensibly to hail the introduction of the National Health Service, that the Tories were 'lower than vermin'. As a result, he received verbal abuse, packets of excrement through the post, a boot in the pants in White's Club from an unhinged aristocrat. By contrast, Benn, Scargill, or Hatton are the darlings of the halls.

After the clash with Gaitskell and Bevan's resignation over NHS charges in April 1951, the fury of the Tory enemy was matched by the hostility of the Gaitskellite right. In the fifties, Bevan re-emerged as a rebel and trouble-maker. In 1955 he was again expelled from the parliamentary party for a time. The group 'Keep Left' and the Bevanite movement became the focus of savage, internecine conflict within the Labour Party. The formal reconciliation with Gaitskell (and the breach with CND) in the last years before Bevan's death did not greatly alter the picture.

Yet this stormy petrel had a magic all his own. In particular, in five and a half years at the Ministry of Health under Attlee he was to prove himself not only a prophet but a great constructive pioneer. He was unusual, almost unique, in the labour movement in combining strong socialist principles with rare creative gifts of practical statesmanship. No less than his fellow-countryman, David Lloyd George, he was to prove himself an artist in the uses of power.

For one abiding theme in his career, from his earliest ventures in constituency politics and local government in the early 1920s, is an urge for power. 'Where does power lie in this particular state of Great Britain and how can it be attained by the workers?' Executive responsibility was no 'trial and burden' for him as it was for poor Keir Hardie. Bevan has left us his well-known humorous description of his unavailing pursuit of the elusive phantom of power, from the backstreets of Tredegar to the corridors of Whitehall. Always he 'saw its coat-tails disappearing round the corner'. Even so, he kept a commitment to 'the principle of action' which aimed to make socialism the mechanism of practical policies, rather than cherish his doctrinal purity in the wilderness of permanent opposition. He had much contempt for the moralistic chastity of the doctrinaire left. He had some vigorous dialectical exchanges with his wife, Jennie Lee, still in the ILP at the time, for her 'virginity' in adhering to her exclusive little sect rather than to the broad church of the Labour movement.

It followed that Bevan had a sense of the compromises and complications that the exercise of power might involve. The language of priorities, the relativism of his political philosophy were essential ingredients of his outlook, no less than the socialist bedrock. His main book, *In Place of Fear* (1952), turns time and again to the realities of socialism in action, including the techniques of economic management, since 'freedom was the product of economic surplus'. Tony Crosland might well have said the same, though less arrestingly. As Minister of Health, and again briefly as Minister of Labour, Bevan was a generally pragmatic figure, prepared to cosset the doctors or even to send troops to the docks. At times in the 1945–51 period, Bevan, the supposed irreconcilable, emerges almost as reconciler-in-chief, the vital link between decision-making in the Cabinet and radical grass-roots pressures in the constituencies. This toughness and empiricism is a part of the real Bevan, too, along with the inspiration, the vision and the enduring, affectionate legend.

He grew up, of course, in the turbulence of the Welsh mining valleys. He broke with the chapel-reared radicalism of his family and moved to the far socialist left, in that tumultuous period between the Tonypandy riots in 1910 and the General Strike in 1926, when South Wales was the cockpit of the class struggle in Britain. However, his socialism took a distinctly original form. It was more eclectic, and genuinely international in inspiration, than was common in the Welsh labour movement at the time. It owed as much to the synd-icalist gospel of workers' democracy proclaimed by Noah Ablett as to the mainstream creed of solidarity and public ownership. As a minister after 1945, he took a great deal more interest in democratic accountability and joint industrial consultation than did most col-leagues. He emerged from the Central Labour College in Regent's Park just after the war as a libertarian Marxist, unlike fellow students like Jim Griffiths or Morgan Phillips. On the other hand, it was Labour Party politics rather than the local world of the South Wales Miners' Federation that captured his youthful imagination. It was here that power appeared to reside. In a notable coup, he won the Labour nomination for Ebbw Vale, and was returned to parliament for this impregnable mining stronghold in the 1929 election.

From the start, he proved himself an eloquent and brilliant spokes-man for the miners and the Welsh labour movement. His early attack on the great Lloyd George during a debate on the coal bill in 1929—'better dearer coal than cheaper colliers'—shook even that veteran and recalled his own youthful onslaughts on Joe Chamberlain. But it was soon clear that the young Bevan had an independent spirit and judgement of his own. Prior to the crisis of 1931, he had a flirtation with the economic ideas of Sir Oswald Mosley, of course, before the latter's anti-democratic and racist views emerged. In the mid-thirties, Bevan's *marxisant* critique of economic collapse and the threat of fascism led him to become one of the major advocates of a Popular Front and a leading figure in the columns of *Tribune*. He was expelled, along with Cripps and Strauss, from the parliamentary party in early 1939. But his deviations, socially at least, followed a more unusual route than simply the narrow pathways of the far left. He also became a familiar of Lord Beaverbrook and a *habitué* of journalistic and other circles far removed from the rigours of working class life in the valleys. Brendan Bracken gaily chided him for being 'a Bollinger Bolshevik'. He successfully proposed marriage to Jennie Lee in the Bohemian surroundings of the Café Royal. One of the great working-class leaders of the century, it was already clear that, as he delighted to proclaim, he was by temperament, if not by ideology, a born aristocrat.

The war years appeared to confirm a pattern of deviation and rebellion, even though, unlike his friend Cripps, he remained unmistakably a Labour man and was soon re-admitted to the fold. He was an unremitting critic of Churchill and the foreign and domestic policies of the coalition government. Like Laski, he argued that the consensus of the war years was stifling rather than advancing the cause of socialism. His powerful tract, *Why Not Trust the Tories?*, published in 1944 under the pseudonym 'Celticus', was a strong indictment of the wartime, as well as pre-war, policies for welfare, employment, and industrial organization. It reveals clearly the very real limits of alleged wartime harmony on post-war objectives. He turned his fire, too, on Labour ministers whom he alleged were being corrupted by the blandishments of high office. Ernest Bevin was a particular target, along with the trade-union leadership generally. One angry foray in May 1944 saw Bevan on the point of further expulsion from the parliamentary party when he condemned Bevin over wartime restrictions on the right to strike. It was a critical moment in his career; Bevan could have chosen to become another Jimmy Maxton. Instead, he was persuaded to offer a kind of apology to the National Executive. In fact, in this later phase of the war, when he was applying his mind intensely to post-war reconstruction, Bevan was moving decisively to a more positive role in the party.

Thus he stood, successfully, for the NEC elections for the constituency section in 1944, and was a significant policy-maker and official spokesman in the lead-up to the 1945 general election. His socialism was not in doubt. More than any of his NEC colleagues, he was committed to sweeping social change and a decisive shift in economic power. The war, he believed (as did Orwell and many others), had provided the instruments and the mood to bring these about. But this was accompanied by a growing conviction that these great goals could be won only through solidarity. Like his disciple and biographer, Michael Foot, some time around 1970, the old left-wing poacher contemplated the virtues of the gamekeeper's role. The socialist society was feasible only through the purposive use of centralized power rather than through glamorous, but futile, rebellion. That was the essential logic of the parliamentary mode of socialism. His appointment by Attlee to the Cabinet in July 1945, to the somewhat unexpected post of Minister of Health, was an endorsement and acknowledgement by Bevan that democratic socialism could only be achieved through office and responsibility.

His time at the Ministry of Health was his finest hour. It was, of course, the National Health Service that was his supreme commitment here. The scheme that emerged from his department at the end of 1945 strongly bore his personal stamp. After all, Labour's plans on health had been far more fluid than, say, for social insurance or perhaps education, prior to the election. Had it not been for the Socialist Medical Association in the thirties, Labour would hardly have had much of a health policy at all. What Bevan now proposed had an original, socialist thrust, more radical in character than the wartime scheme proposed by Willink. He markedly increased the overall control of central government. He provided more encouragement for new group partnerships in 'under-doctored areas', and for local health centres. He was firm that there should be a salaried element in the remuneration of general practitioners, while the sale of practices was to be abolished. Above all, there was the crucial commitment to the nationalization of the hospitals, all of them. In this respect, he triumphed in Cabinet over the resistance of Morrison, Ede, and others who urged that voluntary and municipal hospitals be preserved under local control. The great majority of ministers, not only left-wingers like Ellen Wilkinson but more centrist figures like Arthur Greenwood and Tom Williams backed him up. So did the venerable Addison, a former doctor of much distinction who justified nationalization on the grounds of medical instruction and research. His voice carried weight with Attlee, and the Cabinet endorsed Bevan's scheme overwhelmingly.

As is well-known, the launch of the NHS led to a two-year battle between Bevan and the British Medical Association, led by the elderly chairman of its council, Dr Guy Dain, and its secretary Charles Hill who had won fame on the air as 'the radio doctor'. It was not a distinguished episode in British social history. The doctors, notably wealthier GPs from the suburbs of the south-east, were mulish and self-centred in their intransigence. Bevan himself, much provoked, was not always patient either. In February 1948, after two sterile years, he launched a furious broadside at the BMA representatives as 'a small group of politically poisoned people'. But in the end, he was able to use his special personal relationship with the presidents of the Royal Colleges, Lord Moran of the Physicians, and Webb-Johnson of the Surgeons, to break the impasse. A public affirmation that no whole-time salaried service would be introduced by ministerial regulation, that the fixed element of remuneration of £300 would last only three years, and then be optional only, and that the doctors would have total freedom to publish their views on NHS administration, ended the conflict. Despite further obstructionism by Dain and Hill, the vast majority of doctors in England, Wales, and Scotland, rapidly enlisted in the service. When the NHS was officially launched in July 1948 Bevan was able to announce that 93.1 per cent of the population was enrolled under it.

In retrospect, the medical assault on Bevan, accusations that he was acting like a 'führer' and the like, seem totally absurd. His proposals reflected the broad consensus of the time, with *The Times*, *The Economist*, and most significantly *The Lancet* (the doctors' and consultants' journal) in support. He made concessions galore—far too many in the view of the Socialist Medical Association, which wanted a fully salaried medical profession. Private practice had to be retained, as had pay beds in hospitals, both disagreeable necessities in Bevan's view. The waiving of limits on specialists' fees and the remodelled appeal procedures for doctors coming before NHS tribunals were other signs of the minister's remarkably undoctrinaire attitude. The sum of £60m. equity was provided to compensate GPs for the abolition of the sale of practices. Yet the main socialist thrust of the service remained largely intact. Medical attention would be financed from general taxation, and always geared to needs rather than means. Regional inequalities between different parts of Britain would gradually disappear. A massive landmark in the creation of the welfare state had been created, one which retains its broad popularity (as Mrs Thatcher had to acknowledge in 1983) down to the present time.

As an administrative creation, Bevan's NHS certainly fell short of perfection. The organizational structure, with a three-tier system based on regional boards and executive councils, was cumbersome and unwieldy from the start. Nor was its financial basis precisely conceived. From the first year, 1948-9, expenditure outstripped all forecasts, especially for the labour-intensive hospital service. Naturally, the backlog of decades of neglect would be expensive to remedy, but it did mean that in 1949 the minister had the embarrassment of announcing that the estimates of £228m. had proved inadequate, and that supplementary estimates of £53m. would have to be introduced. This was not popular with his colleagues during the Cripps austerity. As NHS expenditure soared ever upwards, there were threats of prescription charges in October 1949 and of charges on teeth, spectacles, and appliances in February–March 1950. Bevan managed to frustrate both, but at the cost of setting up a specific Cabinet Committee to monitor NHS expenditure, an actual inquiry into its funding, and a ceiling of £392m. being laid down for 1950-1. Finance remained a running sore in the record of the service in its earlier years. For all that, it was obviously, on balance, a triumphant success, a social experiment which met with international acclaim. It also made Bevan's reputation as a radical, but flexible, minister.

Nor was his record on his other major responsibility, housing, to his discredit. This is sometimes thought to be a blot on his record. Slow progress in house-building in 1945-7 was strongly attacked, while Bevan himself gave hostages to fortune by claiming (quite wrongly) that he spent a mere five minutes a week on housing policy. Without doubt, the post-war housing drive began badly. It had several endemic problems, as Douglas Jay and other acute critics pointed out at the time. There were endless difficulties of co-ordinating housing policy, with responsibility scattered variously through the Ministries of Health, Supply, Town and Country Planning, and Works, with the Scottish Office having its own sphere of concern north of the border, and separate arrangements again in Northern Ireland. There was a lack of co-ordination, and needless competition at first for men and materials, between housing, schools, transport, factories in development areas, and many other claimants. However, it was sorted out by the start of 1947. In addition, the crushing financial problems that Bevan faced ought to be given due weight, along with bottle-necks in the supply of timber, bricks, and steel for house building, and a shortage of skilled labour after demobilization. In the circumstances, Bevan's achievement of building over one million permanent houses in the six years to October 1951 (excluding Northern Ireland), together with many temporary 'prefabs' and much renovation of dilapidated or bomb-damaged buildings, was an impressive feature of the post-war social programme, too. It might be noted that the quality of construction was exceptionally high throughout. In housing as in health—though less spectacularly so—Bevan emerged as a commanding, even inspiring minister, with a firm sense of priorities, and a gift, amounting to genius, for winning over key individuals, through sheer force of argument or through the well-known Welsh capacity 'to charm a bird off a bough'.

Bevan was not seriously considered for higher office until February 1950 when Attlee contemplated making him Colonial Secretary. (He finally rejected the idea because he thought Bevan would be too sympathetic to black nationalists.) It is much to Attlee's discredit that he did so little to advance the prospects of one of his most creative ministers, one whom he himself at times (according to Mr Harris's biography) saw as a future party leader. Nevertheless, in this second-ranking department, Bevan rose as a significant force within even this talented government. Apart from his executive successes as a minister, of course, he was popularly acknowledged as the major voice of radical change at the highest levels. He was the darling of the annual party conference, at which he achieved each year flashing triumphs of oratory (even though in 1947 he snubbed the rank and file by reminding them, over the tied cottages issue, that conference could not dictate to a democratically elected government). He had immense backing in the constituencies, while *Tribune* (of which Jennie Lee and Michael Foot became editors) was a vital source of support. In parliament, he was Labour's Rupert of debate, capable of dealing faithfully even with Churchill himself. Bevan it was whom the government would put up to defend them in difficult circumstances such as devaluation in September 1949 (when he launched a sparkling, if largely irrelevant, attack on the Tories), or even the new defence budget as late as February 1951.

As a result, he became a minister of far more than mere departmental importance, especially when Cripps moved to the Treasury. He had much to say in Cabinet on foreign policy, where he criticized Bevin's cold war postures, and on Palestine where he had old Zionist sympathies. In these areas, though, he had not the departmental involvement to make a decision or continuous impact on policy. In any case, by the end of 1948, appalled by Soviet policies in

Czechoslovakia, by the threat to Tito in Yugoslavia, and the Russian blockade of West Berlin, he voiced strong criticism of Soviet policy— as, to some degree, he had done since Yalta. He endorsed the establishment of NATO unreservedly. He had no truck with fellow-travelling dissenters such as Platts-Mills and Zilliacus, and generally endorsed their expulsion from the party. Tolerance did not mean the acceptance of sabotage. Nor did he encourage the dissenting MPs to 'Keep Left'. By the start of 1950, Bevan was almost one of the most hawkish ministers towards Russia. He had advocated the dispatch of tanks through the Soviet zone to relieve West Berlin and its socialist administration. His foreword to Denis Healey's *The Curtain Falls*, written in early 1951, consisted of a ferocious attack on Soviet methods in suppressing social democracy in eastern Europe. Kenneth Younger even surmised that, had Bevan been made Foreign Secretary, he would have turned out an orthodox, anti-Communist, perhaps even right-wing, director of British policy. However, this is probably an exaggerated view in the light of Bevan's strong criticism of British cold war postures in the 1950s, when he followed the line taken by George Kennan and others.

On the home front, also, Bevan by 1950 had become a generally content, if volatile, colleague. Along with Dalton, he fought the good fight against abandoning steel nationalization in 1947, as a token of socialist zeal. He had protested against cuts in the housing programme or proposed health service charges in 1949 and had, on occasion, spoken of resignation. Yet, by the summer of 1950, for all the government's slender majority and his own lack of promotion, he was prepared to accept the main drift of home policy, also. The wage freeze could be made a lever for a planned wages policy. At the party colloquium at Dorking in May 1950, he accepted the need for a mixed economy and concentrating on improving the performance and the public image of the nationalized industries, rather than press for more socialism. As he had done in the past, he even spoke of reassuring private enterprise, to make it more adventurous and freer from the constraints of monopolistic practices. Bevan was certainly critical of parts of the Morrison thesis at Dorking. But in effect, he too was a consolidationist by now.

Until the outbreak of the Korean War, there were scant grounds for supposing that Bevan, while a private critic of the caution of colleagues and wary of the advancement of public school right-wingers like Gaitskell, was seriously at odds with the government.

He set his face against plots to depose Attlee in 1947. He did not believe in palace revolutions, even when orchestrated by his old comrade, Stafford Cripps. Then there began a series of seismic upheavals which led to a prolonged conflict with Gaitskell, who was then backed up by Attlee, Morrison, and most of the Cabinet. A huge chasm was opened up in the winter of 1950–1, and quite unnecessarily so. In many ways Labour has never recovered. Of course, there were personal aspects. Bevan was bitterly—and per-haps legitimately—angry at being passed over, first for the Treasury, then for the Foreign Office, as Cripps and Bevin withdrew through ill-health. He was contemptuous of the upstart Gaitskell—'he's nothing, nothing, nothing'. He was also unhappy with his own move to the Ministry of Labour. In three difficult months, he found himself at odds with the unions over the prosecution of workers for unlawful strike action, over attempted wage restraint for the railwaymen, and, worst of all, over having to implement the manpower side of the swingeing new rearmament programme. Guns, not butter, was hardly a Bevan slogan. His time at the Ministry of Labour was truly 'a bed of nails' for him, as for Ray Gunter later on, and his career suddenly lurched into sharp decline.

But the main reason for his break with colleagues, of course, lay in factors far removed from petty matters of personal ambition or departmental frustration. He suddenly found that the Korean War had stampeded his colleagues into appalling miscalculations, both in foreign and defence policy, and indirectly in welfare policy, too. This was the real price of Attlee's famous visit to see Truman in Washington in December 1950, widely portrayed as a triumph for British common sense in restraining the trigger-happy Americans. The priorities of the government, even the ethic of democratic social-ism itself, were suddenly cast into disarray.

Bevan's eventual resignation was based not on pique, but on a well-argued (indeed, incontestable) critique of the economic and political consequences of a rearmament programme on which the less-experienced Gaitskell stubbornly insisted. Bevan had made it clear in Cabinet as early as 1 August 1950 that he opposed the accelerated defence programme of £3600m. which the Americans demanded. In January 1951 he passionately opposed Gaitskell's plan for a far more awesome budget of £4700m. over the next three years. Throughout that winter, Bevan made it clear that the course of British policy, committing the nation to an aggressive anti-

Communist crusade in the Far East, headed by the volatile and unstable General MacArthur, and at the cost of crushing the economy with vastly excessive defence budgets, met with his total opposition. Among other things, it was no way to fight Communism.

Worst of all, Gaitskell made it clear that he wanted to finance this programme, in part, by an attack on the health service through charges on dental and ophthalmic treatment and appliances. Gaitskell's apparent motive will be considered in the next chapter. Here it may be observed flatly that it was well known by Attlee, Morrison, and Gaitskell that to imperil the NHS (especially by imposing a charge of only £23m., trivial in so huge a budget, though fatally destructive in principle), would mean Bevan's resignation. He had told the Cabinet so, a year previously. To push on with so huge an arms programme, which it was known he opposed, and at the cost of disrupting the basic principle underlying the health service, the glory of the welfare state, would have obvious political consequences. In effect, it is hard to acquit Attlee, Morrison, and Gaitskell of charges of conspiracy to remove Bevan from the government. Certainly nothing was more discreditable afterwards than the false claims spread by Attlee, Dalton, Gaitskell, Shinwell, Gordon Walker, and others that Bevan's opposition to the defence programme, rather than just to the health charges to help pay for it, was a huge surprise, sprung from out of the blue upon unsuspecting colleagues. The written record gives them the lie direct. The Cabinet minutes show Bevan as an articulate and consistent critic of the new rearmament programmes since almost the start of the Korean War, certainly from 1 August 1950. His much-cited speech in the Commons on 15 February 1951, defending the government's policies, dwelt on the war of ideologies rather than the new burden of armaments, which he mentioned only in one imprecise sentence. Yet key ministers pressed on regardless, despite the obvious outcome that they would lose Bevan. It seems that some of them relished, and damned, the consequences.

The result was, of course, bitter and far-reaching. Bevan clashed angrily with his colleagues in the NHS Expenditure Committee and then in full Cabinet. Attempts at mediation by the ailing Bevin or the ageing Addison came to nothing. A furious editorial in *Tribune*, written by Michael Foot, which implicitly compared Gaitskell to the traitor Philip Snowden in 1931, further raised the temperature. Gaitskell's budget speech nevertheless announced the levying of charges on aspects of the health service; on Sunday, 22 April, Bevan resigned. His resignation speech in the Commons the following day seethed with bitterness at government policy and Gaitskell's 'arithmetic of Bedlam'. It was badly received in the House. On the 24th, Bevan raged almost uncontrollably at a party meeting about the attack on 'my health service'. Dalton privately (and at the top of his voice) compared him to Mosley. Shortly afterwards, Bevan, along with Wilson and John Freeman who had also resigned, associated himself with the revived 'Keep Left' group. The Bevanite revolt was born, with the publication of *One Way Only* in July (a pamphlet which now reads extraordinarily mildly) as the proclaimed platform of the new left-wing challenge. Despite Bevan's claim to his Ebbw Vale constituents that he still sought party unity, despite his role as part-author of a very mild election manifesto in October, the result was inevitably a widening chasm of bitterness which was to remain for a further twelve years.

Bevan has commonly been seen as the scapegoat for this historic schism in the party in April 1951. In fact, there is much to be said for his point of view. Initially, a clear majority of the Cabinet accepted that cuts in the health service were unnecessary even if the premise of so huge an arms budget were accepted. There were other ways of securing the needed economies, for example by cutting the pharmaceutical bill. One after the other, ministers like Dalton, Griffiths, and Tomlinson, who had been sympathetic, dropped away. Hilary Marquand, Bevan's successor at the Ministry of Health, was a mild-mannered Professor and accepted the cuts with little demur. Anyhow, he was not even in the Cabinet. Morrison, in charge since Attlee was marooned in hospital with a duodenal ulcer, constantly manoeuvred to weaken Bevan's position, while the premier himself, as noted earlier, offered no leadership. Bevan, naturally, had an overwhelming personal devotion to the Health Service he had created. But, worst of all, it was being sacrificed for a mistaken cause. Gaitskell's sums were wrong. The entire rearmament programme had been put together hastily, and with inadequate thought for the damage that would be done to the economy. By the end of the summer, Gaitskell himself was echoing many of the Bevanite criticisms, for instance about the obvious shortage of machine tools, due to be imported from America, and the effects of rearmament on the balance of payments, once again in dire straits. When Churchill became Prime Minister, he and his Minister of Supply, Duncan

Sandys, promptly began to cut back Labour's rearmament programme sharply. In effect, it was phased over four years, and the
total cost cut by about a third. Civil servants were scathing about the
miscalculations which had accompanied Gaitskell's original, rushed
estimates for defence expenditure at the start of 1951. By mid-1952
they were all Bevanites in effect, but the damage had been done long
since.

The 1950s were an unedifying period for the Labour Party. So
they were also, for most of the time, for Bevan himself. He was caught
up in an endless series of brawls with the centre-right, especially its
trade-union allies, over foreign and defence policy, over German
rearmament, over Far East policy, over the nuclear weapons programme. Gaitskell was moved to compare him to Hitler. After many
narrow escapes, Bevan was briefly expelled from the parliamentary
party in early 1955, accused of attacks on trade-union comrades
and of anti-party activities generally. Even after the 1955 general
election, his relations with colleagues remained difficult. He rejoined
the Shadow Cabinet in February as Shadow Colonial Secretary (Gaitskell turned him down as foreign affairs spokesman), and played an
effective part in ridiculing Eden's and Lloyd's handling of the Suez
operation. Memorably, he congratulated the Foreign Secretary for
sounding the bugle of advance to cover his retreat. Privately, though,
he continued to warn Jennie Lee of the dangers to the party from
Gaitskell's 'reactionary impulses'.

Yet, in fact, in 1957 he and Gaitskell swallowed their pride and
made a concordat. Bevan now had a more congenial role as Shadow
Foreign Secretary where his internationalism could have full rein.
Soon afterwards, he became deputy leader of the party, and retained
this position until his final decline and death from cancer in mid-
1960. However, his reconciliation, such as it was, with the party
right was accompanied by a new series of rows with old left-wing
colleagues—Crossman, Barbara Castle, and, more painfully, with his
most devoted admirer, Michael Foot. Bevan's unexpectedly fierce
rebuke to the unilateralists in the 1957 party conference and his
insistence that Britain should retain her nuclear weapons lest she go
'naked into the conference chamber' led to savage quarrels with the
remnants of the old Bevanite movement. Bevan's troubles were
compounded by some personal strain as well, since Jennie Lee was
suffering acute nervous pressure as a result of her mother's illness.
In part, it was the mediation and personal tact of Jill Craigie, Michael

Foot's wife, which restored some harmony between these leading figures on the left. But it was a bleak decade. Bevan may even have been fortunate in his untimely death. At least, it spared him attendance at the 1960 party conference, when the public brawling between Gaitskell and his CND critics reached new heights of savagery which threatened to destroy the party altogether.

And yet, it was not all bitterness and negative protest. Bevan's call for unity may seem ironic for much of the time. Yet, remove the personal antagonism between him and Gaitskell, erase the memories of what had taken place in April 1951, and the gulf between him and his comrades seems less overwhelming. Bevan was himself a constant critic of Labour foreign and defence policy in the fifties, but he was no pacifist—and, indeed, no unilateralist. His critique in time helped the party evolve towards a more balanced outlook, in which adherence to NATO remained axiomatic, but with a more measured view taken of the defence options. In 1964, Labour under Harold Wilson had a broadly Bevanite defence policy, with a rejection of Britain's so-called independent nuclear deterrent. Extraordinarily enough, it was not until 1983, under the lead of another old Bevanite, Michael Foot, that this non-nuclear policy was fully reaffirmed. On domestic matters, Bevan was not far from the mainstream of Labour thinking. Since, unlike Tony Benn in the 1980s, he did not disavow the work of a Labour government of which he had been a key minister, Bevan could go along with much of the revisionism of the period. He endorsed the *Industry and Society* policy document in 1957, which, in effect, rejected rigid models of nationalization and accepted the need for a mixed economy. It offered simultaneously a radical analysis and revisionist solutions. He accepted, too, the growing emphasis on increased production as a basis of socialism, no less than planned distribution and the ethic of equality. For much of the decade, his contributions to debate on domestic policy were constructive, and well attuned to a more flexible and subtle method of approaching the socialist goal. Meanwhile, beyond the shores of Britain, Bevan remained, more than any other of Labour's leaders, a figure of international stature, on friendly terms with personalities as varied as Mendès-France and Nenni, Ben-Gurion and Walter Reuther, Djilas and Nehru. He was hailed on British and American university campuses as a political giant. No-one more fully symbolized the vibrancy of Britain's 'third way', or the internationalism of its message.

Despite the dismal bickering and sheer waste of much of Bevan's last decade, his appeal still seems an enduring one, of much relevance for the 1980s. He remains, perhaps, the most attractive figure that the British socialist movement has produced in its eighty-odd years of fitful life. Some of the attractiveness, of course, derives from Bevan in power and his remarkable record of social achievement during his time at the Ministry of Health after 1945. But he was also an intellectual force and moral inspiration whose magic, charm, and humour retain all their appeal a generation on. Much of this quality comes across in his one significant book, *In Place of Fear*, published in early 1952. It was reissued in the 1970s and is still well worth close attention by socialists and others.

As a book it is not altogether satisfactory. It was put together somewhat hurriedly during a tour of Yugoslavia in the autumn of 1951, when he and Jennie Lee were personal guests of President Tito. It consists of eight somewhat disparate chapters on a range of domestic and external themes. Some of them, bearing in part on his earlier experiences in South Wales and as a young MP, were written years earlier. They are really introductions to the main theme, often announced but seldom developed. In some ways, too, *In Place of Fear* is too rooted in its time, a product of the forties and thereby somewhat dated. Bevan's concept of socialism is based four-square on the party manifesto of 1945, with public ownership as its centre-piece. His passionate certainties about nationalization strike us now as rigid and remote from current explorations of what socialism means. It is also a somewhat insular book, for all the author's genuine internationalism, with shafts of anti-Americanism well to the fore. It is poignant in these hard times to read of Bevan's conviction that world trade movements in no way 'limit the application of socialist policies to the British economy'. Above all, there is no consistent financial strategy spelt out. Abolish capitalism, it seems, and all else will follow.

Even so, his main themes transcend all these limitations. His message, so sparkling in expression, still has enduring relevance and freshness. First, there is an uncompromising commitment to public expenditure and public enterprise. Public spending, as on health or housing, was the only means available to a democratic society of redressing, by consent, the injustices, inequalities, and sheer stupidities of the social system. Hence the decision to finance the Health Service from general taxation, not from a poll-tax. Secondly, in terms of method, there is a passionate faith in the parliamentary route to socialism, 'government by discussion'. Bevan's view, Jennie Lee has observed, was that of 'a passionate parliamentarian'. He had much contempt for the kind of suppression of free expression from which he himself often suffered at the hands of the party machine. Thirdly, as has been already noted, he was always an agent of power. Power must be sought out, mobilized and used vigorously, constructively, and courageously.

Last—and perhaps most moving to a generation in which national self-confidence seems to have withered—there is Bevan's emotional affirmation of the values of democratic socialism, British style. This is no colourless 'middle way', no pallid alternative to Soviet Communism or Butskellite capitalism. It had its own native traditions and pedigree, traceable back to the libertarian creed of the Levellers. It had its location, too, in socialist traditions elsewhere. Hence, the continuing appeal to him of the South American libertarian philosopher, José Enrique Rodo, a more important influence on Bevan than Marx or Engels were (even though he never repudiated his early debt to Marxism). Bevan's democratic socialism combined planning with vision. He followed Rodo's call in *The Motives of Proteus* to 'consecrate a part of your soul to an unknown future'. Bevan's socialism was vibrant, exciting, and alive—and it was also great fun. Unlike the unsmiling, sexless vanguard of the Militants of the 1980s, cheerfulness and humanity kept breaking in. Bevan had no time for drabness, austerity, or the desiccation of the Webb–Cole tradition. He ate well, dressed elegantly, and conducted himself with style. He was an audacious romantic, perhaps the 'sensual puritan' of Michael Foot's brilliant description. Bevan's political testament, incomplete though it is, lays bare the essence of his faith. As a pioneer, a prophet, and most important, a practitioner of power, Bevan lived out his own generous ideal.

# HUGH GAITSKELL

HUGH GAITSKELL has become stereotyped as the Adlai Stevenson of British politics, intellectually appealing, electorally unfortunate, the best Prime Minister we never had. In the fifties he became the symbol of modern, updated socialism, who supplied half of the name of that famous centrist economist, Mr Butskell. Certainly, no labour leader has ever inspired such respect across the political spectrum, or amongst significant segments of the Tory opposition. Since his death, Gaitskell has been mourned as embodying the spirit of revisionism, that 'sensible socialism' which anticipated the Social Democrats of 1981 and which in time led his disciple, William Rodgers, organizer of the Gaitskellites in the constituencies in the fight-back against CND in 1960–1, to defect from his old party. Of Gaitskell's intellectual force, technical skill as an economist, and charisma for centrist and progressive opinion across the nation and the North Atlantic world, there can be no doubt. Philip Williams's magnificent, if partisan, biography recaptures all those fine qualities. Gaitskell inspired an affection close to love amongst a generation of young Labour activists in the fifties. He remains deeply missed down to the present time.

The more abiding question, however, concerns Gaitskell's qualities as leader of the Labour Party. This, after all, was his crucial political role and claim to eminence. Here, the supra-party charisma somewhat dissolves. For almost his entire period as a front-ranking politician, from October 1950 when he became Chancellor until his tragically early death in January 1963, Gaitskell was embroiled in internal party conflict. He was the major antagonist of Bevan and the Bevanites in the early fifties. At the end of the decade, he was caught up in even more savage civil war, first over Clause Four, then over unilateralism in 1960–1. In 1962 he adroitly withdrew from yet another internal clash when he declared himself against British membership of the Common Market. No doubt many, or most of these conflicts were endemic in the history and outlook of that transitional period of Labour's evolution, when the lessons of the Attlee period were being digested. But there can be no question that Gaitskell threw himself into the fray aggressively and with determination to win. As he put it at the 1960 party conference, during his defeat over the bomb, his style was 'to fight, fight, and fight again'. His combativeness and courage were never in question. Unlike the retiring, almost invisible Attlee, Gaitskell led from the front, going over the top to confront the enemy like a regimental officer leading his men to mass slaughter at the battle of the Somme.

Whether this was the right or best way of leading the party is another matter. Gaitskell eventually won a great victory over the unilateralists; but much blood was spilt on the way, while over Clause Four, another key issue, he got the psychology of the party wholly wrong. The one general election at which he led his party was highly unsuccessful, the campaign marred by a fatal pledge by him that Labour's social plans would not mean higher income tax. Harold Wilson later described him as, by temperament, an administrator rather than a politician. It is very probable that Gaitskell would have made a highly competent, perhaps outstanding, Prime Minister. But he might never have given himself the chance, even when assisted by uncovenanted benefits such as Macmillan's 'night of the long knives'. There is general agreement that Wilson's succession to the party leadership in February 1963, albeit in tragic circumstances, and the much more harmonious mood that spread through Labour's ranks thereafter, were greeted with relief. Labour's Wars of the Roses (or perhaps War of Attlee's Succession) had been wound up at long last.

Gaitskell had advanced to a high position in the party essentially as a backroom technocratic planner rather than through the main avenue in the party. He represented that distinctive strain in British cultural life, the middle-class, public school, leftish Hampstead intellectual. His father was an Indian civil servant of conservative outlook. Hugh went to the Dragon, an élitist (though experimental) school in north Oxford, then to Winchester, where like Cripps, Jay, and Crossman, he imbibed that distinctive Wykehamist ethos of public service. As an undergraduate at New College, he was stirred by the General Strike; but the decisive change in his outlook undoubtedly came with his brief period as an adult education lecturer in the Nottinghamshire coalfield in the late twenties. This aroused all the compassion and social guilt which drove him on throughout his career. Then in 1928 he was appointed to a lectureship in economics at University College, London, where he stayed for the next eleven years.

We have already seen Gaitskell as outstanding among Dalton's group of young planners after 1931, and a major figure in recasting Labour's economic programmes, both on the Finance and Trade Subcommittee and informally. At the same time, his first-hand experience of the fall of social democracy in Vienna and his involvement in the London Jewish community (where he found his future wife) gave him a powerful commitment to the anti-fascist cause. In 1935 he fought Chatham as a Labour candidate. But he remained on the fringes of party politics. During the war he served with distinction in Dalton's two departments, the Ministry of Economic Warfare and the Board of Trade. He was, without question, a superb executant of the wartime consensus for planning and egalitarianism as then understood, with a more profound understanding of the new economics of Keynes than his mentor, Dalton. The war confirmed his enthusiasm for state direction of the economy.

But his was still a cloistered world, removed from the passion and hurly-burly of grass-roots politics in the constituences. He felt an affinity to gifted dons promoted into the public service, men like Oliver Franks and John Maud. Similarly, he found himself at home with centrist civil-service planners like Edwin Plowden and Robert Hall, rather than with more partisan figures. Even the election of 1945, in which he was easily returned for South Leeds, gave him only an indirect experience of political life since he was seriously ill during the campaign. He entered parliament as a back-bencher with powerful contacts with the leadership through Dalton, but an unusually slight knowledge of the grass-roots of the party.

He had risen very rapidly indeed by the end of 1950, as an able and decisive minister. He succeeded Shinwell as Minister of Fuel and Power in October 1947 (which ensured him the undying hatred and inverted class contempt of that politician). He handled gas nationalization with much efficiency, and then became Minister of Economic Affairs, again outside the Cabinet, in February 1950. Here he acquired important new contact with international affairs, notably through the working out of the European Payments Union in the summer of 1950. There was, however, one quite pivotal experience in the making of Hugh Gaitskell. In the sterling crisis during the summer of 1949, along with his close friend and ally, Douglas Jay, he emerged as a decisive and clear-headed advocate of devaluation. At a time when Harold Wilson seemed consumed by political calculation, when Cripps himself was uncertain, and ministers like

Attlee and Morrison offered no real lead, Gaitskell's drive and self-confidence were highly impressive. The result was that he was propelled, over the heads of senior colleagues (including, of course, Aneurin Bevan), to succeed Cripps at the Treasury in October 1950. But the issue that had got him there—and which pushed him on to the party leadership itself, five years later—was the specialist economic issue of the technical factors that governed the correct rate of the pound sterling to the dollar, rather than a theme which bore directly on the broad philosophy or strategy of socialism. Few politicians have moved on to one of the supreme offices of state with less political experience than did Gaitskell in October 1950. Not that he betrayed any doubts or unbecoming modesty. He celebrated news of his promotion by dancing the night away in a Greenwich Village night-club in New York. He was also ambitious enough to ensure that he was recognized as number four in the government, behind Attlee, Bevin, and Morrison, but well ahead of Bevan.

His one experience of high office was his twelve months at the Treasury from October 1950 to October 1951. It was not a happy time for him. He was later recalled as the author of a budget which severely strained the economy, and as the blunt instrument who drove Bevan and Wilson out of the government. What is most striking about Gaitskell's performance as Chancellor, in fact, is that, for all his real claims as an economist of superb technical skill and understanding, his approach to the main problems of the day was overwhelmingly political, inexperienced though he clearly was in wider realms. He was passionately pro-American after the outbreak of the Korean War, more so indeed than Ernest Bevin himself had ever been. From discussions with the Americans over the European Payments Union in the summer of 1950, Gaitskell emerged as almost unthinkingly Atlanticist. His earlier doubts about US international economic policy dissolved in the light of the successful negotiations between the OEEC countries and a surprisingly enlightened US administration. He wrote to Averell Harriman on 24 June 1950 (the day before the attack on South Korea, as it happened) that 'the most important thing in the world is for the United States and Britain to work along together'. The EPU discussions had been 'wonderfully encouraging'. Gaitskell's passion for the United States became almost lyrical henceforth. He felt most at home with what he called 'economist–New Dealer types' like Dean Acheson ('a sensitive and cultured mind'),

Averell Harriman, and George Kennan, whose combination of Rooseveltian liberalism and robust anti-Communism he shared to the full. His first clash with Cabinet colleagues came on a foreign policy issue, America's 'brand China' resolution in the United Nations in January 1951, designed to pronounce that the Chinese were the aggressors in Korea. Almost alone in the Cabinet he was a whole-hearted supporter of the American position. Hugh Dalton felt that his protégé's alarm at the alleged 'anti-Americanism' of Strachey, Ede, Griffiths, Noel-Baker, and other centrist colleagues was somewhat unbalanced.

Gaitskell's commitment as Chancellor to the huge £4700m. rearmament programme in January 1951 was also based on political calculations. In economic terms, Gaitskell himself spelt out to his colleagues on 25 January all the real disadvantages that the rearma-ment programme would bring, for inflation, the balance of payments, long-term investment, the allocation of labour, the export drive, and much else besides. So appalling was his frankness, he might almost have been arguing against his own policies. But devotion to the Anglo-American alliance conquered all other considerations, while the advice of his friend, Oliver Franks, from the embassy in Wash-ington also confirmed his opinions. Gaitskell's budget of April 1951 was sketchily put together, and soon shown to be misconceived. It also included cuts in investment allowances which economists were later to criticize. But the budget rested on political conviction rather than economic rationalism. Gaitskell wanted to show that Britain was America's best and firmest ally, unshakable in its commitment to defence of the free world. On that basis, he would allow any financial sacrifice to drive his message home.

There was also the political sacrifice of Nye Bevan. Gaitskell showed no particular grief at this loss of a clear rival. Indeed, he formulated his plans, including cuts in the health service, in a way which made Bevan's resignation almost a foregone conclusion. Gaitskell was gunning for Bevan from his very first day in the Treasury, when he directed his advisers to cost possible cuts in the social services. He had had a good relationship with Bevan at times in the 1945-50 period. Both were close to Cripps in their different ways, in 1948-9. 'He will be prime minister one day', Gaitskell recorded of Bevan in June 1948. They had stimulating discussions on religious matters, in which Bevan gaily taxed Gaitskell with being an eighteenth-century rationalist whereas he was a nineteenth-century romantic. It was a shrewd, if humorous, comparison. Of the two, Bevan had always the greater imagination, instinctive flair, and perhaps humanity Gaitskell was always an Encyclopaedist; he would have been quite at home with Diderot and Voltaire (though not perhaps with Rousseau) in the Café Procope.

But between these two gifted democratic socialists, tragically for the future, there was always a profound incompatibility. Gaitskell tended to see Bevan as ruthless, overemotional in a Welsh way, volatile, and potentially dangerous. On one extraordinary occasion later on, he was even to compare Bevan to Hitler. In the Cabinet in March–April 1951, he refused to make concessions to Bevan's point of view, even for the sake of a paltry £13m. that his health charges would bring in during the current financial year. Dalton himself was alarmed at the way Gaitskell launched bitter assaults on Bevan and his followers. Dalton shrewdly confided to his diary that Gaitskell, in these attacks, 'thought too little about the Party & too much about the electorate in general'. These words could serve as an epitaph for Gaitskell's entire career. All compromises were brushed aside. Either Gaitskell or Bevan had to go. The more senior man it was who went. An era of civil war was ushered in.

Thereafter, Gaitskell played a more measured role. In the Abadan oil crisis that summer, he found himself aligned with Attlee and Dalton in restraining the gunboat belligerence of Morrison and Shinwell. Here again, though, there was an Anglo-American theme since the US envoy, Paul McGhee, made it clear that Washington was as unhappy with these echoes of British imperialism as was much of the Labour Party (Washington had its eyes on Middle East oil, too). For the same Atlanticist reason, Gaitskell threw his weight strongly behind German rearmament. In the late summer, partly because of the new defence programme he had so incautiously endorsed, Gaitskell found himself in grave economic difficulties. The balance of payments rapidly deteriorated, and he had to travel to Washington, cap in hand, to ask, unavailingly, for financial aid (or 'budget sharing') in meeting Britain's huge defence commitment. It was not forthcoming: Snyder at the US Treasury was too isolationist for that. Gaitskell's relations with Attlee, never all that cordial, now somewhat deteriorated, and he was pointedly excluded from Cabinet discussions on the election date in October 1951 (the timing of which he opposed). In the event, Labour's defeat was a narrow one, and Gaitskell could emerge as a formidable front-bench figure in opposition. But the background was a huge rift in the party, discontent in the grass-roots, and the most charismatic socialist leader of the day in open revolt. For these developments, Gaitskell bore a prime responsibility.

In the carnage of the fifties, as has been noted, he took a leading, belligerent role. It was ironic that his firmest supporters were rugged trade-unionists like Arthur Deakin and Sam Watson. It was precisely with rugged proletarians like these that Gaitskell felt personally most awkward, for all the experiences of his youthful days in the Notts. coalfield. (Partly for this reason, he never really got on with the party secretary, Morgan Phillips, who felt Gaitskell was an Oxford-bred intellectual snob.) He reacted to the Bevanite 'coup' at the 1952 Morecambe conference with much ferocity. He gave an eye for an eye and an NHS denture for denture in these stern encounters. Even his close friends admitted his intolerance. His passions were reinforced by the fact that most of the argument concerned aspects of the Anglo-American alliance—German rearmament, SEATO, the bomb—to which he was so devoted. Bevan was undeniably difficult; but Gaitskell compounded the error by overreacting. Eventually he tried in March 1955 to drive Bevan out of the party altogether (this time for his conduct in the Commons, rather than for organizing 'a party within a party'). But he was saved from himself by the consciences of two trade-unionist NEC members who were Moral Rearmers (as well as German Rearmers). The bitterness, of such a highly personalized kind, continued to rankle years later. It made Michael Foot's second volume of his magnificent biography of Bevan, covering the years 1945–60, very different in tone from his first. The same feeling spills over in Foot's otherwise typically generous volume of essays, *Loyalists and Loners* (1986), in which Gaitskell (unlike even George Brown) is conspicuously not accorded the title of 'Brother Hugh'. There is a tale of Gaitskell and Foot glowering at each other across a square in Portofino where, by chance, they both happened to be holidaying at the same time. The mediator between the two groups, improbably enough, was another British holiday-maker, Sir Maurice Bowra, a friend of Gaitskell's and also the warden of Wadham, Foot's old college. The outcome in the party was that when Gaitskell was elected Labour's leader in December 1955, defeating both Bevan and the veteran Herbert Morrison with some ease, he was regarded, inevitably, as the partisan of the virtuous right over the Utopian left, and to that degree a sectarian candidate. His role, claimed *The Economist*, was 'to turn his back on the age of Keir Hardie', and so he did.

Naturally, as party leader, Gaitskell could afford to take a more detached view and try to bind up the party's wounds. To a considerable degree he did so, with the assistance of that skilful but serpentine fellow-Wykehamist, Dick Crossman. There were various ingenious compromises. One of the more celebrated of these was the so-called Crossman–Padley agreement over unilateral disarmament in January 1961, which Alan Watkins has claimed as being for political commentators what the once-notorious Schleswig-Holstein affair was for students of nineteenth-century diplomacy. In the end, the CND Left and Gaitskell agreed in rejecting it. The most dramatic reconciling gesture, of course, was the readmission of Aneurin Bevan to the fold, and to the Shadow Cabinet. The signs of *détente* were there in 1956 when, first over the row involving the dinner of Khruschev and Bulganin with Labour Party leaders, then over the major issue of Suez, Bevan gave Gaitskell's position a broad endorsement. At the 1957 party conference, potentially explosive, Bevan strongly backed Gaitskell on the two main controversies: the policy document *Industry and Society*, with its retreat from nationalization; and, more spectacularly, the unilateralist demand that Britain give up her nuclear weapons. Bevan now became Shadow Foreign Secretary, and he and Gaitskell became closer than ever before. They even invited each other to lunch—two men whom Crossman noted 'had never had a drink with each other, much less a meal, in their whole lives'. There were many disadvantages that Labour faced in 1959, and which led to a heavy electoral defeat. But conflict between Gaitskellite right and Bevanite left was no longer amongst them.

The main unifying theme in these years, however, was the strong impact that Gaitskell was beginning to make as leader of the opposition. His intellectual gifts were now being turned to political effect. He was able to build on the changing mood of the left in the wake of Crosland's *Future of Socialism*, and on the eve of the formal abandonment of its Marxist commitment by Ollenhauer's German SPD. Democratic socialism could now be redefined. Its keynote would be social equality through new policies for health, education, housing, and the environment; the presupposition was the continuous affluence and economic growth that Keynesians like himself had made possible. Nationalization, physical controls, anything resembling the class war, were set aside, and most of the labour movement seemed to concur. In foreign affairs, Gaitskell proved sufficiently flexible to adapt the Bevan critique in suggesting new initiatives in disarmament, for instance outlined in his 1957 Godkin lectures at Harvard, and building on Britain's role in the Commonwealth to forge new links with the third world and non-aligned states. He expressed sympathy with the Rapacki Plan for a demilitarized zone in central Europe, including the whole of Germany.

The outstanding example of Gaitskell's leadership, of course, was Suez. His first reaction, as is well known, was a strong condemnation of Egyptian nationalization of the canal and a comparison of Nasser with Hitler. Partly after pressure from parliamentary colleagues like Healey and Jay on the right and Barbara Castle on the left, a more measured attitude appeared, and Gaitskell spoke out powerfully against the Anglo-French invasion of Suez. His instinct for collaboration with the Americans, his strong Commonwealth sentiments, his moral belief in the UN, his economist's regard for external financial pressures on the reserves, all played their part. For a time, Gaitskell (along with other figures on the right such as Denis Healey) was a key figure in Tory demonology, at a time when Bevan was being praised in some quarters for moderation and patriotism. Never was Gaitskell more hated by the Tories. Never was he a more effective leader of the party and the movement. He played his courageous role in the eviction of Eden in dishonour, and in the repair of the damage that Suez had done.

Gaitskell was at his best as dynamo of the movement in the later fifties. But the heavy defeat of October 1959 saw the old troubles return. Along with them, Gaitskell's limitations as party leader reasserted themselves. The proposal to abolish Clause Four was a victory for abstract logic over common sense. Rationally, of course, Labour did not intend, and never had intended, to nationalize the whole of the economy, or even the bulk of it. The 'corner shop' of Morrisonian rhetoric would stand secure. In practice, this unheralded attack on the party's commitment to socialism aroused intense alarm, not confined to the left alone. There was, in any case, no evidence that Clause Four had played any part at all in Labour's electoral defeat. Clause Four was an expression of a tendency, a direction, an objective, in achieving long-term social change, even if the means were inevitably to be gradual, piecemeal, and even confused. Labour was setting capitalism on the road to 'ultimate extinction', as Abraham Lincoln so argued about slavery in his debates with Douglas.

Gaitskell's rash decision to raise the issue, along with current talk that even the historic name 'Labour Party' might be abolished as a legacy of an outworn class rhetoric, was a disaster. He had to beat an ignominious retreat. But the old suspicions about his leadership and lack of real understanding of the party had been revived.

This added to his difficulties in the fight with CND in 1960–1, in which many trade-unionists, not necesssarily unilateralist, let along pacifist, turned against his leadership. After defeat at Scarborough, he fought again and won the day decisively at Blackpool in 1961, partly because of the skill of CDS under William Rodgers in using the factional methods of grass-roots permeation usually adopted by the left. At Blackpool, the bulk of constituency party votes, for once, swung to the party's right wing. But the damage done was immense. One outcome was that Harold Wilson, who played a somewhat byzantine role during the CND controversy, seemed to many, even before the event, a more adroit and subtle manager of the party.

These were years in which the Macmillan regime seemed to tumble into disarray, with a cumulation of disasters. The varied forces of the 'pay pause', the governmental shock of the 'night of the long knives', security lapses, television satire, and the extramural activities of Christine Keeler and Mandy Rice-Davies all seemed to mark the twilight of Tory rule, a process well under way even before Gaitskell's death in January 1963. For all that, Labour's morale still appeared fragile. Despite some victories, some of the by-election rewards at Orpington, Montgomery, and elsewhere seemed to be going the way of the Liberals. Labour still looked like a party of losers, with a rare capacity for snatching defeat from the jaws of victory. Gaitskell's last months were preoccupied with trying to patch up further divisions in his party over the Common Market, and, more dramatically, to formulate contingency plans, including the possible use of paratroop forces, to prevent a possible secession by a racialist white regime in Southern Rhodesia. Then came his untimely death. Under Wilson, the tide seemed dramatically to turn. The old left, by misadventure, seemed to have won at last.

Gaitskell was a distinguished, attractive, warm-hearted politician. He had a particular appeal to the intellectual young. As Prime Minister he would probably have been highly successful. But as leader of the Labour Party, he left much to be desired. He came to politics through the universities, the civil service, and technocracy. He was propelled to the Treasury too early for his own good, without acquaintance with policy or politics other than specialized areas of economic planning. He reacted too intolerantly, certainly too dogmatically and ideologically, to the party divisions caused by the Bevanite rupture, and indirectly by his own policy as Chancellor. He lacked the ingredients needed to restore calm to his troubled ranks: Attlee's tranquillity, Wilson's sense of manoeuvre, Callaghan's feel for what the movement would take. He and his party were left exhausted by fighting each other, with insufficient energy in reserve to train their fire on the Tory enemy. Socially, too, his style of life did not endear itself to wide reaches of the party. No doubt life amongst the Frognal set in Hampstead was a good deal less glamorous and exciting than rumour had it. Figures like Crosland and Jenkins gave it rare intellectual panache. Gaitskell, like Crosland, is surely to be commended for setting his face against that puritanism which disfigures so much of the labour movement, and for an outgoing, human enjoyment of parties, dancing, and the company of pretty women. From his early youth, Gaitskell was known as a somewhat raffish *enfant terrible*. No one was less of the 'desiccated calculating machine' of legend. And yet, evidence such as his correspondence with Anne Fleming, a doubtless attractive woman of far-right views and no political understanding (whose relationship with Gaitskell even led to rumours of divorce sometimes being entertained) sheds an odd light on the Gaitskellite ethic, or part of it. However trivial their content, the Fleming–Gaitskell letters must at least throw some doubt on the socialist credentials of Labour's leader at that period. Gaitskell entered the party through intellectual conviction and social compassion. But he always viewed it somewhat from the outside and felt detached in its company. He made an enormous intellectual contribution to the welfare democracy which formed the post-war social consensus. He was an educator, a humanist, a civilized force of palpable honesty and integrity. He was amongst the best of his time. But what many felt he was not, and never should have been, was a leader of the Labour Party.

# MORGAN PHILLIPS

THE apparatchik has not been the best-loved of personalities in the Labour Party, as in other parties. Compared with the glamour of policy-making, mass oratory, and the glare of media attention, the closet activites of the machine man, reminiscent of the household activities of Chamber or Wardrobe so beloved of medieval historians, do not have much appeal. The Tapers and Tadpoles work in an aura of secrecy, manoeuvre, even corruption (so some imply). Their natural habitat is the atmosphere of the smoke-filled room. Party organizers like Sir Robert Sanders, Archibald Salvidge, or Francis Schnadhorst may arouse the academic interest of scholars generations later for the light they and their papers tend to throw on the politics of the past (apparatchiks necessarily tend to be very archivally minded). But, at the time, they are usually unpopular even when respected or feared. Yet, for Labour above all parties, representative of the poorer and less privileged sectors of society, organization is critical. From 1918 onwards, the mechanics of party machine politics have been central to its success in keeping local parties, their funding, and structure in good repair, and in bringing out the vote on time. Few now recall men like Jim Middleton, George Shepherd, Dick Windle, or Len Williams, but they are surely among the unsung heroes of Labour's earlier advance. Failures in the machine were linked with many of the vulnerable features of the party, locally and nationally, in the 1970s and early 1980s. Socialist rotten boroughs gave new outlets for the far left, Militant or otherwise. The Bermondsey by-election, which saw Labour's vote plummet so catastrophically in 1982, is a key exhibit here. One sign of Neil Kinnock's new impact on the party in 1985–6 has been his application of a new professionalism and efficiency to the Walworth Road machine under its new general secretary, Larry Whitty—and rightly so.

It is appropriate, then, when considering key personalities during Labour's high noon of power, to consider the supreme apparatchik of those years, Morgan Phillips, secretary, then general secretary of the party from 1944 until just before his death in 1963. For Phillips, without any doubt, exerted a crucial and all-encompassing role in that period. He may, indeed, be considered among the outstanding professional organizers in the entire history of the party. Only Mac-Donald and (especially) Henderson in the early pioneering days begin to approach him as manipulator and organizer of victory.

Phillips's origins were a classic restatement of the rise of Labour as a significant political force. He was born in Aberdare in 1902, to a Welsh-speaking mining family. He entered the local Rhymney Valley pits, became active in the local ILP and constituency Labour Party, and served as agent for the Bargoed Steam Coal Lodge in the 1924-6 period. He was a student at the famous Central Labour College in Regent's Park in its last two years, and was apparently destined for the typical left-wing role in the miners' union, the Fed, characteristic of the Welsh valleys at the time. But Phillips was unusual in his fascination with politics, and more especially with political organization for which he showed an obvious flair. He entered local London politics, becoming secretary-agent for the West Fulham Labour Party and then for Whitechapel, a member of the Fulham Borough Council and chairman of its Finance Committee. In 1937 he entered Transport House as propaganda organizer of the national party. After a brief period as Eastern Counties' organizer, he became secretary of the party Research Department in 1941. Here he impressed Dalton and others by his clear-headedness and ability to draft cogent position papers and memoranda. In early 1944, at a crucial time in Labour's history, after the reluctant retirement of the aged Jim Middleton, he was elected the party general secretary, over the heads of such notable rivals as the national agent, George Shepherd, and the runner-up, Maurice Webb, party youth officer and a former journalist close to Herbert Morrison.

Morgan Phillips was thus in charge of party organization and the policy-making apparatus in 1945, that year of victory, and a key figure in Labour's landslide triumph. No doubt, Labour would have won anyway, and its electoral triumph was not really due to superior organizational resources. Even in 1945, the Tory machine had most of the money and more salaried full-time officials. But there was broad agreement that the machine—and Phillips himself—did very well during the campaign, and that party workers, both paid and volunteers, had never been thicker on the ground. Dalton, as was his wont, greeted Phillips's appointment as secretary with the faintest of praise. 'He is not a commanding personality. ... And he is very Welsh in the derogatory sense. He is, I understand, a terrific intriguer.'

(a rich remark from such a source!). But he added, patronizingly, 'he may grow and he has a wonderful chance'. The subsequent growth of Morgan Phillips after 1944 dispelled even Dalton's habitual scepticism and unfraternal judgement on fellow comrades. The Attlee years were Phillips's great era. He personified the unity and firm sense of direction that the party enjoyed in its years of power. His very background illustrated the intimate links existing between the political movement and the trade unions who provided the base for the alliance, and which enabled control of the NEC and the party conference to pass naturally to the party's leaders in government. Through a close, but sometimes uneasy, relationship with Morrison (whom Phillips tended to feel had upstaged him in the 1945 campaign), Transport House also remained in close touch with the parliamentary party.

Phillips was a valuable lieutenant for the leadership at all stages, deeply loyal to Attlee himself. This took the particular form of exercising his powers, subtly and urbanely, in support of the leaders at all times. It was Phillips who helped determine the arrangements, including the agenda and motions accepted for debate, for party conference. Phillips, too, was the willing agent of discipline, with an iron hand if needed, to ensure that rebels were swiftly brought to heel. Thus in 1948 he was an effective instrument for the NEC in disciplining the left-wingers, over twenty in number, who had erred by their telegram of support to Nenni during the Italian elections. He was also a vigorous agent of authority in the expulsion of a string of far-left fellow-travellers, Platts-Mills, followed by Zilliacus, Solley, and Hutchinson, in 1948-9. Providentially, there was also a right-winger to expel, Alfred Edwards, who objected to steel nationalization. Phillips's adroitness helped ensure the minimum of inconvenience for the party conference and elsewhere on these matters. Indeed, the expelled rebels were scarcely given any real opportunity to defend themselves publicly. Not that it would have made any differences if they had been. All the key figures in the party, from Morrison to Bevan, were determined that they should pay the maximum price for their deviation. In his eyrie in Smith Square, Phillips cheerfully kept a bulky file on the 'lost sheep' who had been expelled from the fold. His files amply illustrate his skilful and highly efficient control of party discipline in these years. In 1950 *Socialist Fellowship* joined a growing list of 'proscribed organizations'. Phillips was also an expert manager of the media at this period, assisted by his good relationship with the Labour press, particularly the editor of the *Daily Herald*, Percy Cudlipp, yet another Welshman prominent in Labour circles, who had begun his career on the *South Wales Echo*. Phillips, indeed, always had a softish spot for his Welsh countrymen. He took pleasure in proclaiming his Welsh credentials (including his knowledge of the Welsh language) when the Welsh Council of Labour was formed, under the direction of Cliff Prothero, in 1947. This was a concession to local sentiment which Phillips had earlier opposed. The smack of firm government echoed through the movement, even in sleepy rural constituencies. More muffled, but even more potent, was the general secretary's skill in deflecting, or sweeping under the carpet, sheaves of left-wing protests from the constituencies about Bevin's cold war foreign policy, conscription, the need for more nationalization, or the fate of Platts-Mills or (especially) Zilliacus. Later criticism by the Labour left that the right wing was as active in suppressing the left in the 1940s as it was vocal in complaining about similar tactics by its opponents in the 1980s certainly finds support in party archives.

Phillips, however, had wider interests and ambitions. He retained a strong, largely mainstream, interest in policy-making. In 1947 he was active in forwarding to the NEC complaints by regional party organizers that controls, high taxation, rationing, and austerity were alienating the voters, especially the suburban middle class. In 1949 he urged Attlee in the general direction of Morrison-type consolidation, and a brake on more socialism, with the coming general election in mind. He urged a summer election in 1950 but was to be disappointed.

The area of policy in which he took a particular interest was foreign affairs. He served as chairman of the re-formed Socialist International from 1948 to 1957. He took a keen interest in the activities of the International Department at Transport House, whose secretary was Denis Healey. Like him, Phillips was an enthusiast for the main drift of Bevin's foreign policy, and a strong opponent of anything that resembled European integration. He objected to Labour's being represented at the European Unity congress at The Hague in May 1948, addressed by Churchill and other right-wing figures, and sent vigorous reprimands to Labour MPs such as 'Kim' Mackay who did attend. As with other Labour figures on the Socialist International—Morrison and Dalton, for example—Phillips's internationalism was strictly qualified, as was his socialism. He was always intensely interested in foreign policy issues—but sensitive if this was misinterpreted. He angrily rebuked Kingsley Martin in May 1949 for suggesting in the *New Statesman* that he had been 'too busy looking after international affairs'. He pointed out that international conferences had occupied only nine days of his time in the preceding twelve months. On balance, Transport House was a lively place in the 1945–51 period, even intellectually distinguished, with figures like Denis Healey and Michael Young in the research department. Under Morgan Phillips, to some degree at least, Head Office was a powerhouse of ideas and policies, home and abroad, as well as a hub of organization.

The divisions into which the party was plunged in early 1951 had a serious effect on Morgan Phillips as on all other Labour leaders. In the crisis that April, he emerged as a strong ally of the party leadership against his old friend, Aneurin Bevan. He vigorously rebutted criticism from Bevan, Mrs Castle and Mikardo, three left-wingers on the NEC, that he had acted unconstitutionally in announcing publicly the executive's strong support for Attlee and Gaitskell. He had difficult relations with his fellow-Welshman, Bevan, in the early 1950s. In 1954, so Gaitskell recorded in his diary, he broke finally with Bevan who had insulted him during a visit to the Far East by telling him 'You are only a paid servant of the party.' Phillips worked assiduously against *Tribune* after its attacks on Deakin and other trade-union nabobs. On the other hand, he exercised his influence on the NEC and the party generally against a final break with the Bevanites, and argued against Bevan's expulsion from the Parliamentary Labour Party in 1955.

Indeed, temperamentally at least, he was closer to Bevan than to Gaitskell. The latter was wary of Phillips when he first came across him. 'People tell me that he is very, very ambitious and that until recently he had regarded himself as a future leader of the Party, and that at the very least he should become Foreign Secretary ... He has certainly been playing with both sides for quite a time. Nevertheless I must avoid any kind of collision with him and obviously try and work with him.' Phillips was one unsung influence which helped the party cool the temperature during the fierce altercations between Bevan and Gaitskell; he was one of the reconcilers, like his fellow-countryman Jim Griffiths. He worked with Bevan and Gaitskell in trying to negate the influence of CND in the later 1950s. But he never lost his feeling that Gaitskell was an unsatisfactory leader of the party. There was constant friction between the two men during the 1959 election campaign. In May 1960, just before a serious stroke, Phillips was observing about Gaitskell, 'What an impossible man he is.' He added on another occasion, 'It's my own view that the party won't get out of its difficulties as long as Gaitskell's there.' However, his chief *bête noire* was neither Bevan nor Gaitskell but the more ambiguous figure of Harold Wilson, for whom he had conceived a 'pestilential hatred' since 1955. In the end, symbolically, one of Phillips's Transport House secretaries, Marcia Williams (later Lady Falkender), defected to the Wilson camp—'with all her files and secrets' as Crossman cryptically observed.

The later fifties were a less happy period for Phillips generally. He was much criticized, perhaps unfairly, for Labour's poor showing in the 1955 general election. Harold Wilson's report termed the party organization under Phillips 'a penny-farthing in the jet age'. It criticized such matters as the distribution of responsibility between Phillips and the national agent (and later to be Phillips's successor), Len Williams. Even the Labour League of Youth, which Phillips had taken much pride in rebuilding, was criticized for far-left infiltration, and eventually disbanded, to be replaced by the Young Socialists. Phillips also found himself uncomfortably in the spotlight after a somewhat colourful visit to Venice to observe the Italian Socialist Congress in February 1957. Crossman snobbishly noted Phillips's lack of interest either in Venetian architecture or Italian food and wine—'can't stick any of this stuff'—by contrast with Bevan's voluble (if sketchy) expositions on the glories of St Mark's or the delights of Chianti. Bevan, Crossman, and Phillips won a somewhat uncomfortable libel case against the *Spectator*, whose editor, Ian Gilmour, had allowed an article to be printed claiming that the Labour leaders had been drunk during the Venice conference. This case, brought forward at the insistence of Arnold Goodman, their solicitor, brought Phillips and his colleagues £2500 damages each. But it added to a somewhat incongruous reputation for Phillips as a *bon viveur*.

However, the main reason for Phillips's discontent lay in the generally disillusioning character of the party at this period, especially after the 1959 election defeat, when (ironically) the party organization seemed to show up much more strongly. Phillips had long had parliamentary ambitions. He had been prospective candidate for Central Nottingham back in 1931. He tried, unsuccessfully, to win nomination for the North-East Derbyshire mining seat in

1959. He also had strong views on the direction of future party policy. He was the main author (with Peter Shore) of *Labour in the Sixties* (1960), a revisionist booklet which called for Labour to adapt itself to the changing class and generational structure, and to broaden its appeal to white-collar workers, home owners, women, and the young. With its talk of 'a scientific revolution', it anticipated Harold Wilson's later appeal to white-coat, technocratic, and professional support for a revamped Labour Party. Labour was somewhat lukewarm about this document; it was merely 'commended' to the annual conference rather than formally accepted by the NEC. Unusually, it bore the signature of Morgan Phillips alone. Yet it was an interesting, cogent pamphlet, full of the ideas popularized at the time by men like Tony Crosland and J. K. Galbraith. The authors of the 1964 Nuffield election survey comment that Phillips's document 'deserves to rank in significance with R. A. Butler's Conservative *Industrial Charter* of 1947' as an exercise in rethinking.

Phillips's search for a parliamentary foothold was still active when he suffered a serious stroke in late 1960 which virtually laid him low thereafter. The main organizational work was undertaken by Len Williams, the deputy general secretary (Phillips was now known as 'general secretary' rather than merely 'secretary'), with the help of Vic Feather. Phillips made a rare public appearance at the Blackpool party conference in the autumn of 1961, which saw Gaitskell's successful reassertion of his leadership. But in January 1963 Phillips finally died. His memorial service, with addresses by Donald Soper and Jim Griffiths, was noted by Crossman as being notably more human than Gaitskell's funeral service had been a few days earlier.

Morgan Phillips, like much of the Labour movement, passed from exaltation in the 1940s to near-despair in the 1960s. The later period as secretary, from 1951 onwards, was accompanied by the ever-present drum beat of civil war. He suffered the particular personal frustration of not having his potential talents as parliamentarian or policy-maker recognized or fulfilled; Gaitskell, in particular, he felt did not appreciate him. It was left to his widow, Norah, to become a life peer and a government chief whip in the Lords, along with taking a major role on a variety of public bodies. His daughter, Gwyneth Dunwoody, achieved what he failed to do and entered parliament in 1966. The recent streamlining of the Walworth Road machine makes the methods of Transport House in Phillips's time seem relatively amateurish and inchoate. At the time, though, especially between

1945 and 1951, Transport House was a model of most of Labour's strength. It fused the mass working-class vote to party professionalism and officialdom. It drew a clear, intelligible distinction between ideas (and not merely organization) compatible and incompatible with Labour's view of democratic socialism. It helped make a fragmented party a coherent national striking-force as never before (or perhaps since) in its history. Not all its methods were admirable. Apparatchiks may have to evade the Queensberry Rules. The exercise of discipline against the Bevanites, who were clearly in the party mainstream in the 1950s, was a mistake, though as we have seen Phillips tried to modify the process. But in those years Labour married action to purpose at the centre, within a party strong in itself, growing in individual membership, and in harmony with the ethos and the patriotism of post-war Britain. One of the unrecorded heroes of that process was Morgan Walter Phillips.

# RITA HINDEN

Rita Hinden was a very gentle socialist. When she paid tribute to R. H. Tawney for exalting the socialist values of equality, freedom, and human fellowship, she could well have been writing a self-description (had not modesty been another of her conspicuous qualities). She was a deeply moral person, and her vision of socialism was a reflection of this passionately ethical outlook. When she turned her pen to such themes as poverty in the third world and the need for proper overseas aid programmes, she wrote with heart and soul as well as with her considerable intellectual power. Unlike many moral, saintly people, however, Rita was immensely practical, even tough-minded. The description, often applied to her, of being a Utopian socialist, is quite incorrect. She had a common-sense, Fabian approach, both as working administrator and editor, and a tough-minded view of how to enlist the necessary resources to realize the ends for which socialists contended.

There is another unusual feature about Rita as an ethical force as well—she achieved real influence and results. In her earlier years, she helped fill a huge gap in Labour's armoury by directing the attention of her insular comrades, for the first time in the party's history, to a systematic and detailed examination of colonial problems, especially those of her native Africa. In her later years, directly or through the force of her gentle stimulus to other socialists, famous and unknown, she supplied a good deal of the intellectual substance the party needed to update its ideas after the euphoria of the Attlee years and the trauma of the internal battles of the fifties. It was largely through Rita, and people like her, that Labour re-emerged from the darkness to present a credible front again in the sixties. In many ways, the supposedly novel approach presented to the electors by the Kinnock–Hattersley partnership in the mid-1980s is merely a rehearsal of the arguments put forward by Rita Hinden and her journal twenty years earlier. She is a comparatively little-known personality amongst the wider public. But she certainly deserves an honoured place as one of Labour's more creative and loveable leaders.

Rita Hinden's special vision of life derived in part from her ethnic background. She was a South African and a Jew. She was, therefore, directly implicated by birth in two of the major human tragedies of the century. Born in 1909, to a comfortable family in Cape Town (her original name was Rebecca, but Rita was always the name she used), she went to a local seminary and university. When she was eighteen the family, intensely orthodox in its Jewish faith and strongly Zionist, moved to Palestine. But Rita herself went to the London School of Economics, in the great days of Laski, to take a B.Sc. After an interval, she and her new husband, Elchon, stayed on for a while in London, becoming active (and ardently left-wing) members of the Willesden branch of the ILP. They had a lively interest in co-operative, guild socialism, even syndicalism. In 1935, they moved off to Palestine, apparently for good. But in fact the move was unsuccessful and disturbing. Neither Rita nor Elchon felt at home in the intense Zionist atmosphere, and both of them rejected both Zionist nationalism and the Jewish faith. Rita became increasingly an advocate of closer Jewish/Arab understanding. In 1938 they returned to London disenchanted, and there Rita was to remain for the rest of her busy life.

Until the start of the war, Rita's life had been a chequered and, in some ways, disillusioning one. But her main early achievement, writing a doctoral thesis on settlement in Palestine, impelled her towards a major new concern with colonial policy. In 1940, an important new phase occurred with the establishment of the Fabian Colonial Research Bureau (FCRB). Arthur Creech Jones was its chairman and Rita Hinden became secretary, a post which she retained until 1950. Here, she achieved an immense transformation. Labour's claims to have a credible colonial policy at all before this time were without much foundation. Only an emotional anti-imperialism and some involvement of key politicians like Cripps with the Indian Congress movement served as any testimony to a wider international concern. Under Rita Hinden's aegis, all this changed, and very dramatically. A stream of pamphlets, speeches, and briefings for Labour MPs and Colonial Office civil servants made the Fabian Colonial Research Bureau a powerhouse of change.

One of its most important productions was Rita's own book, *Plan for Africa*, published in 1941. The message throughout was for a linked policy, a sustained move towards democracy and self-government for colonized territories in Africa, Asia, and elsewhere, accompanied by a programme of partnership, development, and long-term investment between Britain and its colonial peoples. An abiding assumption was an enduring belief in Britain's brand of parliamentary liberalism. Through the guidance of planners, development economists, and many others, the FCRB became enormously influential on the new progressive consensus emerging during the war. On the Labour Party directly, its impact was somewhat more muted. Rita Hinden's attempt at the 1942 party conference to achieve a colonial charter, comparable with the Atlantic Charter (which had been conspicuously silent on the colonial issue), was unsuccessful. Nevertheless, Labour's policies from 1945 onwards, especially when Creech Jones himself became Colonial Secretary in 1946, were in many ways what Rita and the Bureau had argued. She was a notable pioneer of colonial freedom; Denis Healey genially depicted her as 'Rudyard Hardie'. Looking back on the outcome in 1970, she acknowledged many of the disappointments that had resulted, especially in Africa—the political instability and frequent civil war in Nigeria and elsewhere; the failure of any vision of Pan-Africanism; continued economic and trade difficulties; and a diminishing influence for Britain itself throughout the continent. Characteristically, however, she combined realism and historical detachment with renewed hope. She refused to share the somewhat sour disillusion of her old FCRB colleague, Leonard Woolf. The process of liberation and development had been incontestably right in itself. Freedom was the only way for Africa. What was now required was increased economic and aid involvement by the European powers and the United States, to give it substance and permanence. Rita would have been struck in the 1980s at aid for Africa being reliant on the personal media campaigning of Bob Geldof rather than on government assistance.

In 1950, she retired as secretary of the FCRB and served briefly as a member of the Parliamentary Committee that was investigating developments in British Guiana (now Guyana) amidst the turbulence that accompanied the rise of Dr Cheddi Jagan. On this she took an unexpectedly strong line, in calling for a continued British military presence there until the conditions for stable self-government were achieved. In this respect, she was at odds with the Movement for Colonial Freedom, a left-wing body formed in 1954. Indeed, the left now attacked her for perpetuating what they claimed were cold war attitudes in the underdeveloped world, and for an excessive admiration for the achievements of British colonialism. Her reply was that chaos, or alternatively one-party rule by presidents-for-life, was no foundation for colonial self-government. In any event, her interests were moving to wider areas. She found a new role for herself in the Socialist Union, formed after the fall of the Attlee government in late 1951. In effect, it was the voice of the Labour centre-right in opposition to the Bevanites. Its most important instrument was the monthly periodical, *Socialist Commentary*, a journal originally founded by German refugees in 1942. Rita soon emerged as its editor. It was a post she retained, during all the turmoil in the party, in opposition and then in government, for almost twenty years, until her death in late 1971.

In the fifties and the early sixties, *Socialist Commentary* was usually seen as the right wing's answer to *Tribune*, as the voice of the Gaitskellites and later the Campaign for Democratic Socialism after 1960. Although the *Socialist Commentary* group was always much more informal than the Bevanite/*Tribune* section, this interpretation of Rita Hinden's monthly is generally correct. Gaitskell himself served as treasurer of the 'Friends of *Socialist Commentary*' from 1953 until he was elected party leader in 1955. *Socialist Commentary* strongly backed Gaitskell and opposed Bevan in the early fifties. It advocated all the views with which Gaitskell was identified—the Atlantic alliance and a strong anti-Communism, a mixed economy, an emphasis on social equality, planning, and promoting a sense of community as the way to socialism. On nationalization *Socialist Commentary* was more than consolidationist: it viewed public ownership as largely irrelevant. Only Gaitskell's opposition to the Common Market in 1962 brought a significant divergence between him and his friends in *Commentary*. Rita was the major figure in this process of reassessment and revisionism, especially through the major policy supplements she commissioned, dealing with incomes policy, the social services, overseas aid, and much else besides. Education was given a significantly high priority at a time when Labour policy-making in this area, especially on higher education, was sketchy in the extreme. Rita herself was a vulnerable person, unwilling to draw blood, easily upset by personal attacks or party infighting. Yet she was certainly a leading agent of revisionism, much along the lines proclaimed by Crosland, Jenkins, Healey, Griffiths, and others, in her journal. Along with Michael Young, she commissioned the famous survey by Mark Abrams published in 1960 under the title 'Must Labour Lose?' In effect, it was a further move away from the sterile class-war dogmas of the past.

But too much can be made of Rita's revisionism. During the Harold Wilson years from 1964 onwards, *Socialist Commentary* remained, at best, a candid friend of the Labour government. But its socialism was not in doubt. Both at the high level of abstract principle that Rita herself favoured, and in terms of specific policies, *Socialist Commentary* was never anything other than a journal of the democratic left. It was not at all a precursor of the Alliance of the 1980s. Indeed, what Rita had to say on such issues as the public schools or a wealth tax places her somewhat to the left of the Labour leadership in 1986. Even some of the perceived rightwards deviations were conceived on socialist grounds. Thus, Rita's journal was a consistent advocate of British entry into the Common Market, in part because of the need to formulate a joint socialist foreign policy and to forge new links with the Social Democratic parties of continental Europe. It is significant that the editorial board and contributors to the journal always included some distinguished socialist European *émigrés*. Rita consistently advocated an outward-looking, compassionate European Community, especially in terms of aid to the third world. She was too optimistic about how far the bureaucracy of Brussels would allow this to happen. Again, an incomes policy and reform of the unions on lines advocated by the 1968 Donovan Report were endorsed because they were part of the inescapable framework of socialist planning. A wages free-for-all would only harm the low-paid. She was a passionate advocate of the social wage, financed by a mixture of higher taxes and lower pay rises. In this area, through her co-editor and good friend, Allan Flanders, an Oxford don expert on industrial relations, *Socialist Commentary* proved itself particularly knowledgeable.

The journal's message always related present policies and methods to the old socialist objectives—much heavier social expenditure (which meant, naturally, higher taxes, on wealth as well as income); state intervention in industry and through regional planning; protection of the environment; a strong policy for overseas development and wiping out the legacy of colonialism. Rita's message always emphasized commitment and personal involvement. Nothing was more characteristic than a short piece she wrote in November 1969 in defence of participation in politics. In this, she took issue, in typically mild and good-humoured fashion, with the cynical, anti-political cult among the young at the time. Pressure-group politics, 'participation' in shop floor or neighbourhood communes could be self-indulgent, even escapist. They were no substitute for capturing power and taking office to effect permanent change. In that sense, Rita is frequently misrepresented when published diaries or other works refer to her (usually only in passing or in obscure footnote passages) as the voice of the Labour right. Her intellectual inspiration was Tawney, some of whose essays she edited, and about whose philosophical and theoretical socialism she had no doubts or qualms. Her objectives and principles remained firm to the end. Almost the last piece she wrote, on the Upper Clyde Shipbuilders' work-in, expressed them again. When she died in November 1971, her journal lurched somewhat further to the far right. Soon it went out of circulation altogether. But to regard Rita as the forerunner of the SDP of the eighties would be a profound misinterpretation. Her radicalism, consistency, and sense of solidarity were far too strong. Without a powerful, all-inclusive labour movement, her life and struggles would make no sense.

Rita Hinden could easily be underestimated. She was herself a quietly spoken, modest person. At the *Socialist Commentary* offices, above a café in Great Russell Street—George Gissing land (and the location of London Zionist offices)—she presided benignly over a mixed group from the 'chattering classes'—journalists, dons, lawyers, politicians, with a minority of trade-unionists like Dame Anne Godwin. In the wings there was the formidable presence of Margaret Cole. Sometimes there were private sessions with ministers like Jenkins and Healey as well. Yet Rita's presence was always all-important and reassuring. Without her, the whole enterprise would have had little point. The same applied to *Socialist Commentary* tea meetings at party conference, an annual source of renewal of faith for her. In part, this was because of a remarkably kind, unselfish personality, with a warm gift for friendship, a genius for encouragement of contributors to her journal, and an enthusiasm for young, new faces, and new ideas. In part, it was simply due to the passion and plain good sense of her creed. Her legacy for the modern Labour movement is a considerable one. It lies not so much in policy blueprints or legislation, though Creech Jones's regime at the Colonial Office drew heavily on her work, but on a kind of moral force that her writings and personal influence embody. Labour's best-known journalists tend to be flamboyant figures, outgoing, even aggressively extrovert; from William Cobbett to James Cameron they have sought the limelight and relished public combat. Yet it may be that a more withdrawn, reflective writer like Rita Hinden had an educative impact more powerful than almost all of them. Her own life demonstrated that old socialist ideals of love, comradeship, and respect for humanity could be given new validity in a much-changed world. She could defuse cynicism, triumph over disillusion, and rally the faint-hearts. Almost uniquely in her generation, she had the genius for rekindling new faith in the grand old cause. Her soul marches on with us, shoulder to shoulder.

# HAROLD WILSON

THE rise and fall of Harold Wilson bring vividly to mind the experience of an earlier leader of the left, Lloyd George. Like the Welshman before him, the Yorkshireman Wilson was catapulted to eminence in 1963–4 as the voice of provincial dissent, a vigorous, classless figure with a nonconformist heritage and Northern wit reminiscent of the old music hall. Like Lloyd George, too, indeed far more swiftly, Wilson's decline in public esteem since retirement from office has been precipitate in the extreme. The variegated memoirs of his advisers—Joe Haines and Lady Falkender, amongst others—have cast a lurid light on decision-making at No. 10 in the sixties and seventies. This kitchen cabinet recalls the atmosphere of L.G.'s 'Garden Suburb' fifty years earlier, 'Bronco Bill' Sutherland and all—though conspicuously without the intellectual thrust that Kerr, Grigg, Adams, and others brought to central government then. Wilson, too, like Lloyd George, has been permanently tarred with an honours list of alarming character—at least alarming to the squeamish who take their honours seriously. A remarkably large number of Wilson's class of '76 fell by the wayside, financially or otherwise. More than one met an untimely death. Covert anti-Semitism, alas, added to their discredit. Harold Wilson's last act seemed to many to symbolize the sleaziness and shabbiness of a discredited regime, one (allegedly) under surveillance from MI5.

More generally, Wilson, like Lloyd George, seems in acute danger of becoming a universal scapegoat, hounded by the journalists and editors (with whom, like Lloyd George again, he was obsessed) for all the misfortunes of British life between 1964 and 1976. If a future Dangerfield were to write of the Strange Death of Labour England, it is likely that Harold Wilson would play a starring role. The end, truly, has seemed so cathartic. The commoner has become Baron Wilson, not of the River Dwyfor but of the Cistercian abbey of Rievaulx, a highly-paid Weidenfeld author and television personality. Lloyd George, at least, wrote respected works on the first world war and the peace treaties in his later years. Wilson has offered some unconvincing essays in self-justification and *A Prime Minister on Prime Ministers*, of which A. J. P. Taylor wrote (perhaps harshly) in a review that, had it been written by an undergraduate pupil at Magdalen, it would have been given NS, a fail mark. Other ex-Prime Ministers—Home, Heath, Callaghan, even the nonagenarian Lord Stockton—have continued to contribute in dignified fashion to public discourse (as Lloyd George did for twenty years after his downfall in 1922). But, as regards the other Prime Minister still alive at the time of writing, one can only observe sadly (and making much allowance for ill-health) what a falling off was there.

Since Harold Wilson's stock has plummeted so sharply for so long, one can only suppose that it will some day register an upward movement. It is likely, indeed probable, that historians will take a more charitable and compassionate view of his career and achievements than do commentators who delight in trampling on a man when he is down. Indeed, it is to be hoped that this reappraisal does occur, since Wilson is himself a very kindly and generous man, which led in part to the trouble with his honours lists. But if Wilson's reputation is to be salvaged, the career of this remarkable, unpredictable, and elusive politician must be seen as a whole, with its more puzzling features exposed to full view.

Two of the qualities that brought him to the party leadership in February 1963 were a reputation as a master political tactician with a rare understanding of the party grass-roots, and as a man of the radical left, almost a Bevanite. Both are particularly curious when seen in the context of his early career and eventual rise to power.

The young Wilson, in fact, was not a radical politican, indeed not a politician at all. The son of an industrial chemist, he began life as an academic economist and a technocrat. He won a scholarship from the Wirral Grammar School to Jesus College, Oxford, when he spent his time almost exclusively on his academic studies, to brilliant effect. He won the Webb Medley prize for economics, and (though not reading History) the Gladstone history prize for an essay on railway policy in the 1840s. My own supervisor, R. B. McCallum, a thoughtful Scot, considered Wilson the best student he ever had. He gained an outstanding first-class honours degree in the PPE school. Then he was elected to a junior research fellowship at University College, Oxford, and assisted the master of that college, Sir William Beveridge, in work on a study of unemployment and the trade cycle. Wilson's political views, expressed privately only, were those of a radical Liberal of the Lloyd George school, appropriate for the Welsh milieu of Jesus College. He was in no sense a student politician in the Oxford Union or anywhere else.

In September 1939, soon to be happily married to a wife who adored Oxford, he was apparently destined for the tranquil life of a don. (He was to retire to the Betjeman world of north Oxford in the 1980s.) Just before the war, it is true, he eventually joined the Labour Party; but otherwise the pattern of his life did not greatly change. He spent much of the war in the civil service, in a series of home economics departments. He served successively as head of manpower and statistics at the Ministry of Labour, economic assistant at the Mines Department, and then director of economics and statistics at the Ministry of Fuel and Power. He acted as secretary for Dalton's inquiry into miners' wages, and wrote a short book on the nation-alization of the mining industry, published in 1944. The main imprint on his mind, it seems, came from application of science and tech-nology to public planning. His experience in wartime was an essential point of reference for his later proposals in 1963-4 for harnessing the scientific revolution to the processes of government. After some work in the Fabian Research Bureau, he entered parliament in 1945 for the highly marginal seat of Ormskirk (he moved to rock-solid Huyton after redistribution in 1950), a typical symbol of the centrist planning enthusiasms of the intelligentsia of the time, but in no apparent respect a socialist zealot.

He rose very rapidly during the Attlee years as an exceptionally competent, hard-working technocrat. After junior office at the Min-istry of Works, he caught the attention of Cripps and served under him as the Secretary for Overseas Trade from March 1947. After the major government reshuffle in October, he entered the Cabinet, at the astonishingly youthful age of thirty-one, as President of the Board of Trade. Here, he was a skilful and highly efficient lieutenant of the Cripps policy, presiding over the successful expansion of exports in those years. Not all his initiatives were successful, notably a vain attempt to build up the British film industry independent of the Americans. But in general these were flourishing years. Wilson regu-larly appeared before the Commons as the man with good news, as British exports soared ever upwards and the balance of payments once again went into surplus.

He proved a distinctly flexible, even right-of-centre minister, with a strong commitment to industrial competition and anti-monopoly programmes. He made his biggest impact on the general public as an advocate of decontrol who presided, Guy Fawkes-like, over a 'bonfire' of ration books and official licences. He was sometimes rebuked by the *New Statesman* and *Tribune* for *laissez-faire* tendencies. The main crisis of these years which concerned him directly was the devaluation of sterling in 1949, which has already been discussed in various other contexts. Here it may be noted that Wilson's approach was in no way dogmatic. Indeed, close political and civil-service observers felt that he was less interested in the economics than the politics of devaluation, the timing of the next general election, and his own future standing in the party. He cut a far less resolute figure than did Gaitskell, who duly overtook him in the race to the top. The fact that Wilson was the chosen emissary to take the Cabinet's decision to devalue sterling to Cripps's sanatorium in Switzerland gives a misleading impression of his general stance at the time. Wilson was the messenger boy, but Douglas Jay had written the message for Attlee to sign. Otherwise, Wilson kept his head down and seldom intervened on wider issues, including the Palestine question, for all his professed pro-Jewish sympathies later on. He was not a prominent figure at party conferences, nor was he widely known in the country or the media.

In March–April 1951, Wilson's career underwent a remarkable metamorphosis. He had already been a critic of Gaitskell's fiscal policies, as well as being disgruntled at a rival's being appointed Chancellor. He now partnered Bevan in protesting against NHS charges being levied, and resigned with him from the Attlee government. Later on, Wilson was to play down somewhat the impact of his stand, somewhat to the disadvantage of his reputation. He has repeatedly emphasized that, while Bevan resigned largely on the moral issue of health charges, he, Wilson, the hard-headed economist, concentrated on the material effect of the arms programme on the economy. Certainly he had already voiced his concern at the effects of the stockpiling of strategic and other raw materials by the Americans, with resultant inflating costs which made the £4700m. defence budge almost insupportable. His resignation in the House, unlike Bevan's, focused on economic aspects, and was altogether more balanced in tone. It made a good impression on the House, and also won the private applause of Churchill. On the other hand, the Cabinet record shows Wilson's stand as hardly different at all from that of Bevan. Wilson also took a strong social view of the National Health Service and the fabric of social welfare. There was much idealism in what he had to say. Gaitskell's diary references to Wilson at this time are spiteful and unfair. Whatever the truth, Wilson's career was launched in new directions. Along with Bevan and John Freeman, he attended the revitalized 'Keep Left' group of MPs on 26 April just after the resignations. He was part-author of *One Way Only* in July, and by the end of the year was a clear leader of what came to be called 'the Tribune group', or the Bevanites. As a new-born man of the left, with remarkably little party background, Harold Wilson assumed a fresh identity.

Throughout the Tory years that followed, he was usually placed on the party left, and an adherent of the Bevanite group, pressing for more socialist policies at home and abroad. He argued the case for more nationalization. Even his eventual election as party leader in January 1963, after Hugh Gaitskell's death, was hailed as a delayed victory for the left after the Attlee–Gaitskell years. In fact, this reputation was largely spurious. Wilson in no sense anticipated, for example, the militant postures of Tony Benn from 1970 onwards as a rebel against his own legacy. Even as early as January 1952, three months into opposition, Wilson told his Bevanite associates that he wanted to return as soon as possible to being a front-bench spokesman. His policy was to tread a prudent path through the party minefields over the next few years. In a highly controversial decision which shook the Bevanite camp, he decided to take Bevan's place in the Shadow Cabinet in April 1954, after the latter resigned. While he retained ties of affection and regard with the Bevanites, a gulf had opened up between more determined figures such as Foot, Barbara Castle, and Mikardo, who kept faith with Nye until their hero deserted them in 1957, and the centre-left position carved out by Wilson and Crossman along with less important Bevanites like Stephen Swingler and Hugh Delargy. At the end of 1955, it was known that Wilson canvassed and voted for Gaitskell, not for Bevan, in the leadership contest.

In the later fifties, Wilson, made Shadow Chancellor from February 1956 onwards, was, for all his subtle modulations and shifts of position, located in the broad centre of the party. He was associated not with socialist dogma but with the technical advocacy of an expansionist economic policy, and also with attempts to modernize the 'penny farthing' of the party machine (which earned him the undying hatred of Morgan Phillips). Wilson stood for the leadership against Gaitskell in November 1960 (and was defeated, 166–81), mainly it would seem as a marker for the future and to refurbish his battered leftish credentials, rather than for real policy disagreements over defence. Again he re-emerged as a compromiser. He now became Shadow Foreign Secretary; he was less impressive here than in the economics field, but again it confirmed his central position in the movement. In the leadership contest of February 1963, he defeated Brown and Callaghan for the leadership, as something of a *pis aller*. Foot and other old allies were convinced that the Bevanite cause, such as it remained, had triumphed at last. Wilson himself tried to spread this impression within the left. He told them he 'was running a Bolshevik revolution with a Tsarist Shadow Cabinet'. Amazingly enough, this seems to have been taken seriously. In fact, then and later, Wilson's supposed bias to the left was a total illusion.

What was much more important was the new mood that his election gave the party and the country. Crossman himself spoke of the 'sense of liberation' felt after the tetchy Gaitskellite years. *The Times* was moved to comment in late 1963 on how much more impressive Labour seemed now, with Wilson prepared to delegate as Gaitskell never had been, and showing a powerful instinct for the 'expediencies of party management'. Wilson's speeches that winter struck a powerful chord. They picked up themes hinted at in Morgan Phillips's pamphlet, *Labour in the Sixties*, three years before. They called for planned expansion, modernization, and a science-based government. Many of them sounded much better then than they read now. At the time, Wilson's call at the Scarborough conference for a non-theological approach to doctrine and policy, his insistence that there was no room for 'Luddites' in the movement, seemed impressive. Twenty years later, his claim that 'socialism was about science', to be achieved through computers and automation, seems confused, even incomprehensible. But events were moving his way, aided by the shock to morale from Macmillan's last period, Profumo and other fortunate scandals, and the attraction of youth of the Kennedy mystique. Wilson himself invoked the spirit of American liberalism fashionable in Labour ranks at the time, with ample references to new deals, fear of fear itself, and a hundred days of purposeful, dynamic action. His success in the October 1964 election over the aristocratic premier Douglas-Home was by the narrowest of margins, but it seemed a landmark nevertheless. It took place amidst much goodwill and a mood for change. This unsentimental no-nonsense Northerner, with folksy reminiscences about Huddersfield Town in the age of Herbert Chapman, seemed the perfect leader of a new generation and a new society to sweep away the stagnation and moral degeneracy of the wasted Tory years. The dismal background of Labour's years of fratricide was set aside.

The two Labour governments of 1964–70 that Wilson led are commonly believed to have disappointed these hopes. How far this is really true is debatable. Living standards continued to rise steadily through to the early 1970s. Inflation was mostly under control and unemployment was low, if rising. In many areas, the promise of advance and expansion was fulfilled under the Wilson regime. This was notably true of higher education, where the Robbins Report was implemented, and British universities and polytechnics enjoyed a public esteem and support which contrast with the cultural catastrophes wrought by government in the 1980s. There was a considerable expansion of the social services, and the first significant revamping of the social security system since Beveridge. The dock labour system was radically overhauled. Regional policies were vigorously pursued. South Wales, the North-East, and Clydeside perhaps enjoyed the last of the good years in that period, with pit closures and contraction relatively uncontroversial since new industries were brought in and redundancy payments instituted.

The Wilson years also became famous for the consumerism of the 'affluent society', an ambiguous term replete with images of the Beatles, miniskirts, and the World Cup. Whatever ethical or other misgivings the concept may arouse in some quarters, it clearly implied an extension of personal choice and economic security, including for the children of working-class families, enjoying the fruits (previously forbidden) of a welfare society. Some of the characteristic protests of that period—notably by students anxious either for different foreign and defence policies in Vietnam, or else for greater representation within their own tolerant universities—were products of upwardly mobile, well-subsidized critics previously inhibited or inarticulate. Even the rise of Celtic nationalism, following victories for Plaid Cymru in Carmarthen and for the SNP in Hamilton, are in part tributes to Tocqueville's well-known dictum that the *ancien régime* is in most danger when it tries to reform—though admittedly, with Willie Ross at the Scottish Office and George Thomas at the Welsh, the reformist impetus of the Wilson government was not that easy to detect. In the Harold Wilson era, too, changes occurred in the quality of life in areas which Attlee and his colleagues had quite neglected. The arts flourished under Jennie Lee; the Open University was launched; the Ombudsman was created to protect individual liberties; the Official Secrets Act was modified; capital punishment was at last abolished and penal reform taken seriously; the civil rights of women and homosexuals notably advanced; race and community relations vigorously fostered. It was in many ways a highly civilized era in our history. Victims of the hard times of the 1980s might well look back to the golden age of Harold Wilson.

In retrospect, then, the Wilson period may seem to have been a good time in which to have lived. Wilson's own triumphant return to power in March 1966, with a majority of one hundred, confirmed the optimism and goodwill of the voters across a broad spectrum. Oxford and Cambridge, York and Lancaster, Brighton, Hampstead, even rural Cardiganshire (Liberal continuously since 1880) went Labour. But at the time, it was a period of anxiety and constant crisis. The economy was never really under control, despite Wilson's own expertise in this area. For all the brave words in opposition, there was no coherent policy for the balance of payments or for the exchange rate. The main planning innovation of the Wilson years, the creation of the Department of Economic Affairs alongside the Treasury, was never properly thought out and led to endless confusion. Its origins, in a taxi conversation between Wilson and Brown, were symptomatic. It reflected, too much, the personal rivalry between George Brown and James Callaghan, the respective ministers. Brown's National Plan was another scrap of paper. The new department certainly carried no conviction when Wilson himself took charge of it in November 1967. It eventually fizzled out amidst almost general indifference, along with other innovations in the machinery of government attempted in 1964.

Within its first few weeks in office in 1964, Labour had to raise bank rate to 7 per cent, levy a 15 per cent import surcharge, and embark on a huge loan of $2000m. from the US Federal Reserve Board. At first everything could be blamed on the Tories; but this carried less conviction in a year or two. The payments deficit thereafter was steadily reduced, but at the cost of eliminating entirely the National Plan's optimistic hopes for sustained economic expansion. The centre-piece of Labour's programmes was demolished at a stroke. The worst crisis of all came in July 1966, when a combination of a damaging seamen's strike, rising government expenditure, and some domestic inflation led to a severe run on the reserves and much talk of devaluation. Wilson was temporarily abroad in Moscow, and there were rumours of a ministerial *putsch* against him in his absence. Labour responded, not with devaluation, but with large disinflationary budget cuts, to reduce the annual level of demand by £500m. It was, said *The Economist*, with some exaggeration, 'perhaps the biggest deflationary package that any industrial nation has imposed on itself since Keynesian economics began'. Douglas Jay, for one, felt it to be excessive, and believed that £300m. would have been sufficient. The removal of Callaghan's import surcharge in November 1966 brought further difficulties, as did a major dock strike on Merseyside in October 1967. This encouraged a further bout of pressure against sterling and led to the final, desperate decision to devalue. On 18 November the exchange rate of the pound was brought down to $2.40, following news of worsening trade figures and amidst a ferment of rumours. Devaluation was accompanied by a hasty package of deflationary measures which, says Sir Alec Cairncross, 'were generally regarded as neither coherent nor adequate'. Callaghan left the Treasury at this point. However, his successor, Roy Jenkins, pursued a policy of further prolonged and highly deflationary 'hard slog' which indeed did finally revive the balance of payments and actually produced a current surplus of about £1 billion in 1970. But it made any productive growth in the economy impossible. The 1968 budget, with £923m. tax increases, was much the most severe since the war. Throughout, there was a pattern of a government at the mercy of events, with Wilson himself turning from one expedient to another under a mask of frenetic optimism, coupled with condemnation of the press, the BBC, financial speculators, foreigners, 'politically motivated' spies, and other hand-picked scapegoats, for 'selling Britain short'. His television broadcast after the 1967 devaluation, telling the viewer that 'the pound in your pocket has not been devalued', made an appalling impression.

The converse of this broad record of economic failure was an inability to produce social discipline at home. There were repeated moves to try to invent some version of an incomes policy of the kind Wilson had helped administer under Cripps. But the unions rejected them all, while the TUC general secretary, George Woodcock, proved disappointingly inert. The final confrontation with the unions came in June-July 1969. The government's Prices and Incomes Bill, which included some punitive sanctions along the lines of Barbara Castle's

*In Place of Strife*, now met with strong resistance. This came not only from union leaders such as Jack Jones and Hugh Scanlon, but also from a majority in the parliamentary party, right and left alike, and even within the Cabinet. Even if Wilson himself can hardly be blamed, since he and Barbara Castle fought almost a lone battle on the issue, it was a total humiliation. Following a failure to reform the House of Lords earlier in the year, it was further proof of the government's inability to govern. The greatest casualty was the credibility of the Prime Minister. His supreme talent, a unique knowledge, supposedly, of the movement and the way to control or orchestrate it, was found wanting in its greatest test. He had simply lost contact with his party and with reality.

There was not a great deal else that was triumphant about this administration. Attempts to play a world role, either through Europe or the Commonwealth, or through a supposed special relationship with President Johnson, led to nothing. Britain's external prestige declined steadily throughout the decade, with no clear priority of objectives emerging. Indeed, attempts to maintain extensive overseas commitments were directly damaging, since overseas expenditure, including an 'east of Suez' defence policy, remained disturbingly high. Sheer economic pressure saw this finally reversed in 1969–70. As regards Europe, another attempt was made to enter the Common Market in 1967, but it met with another rebuff from President de Gaulle, while Wilson's diplomatic methods caused much disarray within his own Cabinet. There was also much discord within EFTA from the imposition of the import surcharge onwards. Britain's role as a European power was by 1970 more obscure than ever. In the Commonwealth, the main remaining problem of British decol- onization, concerning the unilateral declaration of independence by the illegal Ian Smith regime in Rhodesia, was another failure. Successive talks with Smith, first on HMS *Tiger*, then on HMS *Fearless* (when the principle of African majority rule came close to being sacrificed) led nowhere. The imposition of economic sanctions by Britain on Rhodesia, which Wilson had boasted would bring victory 'in weeks rather than months', was another ineffective strategy. Attempts to turn the Commonwealth into a more coherent trading unit also came to nothing. Within the British Isles, Northern Ireland was by 1970 lapsing into near-chaos after a praiseworthy attempt to break the power of the Protestant ascendancy at Stormont, while, as has been noted elsewhere, there were nationalist difficulties nearer

home still, in Scotland and Wales. A disunited kingdom was confronted with a divided Europe, a stagnating Commonwealth, and an
alliance with the Americans who treated it almost with contempt.

But what, finally and fatally, damaged Harold Wilson were not
these intractable difficulties associated with an ailing economy, or
redefining Britain's post-imperial role in the world—problems which
baffled every British Prime Minister since 1945, perhaps since 1918.
The blank refusal of union leaders to pay any heed to problems of
wage-induced inflation, the firm direction of southern Africa towards
black self-government, the interminable religious feuds of Northern
Ireland, are all highly complex and have defied solution over many
decades. In each case, Harold Wilson had the correct instincts and
the basis for a possible settlement.

The real cross that Wilson had to bear was rather his highly
personalized style as the Prime Minister. It focused on an intensely
personal method of leadership which brought some talk of 'prime
ministerial government', now identified with Wilson as it had been
earlier with Lloyd George. As noted, he himself unwisely invoked
comparisons with the presidential mode with talk of the 'hundred
days' of Franklin Roosevelt in 1933. The existence of an entourage
of advisers, formal and informal, almost courtiers, in particular the
presence of Marcia Williams so close to the centre of power, further
distorted the conduct of policy at No 10. To Lord Longford, a kindly
commentator, Wilson seemed 'a beleaguered spirit'. The emphasis
from the start seemed to be on intrigue, party manœuvre, and the
settling of old scores. Douglas Jay has recorded how 'unease and
suspicion festered' after 1964, in contrast to the sense of purpose
and unity under Attlee. He refers especially to Wilson's underhand
methods in diplomatic negotiations with the EEC in 1966–7. Lobby
journalists, secret briefings, and unattributable sources loomed large
in the public image of the government. It seemed almost government
by leak. Wilson, as *Socialist Commentary* observed in 1968, was more
concerned with the manipulation, or capture, of power than with
the purposes for which that power might be used. The role of George
Wigg was constantly ambiguous and unsettling in this context.
Invited in 1985 to explain the failure of the DEA in the sixties, Wilson
replied, depressingly, 'Moles. Moles. "Moles" was a phrase we very
often used about the Treasury.' Somehow, the tone recaptures the
frustration and the paranoia of government in that era.

Changes in the administration's personnel seemed to relate less to the requirements of policy than to private considerations. Brown and Callaghan had to be balanced out carefully in 1964; Callaghan, Wilson always believed, needed the most careful watching throughout. Later on, the advance of right-wingers such as Jenkins and Crosland had to be countered by progress for old leftists such as Crossman and Mrs Castle. A remarkably large number of simply inadequate ministers stayed in office as placemen to the end. Frank Cousins as Minister of Technology was certainly no Bevin in office.

Wilson was at his best in 1964–6, when his majority was only two. Thus he was able to deal cunningly with a crisis when the deputy speakership fell vacant in 1965 (imperilling his majority altogether) by alighting unerringly on a Welsh Liberal, the one available candidate. When the majority was one hundred after March 1966, things promptly fell apart. Throughout, the cosmetics of politics took a prime place, with endless personalized feuds and intrigues with press barons, figures in the BBC, and a host of others. The fetid, highly charged atmosphere was reminiscent of the last days of Lloyd George, if not of Pompeii. In short, Wilson's great talent, as was popularly supposed, for political tactics and manœuvre became the cloven hoof of his government. The style of leadership hastened a spread of disillusionment throughout the movement. There was a steady fall in party membership, and weaker ties with the unions and their more militant officials and activists, in contrast to the solidarity of 1945–51. Labour lost only narrowly to the Conservatives in June 1970, and indeed a further Wilson victory was expected by the pollsters right to the very end. But it was a decisive defeat, leaving Wilson discredited and almost alone, if still indispensable. It heralded a headlong decline by the party which took a decade and a half to arrest.

Wilson's last phase was a tranquil and measured one. In some respects, it was perhaps more successful. Certainly there was less intensity about the kitchen cabinet atmosphere. Wilson took a long while to recover from the trauma of defeat; in many ways he seemed almost a crushed figure after June 1970, still brooding over the endless crises and personal vendettas and abuse of the sixties. He was not a vigorous leader of the opposition, and was unable to prevent a lurch to the left, especially after the resignation of Roy Jenkins as deputy leader. Wilson's main concern was that the party did not pull itself apart over the Common Market and defence policy; to a degree he succeeded, although Labour's policy in each case remained unclear.

Somewhat unexpectedly, he became Prime Minister again in March 1974, mainly through the mishandling of the miners' strike by the Heath government and the loss of many Tory votes to the Liberals. Armed with a somewhat nebulous 'social contract' with the unions, in October 1974 he narrowly increased his majority, to make it possible for him to claim, like his old hero Gladstone, that he had led four administrations. This was a more restrained Harold Wilson now. In his favourite footballing analogy, he saw himself as a 'deep-lying centre half', like Herbie Roberts in the Arsenal football team the thirties, rather than a centre-forward. In effect, this meant that he considered himself a co-ordinator, the leader of a team. The Downing Street Policy Unit under Bernard Donoughue improved the quality of central decision-making. With Callaghan, an old rival, Wilson's relationship was now much more harmonious. His main political task was to keep government and party intact over membership of the Common Market. The decision to conduct a national referendum on the EEC issue in 1975, while constitutionally open to debate, was tactically an act of genius. It enabled the government to hold together, despite a proliferation of views on Europe, and enabled Wilson to project himself in Europe as an international statesman. Meanwhile, Britain's relations with the US were distinctly repaired, Callaghan, the Foreign Secretary, building up a good relationship with Kissinger, the US Secretary of State.

The economic news, in the aftermath of the Arab–Israeli war and the hugh increase in oil prices, continued to be grim, but on balance the government coped tolerably well. After the floating pound had fallen, frighteningly, to only two-thirds of its former value, a rescue operation was patched up in December 1975—'the most hectic and harrowing month I experienced in nearly eight years as Prime Minister', Wilson reflected. Special drawing rights of £1000m. were finally negotiated with the IMF under the oil facility, with provision for a further £700m. stand-by credit. Massive cuts were made in public expenditure, and after an agreement with the unions (largely the work of Jack Jones) for a £6 weekly pay increase limit, domestic inflation began to fall after reaching a peak of over twenty per cent. Barbara Castle's Social Security Act of 1975 showed that the government had not lost all its social fervour—she was always Wilson's voice of Bevanite conscience—while impetus was given to regional policy, in Wales, Scotland, and the North. The National Enterprise Board gave new life to the age-old priority of public ownership. When Wilson, quite unexpectedly, retired from the premiership in April 1976, apparently more through fatigue and ennui than anything more sinister, the line had been held and confidence was somewhat on the mend. There were signs that the party and the unions were showing some realism and restraint at last, after the mindless euphoria of the sixties and the period of *In Place of Strife*. The potentially disruptive figure of Tony Benn was first neutralized by the Policy Unit, then skilfully side-tracked by Wilson from the Department of Trade and Industry to that of Energy where he could cope with such problems as pit closures and the spread of nuclear power. Harold Wilson's last phase in office, his least colourful and personally stressful, in some ways saw him at his best—more controlled, all passion spent. The succession of Callaghan, as he wished, seemed to ensure that this mood would continue. With characteristic prudence, Wilson ensured that the seating plan at his farewell dinner in Downing Street (22 March 1976) reproduced the seating in the Cabinet, 'so that no one could read anything into anything'.

Long before he retired from the premiership, and the party leadership, Harold Wilson was commonly seen as an enigma. His settled views, his precise location in the political spectrum, even his basic psychology seemed hard to define. Various personalities seemed to jostle within him. There was Dunkirk Harold in Churchillian garb, white-coated Harold caught in the white heat of technological revolution, Walter Mitty Harold about to amaze the world with deeds that would be the terror of the earth, even World Cup Harold, appealing to the populist instinct for razzmatazz, with mood as a substitute for achievement. He remained elusive to the end. His three volumes of memoirs, opaque in style and with obvious gaps in the story, have not greatly helped in the process of explanation. The diaries of Crossman and Barbara Castle are too narrowly focused to give much guidance on deeper matters. Wilson's own historical survey of prime ministers through the ages is even more confusing, since some of his warmest praise goes to Tories, including Pitt, Disraeli, and especially Churchill, with some incidental nostalgia for the foreign policy of Palmerston. It is an unexpected verdict from Labour's longest-serving Prime Minister.

On balance, Wilson's political viewpoint has always been broadly centrist, even corporatist. He has been committed to the institutional framework—civil service, upper house, monarchy and all. He has never been much of a reformer. One of the major weaknesses in 1964–70 was an excessive reliance on the guidance of the Treasury, the Bank of England, and in other matters, the Foreign Office. However, if the battered instrument has remained much the same, the pianist has changed the tempo, or tried to. Wilson has sought to breathe into ancient usages a new vitality and a classless ethos appropriate for the later twentieth century. It is too easy to forget how appealing and attractive a figure the Wilson of 1963–4 (or perhaps 1963–6) was, with his call for expansion and innovation, coupled with a commitment to growth and articulated with a kind of Coronation Street folksiness and lack of pomposity which got the message across. For a moment, it seemed to change the national psyche, and with it the electoral landscape. Alone of Labour's leaders (other than Attlee around 1945), Wilson seemed capable of making his party the natural majority of the nation and the normal instrument of government. If he had succeeded he would have produced at worst a British version of the French Monnet Plan, at best something like Swedish social democracy, or even the progressive coalition of the American New Deal–Fair Deal programmes. Labour leaders down to Kinnock have tried to recapture the Wilson appeal from that remote era, and translate it into modern garb. And, of course, Wilson won elections, four out of five, with the one defeat a considerable surprise—a feat scarcely conceivable under any other leader in Labour's history.

He failed in the end because of defects both of substance and of style. The substance collapsed because of inadequate planning in detail on the major aspects of policy. To quote Lord Longford again, 'the intellectual guidelines were lacking' (the moral guidelines were shakier still). It is worth noting here that Wilson in the years of opposition was a policy-maker only to a limited extent. He was never really a part of the Crosland-style revisionism, nor of the more creative or visionary side of Bevanism in the fifties. His very isolation from both the Gaitskellite and Bevanite camps was, to that degree, a weakness. His emphasis on 'purposive investment' and 'growth' was to the exclusion of more fundamental questions of social change. Paul Foot, a stern left-wing critic, in 1968 plausibly saw Wilson's view of himself as the executive manager of corporate state capitalism. As regards style, the years 1964–70 may suggest that Wilson, by background a don and by method a technocrat, was not a natural party leader at all. His chosen ground was the enclosed parliamentary arena, with Fleet Street and Annie's Bar in close conjunction, that manic-depressive, hothouse world removed from the party grass-roots and the projection of policies throughout the nation. This was the world into which he plunged in his rapid—much too rapid—metamorphosis after April 1951, when he was suddenly transformed from centrist planner into radical dissenter. The party leadership became too personalized, too fraught with neuroses and phobias to be either stable or subtle. When the style was modified, more effect-ively, in 1974–6, it was too late. The momentum of the early sixties had gone for ever, and Labour's decline was well under way.

It is, indeed, one of Labour's many tragedies that the pace and pressure of events after 1964 undermined perhaps one of the party's most intellectually agile, and in many ways most human and per-sonally likeable, figures. There are still many who recall the Wilson years as a time of some hope and cultural excitement, a civilized interlude in contrast to the 'Victorian values' invented by a harsher regime twenty years on. (Really, it must surely be Wilson, the heir to Peel, Samuel Smiles, Gladstone and the nonconformist conscience, who is the last of the true Victorians.) In the end, public relations superseded public planning, tactics swamped strategy, and cosmetics dominated economics. The old performer, whether as striker or sweeper, retired to the non-league pastures of the Lords, his team under new management, and the great game dragging on incon-clusively. For Baron Wilson of Rievaulx, at least, extra time will not be played.

# 4

# RETREAT AND RENEWAL
## 1970–1987

# JAMES CALLAGHAN

IN the version of British politics in the sixties authorized by the exciting pages of the rival prophets, Crossman and Castle, James Callaghan plays a central, if ambivalent, role. Much of the time he is their whipping-boy, derided for repeated failures at the Treasury and eventually resigning, physically and psychologically broken, after having to concede devaluation; unimaginative, even positively reactionary or racist, at the Home Office; finally, playing a flatly disloyal role in overthrowing his own government's Prices and Incomes Bill in 1969, and intriguing with the unions and all available dissidents in such a way as to make collective responsibility, even parliamentary government itself, quite impossible. Throughout, there are references to Callaghan as a machine politician of the old school, a fixer of the Herbert Morrison type, a regular obstacle to far-reaching change.

The curious fact emerges, however, that, almost in spite of themselves, the diarists finish up with Callaghan's reputation and public stock higher than ever. Even Barbara Castle is forced reluctantly to admit that Callaghan's hostility to the penal sanctions included in her Prices and Incomes Bill struck a chord throughout the movement, and that he had the skill and strength to carry his point, even with the Prime Minister himself in opposition. Crossman, so often patronizing about Callaghan's relative lack of educational or (in Crossman's opinion) intellectual abilities, finds his pages almost dominated by Callaghan at the end, as by no other politician of the time. Callaghan he concludes is 'a big man' (March 1967), 'a wonderful political personality' (September 1969), easily the most accomplished politician in the party. Against all the odds, Callaghan climbed back from the abyss when he resigned as Chancellor. He rebuilt his reputation at the Home Office, notably over Northern Ireland. He even managed to recoup his standing in the Cabinet after the rows over incomes policy; this particularly applied with Callaghan's successful fixing of the recommendations of the Boundary Commission which were to Labour's disadvantage. His premiership of 1976–9 did witness the shattering crisis which brought the intervention of the International Monetary Fund to part-control the economy, and it ended with the shambles over the unions' 'winter of discontent' and a defeat over the Devolution bills for Wales and Scotland. Nevertheless, Callaghan emerged with a distinctly stronger reputation after his three years as premier than Wilson had done. His credentials for statesmanship survived both economic hurricanes and the precarious political base of the 'Lib-Lab' pact concluded with the Liberals. It may be safely predicted that his memoirs, due to be published in 1987, will not damage his reputation or credibility in the way that Wilson's did for their author. As one of the few holders of all the main portfolios, Treasury, Home Office, and Foreign Office, as well as the premiership, he has survived the turmoils of his party with his prestige remarkably intact. As elder statesman, he continues to play a dignified and authoritative part in public debate.

The main point to be made about Callaghan, of course, is that he is a highly professional politician, of a remarkably tough kind. The soubriquet 'Sunny Jim' is as inappropriate a name for this determined man as was 'Uncle Arthur' for the remarkably non-avuncular Arthur Henderson, whom in many ways Callaghan resembles. His political skills are of no ordinary kind. They stem from a remarkable control of his variegated constituency base in Cardiff South (or South-East). To see Callaghan on the move in Cardiff, subtly adapting his approach as he ambles on from proletarian Splott through the mixed residential population of Llanrumney and on to the genteel villadom of Penarth, taking in myriad ethnic minorities in the old dockside communities *en route*, is to see a master craftsman at work, his technique tempered by a genuine humanity and directness. An extreme illustration of his talents came in the 1964 general election when, perhaps for the only time, Callaghan was in some electoral danger, defending a seat whose majority had fallen to below a thousand in 1959. Confronting him as Tory candidate, almost incredibly, was the England cricket captain of the day, Ted Dexter, apparently nominated by Wilfred Wooller and others to appeal to West Indian voters (even though the coloured residents of Cardiff tend to be from West Africa, Aden, or Somalia). The contrast between the unfortunate Dexter and the effortless ease of the Callaghan campaign was an extreme vision of the gap in ability between the sitting member and other, lesser aspiring politicians.

In the House, too, Callaghan has always enjoyed a strong base in the parliamentary party, while his strength among the unions propelled him to the key position of party treasurer in the 1960s. By

1979, his rapport with the unions seemed frail indeed—but, then, the latter, under such notably unpolitical and unthinking leadership as that of Alan Fisher of NUPE and Moss Evans of the TGWU, were almost ungovernable. Callaghan's general approach and style have made him a natural symbol of the solidarity of the movement, and its inmost recesses. Colleagues have spoken, half admiringly, half in jest perhaps, of his affinity with the envelopes, the old ladies, the bad tea, and the peeling walls of committee room politics. Callaghan has, indeed, all of this. But unlike many other machine politicians (including, possibly, Morrison in this context), he has grown impressively with office and departmental responsibility. He is also, as Lord Longford has reasonably claimed, 'the greatest natural orator' amongst recent political leaders, crisp and commanding with seldom a note in sight. While other, more glamorous, politicians were blown away in the whirlwind of Labour politics in the troubled years of Gaitskell and Wilson, Callaghan remained durable and impregnable, probably more consistently attuned to the instincts of the average Labour voter than anyone else in politics.

Callaghan's early life was a classic of self-help. He grew up, if not quite in the classic slum, at any rate in a very poor home in Portsmouth, the son of a widowed mother who also brought him up in a strict Baptist environment. Later in life, one of his talents (particularly useful in Wales) was a wide knowledge of traditional hymns of the more rousing kind. He entered the Inland Revenue as a clerk and rose rapidly in its white-collar union, becoming secretary of the Inland Revenue Staff Federation. He also met Harold Laski, who nurtured his intellectual ambitions—always much more considerable than he is usually given credit for. In his earlier political incarnation, he was considered a man of the left. He endorsed the 'Mikardo resolution' at party conference in 1944 on behalf of sweeping nationalization, and was later fiercely to rebuke the pugnacious Emanuel Shinwell when he dared to cast doubt on the achievements of public ownership. He was elected for Cardiff South in 1945, clad in the uniform of a naval officer, as a voice of the left. In his early period in the House, he voted against the terms of the US loan in December 1945, on broadly socialist grounds. By 1948, however, it was clear that he was not marked out as a radical dissenter at all. He kept aloof from the 'Keep Left' group which had hoped he might join them, and became one of Dalton's rare protégés of working-class origin. He held junior office, first in the Transport Ministry, later in the Admiralty. In the turmoil over Aneurin Bevan's resignation in 1951, Callaghan was a firm loyalist and recognized as such.

In the fifties, he was probably the most effective, non-middle-class exponent of the Gaitskellite point of view. He was a vigorous critic of the Bevanite group and of Bevan personally. He aggressively opposed CND and the unilateralists at the end of the decade. What built up his position further, however, were his clear skills as a front-bench spokesman, especially as Shadow Colonial Secretary. In the key issues of the decade—Kenya, Cyprus, the Central African Federation, Guyana—Callaghan fused empiricism and moralism most effectively. He was also much in demand in public meetings and on university campuses, where he relished the cut-and-thrust of argument with young students. He rose rapidly to become Shadow Chancellor at the end of 1961, when Wilson moved to become spokesman on foreign affairs. In January 1963, he ran for the party leadership on the nomination of Tony Crosland, and his forty-one votes were not only a significant tally in themselves but a powerful claim for Wilson's favours after the latter had been elected. Callaghan in 1963–4 was a powerful, buoyant figure, a man with an international audience in the USA and elsewhere. Much of his energies behind the scenes, however, were expended in prolonged tussles with George Brown over the precise division of responsibility between the Treasury and the DEA in an incoming Labour government. Unhappily, the argument was still unresolved when Labour took office in October 1964.

Callaghan's reputation was commonly thought to have suffered irreparable damage in his traumatic ordeal by fire as Chancellor between October 1964 and November 1967. Of course, it was a period of recurrent, horrendous crises, with the economy never really under control. In the first few weeks (which saw bank rate rise swiftly to seven per cent), again in July 1966, and again in October–November 1967, the Chancellor had to make massive deflationary measures that virtually wiped out all hope of expansion. His fifteen per cent import surcharge at the end of 1964 was an unhappy move which infuriated our EFTA partners. Callaghan was also much criticized for not devaluing the pound until forced to do so by foreign speculative pressure in November 1967. Even then, according to Sir Alec Cairncross, he had hoped to stave off a decision until 1968. Yet, in fact, the economists were much divided on the pound—a minister as authoritative as Douglas Jay, for instance, supported the refusal to devalue in July 1966. In any case Wilson himself had made it clear, for political reasons, that Labour would not again devalue as it had done (indirectly) in 1931 and (directly) in 1949. For much of the time, Callaghan's performance was hailed by many of the experts, notably his success in wiping out a deficit of £400m. on the capital account by the end of 1965, and rebuilding the gold and foreign currency reserves. The Treasury's prestige was much weakened by the July cuts in 1966. Yet Callaghan emerged as politically stronger, since the result was the move of George Brown from the DEA to the Foreign Office, and the control of the enfeebled Economic Affairs department passed to the less contentious hands of Michael Stewart. For much of 1967, Callaghan was again a powerful figure: his budget that April effectively challenged the expansionist economic tenets on which the 1964 election had been fought. He won a great oratorical triumph at party conference as late as 3 October 1967. Finally, of course, he was swept away in the devaluation crisis the next month, his career seemingly finished.

There is no question that the balance of payments was not under secure direction for much of this period, and Callaghan's judgement as controller of the economy was, to that degree, cast into doubt. He had never quite seemed to enjoy the stature of Chancellors such as Cripps in the past, or Jenkins subsequently. One sign of diminished prestige was that the Chancellor had not served as a member of the NEDC at all since Labour came into office in October 1964. Yet it should also be said that he was far from being an inert figure at the Treasury. In the strictly fiscal field, he was a radical reformer, with a rare ingenuity and interest in tax reform dating from his days in the Inland Revenue. His time at No. 11 was marked by widespread taxation changes, new corporation and capital gains taxes, a betting tax, the controversial Select Employment Tax of 1965 (a tax on services which turned out to be unsuccessful). Internationally, Callaghan had negotiated the new drawing rights with the IMF, a more flexible attitude to the role of sterling as a reserve currency, and much international monetary co-operation with the Group of Ten. Elsewhere, Callaghan could point to important white papers on public expenditure and the nationalized industries, to the setting up of the Fulton Committee on the Civil Service, and, in more familiar household terms, to decimal coinage on a £ basis. Unfortunately, he was also known—and damned—for an abiding attachment to the pound, somewhat unfairly so, since it is known that both he and Brown came to accept the need for devaluation at one time (13 July 1966) but were frustrated by the Prime Minister. To that extent, he failed to fight free of the external constraints of British economic policy.

The Home Office is not normally a department in which to rebuild a public reputation. In recent years, down to and including Leon Brittan, it has been a graveyard of hopes. Very few Home Secretaries have gone on to become Prime Minister in the present century, though they make an interesting list—Asquith, Churchill, and of course Callaghan. Yet, on balance, Callaghan rebuilt his reputation here substantially. Years later in 1982, he noted that while he was more 'constrained by hierarchy' at the Home Office, compared with the Treasury and the Foreign Office, his decisions were more promptly translated into action. An early elegiac tone to his speeches, suggesting a kind of swansong to his career, rapidly disappeared. He was known not to be anything like the reformer that his predecessor, Roy Jenkins, had been, and many departmental advisers felt deflated as a result. Indeed, his working-class origins and early Baptist faith combined to make Callaghan notably conservative at the Home Office. He did not much like permissiveness, and spoke out against excesses in drug-taking, sexual experiment, gambling, and much else besides. He was a stern controller of Commonwealth immigration, and enraged many liberals by revoking the passport privileges of Kenyan Asians. As the former parliamentary spokesman for the Police Federation, he took a much firmer stand than Jenkins had done on law and order. Callaghan himself struck a traditional posture here, which inspired comparisons with a popular television serial 'Dixon of Dock Green' which had idealized the traditional British 'bobby' on the beat as a community servant.

On the other hand, Callaghan's distaste for the permissive society, intellectually debatable, was politically prudent. It chimed in with a new mood and was generally popular. In the student and other demonstrations of the late sixties concerned with Vietnam or South Africa, he struck a skilful compromise between free speech and the disciplining of unruly protest. Callaghan was an appropriate symbol for the short-haired, law-abiding, silent majority. In some areas, he did build up a new reserve of reputation as a reformer. This particularly applied in Northern Ireland, when from the first he seemed to move decisively in favour of liberalization and the protection of civil rights for the Catholic minority, including the dispatch of British troops to provide security..His visit to Ulster in September 1969 was a remarkable personal triumph. He was sufficiently impressed by his own experience of the age-old problems of Northern Ireland to make it the theme of his one book to date, a most interesting one entitled *A House Divided* (1973). Elsewhere, he could record firm service to his party in delaying the impact of the Boundary Commissioners until after the next election. He explained privately that he had no intention of giving an electoral present to the Tories as Chuter Ede had wantonly done in 1949. As a result he was accused of gerrymandering. His revival in the highest circles of the party was confirmed by his clear defeat of Michael Foot for the party treasurership.

Much the most traumatic time of his years at the Home Office lay in his opposition to *In Place of Strife*, and Barbara Castle's proposed prices and incomes measure. Callaghan's opposition to his colleagues was remarkably open and direct. His role in many ways recalls Arthur Henderson's break with his colleagues over unemployment benefit cuts in 1931, with again the trade-union alliance the central theme. Callaghan supported Joe Gormley's motion against the Labour government's measure on the NEC. He openly challenged the authority of the Cabinet to legislate. There was talk in April and May 1969 of a back-bench revolt which would make Callaghan Prime Minister, and Wilson's conversation was more than ever replete with talk of plots. Wilson dropped him from the inner Cabinet on 13 May; Crossman urged him to resign. But Callaghan proved far closer not only to the mood of the unions (who voted the government's bill down by a majority of eight to one) but of the parliamentary party and even the Cabinet. Even Jenkins in the end deserted Wilson and Mrs Castle. In impotent rage, Wilson had to restore Callaghan to the inner Cabinet, even as his government's bill as being withdrawn humiliatingly in July, in favour of a (largely worthless) 'solemn and binding' voluntary undertaking by the unions to observe pay restraint. 'Sunny Jim' and 'Solomon Binding' were an irresistible partnership. After the election defeat in June 1970 Callaghan (who had eventually endorsed the early election date) stood higher than ever in the past. Even Wilson had come round to admire his skills. In his book, Callaghan informs us that the Prime Minister told him that his handling of the Northern Ireland question was 'a turning-point in the history of the government'.

Callaghan's strength was not significantly eroded by the inner turmoil in the party during the years of opposition, 1970–4 (nor apparently by a serious prostate operation). On the main divisive theme of the time, the Common Market, Callaghan was a straight agnostic. He was well able to enlist patriotic fervour about the language of Chaucer, Shakespeare, and Milton, to suppress undue enthusiasm by Europe-fanatics. On the other hand, on political grounds, he swung with Wilson towards cautious approval for British membership. Both on Europe and on industrial legislation, his links with the unions made him an essential figure in maintaining party unity. It confirmed for Wilson that Callaghan was his only credible successor. In 1974–6 Callaghan proved to be a vigorous and adroit Foreign Secretary, who relished the freer flow of departmental debate, compared to the Home Office. He handled, with varied success, crises in Cyprus, the Iceland cod war, and attempts to put diplomatic and economic pressure on South Africa. His main theme in these years, like Labour Foreign Secretaries since the time of Bevin, was to build up Britain's close, if unequal, partnership with the United States. To this end, he devoted much time and trouble to cementing a close personal relationship with Henry Kissinger (with whom he shared a common enthusiasm for football, which even survived a visit to see Cardiff City perform). With the withdrawal of Roy Jenkins, he was able to defeat Michael Foot by 176 to 137 in the leadership contest after the resignation of Wilson. He had become Prime Minister at last, against all the odds. It was precisely the result that the outgoing Prime Minister had intended.

Until the last few months of his period in office, Callaghan's position as a minority Prime Minister was remarkably secure. There was little talk of *putsches* as there had been under (and by) Wilson, and far less neurosis over press conspiracies, real or alleged. Peter Shore noted the more 'restful' atmosphere when Callaghan took over and the air of confidence that resulted. With a wife well attuned to the political life, Callaghan was a calm pilot in the storms. He built up, in different ways, strong relationships with his two main lieutenants, Denis Healey and Michael Foot. The open sniping of Tony Benn could be warded off with some ease. The horrendous crisis in November–December 1976, which brought in the IMF, was negotiated at some cost, and after a massive Cabinet division over public spending cuts. After some doubt, Callaghan swung his support for Healey over the Letter of Intent to the IMF. After twenty-six Cabinet meetings, the

Prime Minister carried the day, without a single resignation. It gave the nation a breathing-space, and both the rate of inflation and the balance of payments showed much improvement by the start of 1978. Inflation and unemployment were reduced at one and the same time. The 'pact' with the Liberals in April 1977 also made the government's political position more secure, even if it meant taking on board the albatross of a devolution measure rejected in principle by most Labour MPs, and for which Callaghan himself, as a Welsh MP, had harboured doubts.

Overall, he made a good impression by trying to find a higher ground of public debate. He was the first political leader for many years, perhaps since the time of Cripps, to make a serious onslaught on inflationary pressures and escalating public spending. His speech at the 1976 party conference was a powerful indictment of uncontrolled expenditure, perhaps of the entire premises of oversimplified Keynesianism as it had been dominant since the late 1950s. 'We cannot now, if we ever could, spend our way out of recession', Callaghan observed, in words commonly attributed to his son-in-law, Peter Jay. Unfortunately, for all the alliances of the past and memories of 1969, Callaghan's writ did not extend to the unions. Their officials rejected his attempts to impose a five per cent pay increase limit, and then launched a series of destructive, and sometimes quite unfeeling, strikes in the bitter winter of 1978-9. Amidst overflowing rubbish bins, closed schools, and undug graves, the unions destroyed wantonly a government which could hardly have been gentler towards them, and which had specifically ruled out statutory restraints either on pay or on the internal conduct of union affairs. The unions ensured that the legislative backlash against them from 1980 would be the more severe. Callaghan himself seemed to lose his old political touch at this time, since he quite unexpectedly turned down a general election in the autumn, to the dismay of most ministerial colleagues. He wavered over calling a state of emergency during the lorry-drivers' strike. He also cut an unsatisfactory figure when, returning suntanned from a conference in Guadeloupe at the start of 1979, he appeared to question the very existence of an industrial crisis in this freezing country. 'Crisis—what crisis?' was how the press misreported it. The truth, however, was that Labour's prospects of winning a general election in September 1978 were in any case far from clear. Labour's private polls suggested another hung parliament. Callaghan well recalled how Attlee had guessed wrong both in February 1950 and October 1951. Michael Foot and other key ministers agreed with Callaghan that the best chance lay in soldiering on and hoping that things would improve.

For all his surface optimism, Callaghan had no real hope of victory at the polls in 1979, despite a rugged personal performance. The collapse of pay policy during the unions' anarchic behaviour in the 'winter of discontent' had doomed them and their party. Callaghan's position in the party clearly eroded in 1979–80, and he withdrew from the leadership as conveniently as he could. His last months as leader until November 1980 were uncomfortable, dominated by renewed party turmoil and fierce attacks from Tony Benn and the left on his own prime ministerial methods, not least in the framing of the 1979 party manifesto. Ironically, when Callaghan did announce his withdrawal as leader, there were public pleas by Benn and Heffer of the left for him to stay, since they feared the succession of the more hawkish Denis Healey. Michael Foot, Callaghan's eventual successor, brought a very different, more conciliatory style of leadership, but the party's internal troubles became even worse. In this last phase, Callaghan emerged as a natural elder statesman, rebuking his party for softness on Militant or for drifting towards unilateralism or neutralism. His comments to this effect during the 1983 election campaign maybe added to the burdens borne by Michael Foot. More than most leaders, however, Callaghan's departure from the scene in late 1980 seemed the end of an era, just as the departure of Hubert Humphrey in 1968 marked the end of the old New Deal coalition in America. Callaghan's leaving marked the close not only for the most traditional in style of party leaders, but for the ethic of the Attlee consensus which Callaghan more than anyone else had embodied for thirty years and more.

The Thatcher years, however, serve to give the Callaghan period a new lustre. Certainly he himself remains a figure of much stature and dignity. It is clear that he was not, by instinct, a man for sustained change. He had too much commitment, both to a basic Victorian ethic and to a solid kind of old-fashioned patriotism, to deflect the nation's energies into significant new channels. His links with the unions were also a brake against change. His personal life-style, the substantial farm in Sussex, the friendship with the millionaire Julian Hodge, and directorship of the distinctly controversial Bank of Wales, also did not suggest a tendency towards iconoclasm.

But as interpreter and modulator of the mood of the party—
and perhaps as a vigorous executive minister, too—he was always
formidable. His style was one of balance, qualified by occasional
moves into more dramatic innovation. The policy in Northern Ireland
in 1969–70 was a vivid illustration of the latter tendency. So, too,
was his indirect assault on the premises of traditional Keynesianism
while premier in 1976 by insisting on the need to control the money
supply to reduce inflation. 'Sunny Jim' here seemed almost the first
of the Friedmanites. It was not a new tendency: his 'steady as she
goes' budget of April 1967, by breaking with what was known as
the 'full employment standard', had been hailed by *The Times* as 'the
end of the Keynesian era'. Institutionally, his 'economic seminar' in
Downing Street in 1977–8 was a remarkable, covert attempt,
through Harold Lever and others, to shackle the Treasury's ancient
ascendancy in determining financial policy.

Like Henderson and Morrison in the past, Callaghan was consistently underestimated for much of his career. Like both of them,
and like Stanley Baldwin, he was not obviously 'a clever man',
though he exceeded them all as a communicator. His time as Chancellor was too easily dismissed. Compared with the regimes of Mau-
dling beforehand and Barber afterwards, it almost appears a model
of order. His premiership seemed more an essay in survival than
anything else, though it was not without achievement in difficult
circumstances. Callaghan has been, above all, a notably powerful
symbol—perhaps at times an irreplaceable one—of the links between
the political and industrial wings of the movement, and is prepared
to voice his beliefs lucidly and courageously. In a party of prima
donnas, he won respect as the custodian of traditional values and
practices, close to the heart of the movement. This applies even to
his relatively conservative views on law and order. It was notable
that Labour magistrates and police authorities in working-class areas
tended to be much tougher on crime and punishment than were
more affluent middle-class representatives of Conservative or Alliance
outlook. This was true even of South Yorkshire until the 1984 miners'
strike. Labour's new posture in 1986, enthusiastically endorsed by
leaders of working-class origin like Kinnock and Hattersley, as the
instrument of order and security for the law-abiding ordinary citizen,
is a return to the Callaghan style at the Home Office rather than to
Roy Jenkins's middle-class essays in permissiveness. The same applied
to Callaghan's advocacy of improved basic skills in literacy and

numeracy in education, rather than using schools for experiments in applied sociology. Here and elsewhere, as Crossman was moved to observe after Callaghan's oratorical success at party conference on 3 October 1967, he was 'completely en rapport with the rank and file'. He was the more effective, therefore, in stamping on left-wing critics. Callaghan gave his successors something enduring to conserve. Along with Henderson and Morrison, he gave Labour much of its corporeal identity. It may be left to others to supply the spiritual trappings, if they can.

# MICHAEL FOOT

THE past few years have not been the best of times for Michael Foot. As leader from November 1980, he resembled a beleaguered prophet, born a century out of his time. Militant Tendency and the Praetorian guard of the hard left treated him with the same contempt that they had shown for right-wing figures like Gaitskell in the past. On the right, several key leaders broke away to form the SDP. The 1983 election campaign was a disaster, with Foot a popular scapegoat. Mrs Thatcher, buoyed up by Falklands jingoism, was re-elected with a majority of 140, while Labour, gaining less than twenty-eight per cent of the votes cast, put up its worst performance in elections since it began serious operations in 1918. Shortly afterwards, an almost offhand pronouncement by Clive Jenkins and some other union barons announced, apparently on his behalf, Foot's withdrawal from the leadership. The election seemed almost Michael Foot's Gethsemane, as August 1914 was Keir Hardie's, the cruel end not only to one remarkable career but to an ancient tradition of popular dissent which began with the Levellers at Putney in 1647 and spluttered out with the Bennites at Wembley in 1981.

It is too easy to anticipate the fashionable interpretation already crystallizing to sum up the life and times of Michael Foot. Peter Jenkins once wrote a memorable, if harsh, vignette in the *Guardian* of Foot gyrating at the dispatch box, his hair untidy, his collar askew, his few facts wrong. He seemed to Jenkins the very embodiment of Labour as permanent opposition, the natural heir of such Ishmaels as Hardie and Lansbury, not so much an Anabaptist as a Ranter, nourishing 'the red flame of socialist courage' in the doctrinal purity of the wilderness, but with scant gifts of leadership or of creative statesmanship. More than most of his contemporaries, Michael Foot has been taken as the political paradigm of an innocent abroad. He symbolizes, in one interpretation at least, the apotheosis of the Labour left in all its gesticulating futility, the supreme personification of a party unfit to rule.

Yet it is clear that Foot's career is vastly more complicated, and important, than that. He is personally, of course, a man of immense courtesy, loyalty, and generosity. Perhaps he can even go too far in this respect. In his volume of essays, *Loyalists and Loners* (1986), he was disturbingly gentle towards Enoch Powell, just as *Debts of Honour* (1980) tends to overdo the radicalism of Disraeli (after whom his Tibetan terrier is named). But the genuine affection he has inspired has been a crucial factor in his political progress. He is also a quite brilliant essayist and pamphleteer, part-author of *Guilty Men*, the greatest political tract since the days of Wilkes and Paine, as well as of a moving, if partisan, biography of Aneurin Bevan. This very brilliance, however, has enabled other critics to draw a contrast between his talent on paper and his alleged shortcomings in day-to-day politics.

More important, Foot embodies, and genuinely feels himself to embody, a powerful, creative thrust of populistic radicalism that has been constant in British public life for two centuries (at least as much so as the consensual, soggy centrism that is often claimed to reflect the native political genius). Foot's location in the British dissenting tradition is a complex one, and so is his career. A man who identifies with both the Levellers and with Cromwell, with the Whigs and the nonconformists, who used the style of Tory Democrats like Disraeli, Lord Randolph Churchill, or Beaverbrook to propel himself to the head of the inchoate forces of the British left, is clearly multidimensional, full of the ambiguities of an English heritage of popular protest that partisans both on the left and the right too often oversimplify to the point of parody. Interestingly, the dissenting tradition, as Foot sees it, is a distinctly bookish tradition. It expresses a radicalism of the word. His writing of history is a propaganda of the deed. His particular heroes are Swift, Hazlitt, Byron, Heine, Disraeli as a novelist, Blatchford, Silone, the early Orwell, rather than, say, Wilkes, Lovett, Garibaldi, Keir Hardie, or Blum. His well-lined study in Pilgrim's Lane calls to mind a discriminating man of letters rather than an engaged politician. To this extent, it is socialism by way of rare first editions, the Kelmscott Press, and the Home University Library, but warm, humane, and in important and relevant senses, patriotic.

Again, for an instinctive 'trouble-maker', a somewhat élitist gadfly, Foot is not a natural resident of the outback. He comes from a regional background and a family born to rule. His home was indeed a West-country Hatfield, in the shrewd phrase of Professor John Vincent (conveyed in the *Times Literary Supplement*, not in the egregious *Sun*). Foot has usually been a political realist, like his mentors and

Bevan, never a fellow-traveller nor a pacifist (witness his belligerent response to the Argentine invasion of the Falklands in 1982). At decisive moments, he has thrown his lot in with the mainstream of a Labour Party aspiring for power, rather than with a sectarian and isolated far left. In October 1968, his definition of 'parliamentary socialism' won him the unsolicited applause of the old Gaitskellite organ, Socialist Commentary. Not for nothing did his friend, Alan Taylor, see him as a 'compromiser', steering in times of crisis serenely down the middle of the road. Barbara Castle wrote in her diary of the basic rationalist Liberalism of the 'collective Foot type', amongst the more conformist of nonconformists, heir of Gladstone and Bright as well as of the astonishing Isaac of the Foot tribe. Michael Foot's kaleidoscopic career is a saga of the subtle shifts and contrasts that bear witness to the complexity of a major politician.

A major gap in our literature to date is a proper biography of Michael Foot—though, of course, any biographer would fatally risk comparison with Foot's own dazzling literary skills. The best to date has been Michael Foot: A Portrait by two journalists, Simon Hoggart and David Leigh, in 1977. It is, in fact, distinctly less satisfying than Mark Jenkins's important study of the Bevanites. It also errs by perhaps clothing its subject not only in a donkey jacket but in unduly saintly garb. Such curiosities as the champion of free speech and party tolerance endorsing the expulsion of Platts-Mills and the disciplining of the Nenni telegrammers in 1948 (and, much later in 1982, seeking the eviction of key members of Militant) need more explanation. Generous though he always is, Michael Foot, like every politician, can have his harder side, as Barbara Castle claims to have found out in 1976, and as recent aggressive essays on such targets as Gaitskell, George Brown, David Owen, and George, Lord Tony-pandy bear out. What Hoggart and Leigh have most usefully done is to etch in some personal material. Foot's shy personality; his relationship with young women (including the youthful Barbara Castle, née Betts, with whom he had the depressing experience of reading Das Kapital in a Bloomsbury attic); his filial devotion to such mentors as William Mellor and Beaverbrook; his intense personal loyalty to Cabinet colleagues, and especially to Nye Bevan (not forgetting his devotion to his admirable wife, Jill) are all spelt out in detail. Hoggart and Leigh have provided some helpful nuggets for future authors to follow up.

Four phases were crucial in the making of Michael Foot. The first three were each shaped by one powerful individual. The earliest was overshadowed by father, Isaac, who bequeathed to his four sons (three of whom were to become government ministers) a powerful and secure background of dissenting protest. Radical rural Liberalism, the quasi-pacifist overtones, the obsessions with drink (anti) and Plymouth Argyle (pro), the genuflections to Oliver Cromwell and John Bunyan, on to the dissenting Quaker academy at Leighton Park, and then Wadham College, Oxford, Foot's beloved *alma mater*—all were important. It was a primrose path for a pilgrim of the old left, marked out in 'the valley of the shadow of books' incontinently piled up sky-high by his fanatically bibliophile father. But it was an attractive, comfortable background, without the *angst*, the poverty, or the instinctive class bitterness inbred in the regional bases of Bright, Joe Chamberlain, Lloyd George, or Nye Bevan. Among the more notable features is the capacity for the dissidence of dissent to reproduce within itself as Michael delicatedly veered away from Isaac's Asquithian Liberalism, and as his nephew, Paul, has latterly forsworn his uncle's commitment to orthodox parliamentary socialism in favour of the nostrums of the Socialist Workers' Party. The Foots are never still and they are never dull.

The second phase, of course, was the thirties. They galvanized the young Oxford half-pacifist, fresh from 'King and Country' excitements, into the Popular Front enthusiasms of the time. (Incidentally, Oxford, along with Venice was always been one of his passions.) Finally it led him, with Frank Owen and Peter Howard, to write the *Guilty Men*, the *Junius Letters* of our time. In conventional terms, this period was Foot's formal conversion from Liberalism to Labour, and to the left-wing journalism of *Tribune*. Earlier, he had been sacked by Kingsley Martin, in a quite amazing misjudgement of his brilliant young journalist. The relationship Foot had with Stafford Cripps, that high-Church patrician only recently converted to socialist politics, was decisive here. It anticipated a wide range of unexpected alliances and liaisons over the years, from the Unity Front of the mid-thirties, to (in recent years) an improbable alliance with Enoch Powell. The relationship with Beaverbrook and the editorship of the *Evening Standard* during the war, of which too much has been made by some suspicious critics, were a continuation of this process. Foot admired Beaverbrook's iconoclasm, bohemianism, and his taste in Austrian actresses. This sense of style was as much a part of the dissenting tradition as were the 'little terriers' of the tin Bethels of the West Country. But Foot was never swallowed whole by Beaver-brook (any more than Paul Foot has been totally consumed by Robert Maxwell at the *Mirror*). When the old tyrant tried to stop Michael Foot publishing a wartime exposé of the links of the Tory right with Mussolini, the young editor resigned. It was an act of integrity by an honest man. Characteristically, he bore little rancour towards his former patron, and they were soon reconciled. Michael Foot has never found it as difficult as other politicians seem to do to be loyal to his friends.

The third phase lasted from 1945, when Foot entered the Commons as MP for Devonport (holding the seat until 1955), until 1960 when he re-entered parliament as member for Ebbw Vale. The latter, of course, was Bevan's old constituency, and the great Welsh tribune was obviously the dominant influence on Foot throughout—indeed down to 1963, when Wilson's election as party leader was seen on the left as a belated tribute to the legacy of Nye. There is much to be said about this period, more than is implied in Foot's remarkable biography of Bevan. It is clear that Foot was never an automatic voice for 'Keep Left'. Like Bevan, he was amongst the loyalists, not the loners, after 1945. *Tribune*, indeed, had its official and financial links with Transport House in 1948–50 when Foot and Jennie Lee were its editors. The journal defended the Attlee government loyally down to, and beyond, Britain's entry into the Korean War in June 1950. It may have been Bevan's troubles at the Ministry of Labour as much as the scale of the rearmament programme now adopted that led to a change of stance. At any rate, Foot was at the centre of the storms that followed.

His biting attack on Gaitskell, whom he compared in *Tribune* to the long-established traitor, Philip Snowden, added fuel to the final explosion in April 1951. After Bevan's resignation, Foot was caught up in the furious quarrels over a range of foreign policy and defence issues in the 1950s. Foot's main role here was as a journalist, sparkling in the columns of *Tribune*: he had left the NEC in frustration back in 1950. In the end, of course, the final and most painful breach came between Foot and Bevan himself when the latter turned savagely on the unilateralists at the Brighton conference in 1957. In part, as we have seen, it was the emollient presence of Jill Foot who helped reconcile these two giants of the left. In the ranks of CND, Foot was again immersed in the populistic protest of a democratic crusade, as in the thirties. But, once again, he was never an irreconcilable. The eventual defeat of CND in 1961–3 may almost have been a kind of relief, since it gave Foot a more positive role in the party and in public life. The election of Harold Wilson as leader (whose biography Foot was to write) provided justification. Foot persuaded himself that 'the incredible had happened', and that the old left had won at last. Wilson, Foot, and Crossman drank a private toast to a portrait of the dead Nye Bevan.

The final period of Foot's career is that of the advance to power, from Foot's re-entry to the PLP in 1963, through the years of strained loyalty under Wilson, the decision to stand for the Shadow Cabinet after the 1970 election, and the period of unquenchable loyalty as Cabinet minister from 1974. Foot's election as party leader in November 1980 was the natural outcome of this commitment to responsibility. Too much can be made of Foot's 'change of course' when he became a front-bench spokesman for the first time in 1970. The decisive shift had come with the election of Wilson seven years earlier. The pattern did not greatly change in the 1964–70 period, for all Foot's frequent revolts over incomes policy, Vietnam, reform of the House of Lords, and much else besides. Time and again, he persuaded the left to give Wilson the benefit of the doubt.

His five years as Cabinet minister, as Secretary for Employment in 1974–6 and then as Leader of the House and deputy Prime Minister under Callaghan, were not marked by legislative achievement. Attention to administrative detail has not been his strongest suit, and he fell foul of some journalistic colleagues over his amended Labour Relations Bill which appeared to threaten aspects of the freedom to publish. On the other hand, these were far from being wasted years, with a temporary truce negotiated between unions and government after the brawling of Heath's last year and the miners' strike; such useful creations as the mediation service, ACAS; and a political salvage operation that helped arrest inflation in its most uncontrolled phase, which owed much to a new and unexpected axis between Foot and Denis Healey. Foot's loyalty to government and movement, in marked contrast to Benn's ambivalent attitude, was exemplary throughout. Indeed, leftish ministers like Foot and Shore totally detached themselves from Benn from 1976 onwards. On issues on which he held strong views, such as direct elections to the EEC or wage restraint, time after time Foot gave precedence to solidarity with colleagues. Yet, as a socialist, Foot has never felt it necessary to apologize for the Labour policies of the 1970s either. He has pointed proudly to the public ownership of the aircraft and shipbuilding industries, the abolition of tied cottages, the spread of comprehensive education, extended industrial democracy in the docks, and measures against sexual discrimination as good socialist works from the Callaghan government. He was particularly effective in negotiating the 'pact' with the Liberals in April 1977. He built up an especially strong relationship with the Prime Minister, Callaghan in consequence.

There was also one heroic failure, Foot's attachment to Welsh and Scottish devolution. This last was in large measure, of course, the result of the growth of Celtic nationalism since the mid-sixties. It followed the findings of the Crowther–Kilbrandon Commission on the constitution, and was originally inspired by electoral prudence and the nationalist threat to Labour's Celtic heartlands. But Foot passionately believed in the principle of devolution. Partly this may have been the product of a somewhat uncritical regard for the democratic propensities of the Celts (whom Keir Hardie once described as all being 'socialists by instinct'). Foot has always taken very seriously his role as member for Ebbw Vale (now, incomprehensibly, renamed Blaenau Gwent): perhaps he has done so to excess. As Aneurin Bevan once observed, 'the Welsh are good, boy, but they're not that good!' On devolution, the judgement of rebels like Neil Kinnock was vindicated in the 1979 referendum. Yet dissatisfaction in Wales and Scotland with Whitehall rule has certainly not died away: indeed, pit and steel closures and massive unemployment in the eighties have only intensified it. In 1986 the Scottish Labour party strongly reasserted its commitment to some form of devolution, and Neil Kinnock himself, ironically enough, was led to endorse it. Foot's Rousseauite attachment to small nations, to local democratic accountability, and Celtic cultural values is by no means redundant, and does him credit.

His time as party leader in 1980–3 was difficult throughout. Yet, with powerful splinter elements on the far left and the right, it is hard to see how any leader bent on preserving the unity and mass appeal of a disintegrating coalition could have done much better. Foot pursued a unifying role at the disastrous January 1981 Wembley conference, but it is not easy to understand how a more confrontationist line would have made any impact on the Bennites in the constituency parties. In the 1983 general election campaign, Foot was saddled with a notoriously incompetent party machine, and also with a desperately naïve manifesto (one of the longer suicide notes in history, it has been observed). There were also unhelpful interventions on defence policy from senior figures such as Callaghan and Healey. Even in defeat, Labour's spirit and capacity to rebuild were not extinguished. Foot's period of leadership was unhappy, even inglorious, but it was a fitting end to an experience with power, really developed only in the last phase of Foot's career but nurtured in the instincts and inheritance of a lifetime.

The limitations and strengths of Foot's career have often been spelt out. For much of his life, though far less so after 1970, he appeared a rhetorician rather than a creative politician. His understanding of men and events at times has been deficient. In domestic policy, like most of those on the Labour left, he has taken little serious interest in economics over the years, though party instinct led him to support Denis Healey loyally after the 1976 IMF crisis. Such arcane themes as the exchange rate or the management of the money supply—both highly relevant to the establishment of a socialist society—tend to lead him to populistic denunciations of bankers and multinationals, an updated version of Cobbett's 'THING'.

It is in foreign affairs that Foot's main expertise has usually been thought to lie. *Tribune*, for this reason, was widely considered more authoritative than Martin's *New Statesman* in the late 1940s. Yet, save for the brief flirtation with the notion of a socialist united Europe in 1947–8, which attracted Foot, Crossman, Barbara Castle, Silverman, Warbey, and others, he has tended to be something of a 'little Englander', unduly preoccupied with a notion of lost national sovereignty. This perhaps made his initial response to the Falklands invasion in 1982 too emotional, though he later became more measured. The great error of CND in the fifties and sixties was to exaggerate British international moral influence at the time. But so, too, was it the error of the Gaitskellite right, who overestimated the degree to which the possession of a limited British nuclear strike force would increase the nation's stature and bargaining position in the international conference chamber. The air strikes launched against Libya in April 1986, and growing divergence between even the Thatcher government and the Reagan administration, showed the futility of such a belief. The debate on the bomb in the 1960s was in many ways an extended essay in parochialism; the revival of CND in the 1980s has perhaps been less obviously open to this criticism. Foot, similarly, has never shown the technical interest in overseas politics and economics which has been part of Denis Healey's intellectual equipment since his days in the party's International Department at Transport House.

And yet, Michael Foot has without doubt been a figure of major stature and substance in our public affairs over a very long period. The abuse from some press critics while he was party leader—'Worzel Gummidge', 'the old bibliophile', photographs of Foot hobbling on a stick on Hampstead Heath after breaking his ankle in an accident—seems increasingly absurd, as well as appallingly unfair, in retrospect. Of course, Foot has always been a communicator of genius (and not only to the converted), both as stump orator and as journalist and historical essayist. More than that, the crisis in the party in the 1970s merely underlined his importance, perhaps indispensability, for the democratic socialist movement, and perhaps British public life generally. His very presence and survival at the top made the emergence of the new generation represented by Kinnock all the easier. Foot's very Englishness and insularity have surely been his—and Labour's—strength. He has understood the way Labour has evolved within a native radical tradition. More than most figures on the left, he has understood the nuances of Labour as a movement and not simply as a machine.

His battles with Tony Benn throughout his time as leader, and continued in a powerful essay in *Loyalists and Loners*, revealed an intimate, instinctive feeling for the organic relationship of the various elements in the party. The parliamentary party, the NEC, annual conferences, the unions, the constituency management committees, individual party workers, sympathizers in the professions and the media, have all played their vital parts in sustaining Labour's coalition. The balance between them may shift, or give rise to internal party arguments. But the essence of Labour's appeal as the leading democratic socialist party in the world, ever since it supplanted the Liberals after 1918, has resided in the creative tension between its various elements. As Keir Hardie declared at the 1907 party conference, 'There must be free play between the sections. Otherwise they were in for a spill.' Foot himself put it more effectively in a highly perceptive pamphlet, 'My Kind of Socialism' in January 1982. It is essentially an essay in tolerance and pluralism, or perhaps divided sovereignty. Two sovereign bodies, the conference and the parliamentary party, had been created in the 1918 constitution and, writes Foot, 'neither will bow the knee to the other'. But then neither need do so, if internal party debates are conducted in a spirit of common sense rather than doctrinaire zealotry, and if a mood of comradeship is allowed to prevail. An even better known political author, Aristotle, put much the same point two thousand years ago. 'A *polis*, by advancing in unity, will cease to be a *polis* ... It is as if you were to turn harmony into mere unison, or to reduce a theme to a single beat. A *polis* is an aggregate of many members.' So, truly, is a great party, as Foot fully understands and as the new Platonists of the hard left often do not.

Michael Foot's role as party leader in 1980–3, for all the troubles of those times, was more positive in intent than has often been supposed. Often conducted more effectively within the closed walls of Walworth Road council chambers than in the television studio, it consisted of a prolonged engagement with the self-styled 'New Left'. The missionary crusade conducted by the millenarian disciples of the prophet Benn bade fair to produce that very 'spill' against which the pragmatism of Keir Hardie (not to mention the relativism of Aneurin Bevan) warned years ago. To treat members of parliament, the Shadow Cabinet, even the party's elected leader and prospective Prime Minister, as no more than ventriloquist's dummies, trained to reproduce the ill-thought-out and often contradictory resolutions cobbled together amidst the emotion of an annual conference or through the late-night decisions of Militant-led minorities in the constituencies, was not merely insulting to the dignity of public men and women: it was totally at variance with the vibrant democracy that the Labour Party (especially its ILP wing, which Foot best symbolizes) claimed to represent.

Foot in the years from 1980 was engaged, among other things, in demonstrating that he was simply a better democrat, as well as a better socialist, than Tony Benn, that he had really the more effective 'arguments for democracy'. He did not find it difficult to do so. Despite the electoral disasters of the party down to the 1983 campaign, Foot made a considerable contribution to making Labour newly credible, not through new ideas or policy-making, but through neutralizing the impact of the hard left within the party. To an extent still not properly appreciated, he succeeded. The return to realism of important sections of the left, the 'soft left' as usually defined, including such important figures as David Blunkett, Michael Meacher, and Audrey Wise (and perhaps Ken Livingstone), has in large measure been Foot's work. If there is a renewal of the party under the Kinnock–

Hattersley partnership, as there appeared to be in 1986 at least, it will be Michael Foot who conspicuously helped to that end.

Foot's ultimate task, as orator, pamphleteer, and communicator extraordinary, has been to educate, and to relate the British variant of socialism to a long, but still relevant, history of British libertarian protest—in other words, to the real world. In his respect for parliament, for the rule of law (subject to some very valid doubts about the judgement of the judges), for representative democracy, for the pluralism and tolerance embedded in the culture of his people, he has been in the best sense a force for stability. His view of the role of leader was not based on mere rhetoric. It was entirely rational to show how Keir Hardie, Arthur Henderson, George Lansbury, Aneurin Bevan, almost every great working-class leader the Labour Party has ever produced, all honoured and prized the parliamentary mode of democracy, and regarded it as the key to gaining the commanding heights of power so that a socialist society could ultimately be created. The contrast between these labour giants of the past and the Trotskyist tribunes of the far left, especially their déclassé bourgeois members, is instructive. So, too, is the profound loyalty that Aneurin Bevan always showed towards the achievements of the Attlee government, compared with the Janus-like attitude taken by the heir to Lord Stansgate towards Cabinet colleagues with whom he nevertheless felt able to serve in government between 1974 and 1979. It is, indeed, a moral issue, with perhaps problems for the psychologist as well.

In the years 1980–3, Michael Foot, derided by the weekly columnists and the broadcasting media, made a considerable contribution to the future health of his party and to Britain as a polity. It was one that fitted in precisely with his deeply-felt instinct for the past. He has long seen himself as the Hazlitt of our time, 'an unfrocked romantic' as Heine wrote of himself, rekindling our sensibilities. Citizen Foot might have been much more at home in earlier, revolutionary times, as a kind of Methodist Danton. What he has nevertheless done, by message and by example, is to direct a passionate appeal from the Old Left to the New. He has re-articulated and vindicated a long, creative legacy of protest which in the 1970s seemed close to being corrupted or destroyed. It may seem odd for an old Jacobin like Michael Foot to be cast as the Edmund Burke of Ebbw Vale (let alone the Aristotle of Abertysswg). The Bennite multitude may seem mulish rather than positively swinish. Nor does the defensive role come naturally to Foot. As Hazlitt wrote of Cobbett, he is the Tom Cribb of the journalistic prize ring, best on the attack. Yet, in the later stages of a career which has added lustre, literacy and panache to our public dialogue, he has offered us the promise that the long night may be ending and a new beginning in sight.

# JOE GORMLEY, ARTHUR SCARGILL, AND THE MINERS

THE miners are central to the folklore and the usable past of the Labour Party. The party's vision of itself is inextricably bound up with deep-rooted folk memories of Featherstone and Tonypandy, of years of conflict between the colliers and the coalowners. The miners' strike of 1984–5 aroused such intensity of feeling not only because of the still major role of coal in the nation's energy supplies, but also because of the resonance of history. The strike proceeded on its bitter course, amidst eloquent recollection of the betrayals of Black Friday, and the solidarity of the General Strike. At times, it seemed almost to have more to do with 1926 than with 1984. When the secession of the Notts. miners threatened, and duly took effect with the formation of the UDM, there was immediate talk of the evils of 'Spencerism', the breakaway company-type unionism of the 1920s. Arthur Scargill himself became a history man, though his point of reference was more recent—the 1972 Saltley coke depot, and his flying pickets which forced the police and the state to yield before the mass power of organized workers. The passion of the miners' strike, and its bitter *dénouement*, was intensified because the miners seemed to be reliving their own history, with all its tragedies and all its grandeur.

In some ways, of course, this emphasis on the central role of the miners in Labour's past can be overdone. It is not correct that the party 'was born in the bowels' of the mining industry. The miners in 1900 were dominated by Lib-Labs of the Mabon/Pickard/Edwards type. Not until 1909 did the Miners' Federation affiliate to the Labour Party, the last major manual union to do so. Even then, residual Lib-Labbism, especially in the Midlands coalfields, aroused the suspicion of ILP socialists like Hardie and Glasier before 1914.

The industrial militancy of the miners, too, has sometimes been exaggerated. The story of industrial relations in the mining industry is not one of constant class war and confrontation. Apart from the notable MFGB strike in 1893, conflict was largely confined to the years 1908–26, when coal fell from a dominant role in the economy to a state of structural depression and decline. The national strikes of the mining industry were largely concentrated in this brief, traumatic period. The first came in 1912, when the miners successfully wrung wage minima, district by district, from the Asquith government, with the aid of Lloyd George's mediation. The others were products of the post-war industrial crisis which saw miners' national stoppages in October 1920, April–July 1921, and most tragically, May–November 1926. No national miners' strike occurred—or seemed likely to occur—in the forty-six years from 1926 to 1972. The rundown of the industry in the 1950s and 1960s was accepted with relative acquiescence by the NUM and their successive Welsh Communist general secretaries, Arthur Horner and Will Paynter, although there were several local stoppages. More recently, the miners played no part in the winter of discontent in 1978/9 which brought down the Callaghan government. The really bitter memories among mining folk—Featherstone, Tonypandy, Ammanford, Six Bells, Betteshanger, Cortonwood—were local rather than national in their origins. For most of the time, the miners have been among the less militant of Britain's workers.

Nevertheless, as a result of the savage industrial troubles before and after the First World War, the miners did become uniquely identified with the struggles of the labour movement. They were then the largest workforce in the land, with a unique strength and solidarity. Even after 1945, there were over 700 000 miners at work. The nationalization of the mines, with the running up of the NCB standard over the pitheads on 1 January 1947, vesting day, amidst cries of 'Today, the mines belong to the people', aroused spontaneous rejoicing in coalfields from Betteshanger to Fife. The diminishing influence of the miners within the Labour Party since 1945—after the 1983 election there were only fourteen NUM-sponsored MPs, and one or two of these in Nottinghamshire are now linked to the rebel UDM—has not eroded the miners' central role in Labour's class-consciousness, its sense of its past and its destiny. Hence the special trauma and pain aroused by the struggle and defeat of 1984–5.

The nature of the miners' leadership in the past sheds much light on some of the major changes that have latterly taken place within the mining industry, and in the miners' political relationship to the Labour Party. In particular, the contrast between Joe Gormley, the Lancastrian who presided over the triumphant strikes of 1972 and 1974, and Arthur Scargill, the Yorkshireman who led his men to disastrous defeat in 1984–5, is particularly illuminating. Joe Gormley was fortunate in his time, since he presided over the NUM just before coal entered its recent, fatal decline. But then, according to his autobiography, *Battered Cherub*, he always was a lucky fellow. As the fourth of seven children born to a mining family in Ashton-in-Makerfield, midway between Wigan and St Helens, he was, as he genially puts it, 'born to a negotiating position'. As a youth, he was lucky in fights, lucky with girls he met while 'sparking' in the local hayfields, lucky (sometimes) in his compulsive gambling with horses. Fortune was on his side, generally, during a rapid ascent in the stormy world of the NUM in the 1960s. An unsuccessful attempt to emigrate to Australia in 1953 led him to migrate to the Staffordshire coalfield nearer home, and then become general secretary of the Lancashire Miners in the early 1960s. Rapid promotion to the miners' national executive was soon to follow. Defeated by Lawrence Daly for the NUM general secretaryship in 1968, he bounced back to trounce Mick McGahey in winning the presidency three years later. His Lancashire area actually allowed £12 000 for his campaign. Whether in industrial confrontation or (more characteristically) in deft diplomacy over ale and sandwiches, things usually went his way. After all, as an awestruck NCB official once observed, 'Joe could bargain the buttons off your trousers.'

Like the American Federation of Labor leader, Sam Gompers, whom in some ways he resembled, Gormley's basic demand for the British miners was always 'more'. Under his presidency, the NUM's outlook was worlds removed from the dour, inward-looking strategies of Smillie and Cook half a century earlier. Instead of a desperate fight to ward off punitive wage cuts and victimization by the bosses, Gormley's sights were set on 'a good education for the children, a Jaguar at the front, a Mini at the back to take the wife shopping'. With a blend of cunning and vision, he enabled the miners to make giant strides towards these agreeable bourgeois objectives. Under his leadership between 1971 and 1982, the miners' living standards made dramatic progress. The £100-a-week collier became a reality. Health and pit safety were improved beyond all measure. Despite the controversy that surrounded his career, down to his retirement, Gormley has been, along with Arthur Horner perhaps, the outstanding miners' leader of the post-war period.

From the start, he was a pugnacious 'moderate', a natural diplomat with a good dig in either fist. One Lancashire miners' official considered him 'a gangster'. Out of the timeless working-class world of struggle and poverty in the South Lancashire coalfield, little removed from Mrs Gaskell, with its daily brutalities and terrible pit accidents, Gormley rose with rare ambition. He was Archie Rice and Andy Capp rolled into one. In the more hopeful world of nationalized coal after 1947, new opportunities could open up for a thrusting young area secretary. Now Sam Watson had gone, the NUM right wing needed a leader. Gormley's approach was always expansive and optimistic. He fought selectively against the pit closures of the Robens era; while for the men left underground, and for surface workers, he struck out boldly to win unprecedented benefits. The climax of his career was the two national coal strikes, of February 1972 and February 1974. In 1972, after the Wilberforce findings, with the Heath government admitting defeat, Gormley was as forceful as his Communist colleagues in piling a further twenty fringe benefits on to the basic wage awards, including the ending of the hated 'bonus shift', a source of contention for the miners since 1947.

The 1974 strike ended with an equal flourish. Incidentally, Gormley claims that potentially successful talks between himself and Whitelaw were blitzed by interference from Labour Party leaders— which leads him to join the throng in driving a few more nails into Harold Wilson's reputation. After this strike, the miners were again triumphant, being in effect given a blank cheque by the new Labour government. In passing, Gormley murmurs that these stoppages may have had some undesirable long-term effects in teaching 'the lads' to take precipitate strike action. He was unhappy with Arthur Scargill's violent methods at the Saltley coke depot. But such worries do not detain him for long. The president of the NUM in the late 1970s was a cheerful hedonist, enjoying the good life in Sunbury-on-Thames, honoured by the media and revered by some (though emphatically not all) of his flock. When Tony Benn offered him the chairmanship of the NCB in 1976, it was an appropriate recognition of his qualities. Under his guidance, no doubt, the coal industry would have followed a very different and less abrasive route from the MacGregor regime.

In one important respect, Gormley's career marked almost the end of an era, since he was committed to maintaining in full the links between the NUM and the Labour Party. He did intend, or hope for, a parliamentary career, but he was turned down as Labour candidate for Burnley, owing to his anti-CND views. He followed Sam Watson on to the Labour NEC in 1963. A past chairman of the party's policy and international committees, he has always been one of the more politically aware of the major union leaders. His close links with the Labour Party leadership enabled him to help produce the famous (though later abortive) 'Plan for Coal', with its proposed target of 150m. tons production by 1985, which led to so much debate during the national miners' strike a decade later. His close links with the government during the Callaghan era helped to get the area-based incentive scheme for productivity off the ground, while as late as January 1982 his instinct for 'moderation' and 'sensible socialism' helped win support for an improved wage offer among the miners and avert a national stoppage. Gormley may have been lucky in his time, but he has ridden his good fortune by maintaining the old alliance of the miners and the Labour Party as comrades-in-arms.

Arthur Scargill, from the very start, represented a totally different outlook and strategy. For one thing, of course, he came from a younger generation than Gormley with whom he was locked in conflict for almost a decade. Born in 1938, he became president of the NUM at the remarkably early age of forty-four. His father was a hard-line Communist. Young Arthur himself joined the Young Communist League at the age of seventeen, and soon won the 'Willie Gallacher Cup' for dramatically boosting sales of *Challenge* in the Barnsley area. He does not seem to have had his faith shaken at all by the events in Hungary in 1956. The following year, he went to the World Youth Festival in Moscow. When he met Khrushchev and Bulganin, the young Yorkshire militant took the opportunity to attack them for their denunciation of Stalin a year earlier. He stood as a Communist candidate on the Worsborough Urban District Council in 1960, coming bottom of the poll. In 1963, however, he left the Communist Party, not for libertarian reasons it would seem, but because of attacks by the Kremlin on the reputation of Stalin, including changing the name of Stalingrad. Scargill's departure from the fold seems to have been inspired by ambitious reasons, at least in part, since in 1964 he began the new career which launched him to power when he was elected branch delegate for Woolley within the NUM, with opportunities to make an impact at the national union level as well. For all the moderate views of the Woolley miners, Scargill's brashness, energy, and charisma thrust him to the forefront.

Around this time, he formally joined the Labour Party; he remains a party member, acting as head of the NUM delegation at party conferences. Yet it is clear that his connection with the Labour Party has never been an important factor in his career. The contrast with Gormley is very noticeable. While he may have left the Communist Party in his twenties, Scargill's creed has not changed over the years. He remains a Communist of the hard, Stalinist kind. He feels close kinship with the 'people's democracies' of eastern Europe, and frequently proclaims his comradeship with them. He has a soft spot for Cuba, even for Qaddafi's Libya. In the fierce doctrinal argument within the Communist Party (unlike the Scotsman, Mick McGahey, a party member associated with the Euro-Communist wing) Scargill strongly backed the fundamentalist Stalinist faction identified with the *Morning Star*. He urged that a struggle like the miners' strike of 1984-5, apparently hopeless though it might seem, really represented a powerful advance to socialism on Marxist lines. So far as his social and economic philosophy is concerned, Michael Crick's *Scargill and the Miners*, which is very fair-minded towards its subject, sees Scargill as committed to a wholly Marxist state, with total planning of the economy and social order, and one hundred per cent state ownership. His wife, Anne, would appear to hold the same views. Scargill's outlook is light years removed from the gradualist stance of the Labour Party, as he has always had the honesty to admit. In a particularly intense, doctrinal fashion, he reflects a generation of union leaders totally absorbed in the industrial struggle against capitalism, careless of the parliamentary or political links which earlier miners' leaders, from Smillie to Gormley, had seen as the staff of life.

From the start, Scargill's career as union leader was linked with industrial conflict, often with violence. The mass picketing of Saltley coke depot of 1972 was 'the magic moment' of his life, a physical symbol of the raw power of organized labour triumphing over the capitalist order of a police state. Two years later, still only thirty-four, he was elected president of the Yorkshire miners, and thereafter was a constant advocate of conflict with the NCB, industrial action against the closure of uneconomic pits or on behalf of swingeing wage advances with no regard to finance. Until the 1980s, he was usually narrowly outvoted by a right-wing majority on the NUM executive, however. At times, even Scargill could be taken unawares by the intensity of local protest, as when the Welsh miners launched a series of lightning unofficial strikes in early 1981 against pit closures at Deep Duffryn and elsewhere, forcing even the Thatcher government, momentarily, to give way. His administrative style as president led to some industrial trouble with the NUM clerical staff at Euston Road, after Gormley's relatively relaxed methods. On balance, however, Scargill's credentials as a class warrior and advocate of industrial confrontation remained untarnished. It was in this light that he was elected NUM president by a huge majority over Trevor Bell in 1982, and it was on that basis that he fought the good fight in 1984–5.

The Yorkshire miners' action against the closure of Cortonwood Colliery in March 1984, resisting a clear betrayal of previous pledges given by the National Coal Board, gave Scargill his opportunity. The NUM right now agreed on resisting pit closures by industrial action; but, unlike Scargill, they had no strategy. Without calling a national ballot, which might well have gone against him, he allowed coalfield after coalfield to go its own way. Soon, other than in Nottinghamshire and one or two smaller Midlands coalfields, there was a total stoppage of work. Scargill's gaze was still focused on the heady triumph of Saltley a decade and more before. While somewhat sceptical about the feasibility of a national strike in 1982–3, he still believed in the mystical industrial muscle of King Coal. For generations, industrial action by the miners had brought terror to elected governments, from Asquith's premiership to Thatcher's. As late as the 1950s, the Conservative administration of Churchill himself, through the mediation of Sir Walter Monckton, gave in to the NUM on every issue. Harold Macmillan laid down that the miners, along with the Catholic church and the Brigade of Guards, were an institution with which no Tory government should ever tangle, and he was true to his word.

But the times were very different now. In 1984 Scargill's doctrinaire refusal to acknowledge the changing facts of life and his dogmatic devotion to a Marxist version of miners' power led his men to irreparable disaster. Scargill became central to the greatest defeat the miners had ever suffered, worse even than 1926.

First of all, he failed to take sufficiently seriously the diminished role of coal in the British economy. With the growing advance of oil and (despite continuing controversy) nuclear power since the 1950s, with cheap foreign coal always available, and the falling demand for a labour-intensive product like home-produced British coal, the mining industry's importance was obviously reduced. In 1913, there had been 1 200 000 miners at work. In 1947 there were 700 000.

In 1984, less than 200 000 were engaged in the industry in any form. South Wales, which employed a quarter of a million miners in 1913 (40 000 in the Rhondda alone), was in 1984 employing barely 20 000 (the tally in late-1986, with the closure of thirteen Welsh pits since the end of the strike, is around 12 000). The closing of historic 'Red Maerdy' in June 1986 ended all mining in the Rhondda. Coal output halved between 1955 and 1983, yet millions of tons remained unsold, piling up at pitheads or stockpiled by power stations. The capacity of the miners to defeat the government of the day, so evident under Joe Gormley as under Herbert Smith in the past, was no longer there.

Secondly, the links between the miners and other unions were weaker than ever. Perhaps they had never been that strong anyhow. Even during and after the General Strike in 1926, a miners' strike did not paralyse the nation, partly because dockers continued to unload cheap imported coal from Germany and elsewhere, partly because railwaymen and lorry drivers did not impose a transport embargo on coal movement. The 1984 miners' strike confirmed that appeals to workers' unity did not find much response within an increasingly stratified and bourgeoisified trade-union movement. The industrial recession was another powerful negative factor. Nor did fraternal assistance from foreign trade-unionists (food hampers from France and the like) add up to much, for all Scargill's insistence to the contrary.

Thirdly, the government was clearly far better prepared to face major industrial confrontation with key workers than ever in the past. The new co-ordination and power of the police in meeting mass picketing and industrial disruption marked a profound historical change. The National Reporting Centre provided a unique nerve centre. Mutual aid agreements for the provincial police, harder to implement in the inter-war years, are now standard form. The alarming use of police support units, amounting to nearly ten thousand in July 1984, was another novel element. So, too, were new powers claimed by the police to use stop-and-search methods to intercept peaceful pickets on the open road very far from mining areas, and to place entire pit communities virtually under a state of siege. The government had also new resources in the ability of power stations and manufacturing industry to outface a miners' strike. The Civil Contingency Unit in Whitehall, far more sophisticated than the old anti-strike emergency apparatus of 1920 or 1946, was crucial here.

The miners had lost their central weapon, probably for ever, in the face of a grimly determined, ruthless Thatcher government prepared to use any methods to defeat them.

Finally, within the NUM itself, history fatally reasserted itself. Of course, the strike displayed the intense, deeply moving solidarity amongst the mining communities. Despite a hostile press, despite a government which sharply reduced social security benefits and despite the brute effects of hunger, poverty, and police pressure, well over 100 000 miners remained on strike for almost a year. Families and neighbourhoods were staunch behind them. No other group of workers could have remained so united and so brave for so long. The real cause lay, not in physical intimidation of non-strikers (though clearly this played some part), but in class and occupational unity. At the same time, the strike confirmed something else—the historical divisions within the miners as a group. The miners have always been regionally divided. Regionalism and localism were enshrined in the NUM structure after 1945, as the would-be sequestrators of the miners' funds found out to their cost in 1984–5. Scargill was the leader of nineteen semi-autonomous unions. In the fifties and sixties, Horner and Paynter had tried to unite their men by abolishing divisive piece-rates. The Power Loading Agreement of 1966, Will Paynter's statesman-like achievement, removed one damaging element here. But the productivity bonus scheme of the 1970s reinforced the built-in schismatic tendencies of the various coalfields, implicitly setting region against region and miner against miner. Some of the NCB saw it as a key to blunting the challenge of the left. The Welsh or the Scots, seeking to keep open Ty-mawr Lewis Merthyr or Polmaise, found it difficult to win nationwide support. The 1984 strike opened these regional divisions up into a chasm. The outcome was the breakaway of miners in Notts. and South Derbyshire, to-gether with smaller groups in Durham, Warwickshire, Lancashire, North Wales, and amongst the coke men. The Union of Democratic Mineworkers aroused suspicion in many quarters, and certainly did not swamp the old NUM as its founders intended. But with well over thirty thousand members in relatively thriving coalfields, the UDM confirmed that what Scargill and the NUM had done was to destroy, at least for the moment, the historic unity of the British miners. No longer would the miners work, fight, and die as comrades in a common cause.

In these unpromising circumstances, Arthur Scargill's approach seemed to be to deny the facts and turn his back on realism of any form. He symbolized an ideological and unduly personalized miners' leadership. Whereas the miners' leadership in the past had usually consisted of partnerships—Smith and Cook in the twenties, Lawther and Horner in the forties, Gormley and Daly in the seventies—Scargill stood on a remote pinnacle of his own. (It might be noted that Gormley's own ascendancy during Daly's ill-health in the late seventies had been a contributory factor in building up the power of the president.) The press treated Scargill savagely, and he was seriously and repeatedly harrassed by the police. 'Barnsley's Lenin' was among the more moderate descriptions attached to him in the media. But his position masked the fact that most other NUM leaders, even the Communist Mick McGahey (whose Scottish miners were amongst the first to drift back starting in Lothian with Bilston Glen), were more conciliatory. As McGahey bitterly complained, Arthur Scargill's militant rhetoric and refusal to consider compromise left the miners with no way out. Also, and quite unlike Gormley in the recent past, he ignored the old-established *rapport* between the NUM and the Labour Party, which had operated so powerfully in February–March 1974. Apart from far-left figures such as Tony Benn and Denis Skinner, few Labour politicians gave the miners much encouragement. Many were appalled by the violence, intimidation, and brutality (by police as well as strikers, of course) over which Scargill watched with apparent equanimity and an ever-present Nelsonian blind eye. Neil Kinnock, himself a miner's son from the Rhymney Valley, treated the miners' strike with great reserve, and made only a token appearance on the picket line himself. About Scargill he was scathing, comparing him with a British first world war general in the slaughter at Gallipoli.

For Scargill himself, the media attention was a trap and a snare. He was, of course, very good on television, his wit, charm, and articulateness being in marked contrast to the dourness and bad temper of the ageing MacGregor and his acolytes. Scargill's treatment was uncannily reminiscent of the horrid fascination evoked in the 1920s by another far-left miners' leader, Arthur Cook. The latter was represented in the press as a kind of red Welsh revivalist, Lenin, and Billy Sunday rolled into one, 'an inspired idiot drunk with words' in Beatrice Webb's opinion. Cook became the tragic victim of the general strike, admittedly in part because of ill-health. He died of cancer just before his forty-eighth birthday in 1931. But he had previously had a flirtation with Oswald Mosley's New Party, and had also been censured by the Miners' Federation for the crimes of opportunism and implied betrayal. Arthur Scargill's militant credentials, of course, still remain unimpaired. But the tragic end of the strike, the closure of twenty-seven pits in the first instance with the loss of over thirty thousand jobs, the loss of NUM funds, the deep schism in the union, the helplessness of the miners in the face of aggressive tactics by management and government had potentially put even Scargill's post as president (nominally, beyond challenge until 2004) on the line. He presides over a sadly demoralized union, with productivity records being broken on all sides by men fearful for the future of their jobs and their industry. Scargill is a remarkably tough, resilient, buoyant man, but his career has none the less ended in tears for his followers, if not yet for him.

Joe Gormley and Arthur Scargill clearly represent quite different approaches to the strategy of the miners. Gormley embodies the broad church view, linked with the Labour Party and the TUC, in the main cautious and judicious, and anxious to keep in step with the movement as a whole. Scargill, by contrast, has offered a prolonged cavalry charge into the unknown, urging the TUC and fellow socialists to join in and follow, but with scant apparent concern whether in fact they do or not. Even in June 1986, he was proposing industrial action to the NUM annual conference, but the delegates ignored him. In some ways, of course, to compare Gormley's successes and Scargill's débâcle is unfair. The circumstances were more favourable to the NUM leadership in the early 1970s, with the shock effect of an energy crisis and a quadrupled price of oil: in 1986, oil prices have actually fallen rapidly so that, in real terms, oil is cheaper than in 1972. Gormley's own view of wage bargaining was highly traditional, even antiquated. His memoirs include side by side, in an ambivalence typical of the labour movement, an adherence to economic planning with a total rejection of anything resembling an incomes policy. His career masked the reality of a highly precarious future for coal within the context of a national energy policy, and constant warfare within his executive over ends and means. Under Scargill these differences have come out into the open. It may be guessed that, under any leadership, the miners would have faced severe contraction of their industry, on strictly economic grounds, during the 1980s. Right and left wings alike on the NUM executive shared a common anxiety. Scargill's achievement, however, has been to turn an orderly, controlled retreat into a bloody rout.

The miners have been sad victims of history, geology, and sociology, and prisoners of a deceptive vision of the past. There is no apparent way in which coal can be restored to a prime position in the economy (though it might be noted that, in mid-1986, eighty per cent of the fuel for British power stations still came from coal, while the Chernobyl disaster in Russia posed alarming new questions over the development of nuclear power). But if the miners are to have a decent future, as they should, it can only be won by pragmatism and collaboration with industrial and political allies along agreed lines (including a regional policy for industrial diversification worthy of the name in mining areas). They should forget their history and wipe away memories of past glories, triumphs, and defeats. The miners might also do well to operate more collectively, and ignore the charisma of personally dominant leaders. Unknown soldiers might be more effective guides in directing the miners along the later stages of their tragic odyssey.

# TONY BENN

THE zeal of the convert is always a difficult factor to accommodate to the usages of British politics, as to life in general. Gibbon provided a useful text when he observed of the fanaticism and intemperance of the early Christian martyrs that it was not in this world that they sought to be either agreeable or useful. Naturally, our history shows many cases of significant politicians who, for entirely defensible and genuine reasons over a period of years, have decided that the time had come to change their allegiance and cross the floor. As is well known, Gladstone himself began life as 'the rising hope of the stern unbending Tories', moved into Peelite centrism in middle age, and ended up as the increasingly combative voice of the Liberal left. In his eighties, he was more radical than at any other stage of his life. Such shifts (Joe Chamberlain and Winston Churchill are other instances) are inevitable in political affairs, and the privilege of public men and women. More difficult are very rapid and extreme shifts of position from one party to another. The most spectacular case this century is that of Oswald Mosley who swung violently from Toryism in 1918 to leftwards socialism by 1924, and finally left Labour as well to found his own fascist offshoot in 1931. But Mosley's very rootlessness and lack of a firm base destroyed him as a major figure, leaving intact the political framework as a whole.

The most complicated case of all is a convert who changes his outlook with extreme rapidity, even violence, yet still stays within his original political habitat. There are two notable Labour examples this century, both of patrician origin, Stafford Cripps and Tony Benn. But their moves have been in opposite directions. As noted above, Cripps moved swiftly in 1939–40 from far left, almost fellow-travelling socialism, to a broad centrism which saw him closer to moderate Tories than to his former comrades. Benn, on the other hand, swung with equal velocity the other way, some time during the latter part of 1970. From being a centre, even right-wing member of Labour Cabinets, he became the pied piper of almost every available left-wing cause. He was the apostle of widespread nationalization and state intervention, the voice of the anti-Marketeer, the unilateralist, the supporter of Irish republicanism. By the end of the

1970s, there seemed hardly a fashionable radical cause—that of the black activist, feminist, 'gay lib' or Greenpeace environmentalist—with which he was not passionately identified. Trotskyists readily campaigned on his behalf. After the 1979 election, there came a further seismic movement, with a renewed commitment to internal party democracy and constitutional reform. His election defeat in the deputy leadership contest by Denis Healey in October 1981 was the watershed. Since then he has seemed diminished, physically less vigorous, somewhat outstripped on the left by younger men like Ken Livingstone or the cohorts of Militant. In the miners' strike in 1984–5, during the air strike on Libya or the Wapping industrial dispute in 1986, Benn's views (often humane and basically sensible) appeared no longer to carry the same force. He seemed increasingly marginalized, a spent force.

But of his central importance in the realignment and broad decline of the Labour Party between 1970 and 1983, there can be no question. Long after he has ceased to be a participant in our affairs, the impact of Tony Benn over the restructuring of the British left will be felt. At the same time, the bewildering, quixotic nature of his influence with, as noted, a central interruption in continuity in 1970, makes him almost impossible to compartmentalize. Several personae jostle for prominence within him. There has been Tony Benn the technocratic socialist and a Europeanist through the supreme importance of technological modernity, a gadget man known to Crosland as 'Jimmy' whose enthusiasms ranged from repairing old bicycles to computerizing the Post Office. There was Tony Benn the reformed Congregationalist, the new voice of the nonconformist conscience with which he grew up, a new Wycliffe or Wesley evangelizing, prophesying, crusading with missionary zeal and a Rousseauite faith in direct contact with 'the people'. There are many contradictions. The high corporatist of MinTech days is conjoined with the passionate advocate of direct democracy since the seventies. There is the calm voice of socialist rationalism who is addicted to the mystical Christian antecedents of early socialism, a transcendental guru of the new left. There is the crusader for a planned future commonwealth who is fascinated by the heritage of John Ball, the Levellers, the Diggers and other improbable recruits for the Labour Party in past centuries.

Perhaps most difficult for political colleagues, (especially those like Michael Foot and Mrs Castle who are clearly on the left themselves), there has been Benn the pedantic advocate of strict adherence to manifesto, conference resolution and NEC edict, who nevertheless, in terms of his own career as Cabinet minister and party spokesman in recent years, chose defiantly to pursue his own path, whatever charges of disloyalty might be hurled against him. The fact of Benn's principled conversion to a purer form of socialist theory during late 1970 can be accepted, with all its political and psychological ramifications. But its extreme rapidity, the puzzling or unanswered aspects of his changes in outlook, the allies he has enlisted and the tactics he has adopted, are harder to embrace. His career as a serious politician is more difficult to interpret in consequence.

As is well known, Benn grew up with an impeccable upper-middle-class radical inheritance. His father, William Wedgwood Benn, Lord Stansgate, was a leading Congregationalist of independent views and diminutive stature. He was a vigorous parliamentary debater who seemed at home in the isolation of Liberalism in the early twenties. Eventually in 1927 he joined the Labour Party, somewhat later than radicals of the anti-war UDC school or even an old Coalition Liberal like his fellow East End MP, Dr Christopher Addison. Wedgwood Benn was not an especially radical figure thereafter, despite his nonconformist attachment to the phrase 'Dare to be a Daniel'. He was an effective, relatively right-wing member of both MacDonald's and Attlee's Cabinets. He had charge of important, but unsuccessful, talks with the leaders of the Indian Congress in 1930, and the Egyptian Wafd in 1946.

His son, Anthony, was a product of Westminster School and New College, Oxford (where he was president of the Union and a notably humorous and eloquent debater there). Throughout his career, he has retained the wealth, patrician accent, and public school style of his upbringing. He entered parliament as member for Cripps's old seat of Bristol South East in late 1950, again as an apparently loyalist, middle-of-the-road Labour MP. During the party storms of the fifties and early sixties, he was no Bevanite and no unilateralist. On balance he was aligned with the Gaitskellite camp, and voted for Gaitskell as leader in 1955 even though the latter had a low opinion of his judgement: 'the last person in the world I would go to for advice on policy'. He queried the attempt to do away with Clause Four, however. Benn got on the NEC in 1959, but his attempts to act as bridge-builder between Gaitskell and Frank Cousins over nuclear policy in 1960 cost him his NEC seat for two years. When Labour returned to office in 1964, he had become established as a solid supporter and speech-writer for Harold Wilson in his 'white heat of the technological revolution' vein. He was a prime exponent of the view that socialism was about science, the unlikely offspring of the computer and conveyor belt. Benn's main fame arose from his brilliant campaign to renounce his peerage and to claim his seat in Bristol. In the Peerage Act he won a great constitutional victory with the right to disclaim assured. But it was not an issue that made much impact on the broad working-class public; not did it impel him in any serious sense further to the left.

He served as government minister for six years under Wilson. He was Postmaster-General until 1966 and then Minister of Technology. In October 1969 this last office was much expanded with the functions of the Ministry of Power and (in part) the Board of Trade also thrown in. His view of socialism seemed thoroughly technocratic in concept; he was a Fabian of the old Webb school. In policy, he was the quintessential whizz-kid, developing Concorde with the French, computerizing industry, building up Britain's civilian nuclear energy programme as an enthusiast for fast-breeder reactors. Student audiences marvelled at this pullover-clad minister enthralled by his machines. Technology seemed the key to his vision of politics in general, including defence policy and industrial regeneration. He became a strong supporter of Britain's membership of the Common Market between 1966 and 1970, since it would build up 'an integrated European technology'. The bureaucratic, anti-democratic features of Brussels do not seem to have greatly disturbed him at that stage. On general policies, he was not an influential figure. He was easily dominated by colleagues such as Jenkins, Crosland, or Healey. Richard Crossman, very harshly without doubt, considered Benn to be 'philosophically non-existent' and 'intellectually negligible'. Tony Crosland told him bluntly that, in order to lose a reputation as an intellectual, he would first have to acquire one. He fought the 1970 election as a loyal and acquiescent lieutenant of Harold Wilson, the dutiful technocrat to the end. The one clear asset that had emerged was his undoubted capacity and energy as an executive minister, and his ability to harness the confidence and enthusiasm of his civil servants. Like Edward Heath and other rising figures of the time, Benn's forte was institutional modernization and productive efficiency, rather than social change.

After the poll in June 1970, his political position in the Labour spectrum changed dramatically. The Rt. Hon. Anthony Wedgwood Benn was symbolically recycled into plain Tony Benn, the people's friend; his entry in *Who's Who* was purged of its tell-tale élitist features. He now told Crosland that he felt there was no future in Labour's policy of Wilsonian pragmatism, and that a new socialist impulse was the only answer. In the past, he had been a conspicuous non-joiner. He was never a member of any parliamentary grouping, *Tribune*, Victory for Socialism, or whatever. Now he was zealous for involvement. He would offer himself to the party as Labour's answer to Enoch Powell, a populist guru of the left. By the end of 1971, when he stood for the deputy leadership against Jenkins and Foot (gaining a creditable forty-six votes), he was marked as the clear voice of the political and industrial left, with a strength in the party that he had never previously suggested. We can accept that conviction played the major part in this rapid conversion, rather than mere ambition to be Labour's leader, although it is puzzling to decide precisely why Benn should believe that more nationalization or unilateralist defence policies were likely to be the way for Labour to convince a majority of the electors. It is worth noting that old radicals like Michael Foot had been eloquent on these themes in 1964–70 while Benn was an acquiescent minister. Still, there is every ground for accepting Benn's diagnosis that the sixties had been a shabby, opportunist phase for the movement, that consensus politics had failed, and that new impetus and conviction were required. The allies that Benn would have to enlist in his process, the tactics he would have to use against his colleagues, were another matter.

The reincarnated Benn of the opposition years 1970–4 (he was party chairman in 1971–2) was an interesting, transitional figure. The socialism he embraced was an updated version of his technocratic passions of the sixties. Socialism was linked to planning agreements, investment, technological advance: as chairman of the NEC's Industrial Policy Committee, he was well placed to push these ideas forward. The enterprise board and proposals for nationalizing twenty-five companies put forward by Benn in 1973 and vetoed by Wilson before the election were projections from his experience at MinTech in the sixties. The additional ingredient he now offered was populism. He related these vast, centralized programmes to local accountability and to models of open government. As party chairman, he launched the exercise 'Participation 72'. A variety of proposals were offered, some internal to the party such as the election of the leader or the Shadow Cabinet or granting a dominant policy role to the annual conference. Others related to wider institutions including measures to enforce the disclosure of information by public servants, extend democratic participation within industry, ensure the freedom of the press, impose accountability on judges, the police, bureaucrats, generals, and many others. Many of these suggestions were wholly reasonable in themselves. Benn's demand for Cabinet and other governmental records to be freed from the shackles of the thirty-year (formerly fifty-year) rule were echoed by non-political scholars throughout the land. Civil libertarians of all shades were equally concerned at the growth of a nationally co-ordinated police force with increased executive initiative, free from democratic constraint or public inquiry, and were heartened by Benn's views.

What was more difficult was to make a coherent *mélange* of planning and accountability, nationalization and workers' co-operatives, centralism and populism. It was an attempt to reconcile Jean Monnet with Jean-Jacques Rousseau. In Benn's remarkably volatile personality, technocracy and Congregationalism, industrial order and the dissidence of dissent were fused in one heady, combustible mixture. It was also difficult to find suitable instruments to give the new platform practical effect. Technological advance had to be combined with a wholly uncritical attitude towards the unions, notoriously wedded to antiquated work practices (in contrast to their European counterparts) and resistant to involvement in management. Party democracy had to be equated with the almost farcically undemocratic way in which party conference reached its decisions, the NEC was elected, and local parties were falling into the hands of almost wholly unaccountable management committees, often (as in Bermondsey) the victims of Trotskyist entryism. It was all a great mess. But party workers were desperate for a new vision and a new Messiah. If a 'socialist renaissance' had to be attempted, Benn was realist enough to see that you had to start somewhere.

These approaches meant, of course, a complete disavowal of his former positions on several major questions. He swung from supporting a mixed economy to one largely centralist with affinities with eastern Europe; from support of NATO to neutralism and unilateralism; from agnosticism on Ireland to endorsement of the non-violent side of Sinn Fein. Most spectacularly of all, Benn now became the unremitting opponent of British membership of the EEC, mainly on the political grounds that it was an undemocratic organization which would remove sovereignty from the British people, and overrule British laws, conventions, and usages. Britain would become a colony and its people disinherited. The technological arguments he had himself advanced for British membership in the sixties were not so much renounced as by-passed. The argument vaulted on to another, perhaps higher, plane. The case for technocracy remained, but it was subsumed by other, mainly non-economic, considerations.

Benn served throughout Labour's five years in government under Wilson and Callaghan in 1974-9. He was universally regarded as a personally charming, humorous colleague, notable for his woollen cardigans and mugs of tea. Yet he was at war with his colleagues on virtually every issue of the day. With his Cabinet speeches delivered apparently for posterity and the public records, with his vast archive of tape recordings, his consistent disavowal of Cabinet policies on platforms and in committee meetings throughout the land (while constantly refusing to mention 'personalities'), his mind did not really seem to be on the job. At first, perhaps, it was. As Secretary for Trade and Industry in 1974-5, he had a sphere in which his 'alternative economic strategy' of public ownership, public enterprise boards, planning agreements at home and important controls against foreign manufactures could be put forward. But Wilson skilfully worked to neutralize all this, particularly through his Policy Unit at No. 10, and the economist, Richard Graham, a specifically designated 'Benn-watcher'. In July 1975, following the British decision to support membership of the EEC in the referendum which he had managed to obtain, Benn suffered a decisive set-back to his authority. Despite much pleading on his behalf by Michael Foot (ironically, in the light of later events), he was side-tracked by Wilson to the Department of Energy, and replaced by the notably less powerful figure of Eric Varley. It was an obvious rebuff, and one that hurt Benn very deeply. Yet in fact, there was much to do at Energy. Indeed, as the minister presiding over the first, massive inflow of North Sea oil, his message was more cheerful to the country than that of any other minister; like Wilson at the Board of Trade in 1947-50, Benn was the official harbinger of good tidings. With the 'plan for coal', hydroelectric power in Scotland and Wales, and nuclear power coming on apace, quite apart from North Sea gas, Britain was self-sufficient in energy supplies in a way hardly any other country on earth could match.

Yet Benn in the later seventies was a frustrated, ineffective figure as a member of government. In Michael Foot's view, he had simply lost interest in present-day politics. His position in the Cabinet distinctly waned in the Callaghan era, when keeping the party in office at almost all costs became the essential priority. Benn's credibility was already much undermined by his having been associated with a series of forlorn causes. His advocacy of a string of workers' co-operatives, initially the product of sit-ins by workers threatened with plant closures, led nowhere. A series of them—first, the *Scottish Daily News* and *Daily Express* in Glasgow, then Norton Villiers Triumph motorcycles at Meriden, then Kirkby Engineering on Merseyside, became derided as 'Benn's follies', commercial fiascos one and all. The proposal to inject £3.9m. into Kirkby Engineering (which, incomprehensibly, produced orange juice as well as car radiators) had earlier led to a public row between Benn and his Permanent Secretary, Sir Anthony Part. Only the Meriden venture lasted for any length of time. In each case, there were no real market prospects for profitability or survival. Proposals for more Treasury money to be invested into a further range of failing concerns, including Bear Brand stockings and Triang Toys, did not get off the ground. A National Enterprise Board was, indeed, set up, with Donald Ryder as its head, but with far less extensive powers than Benn himself had urged. Heffer resigned from the government on this point, though Benn fatalistically stayed on.

During the IMF crisis in October–December 1976, Benn, along with other ministers, bitterly opposed the Treasury's plans for deflation and huge expenditure cuts; but his advocacy of an 'alternative strategy' was easily cut to pieces by Healey. Shore and Crosland were far more authoritative critics. The main political issue of the later 1970s, the Lib-Lab pact, negotiated by Callaghan and Foot with the Liberals, Steel and Pardoe, saw Benn in unavailing opposition. For all his concern for more local democracy, he took little part in the devolution debate. The general record of these years, as far as he was concerned, was entirely negative. 'He was simply agin it', in Healey's phrase. He showed, colleagues felt, a consistent lack of realism, a blank refusal to admit that there were deep-seated problems in the economy, in work practices, in the unions, and in the procedures for pay bargaining, coupled with a denial of the simple facts of inflation or external financial weakness. Indeed, there was every sign that Benn himself welcomed this bleak outcome and his own resulting political isolation. He projected himself to the party faithful as the lone voice of socialist purity, repeatedly spurned by opportunist colleagues. He took relish in denouncing the Wilson and

Callaghan governments, in which he had served and in which he had accepted the premisses of collective responsibility, for betraying their manifesto, their mandate, their moral obligations to the present and past of the movement. He was truly *le mauvais coucheur* incarnate.

In so many ways, this record of embittered isolation was a tragedy for him and the nation. It meant, for example, that his powerful criticisms of the effects of the Common Market upon British manufactured exports and the balance of payments, some sensible ideas he had for reversing the tide of unemployment and deindustrialization, were given scant attention. The 1970s were a bleak time for British political and economic prospects, and there were many initiatives, socialist and non-socialist, which could have effected a partial reversal. However, the Labour Party unhesitatingly consigned Benn to the wilderness. It was a location which, in any case, by psychological make-up, he preferred. The result was that one of the most fertile minds in public life was committed to a sterile, querulous role, with only the hard-left minority to offer consistent applause.

After Labour's defeat in 1979, Benn had neither a viable national role nor a short-term future. After all, though eternally youthful in image, he was in his mid-fifties. He opted now for nationwide party campaigning and the long haul. He aligned himself with the grass-roots Campaign for Labour Democracy, and with constitutional reforms within the party to make the selection of MPs, the parliamentary party, the party programme, and the leader of the party subject to popular election or dictation. In 1979 alone, he addressed 215 meetings on behalf of these objectives. The main achievement was the extraordinary electoral college arrangement, originally proposed by Neil Kinnock, and cobbled together soon after the 1980 party conference. It was hardly democratic in any meaningful sense, especially in the half-corrupt trade-union section: but it undoubtedly showed a distinct move in the Bennite direction. He did not stand for the party leadership in November 1980. For tactical reasons, he supported Foot against Healey, even though Foot's brand of orthodox parliamentary socialism is as remote from Benn's creed as was that of Healey. However, the election for the deputy leadership that followed left him with no choice but to campaign across the land as the voice of the left. He received massive endorsement from party activists in the constituencies, but only limited support from parliamentary colleagues. A left-winger like Kinnock fiercely attacked his divisive methods. To Labour voters generally, in part perhaps because of a furious press campaign which showed Benn as an extremist, almost a lunatic, he was unpopular, even hated. As the apostle of party unity, Benn of all people did not carry conviction.

The result reflected his weakness. He won heavily against Healey in the constituency section amongst the zealots. He was defeated amongst the MPs. Amongst the unions, he did best where there was no nation-wide test of opinion. The advocate of direct democracy found that his strongest advocates came from the most undemocratic echelons of the party. His defeat in the poll was narrow, but decisive. Thereafter, especially after Kinnock replaced Foot as party leader in 1983, Benn was relegated increasingly to the sidelines. He was isolated even on the NEC by 'soft-left' supporters of Foot, and finally moved as chairman from the important Policy Committee. The logic of his cause compelled him to take the most leftwards position on all issues—the Falklands, the miners' strike and its accompanying violence, incomes policy, legislation on the unions, the expulsion of Militant supporters. Logic, equally, led to his being increasingly discredited. After his defeat in the 1983 election (he returned as member for Chesterfield in 1984), he had forfeited his old parliamentary dominance. Equally, he was removed from his traditional bastions on the key committees of the NEC. By 1986, only the inchoate masses remained as a return route to the leadership, but, like Enoch Powell, his model in 1970, he seemed to have lost zeal for the fight. No doubt, ill-health played its part in this. Amongst the Shadow Cabinet, he was distrusted and discredited as few had been since the worst days for Cripps in the late thirties. The party had been formally remodelled. Mandatory reselection and other institutional novelties had been implemented. The people had spoken. But Tony Benn had become their victim and scapegoat, not their residuary legatee.

Benn has tried consciously to build a New Left since 1970. He rejected not only the parliamentary pragmatism of Labour leaders from Attlee to Callaghan, but also the Old Left of Bevan, Foot, and Mrs Castle. He has conspicuously failed, in his message if not in his methods. If he is compared with the Bevan of the fifties, he cuts a less impressive figure. Bevan's democratic socialism unhesitatingly drew firm distinctions betwen varieties of socialism which followed the parliamentary route, and those that relied on coercive or revolutionary methods. 'The Communist Party is the sworn enemy of Socialist and Democratic Parties', wrote Bevan in 1951. Bevan was a tolerant, charitable relativist, but not to the point of conflating totally opposed systems of socialist belief. In terms of method, Bevan's approach was parliamentary, persuasive. He favoured open debate, not indirect dictation by the caucus, the management committee, or the union barons. He could never have endorsed Benn's views that parliament could become largely irrelevant, with the workers satisfying their aims outside it. Bevan's style of socialism, even in the worst years of party civil war, reflected a mainstream variety of belief, fully capable of being reconciled with the movement as a whole. Further, he never combined his criticism of present leaders with disloyalty or disavowal of ministers with whom he had served. His whole approach to the Labour government of 1945–51 was in stark contrast to Benn's attitude to the governments of 1974–9. Michael Foot's fierce onslaught on 'Brother Tony' in 1986 was a commentary on the gulf between the ethic of the Old Left and the New.

Benn, far more than Bevan, is by instinct a dissident, an individualist, almost an anarchist. His socialism is mystical in concept rather than rigorously argued or intellectual in substance. It evokes sentiments reminiscent of William Morris's 'A Dream of John Ball'. It has taken him down many courageous paths, including criticism of the Falklands war at a time when 1940-style jingoism prevailed on the Labour front-bench. But it has also led him into methods and alliances which contradict his purposes and values. 'Bennery' has become the negation of the negation, a broad pasture within which any variety of Trotskyist, Provisional Sinn Feiner, animal rights' activist or picket-line brawler may safely graze. It is Entryism run mad. Technocracy had driven him away from grass-roots labourism in the 1960s. A half-religious commitment to populism drove him away from most of his parliamentary colleagues in the 1970s. He is not a major thinker. Even as a prophet of a British version of democratic centralism, he does not carry conviction. His book, *Arguments for Socialism*, full of interesting perceptions on incidentals, largely evades its professed theme. It consists of a series of disjointed fragments on industrial planning agreements, the Common Market, nuclear energy and other topics; what the book conspicuously does not argue for is socialism. Indeed, the only extended treatment at all comes at the start, with some reflections on the relationship of socialism to Christianity from biblical times onwards. Somewhere around the mid-seventeenth century, the author loses interest in socialism as an idea.

A uniting theme in his vision of socialist advance is a fascination with mechanisms and structures. This makes *Arguments for Democracy*, with its critique of the civil service, the security services, the press, and much else besides, a more coherent book. Benn has been obsessed with the inner mechanics of the party, on and off, until the 1980s. He has been similarly preoccupied with harnessing technology to industry. If the mechanics are right, it seems, the social consequences will follow. Planning agreements will ensure industrial harmony; scientific consultative procedures will mean a sensible nuclear power programme; procedural electoral reforms will automatically enable the people to speak with undivided voice. The 'transition to democratic socialism' is spelt out wholly in negative terms of disengagement by the labour movement from the EEC, NATO, the House of Lords, government planning bodies, and large parts of the civil service. The state must be dismantled before it is remade. The approach is extraordinarily abstract, with no cultural insight or any real sense of history either. Humanity, above all, is lacking. There is no ghost in these machines, little hint of what kind of society or what kind of democracy might emerge from their mighty operations. There would indeed be 'Freedom of Information', but personal freedom (at least for minorities of whom Benn does not approve) is not obviously on the agenda.

In pursuit of his goals, Benn has magnified or created structural tensions within his party unique in its history. He has openly challenged the sensitive pluralism which made the Labour alliance effective. His approach has been presented in a tone of illiberal dogma which recalls the puritanical excesses of the Fifth Monarchy men: 'unctuous pride' was Barbara Castle's favoured description. As a result, canvassers on the doorstep in 1979 and 1983 found that his approach to politics had become Labour's main electoral liability. To attribute this, in paranoid fashion, simply to distortion by the media, the power of capitalist barons and the multinationals, or the coercive pressures of a police state implies a singular lack of faith in a literate public from a professed democrat. In consequence, this attractive, articulate, and energetic man has had a largely unsatisfactory and shapeless career. In some ways, he conforms to the pattern of the 'True Believer' of the American writer Eric Hoffer—the Messiah who can 'harness men's hopes and fears in the service of a holy cause'. But the gulf between a creative mass leader and a destructive fanatic is a narrow one. The believer also needs, so Hoffer reminds us, faith in humanity. 'For no one can be honourable unless he honours mankind.'

# DENIS HEALEY

DENIS HEALEY has always been an aloof figure in the Labour movement, a cat that walks by himself. Crossman, wrong in many assessments, perhaps got him right in October 1963—'a very lone mover, completely on his own'. Intellectually and personally, Healey has tended to pursue his own furrow. A Communist while an Oxford undergraduate, he retained something of the rigid, dialectical thought-processes of that party long after he had moved to the far right of the Labour Party. A robust anti-Bevanite in the party divisions of the fifties, he was, nevertheless, not one of the real Gaitskell intimates in the way that Jenkins, Jay, and Crosland were. Although the Healeys and Gaitskells holidayed together, he was never quite in the so-called 'Hampstead set'. 'I was never a member of Hugh's personal court', he recalled. He had two long spells in Cabinet, at Defence in 1964–70 and at the Treasury in 1974–9. In both portfolios, his own temperament as much as the exigencies of office made him relatively isolated, though enormously respected, even feared. He alienated even his admirers in the parliamentary party, through a reputation for intellectual arrogance allied to an aggressive, even bullying, personal manner. In the 1976 leadership election he ran a poor third, far behind Callaghan and Foot. Even in 1980, when he was manifestly the standard-bearer of the centre-right, he campaigned in a curiously wooden fashion, and was overtaken by the more charismatic debating qualities of Michael Foot.

Only in 1981, when he and Tony Benn found themselves locked in a herculean contest for the soul of the party, did Healey, for the first time in his career, throw himself uninhibitedly into nation-wide campaigning amongst shop-floor trade-unionists and constituency activists. Here, he proved remarkably effective. His victory over Benn was much more conclusive than the bare figures suggested. They were largely concealed by manipulation by union executives such as in Moss Evans's TGWU, which fudged the fact that every union which had conducted a poll among its members (including Alan Fisher's NUPE) had seen Healey come out on top. Healey's belated conversion to populism had paid rich dividends. Even so, his relative detachment from the party hurly-burly has continued. In 1983 he stood aloof from the contest for the leadership between Kinnock and Hattersley. He pronounced himself content with the position, long sought, of Shadow Foreign Secretary, a unique elder statesman role and the self-proclaimed status of 'Labour's Gromyko'. Despite a Yorkshire folksiness in manner, his interests remain highly specialized, including a remarkably erudite knowledge of twentieth-century art. A stern independence of spirit has governed his style down to the present time.

Denis Healey, then, is not a natural democrat. He has carved his unique, almost irreplaceable niche in the Labour hierarchy through sheer force of intellect and political application. He is, indeed, the most formidable intellectual influence in the party since the heyday of Crosland in the fifties. What is most remarkable of all is that Healey's extraordinary political strength was built up in an area of policy which, perhaps above all others, the British left has traditionally most distrusted, even despised—defence and armaments. Labour's advance after 1918, after all, was bound up with dreams of disarmament and hatred of the merchants of death. Pacifism, or at least anti-militarism, was deeply ingrained in the party's leaders down to the late thirties. Even though Labour accepted the huge arms expenditure implied in Bevin's foreign policy after 1945, it went against the grain. The furore caused by Gaitskell's budget of 1951, linked as we have seen, with a vastly accelerated arms programme, reawakened in wide reaches of the left an instinctive distaste for the politics of power. Anti-militarism lay behind many of the rows in the party in the fifties, including German rearmament and, of course, the traumatic arguments about the bomb. This last was coloured with horror that it was a Labour government, headed by the venerated Attlee, which had secretly, and with scant consideration of the military, scientific, or human consequences, committed Britain to participation in the thermonuclear arms race. Reducing the burden of armaments was a popular Labour theme in buttressing the case for more social spending at home in the 1950s and early 1960s. Harold Wilson campaigned in 1964 to the effect that Britain would renounce her 'so-called independent, so-called deterrent'. Labour's manifesto bitterly attacked Macmillan's defence policy, including the 1957 Nassau agreement with the Americans and his successive, vastly expensive dependence on Blue Streak, Skybolt, and finally the Polaris missiles. Defence, then, was not the most promising special interest on which to build a towering reputation within the Labour Party in these years. It is testimony to Healey's honesty, force of personality, and brute intellectual strength that he was able to do so.

He emerged from a middle-class family in Keighley: his father was principal of the local technical college. He went on from Bradford Grammar School in the mid-thirties not to Queen's, that haven of Oxford Yorkshiremen, but to Balliol. At Oxford he became and remained for some years a Communist, the political and dialectical opponent of other contemporaries such as Jenkins, Crosland, or Heath. It was not rare for an idealistic young man to join the Communist Party at Oxford in the thirties (it was a process usually free from the self-indulgent narcissism and sexual deviation that marked the Blunt group at Cambridge at the same period). What was more unusual was that Healey remained a Communist for some years, through the war in Spain, beyond the Nazi–Soviet pact and the Russo-Finnish war. Not until some time in 1940 did he finally revert to the Labour Party. But the dialectical rigour, combined with a somewhat Germanic, even Hegelian, devotion to intellectual structures of a formal kind, left their stamp upon him. Crossman in 1953 noted how Healey still showed evidence of his Marxist background—'between good and evil'. Wilson quoted Nye Bevan on Healey's qualities: 'like one of those Trojan cars [sic], boy—once they get on the tramline they go straight back to the depot'. Healey was evidently a man of the far left throughout the war. Adopted Labour candidate for the relatively forlorn hope (even in 1945) of Pudsey and Otley in Yorkshire, he created a stir at the 1945 party conference, when, as Major Healey MBE, a delegate in military uniform just back from the Italian front, he called for Labour to promote socialist revolution throughout continental Europe.

It was not surprising that Healey lost at Pudsey and Otley, though he came within a whisker of winning and joining Gaitskell, Wilson, Callaghan, and others in the 'class of '45'. Instead of junior office and ministerial experience, he had to find another political outlet. Surprisingly, it came in Transport House. He served from January 1946 until the end of 1951 as secretary of the Labour Party International Department, directly responsible to Morgan Phillips. In fact, this was a fortunate choice. Healey became well known to Hugh Dalton and other party leaders at the time, accompanying Dalton to Strasburg more than once. He also became an unusually influential force on party policy for so young an apparatchik, only just out of his twenties. Healey already had considerable knowledge of international politics, reinforced by his acquaintance with Italian partisans gained during wartime service as a staff officer with the Eighth Army. As the head of Labour's International Department, he was much involved in building up the Socialist International (COMISCO) and re-establishing links through it with European socialist parties, including those in eastern European countries like Poland, Hungary, and Rumania. He also sought to build bridges to the German Social Democrats, largely ostracized during the war at the hands of the fierce anti-Teutonism of William Gillies, Healey's predecessor as International Secretary. Healey had the controversial Kurt Schumacher, the distinctly nationalistic head of the German SPD, invited to Britain in 1948, despite Dalton's opposition. He also became friendly with Willy Brandt.

Healey had now become a belligerent supporter of Bevin's stance in foreign affairs. He devoted the same aggressive logical rigour to anti-Communism that he had shown in defence of Comintern policy during the thirties. His powerful pamphlet, *Cards on the Table* (May, 1947) spelt out forcefully the growing Russian take-over in eastern Europe: it was a document strongly attacked by Laski and a few others, but warmly applauded by Attlee, Bevin, and the Cabinet as a whole. It helped silence critics on the party left. He repeated this theme, equally forcefully, in his edited work, *The Curtain Falls* (1951), a stinging critique of Communist take-over methods in Poland, Hungary, and Czechoslovakia; remarkably enough, it had a vigorously anti-Communist introduction by Aneurin Bevan. Healey was an emphatic supporter of the Atlantic alliance, of the growing US commitment to western defence, of the Brussels Treaty and the founding of NATO. His Atlanticism, as with other Labour figures of the right, led to a cool, even hostile, attitude to proposals for European integration. His pamphlet, *European Unity*, published on 13 June 1950, caused a stir with its vigorous assault on the basic idea of the Schuman Plan. Attlee had to explain to the Commons that it was a Transport House product rather than an official paper from government. But it undoubtedly captured and reflected the mood of the party.

Healey entered parliament in February 1952 as member for Leeds South East: the nomenclature changed to Leeds East in 1955. His main problem was winning the Labour nomination in the face of his known Transport House connections. He has retained this West Riding constituency without difficulty for thirty-five unbroken years.

Through the fifties, as we have seen, although clearly on the dominant right-wing of the party, a strong defender of NATO including its nuclear strike capability, Healey remained a detached figure. Not until 1959 did he rise to Shadow Cabinet rank. He was never a serious runner for the national executive. What was unique about his rise was that it was based almost entirely on expertise in foreign and defence policy. He emerged as remarkably knowledgeable here, with close contacts with American and European politicians, chiefs of staff, journalists and others, with a flow of important articles and conference papers in North American and European journals. He helped start the Ford-financed Institute of Strategic Studies in 1958. His fundamental diagnosis was spelt out in an important essay, 'Power Politics and the Labour Party', published in Crossman's edition of *New Fabian Essays* in 1952 and in his pamphlet, *Neutralism* (1955). As elsewhere, Healey here took a tough, unsentimental, post-Marxist view, unusual on the left, about the realities of international and strategic power. He poured scorn on the pacifism, parochialism, and Utopianism which had been a substitute for serious thought on foreign affairs within the party since the thirties. He launched withering attacks on naïve advocates of 'a socialist foreign policy', whatever that might mean.

For too long, he argued, Labour had ignored the inescapable realities in world affairs. It had expected capitalist states to behave more altruistically and peacefully than any groups had ever behaved in the whole of recorded history. He also cast doubt on how far, even within the agreed confines of the military alliances with America, Communism could or would be repelled by social reform, economic aid to the undeveloped world and anti-poverty programmes. He thus challenged a famous sacred cow of the left. Power, force, nationalist rivalries—these would continue as the abiding realities. On the other hand, he also argued that an excessively rigid commitment to power-bloc systems ignored the growth of a more fluid international order, with the growing refusal of ex-colonial countries to align themselves with East or West. He remained an unflinching advocate of the alliance with the USA as the pivot of British policy, but with full regard also for the new fluidity emerging above all in the Middle East, but also in south-east Asia, and perhaps in disturbances within the Communist bloc as well, in eastern Europe or perhaps even in Sino-Soviet relations.

His key crisis in the fifties, as for the Labour right generally, was

Suez, when both the Anglo-American alliance and an appropriate modern-minded response to the new nationalist regimes were threatened. His attacks on Eden and Lloyd in the Commons were more savage than those of the left. Within the party, he and Douglas Jay put pressure on Gaitskell to stiffen his opposition to the use of force against Egypt. The Soviet invasion of Hungary at the same time added fury to Healey's views on the Suez operation. Nor, as an old Bevin loyalist, was his intellectual baggage unduly cluttered by Zionist sentiment, for all the Jewish support he received in his Leeds constituency. On balance, he won respect, often grudging, in the Tory years for a hard-headed advocacy of realism, preparedness and geopolitical awareness of changing currents in world affairs, as opposed to the emotionalism (and, as Healey saw it, the revived Utopianism) of CND and the ex-Bevanite left.

Defence became his key specialism. With wide links with American and western European defence experts and systems analysts, by 1964 Healey had developed an expertise unique in British political life. He was a close friend, amongst others, of the US Defence Secretary, Robert McNamara. He expected, and got, the post of Minister of Defence under Wilson. The next six years were, perhaps, less traumatic for Healey than for many colleagues. He was never one of the inner group of Wilson, Brown, and Callaghan (with Jenkins and Mrs Castle later coming in). He was removed from direct implication in the main economic crises in this period, including the sterling crisis of July 1966 and devaluation in November 1967. He became very restless towards the end, but was kept at Defence for the whole span of six years, partly because his removal would disturb the sensitive political balance that Wilson sought to maintain in the Cabinet. Healey boldly demanded the Foreign Secretaryship in 1969. He might well argue that he would be more effective than Gordon Walker, Brown, and Stewart (twice), the varied incumbents of the Foreign Office in the Wilson years; while as Defence Secretary and with his long experience going back to Transport House days, he was uniquely knowledgeable on international affairs. He even told Wilson who his successor at Defence should be (George Thomson). But he was frustrated in his hopes, time and again.

Even so, as Defence Secretary, he was very closely involved in many of the key political events of the 1964–70 period, including military operations in Malaya, North Borneo, and Aden; arms sales to South Africa (which he endorsed); contingency military planning for Rhodesia; security arrangements in Northern Ireland; arms supplies to Nigeria during the civil war with Biafra—even the sinking of the ship *Torrey Canyon*, a stricken oil tanker whose sticky cargo threatened to pollute the beaches of half Cornwall. Above all, he put a powerful personal stamp on defence policy, the more impressive since the Conservative years had shown a sequence of nine Defence ministers in thirteen years, and bewildering changes of policy. Healey was very much his own man, independent of guidance from the chiefs of staff. Defence experts came to consider him easily the outstanding post-war service minister.

His policy, as launched in a major Defence White Paper of January 1965, was to give value for money, to match Britain's military deployment both to the available economic resources and to an updated assessment of Britain's role in the world. His analysis gained from the adoption of modern techniques of cost-benefit assessments, and new management and budgetary methods. Defence expenditure was duly cut by £56m., the first real cut since the early fifties; integration between the services was much extended; the main new spending plans would focus on fighter aircraft, notably the US-built Phantoms and the British Buccaneers. The British-built TSR2, designed to carry airborne nuclear weapons, it was announced on 6 April 1965, was to be scrapped. There were numerous other casualties in the 1966 Healey Defence Review. The navy suffered several blows, including the decision to end the further building of aircraft carriers (a decision which cost the government the Minister of State, Christopher Mayhew, who resigned, and which almost brought disaster in the south Atlantic war in 1982). On home ground, the Territorial Army, a legacy of Haldane's days at the War Office before 1914, was also abolished. In Cabinet, Healey battered down the opposition of mild-mannered Sir Frank Soskice, who was (wrote Crossman) 'no match for this rough, rather ruthless, young man'.

The purpose was to end a situation under which Britain had only sketchy protection, yet with the cost extending far beyond her real resources. A cut in real defence spending of £400m. by 1970 was the proclaimed objective. Remorselessly and logically, Healey spelt out the contradictions; he repeated, in effect, Bonar Law's famous dictum of 1922 that Britain could no longer act as policeman of the world. Britain's military involvement, Healey later claimed, indeed had prevented war between Malaysia and Indonesia spreading through south-east Asia in the 1960s. But the cost had been the deployment of one hundred thousand civilian and military personnel in an area where the changing roles of the United States, Russia, and China made Britain's position more and more marginal. On the other hand, his premises still assumed a more interventionist role for Britain at this period than many felt that the political or economic facts warranted. The cancellation of the contract for F/111 strike aircraft was forced through by Roy Jenkins in January 1968 over Healey's vehement objections. Defence spending remained remarkably high; the British nuclear deterrent was extended, not abolished, quite contrary to the 1964 manifesto; American Polaris submarines, far from being rejected were duly based at Holy Loch.

The legacy of colonialism also took a long time to wipe clean. The British army was heavily involved in Aden and South Yemen until the end of the decade, while the 'east of Suez' defence commitment continued until 1969–70. Military experts were heard to criticize Healey's 'Indo-Pacific' bias in strategy. Not until January 1968 did he, very reluctantly, agree to remove the remaining British presence in the Persian Gulf and south-east Asia. He himself wanted to delay these withdrawals, and British troops to stay on in Singapore and the Persian Gulf until at least 1972, to ward off possible nationalist insurrection. So did Brown, Callaghan, and Stewart. One important factor, no doubt, was that the Americans were most anxious for the British military commitment there to continue.

In spite of these vagaries of policy, Healey emerged in 1970 as a Defence Secretary who, despite being a major architect of western multilateral nuclear strategy, had actually cut defence spending. He returned to opposition in a relatively commanding position in the party. The main crises of the 1970–74 period saw him more or less in the mainstream of opinion. Like Labour generally, he had been instinctively hostile to the EEC and repeatedly argued against British membership in the fifties and sixties, not least because its inward-looking arrangements conflicted with his vision of the Atlantic alliance. In the end, like Wilson and Callaghan, he moved warily to endorse British membership in principle on the basis of some renegotiation, more for political than for economic reasons, and to secure a stronger European voice on defence issues. However, he was never among the more zealous Europeans, never remotely a Euro-fanatic. The European controversy, however, did clear the path for him within the party hierarchy. The resignation of Jenkins from the front-bench in 1972 meant that Healey could now become Shadow Chancellor, since Callaghan was guaranteed the post of foreign affairs spokesman which he had always coveted. Healey had not been a specialist on economic policy at all hitherto. But he built up a strong team, including the legendary pair of Joel Barnett and Robert Sheldon, while his formidable intellectual powers enabled him to master many of the complexities of external economic policy while at Defence. So he regained Cabinet office, first under Wilson in March 1974, then under Callaghan from April 1976, as Chancellor of the Exchequer, and remained there for five years. The trials he was to face then placed his reputation and judgement again under the most intense scrutiny. Unlike Callaghan in the sixties, however, these economic crises, on balance, were to enhance his public standing even further.

At first, he found some difficulty in stamping his authority on the Cabinet as he had done at Defence. After all, formidable economists such as Crosland, Jenkins, and Shore were amongst his colleagues; the Prime Minister was a former Chancellor, too. But Healey's command steadily grew. His speech at East Leeds on 10 January 1975, in which he urged that monetary policy must be geared to reducing inflation, that a fall in unemployment would come from moderating the growth of real pay, and that growth in the money supply must be curbed, made a considerable impact, if bringing much flak from the left. Healey's five years at the Treasury were far from being wholly grim. The 'short parliament' of March–October 1974 saw a somewhat relaxed approach, with social rewards to fulfil the supposed 'contract' with the unions. In his last year, 1978–9, there was again a mood of repose—almost of euphoria in the summer of 1978, with talk of an early election. The balance of payments was now back in surplus by £1000m.; North Sea oil revenue was flowing in; inflation was falling fast; the index of industrial production rose steadily; even unemployment showed a downward turn.

But for much of the time it was a period of hard slog which surpassed even the rigours of Cripps, Callaghan, and Jenkins in the past. In this fearful tension, Healey's very survival at all was a tribute to his mental toughness and physical fitness, and total refusal to wallow in self-pity. As inflation reached a high tide of over twenty per cent in 1975, in the wake of the oil price rise and totally irrational trade-union pay claims, special drawing right of £1000m. were negotiated with the IMF at the end of the year, with a further stand-by credit of £700m. Healey's policy became one of stern and consistent deflation. Perhaps it should have been even more severe. Joel Barnett, the Treasury minister responsible for swinging the axe on public spending, criticized the April 1976 budget for being insufficiently rigorous on expenditure cuts, and for actually increasing spending on social security. In the defence field, Chevaline, which was eventually costed at no less than £1000m., was allowed to go ahead. The flight from sterling and the drain on the reserves were relentless in the latter months of 1976. Healey's 'July package', which cut spending by £1 billion, with a further £1 billion cut in effect through a two per cent increase in employers' national insurance contributions, did not stem the tide.

Healey's *Götterdammerung* was the talks with the IMF in October–December 1976. As is well known, they led to bitter argument within the Labour Cabinet, with right-wing ministers such as Crosland and Shirley Williams joining left-wingers such as Benn and Shore in protest. Relations between Healey and Callaghan became strained over raising MLR in early October, and there was some talk in the press of Healey being replaced. In the end, his own persistence, Callaghan's backing, and the very severity of the crisis led Healey to get his way. He announced the 'letter of intent' to the IMF on 15 December, and prepared the way thereby for a further £3 billion cuts in spending, consisting of £1 billion in 1977–8, a further £1.5 billion in 1978–9, and an additional £500m. from the sale of BP shares. It was a horrifying package, accepted without enthusiasm or endorsement by the PLP, the TUC, and the party outside. Only the threat of resignation kept the party loyal. Healey emerged in a strong, but confined position. Among other things, it meant that he would have to soldier on at the Treasury rather than move on to the Foreign Office. When Crosland died in early 1977, it was the youthful David Owen who took on that portfolio.

In 1977–8, the medicine seemed to be working. Healey's October 1977 budget was actually reflationary, reinjecting some £1 billion back again into the economy. That of April 1978 was expansionist. The government seemed back in control of their destiny. Healey now spoke (correctly) of growth and falling inflation, rising output and a stronger pound. Labour was level with the Tories in the polls, and hopeful of retaining power in an autumn election. There was much dismay when, as noted above, Callaghan declined to call an election and announced a postponement until 1979. In fact, the economic indices remained very mixed, as Healey well knew. Inflation was still too high, compared with our foreign competitors. Healey's package depended, above all, on wage restraint by the unions, and there were grounds for believing that he and his ally, Foot, had converted the TUC to the need for a five per cent wage increase limit. But the outcome, as has been seen, was totally different, with the notorious 'winter of discontent', a pay policy in ruins, and Labour ejected from office at the hands of a resolute Mrs Thatcher.

The left saw Healey as the villain of the drama, not surprisingly in view of the expenditure cuts. In the November 1980 leadership election, the left duly exacted full revenge. Thereafter, under Foot's leadership, Healey had to concede much ground to remain a figure of substance. On defence, he renounced Chevaline, Trident and Cruise. He admitted in 1982 that he ought to have killed off the Chevaline system while Chancellor eight years earlier. He apparently accepted the potential removal of US nuclear bases in Britain, in flat contradiction to his earlier position about the threat of the Russian SS 20s, and his general stance on defence issues since the sixties. Evidently, he had acquired the arts of flexibility, to use no more blunt a word. He stayed on as foreign affairs spokesman, easily outshining the passive figure of Geoffrey Howe, the original 'dead sheep' at the dispatch box. On South Africa, Libya, and many other issues, Healey was a commanding figure. He served as deputy leader in 1981-3 after defeating Benn. But he had not become party leader, and joined Rab Butler as a major figure whom the glittering prize had always eluded. It was, without doubt, his experience as Chancellor that had led to this frustration.

Denis Healey has been Labour's most powerful policy-maker over the past twenty years, and seems destined to remain so for some time to come, health permitting. At Defence, he was able to take on board, intellectually, the most sophisticated systems analysis of the time, and to become a towering figure in the Atlantic world. He revolutionized strategic ideas and planning for defence, notably by separating defence policy from operational and contingency planning within his department. At the Treasury, with some difficulty, he was able to rebuild the prevailing Keynesian orthodoxy, embodied by Sir Douglas Wass amongst his advisers. But his legacy, necessarily, is a somewhat mixed or controversial one. At Defence, one outcome was a continued perseverance in a world role many felt was still beyond the nation's capacity. It was linked to the notion of a special relationship with the Americans which the facts since 1945 (perhaps since 1783) have not warranted. His emphasis on nuclear deterrence, however 'flexible' the 'response', somewhat weakened the case for conventional ground forces. He was, through the Nuclear Planning Group of NATO, the author of a western nuclear posture which aroused many fears at the time, not only from unilateralists, and which by 1986 he seemed largely to have abandoned himself. At the Treasury, he was the first monetarist, and Labour's first privatizer, with reference to BP. He inverted the post-1944 conventional wisdom about management of the economy. His programme was one of severe cut-backs in social and other spending, cash limits in all their rigour, an enthronement of the Public Sector Borrowing Requirement as the determinant of policy. Such a record won respect for its courageous author, but hardly affection, or even perhaps conviction.

Nor has his style helped his cause. He operates naturally at the summit of policy-making and power bargaining—with Robert McNamara and NATO, with Jack Jones and the TUC General Council, with Alan Whittome and the IMF. He has never approached either the political skills of a Callaghan with the grass-roots or the command of a Foot over the party conferences. His authority in the parliamentary party has not been helped by some lack of flexibility at the dispatch box; nor does his rich grasp of four-letter abuse win friends. His manner in Cabinet contributed to his defeat by Roy Jenkins over the F/111 in 1968. His ability to offend civil servants became legendary. 'Have I insulted everyone round this table?' he once asked, rhetorically and unnecessarily, since he obviously had. His brawls with the equally pugnacious John Pardoe rocked the 'Lib-Lab' pact in 1977–8; Healey, after all, is by origin an Irishman, thoroughly at home in Donnybrook Fair. He can be maladroit with the media on occasion. His comments on Polaris did not help Foot during the 1983 election campaign, while an interview with an Italian journalist in 1986, focusing in part on Kinnock's 'inexperience', showed an odd lack of judgement. His change of stance on defence policy since 1981 seems primarily opportunist rather than principled.

On balance, though, Labour has surely gained the maximum benefit from the talents of this proudly independent, strong-minded man. Right-wing commentators who lamented his defeat by Foot in 1980 have seldom noted that the main task of a party leader is to lead his party. Healey's rigorous, dialectical, almost scholastic method is unlikely to have been very successful in doing so. Even his close colleague and admirer, Joel Barnett, admitted he was not 'a good leader of a team'. Healey, however, is supremely equipped as a highly original policy-maker, both in detail and in long-term implications, and distinguished for an unsentimental toughness in the execution of power. He is, indeed, a very strong politician, the strongest of his time. He alone could have stood up, without flinching, to the violent attacks of the Bennites in 1980–1. He has risen to the top on his own, without factions, time-servers, or trade-union barons to promote his cause. More than any other politician of his generation, he is outstandingly qualified for every high public office, except possibly a Labour premiership. But he has done something more important than win the leadership. More than anyone else, living or dead, he has made his fractious, introverted comrades capable of looking out to confront the twenty-first century.

# ROY HATTERSLEY

LABOUR autobiographies are not what they used to be. Earlier in the century, they would tend to follow a common pattern, perhaps bearing some such title as *Adventures of a Labour Leader*, rather as superannuated generals would call their memoirs *Annals of an Active Life*. If the Labour leader was working class (Smillie, Hodges, Kirkwood, Shinwell, etc.), his story would trace his career through years of industrial toil, climactic confrontations with brutal employers, the breakthrough into power, either in the union or into parliament, and usually a prolonged mellowing process thereafter which could lead anywhere from a southern coastal resort to the House of Lords. If the Labour leader were middle-class (the Webbs, Sam Hobson, Dalton, Fenner Brockway, etc.), a conventional childhood would be transformed by dramatic and conclusive engagement with the thrilling creed of socialism, either through personal witness of urban poverty or through philosophical conversion, or some combination of the two. In each case, there would be a clear thread of explanation to account for the author's socialist ideology or practical involvement in the political or industrial wings of the labour movement. The autobiographies would exist less as forms of literary self-indulgence than as keys to amplifying a belief in social change and a career of constructive protest.

Nowadays, however, Labour autobiographies follow a very different style. Of none is this more true than Roy Hattersley's engaging memoir, *A Yorkshire Boyhood*, the record of the first eighteen years of a prominent (and far from elderly) Labour politician of the present time, currently deputy leader and Shadow Chancellor. It is a very readable and attractive book, admirably produced by the publishers. Yet a striking feature of it is the dog that does not bark. It does not directly explain what impelled the author into Labour, or any other, politics, and a commitment to democratic socialism. Admittedly, Hattersley has turned his ever-active pen to this fascinating theme elsewhere, in addresses to the Fabian Society and on other occasions. His autobiography, ending somewhat ambiguously with his departure from home and family in Sheffield, either for university or for national service (it is not clear which, though in fact Hull University was where he eventually ended up), seems to cry out for an early sequel. For all that, readers pulverized by the electoral volatility of the 1980s, seeking fresh guidance on the roots and relevance of the British labour movement, will have to ponder further and probe more deeply.

Roy Hattersley's book is a very agreeable, civilized account of his early years in Sheffield, the citadel of steel. It is full of rich detail on the personalities and mores of that great city (latterly, the capital of the 'socialist republic' of South Yorkshire), which makes the book vividly instructive for the non-Yorkshire reader. He is less secure on other parts of England. An authoritative discussion of Sheffield Wednesday FC in the 1940s must be weighed against a somewhat erroneous passage on the Arsenal team of the same period. He is better on Jackie Robinson than on Jimmy Logie, as one would expect. The Hattersley household was a secure, happy one. Young Roy, an only child, was doted on by his father (a lapsed Catholic priest, remarkably enough) and an apparently formidable mother, who later became mayor of Sheffield. In a series of deft sketches, South Yorkshire in the years before, during and just after the second world war, comes vividly to life. Among other things, the historically inclined reader will note that, for schoolchildren like young Roy (and the present writer), the years of so-called 'austerity' under the Attlee government were by no means a time of unrelieved gloom. They saw generally rising living standards, and much cheap popular entertainment, notably sport and the cinema. The ethos and aspirations of the Hattersley household emerge as strictly bourgeois. They live in Hillsborough, the up-market end of working-class Sheffield, unlike Attercliffe or Brightside. They own their semi-detached house. Roy spends five years at a fee-paying local prep school, then wins a scholarship to the city grammar school. He extols the pride of possession of a traditional school uniform. He collects stamps and learns Latin. He is urged by his mother 'to do well', like the young Lloyd George being told to 'get on' by his remarkable Uncle Lloyd. Roy captains the school cricket team, he confronts both sporting success and local girls without disaster, and finally wins admission to Hull University.

In all this comfortable saga of suburban folk, it comes as quite a surprise to learn that the Hattersleys were committed to 'Labour' (never 'socialist') politics, that young Roy attended a Socialist Sunday School, and joined the Labour League of Youth in its new-model Morgan Phillips guise. We are given little further explanatory detail, apart from a brief sketch of campaigning in the 1950s for the election of George Darling (Labour and Co-op), for the Hillsborough division, and praise of one Sid Osgothorpe, a self-improving Sheffield steel artisan who represents for Hattersley the abiding values of the British working-class movement. Beyond this, the message of the Labour Party or the purpose or appeal of socialism for an impressionable, intelligent young schoolboy are not elaborated. He explains his enthusiasm for party canvass returns in much the same terms as for Yorkshire cricket score cards. No conviction politics here. It is simply a good-humoured, tolerant, profoundly unideological, almost laconic book by a highly sympathetic man of the centre-left, looking back without the least trace of anger.

To a degree, his career since 1964 has tended to reproduce this pattern. He has seldom deviated from the progressive centre, anxious largely to retain the heritage of the Attlee years of the welfare state through which he lived as a young boy. Nor do his humorous, engaging columns in the pages of the weekend *Guardian*, *Punch*, and other publications, with their ruminations on Jane Austen, Sheffield Wednesday, and the varieties of the English landscape, suggest a man in any sense at war with his society. His solid physical presence, like that of Cobbett, is in itself a comforting sight, testimony to the inevitability of gradualness in the engaging ambience of the 'Gay Hussar'. In junior office under Harold Wilson in the sixties, then as minister, at the Foreign Office and then (in the Cabinet) at Consumer Affairs between 1974 and 1979, Hattersley always was viewed as a spokesman of the Labour right. In the sixties, Barbara Castle wrote darkly of him as 'a Jenkins man', though the bond weakened later in that decade. Marcia Williams, typically, condemned him as 'a conspirator' and 'a Gaitskellite'. The latter, at least, may be accepted without demur. As a NATO man, a strong opponent of unilateralism, an enthusiast for entry into the Common Market, an advocate of incomes policy and a non-ideological approach towards state intervention, Hattersley rearticulated the priorities of much of the Labour right of Gaitskellite days, with his Europeanism placing him in a distinct category in that wing. Sometimes there were radical deviations, notably in some sharp remarks on Northern Ireland during the Heath years, and in some powerful statements on civil liberties issues (notably the British Nationality, and Police and Criminal Evidence Acts) while Shadow Home Secretary 1980–3. But, in general, Hattersley has an unblemished record as the voice of the right.

In the leadership election of 1983, Hattersley laid down his support for British membership of NATO and the EEC, and his support for a national minimum wage as part of a voluntary incomes policy. This was balanced by attacks on public schools and private medicine. He was supported by most of the right-led unions, which enabled him to defeat Michael Meacher quite comfortably in the contest for the deputy leadership, while losing heavily to Neil Kinnock in the leadership contest itself. Hattersley's campaign references to the 'broad-church' character of the Labour Party were clearly directed against the sectarian left, whom he did not hesitate to take on in public debate, often with surprising belligerence. Later on, despite the sensitive ethnic balance in his Birmingham constituency, he argued strongly against having black sections within the party. Since 1983, he and Kinnock have, to all appearances, worked in close harmony and with a united outlook. This can only be because, in large measure, the party's strategy and approach have been recast in Hattersley's Gaitskellite image. Indeed, *A Duty to Win*, a selection of Hattersley's speeches and articles edited by Giles Radice and published in September 1983, bore an extremely close resemblance to Labour's provisional election manifesto, three years later. The determination that Labour will be staunch on inflation and wage restraint, cautious on public ownership, tough on law and order, and a powerful champion of individual liberties and private property, including home ownership for council tenants and others, reflect the essence of the Hattersley ethos. It is probably close to the general will of the nation. The rejection of any form of class war, the emphasis on reform, and moderation have subtly remodelled the party, at least at the summit. When asked by Elizabeth Durbin to write on the Gaitskell–Durbin–Jay group of young economists of the thirties, Hattersley commended above all their 'practicality'. It is the emphasis on 'practical policies' which has dominated his speeches and writings for the past two decades.

The main problem about Roy Hattersley's career must surely be why, given his professed views and background, he did not join the Social Democrats, along with politicians like Shirley Williams and Roy Jenkins, with whom his views were so closely aligned. In fact, there was never the slightest of suggestions that he would so do. No doubt, a variety of motives combined to produce this effect. Like other young politicians, Hattersley was naturally ambitious and trod skilfully through the minefield of conflicting policies during the

Harold Wilson era. Wilson himself, of all people, criticized him for
undue flexibility. Ambition, indeed, has been an accusation often
thrown at Hattersley from the sixties onwards, though it is hard to
see anyone committing himself or herself to the rigours of the political
life at all if ambition did not play a part. Hattersley is hardly unique
in this regard, while his policy pronouncements during the 1983
leadership campaign—notably his strong attack on the 'national
economic assessment' under which Labour nominally fought the
1983 general election, as 'literally incredible'—showed much courage and common sense. In the leadership contest, indeed, Hattersley's
policy declarations were a good deal more outspoken and iconoclastic
than those of Neil Kinnock. Certainly they were not obviously the
statements of a man consumed by ambition to the exclusion of
principle. As Shadow Chancellor, his calls for a new Labour government to rein in public expenditure are no obvious route to easy
popularity. Nor are his views on nuclear weapons.

It is fair to say, too, that, moderate though he certainly is,
Hattersley's brand of the Attlee–Gaitskell style of social democracy
stops well short of the SDP admiration of the 'social market'; his Fabian
lecture, 'Socialism and Markets' (19 November 1985) illustrates the
point. There is a clear ideological gulf between Hattersley's position
and what appears to emerge from the SDP's *mélange* of views on social
and economic matters. In August 1983, Hattersley took sharp issue
with the SDP view that equality of opportunity should be the governing principle in educational and other policy; he emphasized instead
equality of outcome. He disputed that meaningful equality of opportunity was feasible without a broader social equality. Not for nothing
is his wife an influential head of a comprehensive school. On defence
policy, too, for all his multilaterialism, Hattersley takes a distinctly
different position from the commitment to Trident and an independent British nuclear strike force that Dr David Owen is attempting
to impose on his unhappy flock. Even so, the precise personal or
ideological factors which have seen Shirley Williams, Jenkins, and
Rodgers move one way, but Hattersley, Healey, and John Smith
stand firm to the old party require an alternative instrument of
measurement.

Perhaps to understand Hattersley's underlying motives, we ought
rather to turn to sociology, psychology, even simple instinct. In this
respect, it may be that *A Yorkshire Boyhood*, even though obviously
a light literary piece designed for the general reader at the station

bookstall, may be a more important political document than at first sight appears. Within its pages, it does convey a powerful commitment to a special kind of industrial community, organic, integrated, with its own sense of local and civic pride. It was animated, as were South Wales, Tyneside, and other Labour strongholds (Liverpool always somewhat excluded, for ethnic and other reasons) by the ethos of the artisan, self-improving, devoted to educational and professional advancement, but with an unshakeable sense of place and of history. In Sheffield's light industrial trades, this was especially marked. To a young boy brought up in such an atmosphere, a more genuine community than the middle-class ghettos of Islington or Hammersmith from which many of the hard-left ideologues of the 1980s derived, the labour movement was what gave shape, rhythm, and meaning to life. So it has been through the generations: by 1926, Sheffield was unmistakably a Labour city, the first such in England. Thus in 1945 Labour urged the voters, 'Ask your Dad'.

Sheffield in the 1940s, still industrially thriving, its steel furnaces active in the post-war export boom, its workforce fully employed both in light and heavy industry, embodied the best of the Lib-Lab ethic of the past, its sense of local pride and indelible class-consciousness, without extending the deference to Liberal capitalism that made the old Lib-Labbery a dead creed by 1914. The significance of this ethic lies deep below the surface structure or institutions of a society. We should, perhaps, look for what French historians have taught us to regard as the *mentalité* of industrial Sheffield. Perhaps it would take a Richard Cobb to probe the real dignity and cultural seriousness of Sid Osgothorpe and his mates.

Not all products of that kind of culture reached the same political conclusions. Roy Jenkins of Abersychan, whose father was a miners' agent imprisoned for nine months for his role during the General Strike, seems to have forgotten his background with some speed, certainly as soon as he reached Balliol. A brief interlude at University College, Cardiff, to which he travelled daily by bus from Pontypool, left no imprint upon him. Welsh mutton soon gave way to Mouton Rothschild. By the time of his entry into parliament as an SDP member in 1982, with some years of Euro-bureaucracy behind him, Jenkins had apparently forgotten his Welsh origins. He had played virtually no part in the social or cultural life of South Wales for many years; in a disastrous moment during the Hillhead by-election he had to be reminded that he was a Welshman at all. He is the biographer of Asquith, of course, and his book records his subject as observing that 'I'd sooner go to hell than to Wales' and that 'Peter was a Celt'. On Asquith's burial at Sutton Courtenay, Jenkins wrote that, whilst Asquith 'had started on a bleak Yorkshire hillside' and had been a Scottish MP, 'a South of England resting-place, within ten miles of Carfax Tower, was nevertheless wholly appropriate'. Hattersley, by contrast, went to Hull not to hell, and served for some years on the Sheffield City Council. For all his translation to a Birmingham constituency and to London political and journalistic circles, he has manifestly not forsaken his roots, however whimsically he may recall them. Indeed, they form a broad explanation of why he is in the Labour Party at all. The route from the Lib-Labs of the late Victorian period to the democratic socialists of today is a tortuous one; many have failed to complete it and fallen by the wayside. Hattersley, though, appears to have arrived successfully. He has also, if only indirectly, helped us to understand why, by writing a book that gives a new twist to Labour autobiography as an art form.

# NEIL KINNOCK

THE present Labour leader's main characteristic as a politician, we are often told, is his inexperience. Born as recently as 1942, Neil Kinnock represents a manifestly new generation, unacquainted with power. Some may well consider this a grave, perhaps fatal, liability. British politics has seldom given much encouragement to youth since the heady experience of the Younger Pitt in 1783. The Labour Party, in particular, has tended to emphasize length of service to the move- ment, whether effective or not, and to be suspicious of young men in a hurry. Nye Bevan was still regarded as a coming man when he was in his early fifties. None of the six Labour governments to date has given much encouragement to untried talent. The Attlee regime (with the conspicuous exception of Harold Wilson) was almost a gerontocracy, with sexagenarians and septuagenarians thick on the ground. Government, in the long-held view of the people's party, is no job for a boy. Conversely, it could well turn out that Neil Kinnock's very remoteness from power during the past two troubled decades may prove his greatest asset, not least amongst those millions of voters not yet born when Wilson took office in 1964. More con- vincingly than Wilson in the 1963–4 period, Kinnock has won public support and sympathy for his being a fresh, cheerful face, with an attractive, articulate wife, and pleasant young children. He seems born free, relatively detached from the party infighting of the sixties and early seventies, untrammelled by the sterile dogma of the past. Nor is he stunned into awed deference before the Whitehall machine. Compared with him, even the eternally boyish David Steel (who, after all, has been Liberal leader for a full decade) looks relatively shop-soiled.

But, of course, the very novelty of Kinnock, which makes him the least known Labour leader there has been since the advent of Keir Hardie (and perhaps the least tried major party leader since Margaret Thatcher!) makes an assessment peculiarly difficult. It is hard to say whether he belongs more truly to the prophets, to such politicians of protest as Hardie, Lansbury, or Maxton, or to the pragmatic parliamentarians, such as Attlee, Wilson, or Callaghan, concerned with winning and mobilizing power. The former are attacked, in

Ernest Bevin's pithy phrase, for 'letting their bleeding 'earts run away with their bloody 'eads'. The latter, by their very calculation, have been condemned at times for appearing to have no heart at all. Labour needs the special qualities of both types of leader—perhaps Aneurin Bevan was close to fusing the two in his last years. But into which, if any, category, Kinnock will fall, his approach towards the conquest and uses of power, remain singularly hard to determine.

Hitherto, we have had two workmanlike biographies, by G. M. F. Drower and Robert Harris, which both provide valuable background information. Beyond that, they cannot take us very far, save to underline the obvious truth that, at all costs, Neil Kinnock should never be underestimated. In his early period as Labour's leader, he was usually dismissed as the archetypal Welsh windbag, a prolix lightweight who preferred the limelight of the media (including, rather extraordinarily, a pop video with Tracy Ullman) to solid thought about policy. To use his own term, Kinnock was no natural 'plodder'. Since 1983, however, this judgement has seemed much less tenable. Indeed, Kinnock, by the time of his stinging attacks on the Liverpool Militants in the 1985 party conference was widely praised for showing not only a courage but also a wisdom which the combined gifts of Attlee, Gaitskell, Wilson, Callaghan, and Foot had failed to generate in the past. Nevertheless, it is still common to hear observations—on the basis of what evidence it is hard to say—to the effect that Mrs Thatcher's prime ministerial authority, however stridently and repetitively expressed, shows up young Neil as an inexperienced tyro time after time. Even this judgement seems thread-bare, and will no doubt join past dismissals on the scrapheap of history (located, perhaps, in the recesses of Annie's Bar). What cannot reasonably be disputed is that Kinnock has retained a con-sistent capacity to surprise and to mature, that he has constantly grown with responsibility, and that this process is still very far from over.

He comes, of course, from the mining and steel valleys of South Wales, from one of Labour's most traditional heartlands. In particu-lar, he comes from Tredegar in the Rhymney Valley, a cradle of Welsh socialism. Welsh historians over the years have perhaps been unduly besotted with the unique role of Merthyr Tydfil as the matrix of Welsh popular radicalism, home of the martyr, Dic Penderyn (executed in 1831), the parliamentary seat of Henry Richard, Keir Hardie, and later S. O. Davies. Merthyr has always been a private world, perched on the rim of the coalfield. Perhaps we should be casting our gaze further east, to the Gwent valleys, the heart of revolutionary consciousness at the time of the Scotch Cattle and the Chartist uprising, the fount of Tom Jones's 'Rhymney memories', the base for Aneurin Bevan and now Neil Kinnock. His family, typically of his community, was poor, and scarred by experience of personal tragedy in the mines. His father, a miner, died young; his mother, a nurse, had to support the family. From this background, Kinnock gained his most precious political quality, an intense sense of involvement with this working-class community. Unusually among Labour's leaders, he is an authentic proletarian in the people's party, with his mother's insistence on short haircuts and polished shoes as a further tribute to South Wales working-class canons of respectability. No donkey jacket at the Cenotaph for him. Only the piano in the front parlour seems to have been missing in his upbringing.

But Kinnock comes from a new South Wales, an updated, upwardly mobile, welfarized society, the product of the Labour revolution after 1945. He grew up in the fifties and sixties in a world of full employment, with the old solidarity of the pits diminishing fast. (The main pit at nearby Bargoed closed in the late sixties, which helped on a brief resurgence by Plaid Cymru in the area.) His rise to power followed a suitably modern route in consequence. Along with the typical 'macho' world of the valleys, 'poems and pints', and always rugby, there was also the fact that young Neil went to a prestigious old Welsh grammar school, Lewis School, Pengam, once hailed by Lloyd George as 'the Eton of Wales'. Kinnock did well enough to gain decent A levels and to move on to University College, Cardiff, to study history. By all accounts (including his own) he made little effort to be a scholar, and his degree was a poor one. But this university did introduce him to the bourgeois world of politics. It is through student elections and campaigning in the Student Union that he came to the Labour Party rather than through grass-roots politics in the Rhymney Valley, which he was already in some sense beginning to leave behind. After all, Cardiff tends to be the Ellis Island for able products of the valleys, processing them for a wider, anglicized world. At university, in particular with the remarkable Glenys Parry, whom he shortly married, Kinnock learnt the vocabulary and syntax of modern machine politics.

After university he became a WEA lecturer in economics in South Wales. Adult education was an ideal base for a political career, as it always has been, no less than the solicitor's career for the young Lloyd George in North Wales long ago. When he was, somewhat remarkably or even fortuitously, adopted for the impregnable Labour seat of Bedwellty at the tender age of twenty-eight in place of the venerable retiring member Harold Finch, Kinnock was already committed to the style and substance of a politics recognizably contemporary, almost classless, subtly removed from the traditional South Wales labour movement where canvassing, like the Tory Party, was redundant. He was, far more than most ambitious young politicians, a complete professional.

In the 1970s, he advanced rapidly and confidently up through the echelons of the party. By 1974 he was a formidable orator (and cabaret wit) at party conference. He was a vocal advocate of the standard left-wing position on nuclear weapons, the Common Market, public ownership, incomes policy, arms to South Africa, Chile, El Salvador, and much else besides. He also emerged as a fluent and persuasive performer in the television studio, able to deal faithfully with senior figures like Lord Hailsham; he also became a firm favourite with the press lobby, always sociable, good humoured, and lacking in pomposity. In 1977 he was elected to the constituency section of the NEC, apparently a firm supporter of the leftish movement associated with the Benn supporters. The main criticism of him in these years was that he was strong on rhetoric, weak on the nuts and bolts of policy-making, whether defence, foreign policy, or economics. He declined the offer of minor office under Callaghan in 1976. When he was later appointed shadow spokesman for education in 1979, he was not always famous for his care in presentation and attention to detail. On occasion he managed to make the then Conservative minister, Mark Carlisle, look impressive. But he soon established himself as a powerful front-bench performer, with original things to say on further education, industrial retraining, and other themes. Even his critics conceded that any shortcomings were overshadowed by a kind of star quality and courage which gave new heart to the party even in the miserable years of turmoil and tension in the late seventies and early eighties.

Sometimes he was compared (including by himself) to Aneurin Bevan. Indeed, he underlined the comparison with that old hero of the left by writing a foreword to a new printing of *In Place of Fear*, and even threatening to write a full-scale biography. But a careful examination of his career, at least from 1977, showed a more complicated relationship. If he is to be compared with Bevan at all—and it may well be that the comparison does not take us very far—it may be more appropriate to link him not with the demagogic Bevan of Popular Front days, but with the more reflective democratic socialist concerned with the uses of power who emerged in 1945 and bequeathed the movement an enduring testament. Allied to Bevan's early commitment to South Wales was an outgoing cosmopolitanism and a restless experimentation with the practicalities of socialism. It is this later Bevan which Kinnock perhaps best resembles, more of a relativist than a revivalist.

Realism has always been central to Kinnock's socialist vision. He quoted enthusiastically in a Welsh radio programme Keir Hardie's dictum that socialists should seek to use power, not to destroy it. Kinnock was in no sense the heir of the anarcho-syndicalists of the *Miners' Next Step*; it was a parable for his views on Militant in his own times. At key moments in the period 1977–83, Kinnock emerged as a mainstream socialist, realistic though never right-wing, committed above all to the unity and coherence of a broad-based party. His response to electoral defeat in 1979 was quite different from that of Tony Benn in 1970. Kinnock now turned against what he saw as the destructive activities of the Campaign for Labour Democracy of which he had been a founder member. He disavowed attacks on the Shadow Cabinet and the party leader, especially when his close friend, Michael Foot, succeeded Callaghan. He flatly opposed the endorsement of Peter Tatchell as Labour's candidate in Bermondsey in 1981, some kind of litmus test which divided the soft (or Old) from the hard (or New) left. Kinnock also spoke out strongly against the entryist activities of minority 'vanguard' groups such as Militant, and upheld the rule of law and the parliamentary approach to socialism. As shadow education spokesman, at some personal cost, he reminded his zealous comrades of the need for economic prudence in the use of available resources for investment. Most decisively, and characteristically, at the Brighton party conference in 1981, he acted with other moderate left Tribunites such as Joan Lestor and Stan Orme to prevent the election of Benn as deputy leader. They voted for John Silkin in the first ballot and, crucially, abstained in the second, thus ensuring Benn's defeat. Kinnock evidently was a plausible Bevanite, but a most implausible Bennite.

He thus showed himself a more complicated figure than many critics had imagined, an interesting man for interesting times. He could brave the wrath of old allies on the left, and take them on (physically, if necessary, if accounts of an episode in the men's lavatory at the Brighton conference are to be believed). He was also no time-server. Towards the unions, he was respectful but never subservient (which won him the unlikely endorsement of Frank Chapple in the leadership contest in 1983). An illuminating episode came in Kinnock's strong opposition to the passage of the Welsh devolution bill in 1976-9 when, with five Welsh colleagues, he campaigned strongly against his own government. He differed sharply even from his mentor, Michael Foot, on this issue, though it left no scar in their relations. It was, without doubt, opposition based on principle. Kinnock felt deeply that devolution must mean the negation of central socialist planning and real institutional reform. He faced fierce attacks within the party, even in anglicized Bedwellty. But his very force of argument took him to a higher plane of debate than those such as Leo Abse who took refuge in *ad hominem* attacks on the Welsh-speaking minority (after all, they include Glenys Kinnock). Neil Kinnock won the devolution argument, through force of persuasion and dialectical talent, not through racial or linguistic prejudice more appropriate for Ulster. Eighty per cent of his countrymen (probably even more now) agreed with him in the end.

It was these wider qualities which made Kinnock so readily acceptable across the spectrum of the party as the elected successor to Michael Foot in October 1983. Since that time he has become increasingly effective. If he had been the simple-minded ranter of journalistic invention this could never have happened. Nor could it had he been the ill-informed neophyte scorned by the right. After a very difficult first phase, which included the miners' strike that posed particular problems close to home, he has sought to free his party from sterile class-war postures, just as South Wales itself has been liberated, the miners' stoppage and the sentimentalism of some academics notwithstanding. Kinnock has always crusaded against sectarianism, whether from a union leader like Scargill or a middle-class maverick like Benn, or local government barons like Hatton or Mulhearn. He robustly disowned Livingstone's expressions of sympathy for Sinn Fein. He has worked to make his party credible as an alternative instrument of power. *The Times* in October 1985 defined his position (in terms that he himself would perhaps reject) as 'Gaitskellism from the left of centre'. One can see what is meant.

Ideologically, Kinnock has travelled fairly light. By mid-1986, his party's priorities have largely modified nationalization or extensive state intervention in the economy. A modest 'social ownership' is offered in place of Morrisonian 'socialization'. A wealth tax, even ending tax relief on house mortgages, are not on the agenda. Membership of the Common Market is no longer seriously in dispute, while Kinnock, as the friend of European socialist premiers like Gonzales in Spain and Papandreou in Greece, is no isolationist. Although the renunciation of nuclear weapons is firm party policy, together with the rejection of Trident, so too is the commitment to NATO and (if feasible) the retention of non-nuclear US bases on British soil. Clearly, Kinnock is engaged in adjusting his slow-moving, stereotyped party, caught up for too long in destructive introspection, to a changing society and ideological mood. His programme is almost indistinguishable from the distinctly Gaitskellite prescription offered by Hattersley in 1979–83. He wants to identify the aspirations of the party with the relatively affluent majority who are employed, own their own homes, worry about mortgages and vandalism and the standards in neighbourhood schools, and are anxious for the pleasures of a consumer society, as well as the hard-hit minority dependent on public welfare. Labour must appeal, as Kinnock put it in a Fabian lecture in November 1985, to modern workers 'whose upward mobility, increased expectations and extended horizons are largely the result of opportunities afforded by our movement in the past'. In a much more compassionate form, no doubt, Labour is observing what the American Democrats came to discover in McGovern's idealistic but disastrous campaign in 1972, that the majority of the nation is 'unyoung, unpoor and unblack'.

Labour's manifesto at the next election seems certain not to repeat the lengthy list of minority themes put forward in 1983. It will focus on a few essentials: employment, health, education, housing. The clear emphasis under Kinnock has been on personal freedom and security, including law and order, never one of Labour's stronger suits. Nuclear weapons will be scrapped (Kinnock appears to be a Labour leader who really does mean to abandon Polaris) but much more spent on conventional forces, especially the ever-popular Royal Navy. The party has now merged with a progressive consensus which can even identify (in the unguarded chat of a television programme) with Franklin Roosevelt's New Deal. Neil Kinnock is still to be classed as a socialist, but a distinctly flexible and modernized one. Appropriately, one of his priorities has been to overhaul the party machine and the presentation of policy, both of which in 1983 were a shambles. But there is nothing either incongruous, or ignoble, about the stance Kinnock has adopted as party leader. It is consonant with his pragmatic make-up and the political shrewdness he has shown since he entered students politics in the Cardiff Union (and the bar of the 'Arcade') twenty years ago. It is the only way a new-born politician can react. It is perhaps his only feasible route to power.

During the controversy over the air strike on Libya in April 1986, it began to be noted that Kinnock seemed now thoroughly settled in as leader. On more arcane economic and international matters he was more assured and better informed. The prospects of the Kinnocks at No 10, throwing a rugby ball around the lawn where Lloyd George's 'garden suburb' once took root, is less incredible now, even if an overall Labour majority in the next election, needing a net gain of 117 seats, would be an astonishing result indeed. How Kinnock would then fare as Prime Minister cannot, of course, be predicted. But past experience suggests that he would not flinch from the challenge of power. He is not obviously an intellectual nor (despite a well-advertised penchant for Brahms's symphonies) is he an enthusiast for the arts. He is sometimes derided in clubs and common rooms—but, then, dons are notoriously bad judges of popular politics, even when their own profession is at stake. There are no grounds for supposing that Kinnock would be a better leader if he did have these qualities. Leading the Labour Party, his prime responsibility, is no place for over-fastidious academics or refined aesthetes. His political sure-footedness over the past three years has been consistently more impressive than the undoubtedly more intellectual and artistic Denis Healey, as the 1986 party conference amply showed.

Kinnock senses something profoundly important. A party leader should respond to currents of new ideas, rather than necessarily generate them. He should concentrate on policy positions rather than policies. In this context, Kinnock's Fabian lecture in 1985 was not at all a shoddy attempt to explore traditional socialist dilemmas about reconciling individual freedom with collective provision, or using the latter as 'the agent of individual emancipation' in Kinnock's words. In his stress on the dangers of centralization and 'unaccountable bureaucracies' he struck a powerful chord with many Labour voters. Kinnock might prove a very good Prime Minister if circumstances allowed, more decisive than Attlee, more principled than Wilson, more innovative than Callaghan, and a better butcher than any of them. He has said that he would strengthen the Prime Minister's office, and restore the 'think tank'. Harold Wilson once referred to the two roles he had played as Prime Minister—'centre forward' in 1964, 'deep-lying centre-half' in 1974. Kinnock, one guesses, would neither be so rash as to pursue the first role, nor so timid as to lapse into the second. In sporting parlance, he might be more of an old-fashioned leader of the forward line, like Tommy Lawton of yore, working collectively with colleagues whose individual skills he respected. He has another quality, also—pertinacity, not always found in Wales; like his countryman, Henry VII, what he minds he compasses.

For nearly forty years, Labour was dazzled by the glories, real or imagined, of 1945, unable either to develop its politics or modernize its image much beyond that basic point of historic reference. Kinnock—along with Hattersley, John Smith, and other similarly unencumbered colleagues—has succeeded in making the party look fresher and much more credible, at least for the moment. If it regains power at the polls—or even if it merely re-establishes its credentials as the essential voice of anti-Tory opposition—then not only Kinnock himself, but also the rhetoric and practice of the movement will truly have come of age, eighty-seven years on.

# APPENDIX: BIOGRAPHICAL DATA

ABLETT, NOAH (1882–1935): executive member, South Wales Miners' Federation, 1910–35; part-author, *Miners' Next Step* (1912); miners' agent for Merthyr, 1918–35; executive member, Miners' Federation of Great Britain, 1921–6.

ADDISON, DR CHRISTOPHER (1869–1951): MP (Lib.) for Hoxton, 1910–22; (Lab.), Swindon, 1929–31 and 1934–5; created a viscount, 1935; held various ministerial posts under Asquith and Lloyd George, notably Minister of Health, 1919–21; Minister of Agriculture, 1930–1; Dominions Secretary, 1945–7; Commonwealth Secretary, 1947; Lord Privy Seal, 1947–51; Paymaster-General, 1948–9; Lord President of the Council, 1951; leader of the Lords, 1945–51.

ATTLEE, CLEMENT R. (1883–1967): MP for Limehouse, 1922–50; Walthamstow West, 1950–5; Chancellor of the Duchy of Lancaster, 1930–1; Postmaster-General, 1931; Lord Privy Seal, 1940–2; Dominions Secretary, 1942–3; Lord President of the Council, 1943–5; Deputy Prime Minister, 1942–5; Prime Minister, 1945–51; created an earl, 1955.

BENN, TONY (1925– ): Anthony Neil Wedgwood Benn, heir to Lord Stansgate, but disclaimed peerage, 1963; MP for Bristol South-East, 1950–60 and 1963–83; Chesterfield, 1984– ; Postmaster-General, 1964–6; Minister of Technology, 1966–70; Secretary of State for Industry, 1974–5; Secretary of State for Energy, 1975–9.

BEVAN, ANEURIN (1897–1960): MP for Ebbw Vale, 1929–60; Minister of Health, 1945–51; Minister of Labour, 1951; resigned from government, 1951; deputy-leader of the Labour Party, 1959–60.

BEVIN, ERNEST (1881–1951): secretary, Transport and General Workers Union, 1921–40; MP for Wandsworth Central, 1940–50; Woolwich East, 1950–1; Minister of Labour, 1940–5; Foreign Secretary, 1945–51; Lord Privy Seal, 1951.

CALLAGHAN, JAMES (1912– ): MP for Cardiff South, 1945–50; Cardiff South-East, 1950–83; Cardiff South, 1983– . Chancellor of the Exchequer, 1964–7; Home Secretary, 1967–70; Foreign Secretary, 1974–6; Prime Minister, 1976–9; leader of the Labour Party, 1976–80.

CRIPPS, SIR R. STAFFORD (1889–1952): MP for Bristol East, 1931–50, and Bristol South-East, 1950; Solicitor-General 1930–1; ambassador to Soviet Union, 1940–2; Lord Privy Seal and Leader of the House, 1942; Minister of Aircraft Production, 1942–5; President of the Board of Trade, 1945–7;

Minister of Economic Affairs, 1947; Chancellor of the Exchequer, 1947–50.

DALTON, HUGH (1887–1962): lecturer, then professor at London School of Economics; MP for Peckham, 1924–9; Bishop Auckland, 1929–31, 1935–59; Minister of Economic Warfare, 1940–2; President of the Board of Trade, 1942–5; Chancellor of the Exchequer, 1945–7; Chancellor of the Duchy of Lancaster, 1948–50; Minister of Town and Country Planning, 1950–1; Minister of Local Government Planning, 1951; created Baron Dalton, 1959.

DURBIN, EVAN F. M. (1906–48): economist; MP for Edmonton, 1945–8; drowned in a holiday accident.

FOOT, MICHAEL (1913– ): editor of Evening Standard, 1941–3, and Tribune, 1948–52, 1955–60; MP for Devonport, 1945–55; Ebbw Vale, 1960–83; Blaenau Gwent, 1983– ; Secretary of State for Employment, 1974–6; Lord President of the Council and Leader of the House, 1976–9; leader of the Labour Party, 1980–3.

GAITSKELL, HUGH T. N. (1907–63): economist and civil servant; MP for Leeds South, 1946–63; Minister of Fuel and Power, 1947–50; Minister for Economic Affairs, 1950; Chancellor of the Exchequer, 1950–1; leader of the Labour Party, 1955–63.

GORMLEY, JOE (1917– ): elected secretary, Lancashire Miners, 1961; president National Union of Mineworkers, 1971–82; member of Labour Party national executive, 1963–73.

GRAYSON, VICTOR (1882–?): MP for Colne Valley, 1907–10; precise date and place of death unknown.

GRIFFITHS, JAMES (1890–1975): President of South Wales Miners' Federation, 1934–6; Minister of National Insurance, 1945–50; Colonial Secretary, 1950–1; Secretary of State for Wales, 1964–6.

HARDIE, JAMES KEIR (1856–1915): MP for West Ham South, 1892–5, and Merthyr Tydfil, 1900–15; chairman of Independent Labour Party, 1894–1900; first chairman, Parliamentary Labour Party, 1906–8.

HATTERSLEY, ROY (1932– ): MP for Sparkbrook, 1964– ; Minister of State, Foreign and Colonial Office, 1974–6; Secretary for Prices and Consumer Protection, 1976–9; deputy leader of the Labour Party and Shadow Chancellor since October 1983.

HEALEY, DENIS (1917– ): International Secretary of the Labour Party, 1946–52; MP for Leeds South-East, 1952–5; Leeds East, 1955– ; Defence Secretary, 1964–70; Chancellor of the Exchequer, 1974–9; deputy leader of the Labour Party, 1980–3.

HENDERSON, ARTHUR (1863–1935): general secretary, Ironfounders; MP for Barnard Castle, 1903–18; Widnes, 1919–22; Newcastle East, 1923;

Burnley, 1924–31, Clay Cross, 1933–5; secretary of the Labour Party, 1911–34; President of the Board of Education, 1915–16; Postmaster-General, 1916; Minister without portfolio, 1916–17; Home Secretary, 1924; Foreign Secretary, 1929–31; leader of the Labour Party, 1908–10, 1931–2.

HINDEN, RITA (1902–71): secretary, Fabian Society Colonial Research Bureau, 1940–50; editor of *Socialist Commentary*, 1951–71.

JAY, DOUGLAS (1907–   ): economist and journalist; private secretary to Attlee, 1945–6; MP for Battersea North, 1946–83; junior minister at the Treasury 1947–51; President of the Board of Trade, 1964–7.

KINNOCK, NEIL (1942–   ): MP for Bedwellty, 1970–83; Islwyn, 1983–   ; leader of the Labour Party since October 1983.

LASKI, HAROLD (1893–1950): professor at London School of Economics, 1926–50; prolific author on political topics; member of National Executive, Labour Party, 1936–49.

'MABON' (WILLIAM ABRAHAM) (1842–1922): MP (Lib.-Lab., then Lab.) for Rhondda, 1885–1918; Rhondda West, 1918–20; first president of South Wales Miners' Federation, 1890–1912; Welsh-speaking nonconformist.

MACDONALD, JAMES RAMSAY (1866–1937): MP for Leicester, 1906–18; Aberavon, 1922–9; Seaham, 1921–31 and (Nat. Lab.) 1931–5; Scottish Universities, 1936–7; secretary of Labour Party, 1900–11; chairman, Parliamentary Labour Party, 1911–14 and 1922–31; Prime Minister and Foreign Secretary, 1924; Prime Minister, 1929–35; Lord President of the Council, 1935–7.

MORRISON, HERBERT (1888–1965): leader of London Labour Party, and leader of LCC, 1934–40; MP for Hackney South, 1923–4, 1929–31, and 1935–45; Lewisham East, 1945–50; Lewisham South, 1950–9; Minister of Transport, 1929–31; Minister of Supply, 1940; Home Secretary, 1940–5; Lord President of the Council, 1945–51; Foreign Secretary, 1951; created Baron Morrison, 1959.

PHILLIPS, MORGAN (1902–63): secretary (later general secretary) of the Labour Party, 1944–61; chairman of the Socialist International, 1948–57.

SCARGILL, ARTHUR (1938–   ): President, Yorkshire Miners, 1973–82; President, National Union of Mineworkers, since 1982.

WEBB, BEATRICE (1858–1943): *née* Beatrice Potter, married Sidney Webb, 1892; a leading Fabian and author on social themes for over fifty years.

WEBB, SIDNEY (1859–1947): member of the Fabian Society from 1885; MP for Seaham, 1922–9; President of the Board of Trade, 1924; Dominions Secretary, 1929–30 and Colonial Secretary, 1929–31; created Baron Passfield, 1929.

WILKINSON, ELLEN (1891–1947): MP for Middlesbrough East, 1924–31, and Jarrow, 1935–47; parliamentary secretary, Ministry of Home Security, 1940–5; Minister for Education, 1945–7.

WILSON, J. HAROLD (1916–   ): MP for Ormskirk, 1945–50; Huyton, 1950–83; President of the Board of Trade, 1945–51; Prime Minister, 1964–70 and 1974–6; leader of the Labour Party, 1963–76; created Baron Wilson of Rievaulx, 1983.

# SELECT BIBLIOGRAPHY

THIS book is based on a vast range of manuscript and printed primary and secondary materials, together with oral evidence, studied over many years. To record them in detail would be of overwhelming and quite disproportionate length. An exception, however, must be made of the Labour Party archives still housed (in 1986) at Walworth Road; and my thanks are due to their admirable archivist, Stephen Bird, together with Ruby Ranaweere of the Labour Party library. Individual works on, and by, the people discussed in this book are recorded below. However, students might also welcome some guidance on more general secondary works to provide background.

## GENERAL WORKS ON THE LABOUR PARTY

Books surveying the history and ideology of the Labour Party as a whole include Carl Brand, *The British Labour Party: A Short History* (Oxford, 1965); Henry Pelling, *A Short History of the Labour Party* (London, 1961); Chris Cook and Ian Taylor (eds.), *The Labour Party* (London, 1980); R. T. McKenzie, *British Political Parties* (London, 1963); Samuel Beer, *Modern British Politics* (London, 1965); Ralph Miliband, *Parliamentary Socialism* (London, 1961); Kenneth D. Brown, *The English Labour Movement, 1700–1951* (London, 1982); David E. Martin and David Rubinstein (eds.), *Ideology and the Labour Movement* (London, 1979); James Hinton, *Labour and Socialism* (London, 1983); A. D. Wright, *British Socialism: Socialist Thought from the 1880s to the 1960s* (London, 1983); H. M. Drucker, *Doctrine and Ethos in the Labour Party* (London, 1979). Two celebrated early works by overseas observers were Robert Michels, *Political Parties* (new edn., 1966); and Egon Wertheimer, *Portrait of the Labour Party* (London, 1929). A later one is Maurice Duverger, *Political Parties: Their Organization and Activity in the Modern State* (London, new edn., 1964).

For all periods of Labour history, two marvellous guides are Joyce Bellamy and John Saville (eds.), *Dictionary of Labour Biography*, vols. i–vii (London, 1972–84); and Royden Harrison, Gillian Woolven, and Robert Duncan (eds.), *The Warwick Guide to British Labour Periodicals, 1790–1970* (Hassocks, Sussex, 1977).

## 1900–31

For this period, major works include R. Moore, *The Emergence of the Labour Party, 1880–1924* (London, 1978); Henry Pelling, *Origins of the Labour*

*Party, 1880–1900* (London, 1954); Frank Bealey and Henry Pelling, *Labour and Politics, 1900–1906* (London, 1958); Henry Pelling, *Popular Politics and Society in Late Victorian Britain* (London, 1968); Keith Burgess, *The Challenge of Labour* (London, 1980); David Howell, *British Workers and the Independent Labour Party, 1888–1906* (Manchester, 1983); *idem, A Lost Left: Three Studies in Socialism and Nationalism* (Manchester, 1986); Asa Briggs and John Saville (eds.), *Essays in Labour History, 1886–1923* (London, 1971); Eric Hobsbawm, *Labouring Men* (London, 1964), and *idem, Worlds of Labour* (London, 1984); H. Clegg, A. Fox, and A. F. Thompson, *A History of British Trade Unions since 1889*, vol. 1 (Oxford, 1963); H. Clegg, *A History of British Trade Unions since 1889*, vol. 2 (Oxford, 1985); E. H. Phelps Brown, *The Origins of Trade Union Power* (Oxford, 1983); Kenneth D. Brown (ed.), *The First Labour Party, 1906–1914* (London, 1985); Kenneth O. Morgan, 'The New Liberalism and the Challenge of Labour', in Kenneth D. Brown (ed.), *Essays in Anti-Labour History* (London, 1974), and *idem*, 'Edwardian Socialism' in A. J. P. Taylor and D. Read (eds.), *Edwardian England* (London, 1982); R. I. McKibbin, *The Evolution of the Labour Party, 1910–1924* (Oxford, new edn., 1985) and *idem*, 'Why Was There no Marxism in Great Britain?', *English Historical Review* (April 1984); J. M. Winter, *Socialism and the Challenge of War* (Cambridge, 1974); Marvin Swarz, *The Union of Democratic Control in British Politics during the First World War* (Oxford, 1971); Kenneth O. Morgan, *Consensus and Disunity* (Oxford, new edn., 1986); Richard W. Lyman, *The First Labour Government, 1924* (London, 1957); G. A. Phillips, *The General Strike* (London, 1976); Robert Skidelsky, *Politicians and the Slump* (London, 1967); and R. I. McKibbin, 'The Economic Policy of the Second Labour Government', *Past and Present* (August 1975).

## 1931–45

For this period, see Asa Briggs and John Saville (eds.), *Essays in Labour History*, vol. 3 (London, 1977); David Howell, *British Social Democracy* (London, 2nd edn., 1980); Ben Pimlott, *Labour and the Left in the 1930s* (Cambridge, 1977); Elizabeth Durbin, *New Jerusalems* (London, 1985); John F. Naylor, *Labour's International Policy: The Labour Party in the 1930s* (London, 1969); A. J. P. Taylor, *The Trouble-Makers* (London, 1957); Robert Dare, 'Instinct and Organization: Intellectuals and British Labour after 1931', *Historical Journal* 26, no. 3 (September 1983); Paul Addison, *The Road to 1945* (London, 1976); Angus Calder, *The People's War* (London, 1971); Henry Pelling, 'The 1945 General Election Reconsidered', *Historical Journal* 23, no. 2 (June 1980).

## 1945–70

For this period, see Kenneth O. Morgan, *Labour in Power, 1945–1951* (Oxford, 1984); Henry Pelling, *The Labour Governments of 1945–51* (London,

1984); Michael Sissons and Philip French (eds.), *The Age of Austerity, 1945–1951* (London, 1963); Kenneth O. Morgan, 'La Politique de nationalisation en Grande-Bretagne', *Le Mouvement social* (Janvier–Mars 1986); Jürgen C. Hess, 'Zwischen Revolution und Reform', *Vierteljahrschefte für Zeitgeschichte* (1985); Chris Cook and John Ramsden (eds.), *Trends in British Politics since 1945* (London, 1977); Martin Harrison, *Trade Unions and the Labour Party since 1945* (London, 1960); Partha Sarathi Gupta, *Imperialism and the British Labour Movement* (London, 1975); Rodney Barker, *Education and Politics, 1900–1951* (Oxford, 1972); Alan Butt-Philip, *The Welsh Question, 1945–1970* (Cardiff, 1975); Mark Jenkins, *Bevanism* (London, 1979); Stephen Haseler, *The Gaitskellites* (London, 1969); Vernon Bogdanor and Robert Skidelsky (eds.), *The Age of Affluence, 1951–1964* (London, 1970); Alec Cairncross, *Years of Recovery* (London, 1985); Wilfred Beckerman (ed.), *The Labour Government's Economic Record, 1964–1970* (London, 1972); Samuel Brittain, *Steering the Economy: The Role of the Treasury* (London, 1969); Peter Jenkins, *The Battle of Downing Street* (London, 1970).

## 1970–86

For this period, see Martin Holmes, *The Labour Government, 1974–1979* (London, 1985); Phillip Whitehead, *The Writing on the Wall* (London, 1985); Austin Mitchell, *Four Years in the Death of the Labour Party* (London, 1981); Denis Kavanagh (ed.), *The Politics of the Labour Party* (London, 1982); David Kogan and Maurice Kogan, *The Battle for the Labour Party* (London, 1982); Paul Whiteley, *The Labour Party in Crisis* (London, 1983); Lewis Minkin, *The Labour Party Conference* (London, 1978); John Osmond (ed.), *The National Question Again* (London, 1985); Barry Jones and Michael Keating, *Labour and the British State* (Oxford, 1985); K. D. Ewing, *Trade Unions, the Labour Party and the Law* (Edinburgh, 1982); Ben Pimlott and Chris Cook (eds.), *Trade Unions in British Politics* (London, 1982), Ben Pimlott (ed.), *Fabian Essays in Socialist Thought* (London, 1984); Peter Byrd, 'The Labour Party in Britain', in William E. Paterson and Alastair H. Thomas (eds.), *The Future of Social Democracy* (Oxford, 1986); and Peter Hennessy, *Cabinet* (Oxford, 1986).

### KEIR HARDIE

Apart from thousands of articles, pamphlets, and leaflets, Hardie wrote two books which are well worth reading: *From Serfdom to Socialism* (London, 1907, reprinted Hassocks, Sussex, 1974), and *India: Impressions and Suggestions* (London, 1909, second edn., 1917). Of the many biographies of Hardie, *J. Keir Hardie* by William Stewart, the work of a contemporary with a foreword by Ramsay MacDonald (London, 1921), contains much fascinating information, as does Emrys Hughes, *Keir Hardie* (London, 1956), written by

Hardie's son-in-law. Kenneth O. Morgan, *Keir Hardie: Radical and Socialist* (London, 1975; paperback edn., 1984) relates Hardie's socialism to Edwardian progressivism. Iain McLean, *Keir Hardie* (London, 1975) takes a largely similar view. By contrast, Fred Reid, *Keir Hardie: The Making of a Socialist* (London, 1978), covering the period down to 1895 only, regards his subject as a doctrinaire socialist; a similar view emerges in the same author's 'Keir Hardie and the *Labour Leader*, 1893–1903' in Jay Winter (ed.), *The Working Class in Modern British History: Essays in Honour of Henry Pelling* (Cambridge, 1983). Laurence Thompson, *The Enthusiasts* (London, 1971), a study of Bruce and Katharine Glasier, contains primary material on Hardie.

## RAMSAY MACDONALD

In addition to his many articles and occasional pieces, MacDonald wrote several books. None is easy to read, although they all provide useful insights into MacDonald's political philosophy. Imperial and external themes emerge in *Labour and the Empire* (London, 1907), *The Awakening of India* (London, 1910) and *National Defence* (London, 1917). His view of socialism is treated in several, rather repetitive works, *Socialism and Society* (London, 1905), *Socialism and Government* (London, 1909), *The Socialist Movement* (London, 1911) and *Socialism: Critical and Constructive* (London, 1921). *The Zollverein and British Industry* (London, 1903) deals with the tariff reform controversy. In a totally different category is MacDonald's moving memoir of his wife, *Margaret Ethel MacDonald* (London, 1911). An outstanding and comprehensive biography has been written, David Marquand, *Ramsay MacDonald* (London, 1977). This makes all other biographies redundant, although L. McNeill Weir, *The Tragedy of Ramsay MacDonald* (London, 1938), a hostile account by his former secretary, is a fascinating period piece. A sympathetic handling of the 1931 crisis appears in Reginald Bassett, *1931: Political Crisis* (London, 1958), while Robert Skidelsky, *Politicians and the Slump* (London, 1968) is a stimulating treatment of the failures of the second MacDonald government. An important article is R.I. McKibbin, 'James Ramsay MacDonald and the Problem of the Independence of the Labour Party', *Journal of Modern History* 42, no. 2 (June 1970).

## THE WEBBS

The Webbs were inexhaustible writers, including upon themselves. Four, somewhat abridged, versions of Beatrice Webb's diaries appeared earlier on, *My Apprenticeship* (London, 1926); *Our Partnership, 1892–1911*, edited by Barbara Drake and Margaret Cole (London, 1948); *Beatrice Webb's Diaries, 1912–1924*, edited by Margaret Cole (London, 1952); and *Beatrice Webb's Diaries, 1924–1932*, edited by Margaret Cole (London, 1956). These have now been quite superseded by Norman and Jeanne MacKenzie's magnificent four-volume edition, *The Diary of Beatrice Webb*: vol. i, 1873–92; vol. ii, 1892–1905; vol. iii, 1905–24; and vol. iv, 1924–43 (London, 1982–5). Also a vital primary source is Norman MacKenzie (ed.), *The Letters of Sidney and Beatrice Webb* (3 vols., Cambridge and London, 1978). Norman and Jeanne MacKenzie, *The First Fabians* (London, 1977), draws on much primary material. An interesting document is *Beatrice Webb's American Diary, 1898*, edited by David Shannon (London, 1963). Three important, if dullish, works by Margaret Cole are *Beatrice Webb* (London, 1945); *The Webbs and their Work* (London, 1949); and *The Story of Fabian Socialism* (London, 1961). A sympathetic and attractive study is Lisanne Radice, *Beatrice and Sidney Webb: Fabian Socialists* (London, 1984). Many major books on the Fabians deal extensively with the Webbs. Among them are A. M. McBriar, *Fabian Socialists and English Politics, 1884–1918* (Cambridge, 1963); Eric Hobsbawm, 'The Fabians Reconsidered', reprinted in *Labouring Men* (London, 1964); Willard Wolfe, *From Radicalism to Socialism* (Newhaven, Connecticut, 1975); Ian Britain, *Fabianism and Culture* (Cambridge, 1982); and Patricia Pugh, *Educate, Organise: 100 Years of Fabian Socialism* (London, 1984).

### VICTOR GRAYSON

Much the best book on Grayson is David Clark, *Labour's Lost Leader: Victor Grayson* (London, 1985). Also helpful is the same author's *Colne Valley: Radicalism to Socialism* (London, 1980). An early study was William Thompson, *The Life of Victor Grayson* (Sheffield, 1910), while Reg Groves, *The Strange Case of Victor Grayson* (London, 1975) makes enjoyable reading. Grayson himself wrote a few pamphlets, of which perhaps *God's Country* (Stockport, 1908) is the most interesting.

### MABON AND NOAH ABLETT

Mabon has a worthy biography, Eric Wyn Evans, *Mabon* (Cardiff, 1959); also relevant is the same author's *The Miners of South Wales* (Cardiff, 1961). Ablett is best approached through a splendid entry on him by Joyce Bellamy and John Saville in Bellamy and Saville (eds.), *Dictionary of Labour Biography*, vol. 3 (London, 1976). Also useful are Peter Stead, 'Working-Class Leadership in South Wales, 1900–1920', *Welsh History Review* 6, no. 3 (June 1973); Kenneth O. Morgan, 'Socialism and Syndicalism: The Welsh Miners' Debate', *Society for the Study of Labour History*, Bulletin no. 30 (Spring 1975); and Martin Barclay, '"Slaves of the Lamp": the Aberdare Miners' Strike, 1910', *Llafur* 2, no. 3 (1978). A general treatment of Welsh social and political developments in the period is given in Kenneth O. Morgan, *Wales in British Politics, 1868–1922* (Cardiff, 3rd edn., 1980) and *idem, Rebirth of a Nation: Wales, 1880–1980* (Oxford and Cardiff, paperback edn., 1982). A general treatment of Welsh mining trade-unionism is given in R. Page Arnot, *The South Wales Miners: The South Wales Miners' Federation, 1898–1914* (London, 1967); *idem, The South Wales Miners: The South Wales Miners' Federation, 1914–1926* (London, 1976); and Hywel Francis and David Smith, *The Fed* (London, 1980). There are plenty of lively ideas in Dai Smith, *Wales! Wales?* (London, 1984), and Gwyn A. Williams, *When Was Wales?* (London, 1985). For a contrasting Welsh view, see Peter Stead, 'Vernon Hartshorn: Miners' Agent and Cabinet Minister', in Stewart Williams (ed.), *Glamorgan Historian*, vol. vi (Cowbridge, 1969), and *idem*, 'Working Class Leadership in South Wales, 1900–1920', *Welsh History Review* 6, no. 3 (June 1973). Also see D. Egan, 'Noah Ablett', *Llafur* (1986).

## ARTHUR HENDERSON

Henderson's writings were ephemeral, but *Labour and Foreign Affairs* (1928), *Consolidating World Peace* (Oxford, 1932) and *Labour's Way to Peace* (London, 1935) give the flavour of his internationalism. We desperately need a proper biography of him, Chris Wrigley is currently writing one. In the meantime, all we have is the interesting personal study by Mary Agnes Hamilton, *Arthur Henderson: A Biography* (London, 1938); the same author's *Remembering my Good Friends* (London, 1944) also has much fascination. For Henderson's work as party secretary, a superb account is R. I. McKibbin, *The Evolution of the Labour Party 1910–1924* (Oxford, new paperback edn., 1985). A powerful treatment of wartime trade-union developments appears in Chris Wrigley, *David Lloyd George and the British Labour Movement* (Hassocks, Sussex, 1976). Detailed studies of particular aspects are J. M. Winter, 'Arthur Henderson, the Russian Revolution and the Reconstruction of the Labour Party', *Historical Journal* 25, no. 4 (December 1972); Christopher Howard, 'MacDonald, Henderson and the Outbreak of War, 1914', *Historical Journal* 20, no. 4 (December 1977); and *idem*, 'Expectations Born to Death: Local Labour Party Expansion in the 1920s', in J. M. Winter (ed.), *The Working Class in Modern British History*. Foreign policy is dealt with in Elaine Windrich, *British Labour's Foreign Policy* (Palo Alto, Calif., 1952); David Carlton, *MacDonald versus Henderson* (London, 1970); and Henry R. Winkler, 'Arthur Henderson', in G. A. Craig and F. Gilbert, *The Diplomats, 1919–1939* (Princeton, New Jersey, 1953).

## HAROLD LASKI

Laski should be approached through his own extensive and wide-ranging writings. His major academic work was *Political Thought in England from*

*Locke to Bentham* (London, 1925). His views on the state, sovereignty, pluralism, and political philosophy in general appear in *Authority in the Modern State* (London, 1919), *A Grammar of Politics* (London, 1925), *Communism* (London, 1927), *Liberty in the Modern State* (London, 1930), *The Foundations of Sovereignty* (2nd printing, London, 1931), *Studies in Law and Politics* (London, 1932), *The State in Theory and Practice* (London, 1936), *The American Presidency* (1940), *The American Democracy* (London, 1949), *Reflections on the Constitution* (London, 1951), and in a host of lesser publications. His ideas on current issues of concern to socialists were outlined in *Democracy in Crisis* (London, 1933), *Where Do We Go from Here?* (London, 1940), *Reflections on the Revolution of Our Time* (London, 1943), and *Faith, Reason and Civilization* (London, 1944). There is a study of his political philosophy in Herbert A. Deane, *The Political Ideas of Harold J. Laski* (London, 1955). Laski has no really good biography. The best available are Kingsley Martin, *Harold Laski* (London, 1953), and Granville Eastwood, *Harold Laski*, with a foreword by James Callaghan (London, 1977). A marvellous personal source is Mark Howe (ed.), *The Holmes–Laski Letters* (2 vols., Oxford, 1953). *The Laski Libel Action: Verbatim Report* (London, ?1947) is a fascinating document. John Saville includes a perceptive comment on Laski as a teacher in Martin and Rubinstein (eds.), *Ideology and the Labour Movement*, cited above, p. 346.

### ELLEN WILKINSON

Ellen Wilkinson's most famous book was her work on Jarrow, *The Town that was Murdered* (London, 1939), but her *Peeps at Politicians* (1930) and *How the People Can Win the Peace* (1945) are also of interest. Her article 'Socialism and the Problem of the Middle Class' in G. E. G. Catlin (ed.), *New Trends in Socialism* (London, 1935), distinguished between 'the worthwhile middle class' and the *lumpenbourgeoisie*. A quite excellent biography is Betty D. Vernon, *Ellen Wilkinson* (London, 1982). Some personal insights appear in Billy Hughes, 'In Defence of Ellen Wilkinson', *History Workshop 7* (1979), while a contrasting view appears in the same journal, David Rubinstein, 'Ellen Wilkinson Reconsidered'.

### THE PLANNERS

The thirties' planners are best discovered directly through their own powerful works. Evan Durbin's writings, *Purchasing Power and Trade Depression* (1933), *The Problem of Credit Policy* (1935), *How To Pay for the War* (1939) and *Problems of Economic Planning* (1949) are all distinctly technical, but *The Politics of Democratic Socialism* (1940) is a wide-ranging, illuminating book. His article, 'The Economic Problems, Facing the Labour Government', in Donald Munro (ed.), *Socialism: The British Way* (London, 1948) is of much importance. Douglas Jay's *The Socialist Case* (London, 1937; 2nd edn. with a foreword by Clement Attlee, London, 1946) was an immensely influential work, then and later. It should be compared with Jay's *Socialism in the New Society* (London, 1962); *After the Common Market* (Harmondsworth, 1968); his most interesting memoirs, *Change and Fortune: A Political Record* (London, 1980); and *Sterling* (London, 1985). Gaitskell's role in the thirties is covered rather sparsely in Philip Williams, *Hugh Gaitskell* (London, 1979); more illuminating is Nicholas Davenport's account in *Memoirs of a City Radical* (London, 1974). James Meade's two works, *The Rate of Interest in a Progressive State* (1933) and *Economic Analysis and Policy* (1936), were the product of a leftish economist of immense intellectual distinction (and a later Nobel Prize winner). Easily the outstanding secondary work is Elizabeth Durbin's *New Jerusalems* (London, 1985), an absorbing treatment of the 1933–8 period by the daughter of one of the pioneers of the thirties. An interesting discussion is A. F. Thompson, 'Winchester and the Labour Party: Three "Gentlemanly Rebels",' in R. Custance (ed.), *Winchester College: Sixth Centenary Essays* (Oxford, 1982).

## HUGH DALTON

Of Dalton's books, *Practical Socialism for Britain* (1935) is of central importance, but his classic *Principles of Public Finance* (1923) is also well worth re-reading. His published diaries are an inescapable source for the history of the British labour movement: vol. i, *Memoirs 1887–1931: Call Back Yesterday* (London, 1953); vol. ii, *Memoirs, 1931–45: The Fateful Years* (London, 1957); and vol. iii, *Memoirs, 1945–60: High Tide and After* (London, 1962). Ben Pimlott is now publishing a two-volume edition of his diary in much greater detail. *The Second World War Diary of Hugh Dalton 1940–45* (London, 1986) has so far appeared. As a biography, Ben Pimlott, *Hugh Dalton* (London, 1985) is quite outstanding, perhaps the best study of a Labour leader to have appeared since the Second World War. The DNB entry on Dalton by Nicholas Davenport, *DNB Supplement, 1961–1970*, is full of rich detail. Pimlott's second volume of the edited diary appears in early 1987.

## CLEMENT ATTLEE

Attlee's own writings have more punch and stimulation than might be supposed. In particular *The Social Worker* (1920), *The Will and the Way to Socialism* (1935), and above all, *The Labour Party in Perspective* (1937) are of much interest. Also see his 'Local Government and the Socialist Plan' in *Problems of a Socialist Government* (London, 1933). Some of his speeches were published under the title *Purpose and Policy* (London, 1947), with an introduction by Roy Jenkins. However, Attlee's memoirs, *As It Happened* (London, 1954) are very disappointing, and Francis Williams's book based on interviews with Attlee, *A Prime Minister Remembers* (London, 1961), is distinctly guarded. There is an excellent biography, Kenneth Harris, *Attlee* (London, 1982, paperback edn., 1984), with valuable family material. A more recent one is Trevor Burridge, *Clement Attlee* (London, 1985), while a contemporary work was Roy Jenkins, *Mr Attlee: An Interim Biography* (London, 1948). Harold Wilson discusses Attlee in *A Prime Minister on Prime Ministers* (London, 1977). Two instructive pieces on his early career are W. Golant, 'The Emergence of C. R. Attlee as Leader of the Labour Party in 1935', *History Journal* 13 (1970); and *idem*, 'C. R. Attlee in the First and Second Labour Governments', *Parliamentary Affairs* (1973). Granada Television, *Clem Attlee: The Granada Historical Records* (Panther Records, 1967) is helpful on some points. Some personal insights appear in Sir George Mallaby, *From My Level: Unwritten Minutes* (London, 1965). Peter Hennessy and Andrew Arendts, *Mr Attlee's Engine Room* (Strathclye Papers, Glasgow, 1983) discusses Attlee's Cabinet committee structure.

## ERNEST BEVIN

Bevin was (almost literally) unable to write, and left virtually no private papers. Fortunately, we have Alan Bullock's magnificent three-volume biography, *The Life and Times of Ernest Bevin*. The third volume (London, 1983) covers Bevin's period as Foreign Secretary, 1945–51, in rich detail. Several works give insights into Bevin's ideas and methods at the Foreign Office. Among them are Lord Strang, *Home and Abroad* (London, 1956); Sir Ivone Kirkpatrick, *The Inner Circle* (London, 1959); Piers Dixon, *Double Diploma: The Life of Sir Piers Dixon* (London, 1968); Dean Acheson, *Born at the Creation* (London, 1970); Sir Roderick Barclay, *Ernest Bevin and the Foreign Office* (London, 1975); and Sir Frank Roberts, 'Ernest Bevin as Foreign Secretary' in Ritchie Ovendale (ed.), *The Foreign Policy of the British Labour Governments, 1945–1951* (Leicester, 1984). An interesting recent study is John W. Young, *Britain, France and the Unity of Europe, 1945–51* (Leicester, 1984). Also see Robert Frazier, 'Did Britain Start the Cold War? Bevin and the Truman Doctrine', *Historical Journal* 27, no. 3 (September 1984). A powerful monograph is William Roger Louis, *The British Empire in the Middle East, 1945–1951* (Oxford, 1984).

## STAFFORD CRIPPS

Cripps's approach to politics in the thirties can be partly gleaned by chapters he wrote in collective books: 'Parliamentary Institutions and the Transition to Socialism' in *Where Stands Socialism Today?* (London, 1933) and 'Can

Socialism Come by Constitutional Methods?' in *Problems of a Socialist Government* (London, 1933). Ben Pimlott, *Labour and the Left in the 1930s* (Cambridge, 1977) deals critically with Cripps's Popular Front phase. A proper biography of Cripps is desperately needed; it is to be hoped that Maurice Shock eventually produces one. In the meantime, we have to make do with Eric Estorick, *Stafford Cripps* (London, 1949) and Colin Cooke, *The Life of Richard Stafford Cripps* (London, 1957). Gabriel Gorodetsky, *Stafford Cripps' Mission to Moscow, 1940–42* (Cambridge, 1984) covers an important phase of Cripps's career. Cripps's period at the Treasury is fascinatingly discussed in Douglas Jay's *Change and Fortune*, referred to above.

## HERBERT MORRISON

Of Morrison's writings, easily the most important and influential is his *Socialisation and Transport* (London, 1933), though 'Socialism Today' in B. Russell *et al.*, *Dare We Look Ahead?* (1938) is interesting. A book of his speeches, *The Peaceful Revolution*, appeared in 1949. His *Government and Parliament* (London, 1954) is somewhat conventional, while his *Autobiography* (1960) is rather disappointing. There is, fortunately, a good biography by Bernard Donoughue and G. W. Jones, *Herbert Morrison: Portrait of a Politician* (London, 1973). The DNB entry on him by J. P. Mackintosh, *Supplement, 1961–70*, is also very instructive. J. T. Murphy, *Labour's Big Three* (London, 1948) deals with Morrison, along with Attlee and Bevin. John Rowett is now writing an important new study of Morrison's career.

## LORD ADDISON

Addison's period as Leader of the Lords is covered in Kenneth and Jane Morgan, *Portrait of a Progressive: The Career of Christopher, Viscount Addison* (Oxford, 1980). Some personal insights appear in Lord Pakenham, *Born to Believe* (London, 1953). The Lords in the post-war period is treated in P. A. Bromhead, *The House of Lords and Contemporary Politics* (London, 1958). None of Addison's own writings bear on his time as Leader of the Lords, but apart from his fascinating published diaries on the First World War period, his book, *A Policy for British Agriculture* (London, 1939) was a pioneering work in its day.

## JAMES GRIFFITHS

A new biography of James Griffiths is being written by Peter Stead. Pending its appearance, we have Griffiths's somewhat guarded memoirs, *Pages from Memory* (London, 1969), and an interesting symposium, J. B. Smith and others, *James Griffiths and his Times* (Cardiff, 1978). Griffiths's wife, Winnie, published privately *One Woman's Story* (1979). Some wider considerations emerge in Kenneth O. Morgan, *Rebirth of a Nation: Wales, 1880–1980* (Oxford and Cardiff, 1981) and *idem*, 'Twf cenedlaetholdeb fodern yng Nghymru' in Geraint H. Jenkins (ed.), *Cof Cenedl: Ysgrifau ar Hanes Cymru* (Llandysul, 1986).

### ANEURIN BEVAN

Bevan was less sparkling on paper than he was verbally, but his tract, *Why Not Trust the Tories?* (London, 1944) and especially his most stimulating collection of essays, *In Place of Fear* (London, 1952, reprinted Wakefield, 1976) are basic reading for all socialists. Michael Foot's biography, *Aneurin Bevan* (2 vols., London, 1962 and 1973) is passionately exciting from first to last. Lesser studies are Vincent Brome, *Aneurin Bevan* (London, 1953) and Mark M. Klug, *Aneurin Bevan: Cautious Rebel* (London, 1961). Bevan's wife, Jennie Lee, wrote two important works of autobiography, *This Great Journey* (London, 1963) and *My Life with Nye* (London, 1980). Kenneth O. Morgan, 'Aneurin Bevan', in Paul Barker (ed.), *Founders of the Welfare State* (London, 1985), covers the period at the Ministry of Health, while Mark Jenkins, *Bevanism: Labour's High Tide* (London, 1979) is a good study. A new biography is currently being written by John Campbell, and is due to be published in 1987.

### HUGH GAITSKELL

Gaitskell's own writings are disappointing, other than 'At Oxford in the Twenties' in Asa Briggs and John Saville (eds.), *Essays in Labour History* (London, 1967) and 'Socialism and Nationalization' (Fabian Society Tract 300, 1956). An interesting early piece is 'Financial Policy in the Transition Period' in G. E. G. Catlin (ed.), *New Trends in Socialism*. Gaitskell's diary has been superbly edited by Philip Williams, *The Diary of Hugh Gaitskell, 1945–1956* (London, 1983). Philip Williams's authorized biography, *Hugh Gaitskell* (London, 1979) is a powerful work, but unduly partisan and perhaps overlong. An attractive work is W. T. Rodgers (ed.), *Hugh Gaitskell, 1906–1963* (London, 1963). Many insights into Gaitskell appear in the memoirs of Douglas Jay and Nicholas Davenport, cited above; in Susan Crosland, *Tony Crosland* (London, 1982); and in Janet Morgan (ed.), *The Backbench Diaries of Richard Crossman* (London, 1981). Stephen Haseler, *The Gaitskellites* (London, 1969) is highly informative.

### MORGAN PHILLIPS

The best way of exploring Phillips's career is through his personal papers, currently in the Labour Party headquarters at Walworth Road. His pamphlet, *Labour in the Sixties* (London, 1960) is valuable. An excellent entry on him by John Saville appears in the *DNB, Supplement, 1961–70*.

### RITA HINDEN

Rita Hinden wrote extensively on colonial policy in her early years. Among the more important of her writings are *Plan for Africa* (London, 1941); her edition of *Fabian Colonial Essays* (London, 1945); *Socialists and the Empire* (London, 1946) 'The Labour Government and the Empire', in Donald Munro (ed.), *Socialism: the British Way* (London, 1948); *Empire and After* (London, 1949); and *Common Sense and Colonial Development* (London, 1949). Her idea of socialism generally comes across in *Twentieth-Century Socialism* (ed. with Allan Flanders, London, 1956); *Must Labour Lose?* (with Mark Abrams and Richard Rose, London, 1960); and her editor's preface to R. H. Tawney, *The Radical Tradition* (London, 1964), apart from innumerable contributions to *Socialist Commentary* and other journals. There is a fine obituary by Allan Flanders in Joyce Bellamy and John Saville (eds.), *Dictionary of Labour Biography* ii (London, 1974), and several appreciations in the January 1972 issue of *Socialist Commentary*. Also see a thesis by K. Lewis (Ruskin, Oxford).

### HAROLD WILSON

Wilson's own volumes of memoirs, *The Labour Government, 1964–70: A Personal Memoir* (London, 1971) and *Final Term: The Labour Government, 1974–1976* (London, 1979) are copious but unreliable. A third, *Memoirs: The Making of a Prime Minister* (London, 1986) appeared while this book was in the press. A volume of collected speeches, *The New Britain: Labour's Plan Outlined by Harold Wilson* (Harmondsworth, 1964) conveys his ideas in the 'white heat' phase, while *The Governance of Britain* (London, 1976) has some first-hand information. No biography to date can be considered satisfactory. Dudley Smith, *Harold Wilson: A Critical Biography* (London, 1964) is a right-wing attack; Leslie Smith, *Harold Wilson: The Authentic Portrait* (London, 1964) is unduly favourable, as is Anthony Shrimsley, *The First Hundred Days of Harold Wilson* (London, 1965). Paul Foot's *The Politics of Harold Wilson* (London, 1968) is much the best book to date, written from a far left-wing standpoint. Andrew Roth, *Sir Harold Wilson: Yorkshire's Walter Mitty* (London, 1977) is engaging but somewhat lightweight. Personal insights, some of them alarming, appear in Marcia Williams, *Inside Number 10* (London, 1972); Joe Haines, *The Politics of Power* (London, 1972); Cecil King, *The Cecil King Diaries 1965–70* (London, 1972); and Marcia Falkender, *Downing Street in Perspective* (London, 1983). Much information appears in Janet Morgan (ed.), *Richard Crossman: The Diaries of a Cabinet Minister* (3 vols., London, 1975–7) and Barbara Castle, *The Castle Diaries, 1964–70,* and *The Castle Diaries, 1974–76* (London, 1984, and 1980).

### JAMES CALLAGHAN

James Callaghan is presently writing his autobiography (due to be published in 1987). To date, his writings have been sparse, but there is much of interest in his chapter, 'The Approach to Social Equality' in Donald Munro (ed.), *Socialism: The British Way* (1948), and his book *A House Divided: The Dilemma of Northern Ireland* (London, 1973). Also see 'Challenges and Opportunities for British Foreign Policy' (Fabian Society Tract 439, 1975), and Callaghan's very interesting reflections on his time at the Home Office, 'Cumber and Variableness' in *The Home Office: Perspectives on Policy and Administration* (Royal Institution of Public Administration, Bicentenary Lectures, 1982). Discussions of Callaghan, sometimes erratic, appear freely in the Crossman and Castle diaries. A compatively unsympathetic biography is Peter Kellner and Christopher Hitchins, *Callaghan: The Road to Number Ten* (London, 1976). Some insights appear in 'The Prime Minister Talks to the *Observer,* interviewed by Kenneth Harris' (London, 1979), and Lord Longford's *Eleven at No. 10* (London, 1984).

### MICHAEL FOOT

Michael Foot is a marvellous writer whose ideas and personality leap at you from the printed page. Apart from his remarkable tract, written with Frank Owen and Peter Howard, *Guilty Men* (1940), and his biography of Swift, *The Pen and the Sword* (London, 1957), the reader will enjoy his highly personal biography of Aneurin Bevan, referred to on p. 356, and his two volumes of collected essays, *Debts of Honour* (London, 1980), and *Loyalists and Loners* (London, 1986). His pamphlet, *My Kind of Socialism* (*Observer* reprint, 1982) is illuminating. *Another Heart and Other Pulses* (London, 1984) is an account of the 1983 election. The only biography of significance to date is Simon Hoggart and David Leigh, *Michael Foot: A Portrait* (London, 1981). The Castle diaries are important guides: so is Peggy Duff, *Left, Left, Left* (London, 1971).

### GORMLEY, SCARGILL AND THE MINERS

Gormley's autobiography, *Battered Cherub* (London, 1982) is an interesting and informative book. For Scargill, the best available work is Michael Crick's lively *Scargill and the Miners* (Harmondsworth, 1985). Scargill gave his views in *New Left Review* 92 (July/August 1975) and in *Marxism Today* (April 1981). A hostile view appears in N. Hagger, *Scargill the Stalinist* (London,

1984). Interesting recent works on the mining industry include Tony Hall, *King Coal* (Harmondsworth, 1981); Andrew Taylor, *The Politics of the York-shire Miners* (London, 1984); Roy Ottey, *The Strike: An Insider's Story* (London, 1985); and John Lloyd, *Understanding the Miners' Strike* (Fabian pamphlet, London, 1986). An excellent recent work is Martin Adeney and John Lloyd, *The Miners' Strike, 1984–5* (London, 1986).


## TONY BENN

Benn's major writings include 'The New Politics: A Socialist Reconnaissance' (Fabian Society Tract 402, 1970); *Industry and Democracy* (London, 1978); *The Right to Know* (London, 1978); *Arguments for Socialism* (ed. Chris Mullins, London, 1979); *Arguments for Democracy* (ed. Chris Mullins, London, 1981); and *Parliament, People and Power: Agenda for a Free Society* (London, 1982). A sympathetic treatment appears in Michael Hatfield, *The House the Left Built* (London, 1975); Robert Jenkins, *A Political Biography: Tony Benn* (London, 1980); and Sydney Higgins, *The Benn Inheritance: The Story of a Radical Family* (London, 1984). Benn is dealt with more harshly in David Kogan and Maurice Kogan, *The Battle for the Labour Party* (London, 1982); Alan Freeman, *The Benn Heresy* (London, 1982); and 'Brother Tony' in Michael Foot, *Loyalists and Loners* (1986). Unusual (and attractive) sidelights on Benn's personality appear in Susan Crosland, *Tony Crosland* (London, 1982).


## DENIS HEALEY

Healey's own writings on foreign and defence policy in the fifties and sixties were of much weight. Critical is 'Power Politics and the Labour Party', in R. H. S. Crossman (ed.), *New Fabian Essays* (London, 1952); also see *The Curtain Falls* (London, 1951); *Neutralism* (London, 1955), and 'A Labour Britain and the World' (Fabian Society Tract 352, 1964). An interesting study is B. Reed and G. Williams, *Denis Healey and the Policies of Power* (London, 1971). Some insights into Healey's period as Chancellor appear in Joel Barnett, *Inside the Treasury* (London, 1983), to be read in conjunction with Healey's own lecture, *Managing the Economy* (London, 1980), and Sir Douglas Wass's Reith lectures, *Government and the Governed* (London, 1984).


## ROY HATTERSLEY

Hattersley's own articles and press columns are too ephemeral in the main to warrant inclusion, but his memoirs *Goodbye to Yorkshire* (London, 1976) and *A Yorkshire Boyhood* (London, 1983) are revealing and highly readable. His foreword to Elizabeth Durbin, *New Jerusalems*, referred to on p. 353, affords clues as to his political outlook, as does 'Labour's Choices' (Fabian

Society Tract 489, 1983). An important selection of his speeches and articles, edited by Giles Radice, was published under the title, *A Duty to Win* (London, 1983). A full-length statement of Hattersley's philosophy, *Socialism and Freedom*, is being published by Michael Joseph early in 1987. His introduction to a new edition of Stephen Reynolds, *A Poor Man's House* (Oxford, 1982) is also of interest.

## NEIL KINNOCK

Of Kinnock's various writings, apart from newspaper articles, his introduction to a paperback reprint of Aneurin Bevan's *In Place of Fear* (London, 1978); *Why Vote Labour?* (with N. Butler and T. Harris, London, 1979); 'Which Way Should Labour Go?', *Political Quarterly* (October/December 1980); 'Labour's Choices' (Fabian Society Tract, 489, 1983); his interview with Eric Hobsbawm in *Marxism Today* (1984); the contributions to James Curran (ed.), *The Future of the Left* (London, 1984); and his Fabian lecture, 'The Future of Socialism' (Fabian Tract 509, 1986), shed light on his evolving political creed. Two workman-like biographies are G. M. F. Drower, *Neil Kinnock: The Path to the Leadership* (London, 1984), and Robert Harris, *The Making of Neil Kinnock* (London, 1984). Others are presently under way. A book of Kinnock's was recently published: *Making our Way: Investing in Britain's Future* (Blackwell's, Oxford, 1986).

# INDEX

Main references to individuals on whom chapters are written are in **bold**